THE FRANK W. PIERCE MEMORIAL CONFERENCE
AT CORNELL UNIVERSITY

November 16-17, 1973

Union Power and Public Policy

The Frank W. Pierce Memorial Lectureship
and Conference Series, at the New York
State School of Industrial and Labor
Relations at Cornell University, is made
possible through the generosity of the Teagle
Foundation, Incorporated.

The conference at which the papers in this
volume were presented was organized to
honor George W. Brooks, Alice H. Cook,
Vernon H. Jensen, Milton R. Konvitz, Jean
T. McKelvey, and Maurice F. Neufeld.

Union Power
and
Public Policy

DAVID B. LIPSKY

editor

New York State School of Industrial
and Labor Relations
Cornell University
Ithaca, New York

1975

Copyright© 1975 by Cornell University
All rights reserved

Library of Congress Catalog Card Number: 74-620171
ISBN: 0-87546-057-7
Price:$8.00

ORDER FROM
Publications Division
New York State School of Industrial and
Labor Relations, Cornell University
Ithaca, New York 14853

Library of Congress Cataloging in Publication Data
Main entry under title:

Union power and public policy.

(Pierce lectureship and conference series; no. 4)
Includes bibliographical references.
1. Trade-unions—United States—Addresses, essays, lectures. 2. Labor laws and legislation—United States—Addresses, essays, lectures. I. Lipsky, David B., 1939 – ed.
II. Series.
KF3389.A2U55   331.8'0973   74-620171
ISBN 0-87546-057-7

COMPOSITION BY UNION PRESS
PRINTED IN THE UNITED STATES OF AMERICA BY
THE W. F. HUMPHREY PRESS

Contents

Foreword

The School of Industrial and Labor Relations is in the process of marking the end of an era, which began toward the close of World War II with the founding of the school and which is ending now as the "founders" and other prominent long-term members of the faculty retire from full-time employment.

The magnitude of the transition can be gauged by the fact that the six outstanding professors in whose honor this volume is published make up one-third of what is, by far, the school's largest department. In many respects the Department of Collective Bargaining, Labor Law, and Labor History is the "engine room" of the ILR School, involved in the area of research and teaching most people think of when the field of industrial and labor relations is mentioned. As its long title suggests, many fields of inquiry are pursued from many perspectives within this department. It is a department composed of experts on the bargaining process, labor lawyers, labor historians, and analysts of the union movement. All of these perspectives are represented in the group that is leaving our midst.

The accomplishments of these half-dozen researchers, mentors, teachers, and problem solvers speak for themselves in the form of numerous books, ably trained protégés, distinguished alumni, and hundreds of arbitration and factfinding reports.

George W. Brooks, who came to the faculty in 1961, brought with him several years of experience as research and education director of the International Brotherhood of Pulp, Sulphite and Paper Mill Workers (AFL-CIO). He is a provocative teacher, whose courses rate a "must" among the students, and a writer of stimulating pieces on decentralized collective bargaining and the security of worker institutions. He has been chairman of several key task-force committees within the school on long-range planning and fieldwork. Currently, he is involved in a research project that is studying union mergers and their impact on collective bargaining, which is sponsored by the Department of Labor.

Alice H. Cook joined the faculty in 1952 as director of a labor education program for the Extension Division and, in line with her great interest in this subject, spent her last semester before retirement as director of the school's Credit and Certificate Program in New York City. One of the foremost students of Japanese trade unionism in this country and an expert on the role of women at work, she has published extensively in these areas. She was Cornell University's first ombudsman. She has traveled extensively and her most recent trip, sponsored by the Ford Foundation, involved an around-the-world study of the role of women in the work force of other countries.

Vernon H. Jensen, a prolific researcher who joined the faculty in 1946, was associate dean of the school from 1966 to 1971. The most recent of his many publications are *Decasualization and Modernization of Dock Work in London* and *Strife on the Waterfront: The Port of New York since 1945.* He has been a member of a presidential board of inquiry into a longshore industry dispute and served as chairman of the New York State Advisory Council on Employer and Union Improper Practices. He is an active arbitrator and member of the National Academy of Arbitrators.

Milton R. Konvitz also joined the faculty in 1946. The well-known teacher of two famous courses in American ideals, which have left a lasting impact on students, he has received honorary degrees from six universities and has held fellowships from the Guggenheim Foundation, Ford Foundation, Fund for the Republic, Institute for Advanced Study at Princeton, and Center for Advanced Study in the Behavioral Sciences at Stanford. His writings, covering a wide range of subjects, include *Fundamental Liberties of a Free People, Expanding Liberties,* and *The Constitution and Civil Rights.* He was the first editor of the *Industrial and Labor Relations Review.*

Jean T. McKelvey, teacher of key courses in dispute resolution and mentor to almost 15 percent of all graduate students trained at the school, joined the faculty in 1946. She has served on advisory committees to the U.S. secretary of labor and as a member of a number of presidential railroad emergency boards. Past president of the National Academy of Arbitrators, she started and for eight years served as editor of the *Annual Proceedings* of the academy. She is still an active arbitrator, mediator, and factfinder, and is a member of the Public Review Board (UAW) and of the Federal Service Impasses Panel.

Before Maurice F. Neufeld joined the faculty in 1946 and became relied on for advice and counsel on university-wide matters, he had an illustrious career with several top agencies of the state of New York. A translation of Sophocles' *Antigone* into English poetry, *The House of Labor, Italy: School for Awakening Countries,* and *A Representative Bibliography of American Labor History* are among the titles published during his active research career. Currently labor relations consultant to the Xerox Corporation, he is working on "Realms of Thought and Organized Labor in the Age of Jackson."

Our many thanks go to David Lipsky who first conceived of this project — a *Festschrift* to honor our retiring colleagues. He chaired the planning committee and edited and interpreted the papers with great effectiveness. He and his six authors are to be complimented for the fine volume that follows.

Grateful appreciation is also extended to the Teagle Foundation for financial support to the Frank W. Pierce Memorial Conference and Lectureship fund, which made the seminar and this volume possible. It is appropriate that support for this endeavor should come from a fund named in honor of Frank Pierce. This fund was created to honor a distinguished practitioner with substantive presentations about the problems and developments of the field of industrial and labor relations. Mr. Pierce was a director of the Standard Oil Company (New Jersey) until his retirement in 1954 and also was affiliated with Industrial Relations Counselors, Incorporated (now Organization Resources Counselors, Incorporated), a nonprofit research and education firm in New York City. He died in 1964 at the age of seventy.

In honoring these six academics with these six papers we feel we have added to the knowledge of the field; at the same time underscoring the fact that it has become a field because of the pioneering work on the practitioner side by individuals such as Frank Pierce and because of the efforts and dedication on the academic side of professors like George Brooks, Alice Cook, Vernon Jensen, Milton Konvitz, Jean McKelvey, and Maurice Neufeld.

ROBERT B. MCKERSIE, *Dean*
New York State School of
Industrial and Labor Relations

Introduction

In 1944 the New York State Legislature authorized the establishment of a school of industrial and labor relations at Cornell University. The legislature saw clearly that the postwar era would require new efforts to understand the problems that afflicted relations between employers and employees. It was hoped that an institution devoted to teaching and research in the field of industrial relations would help promote mutual understanding between unions and employers.

The New York State School of Industrial and Labor Relations was a unique institution. The establishment of a specialized school with a full undergraduate and graduate program in a new and controversial academic field was a risky undertaking for the legislators. The success of the school could by no means have been assured from the outset. One needs only to recall any of a number of other educational experiments that proved embarrassments to their sponsors to understand the dimensions of the risk.

Thirty years later the institution stands respected throughout the world for its academic achievements. Many factors have contributed to the ILR School's success, not the least important being the state legislature's continuing support. But if success has "a thousand fathers," paternity in this instance is not particularly difficult to identify. It rests principally with a handful of faculty who were recruited during the school's early years and stayed to mold the institution into its current preeminent position. The old maxim holds that a college is no better than its faculty; if so, the ILR School can never exceed the standards set by its founding faculty members.

A few years ago, the Department of Collective Bargaining, Labor Law, and Labor History of the ILR School realized it would lose six of its senior members because of retirement: George W. Brooks, Alice H. Cook, Vernon H. Jensen, Milton R. Konvitz, Jean T. McKelvey, and Maurice F. Neufeld. The retirements would be occurring at regular intervals between 1972 and 1978. No one who has followed the development of scholarship in the field of industrial and labor relations needs to be reminded of the important contribution these individuals have made. We in the ILR School are also keenly aware of the high standard of classroom teaching maintained by each — in fact, several of us had our first courses in industrial relations with them. Although each remains vigorous and active, and will continue to contribute to our understanding of labor problems for many years to come, soon we will perforce lose their full-time participation in our institution.

It hardly needs to be said that the retirees cannot be replaced, either individually or collectively. The sum of their experiences includes, but is not limited to, organizing for the labor movement in the 1930s; arbitrating under the War Labor Board; fighting discrimination before most Americans were conscious of the depths of the problem; working closely with such historic figures as Herbert Lehman, Sidney Hillman, and Irving Ives; helping to shape the first NLRB; and building the professional status of the neutral in the postwar period. This list could be extended to several pages. Nevertheless, the point is clear: never again will the ILR School be able to tap the rich variety of these unique experiences.

A special conference seemed to be a particularly appropriate vehicle for honoring our retiring colleagues and for marking the transition of the collective bargaining department. Two years ago, I was appointed by Dean Robert McKersie as chairman of a committee to organize a Frank W. Pierce Memorial Conference. It was recognized from the beginning that no single conference would be a sufficient tribute to our senior members. Each truly deserved to be recognized individually. Yet it was hoped that a conference of high academic quality would stand by itself as a token of our great respect for the senior members of the department.

Accordingly, the organizing committee set out to enlist the services of the very best scholars in our field to prepare papers for the conference. In shaping the conference, the committee followed these guidelines: the subject matter of the conference should be clearly within the boundaries of our department, namely, collective bargaining, labor law, and labor history; the scholars selected should have research interests roughly parallel to those of our senior colleagues, and should be in the process of completing research projects on new and interesting topics. New topics would reflect, we hoped, the remarkable changes occurring in labor relations and thus symbolize the transition occurring within the collective bargaining department. We set no specific theme for the conference, but rather hoped to give the chosen scholars maximum latitude in developing their projects. The selection process itself would delimit the range of possible themes for the conference.

The organizing committee was especially fortunate in its work. With very little difficulty, we induced the six authors represented in this volume to participate in the conference. Each was a name included on the committee's initial brief list of "first choices." The mix of participants was just what we had wanted: two labor historians, two labor lawyers, and two labor economists with strong institutional interests. In addition, two were colleagues from the ILR School, two were former students of one or more of the retirees, and all were close friends who were anxious to participate in this collective *Festschrift*.

Each of the papers in this volume is the fruit of a major research project. The length of the papers, which in most cases is two or three times the length of an average scholarly journal article, reflects the ambition and scope of the author's research. This is consistent with the organizing committee's desire to provide the participants with a forum that they could use to maximum advantage, taking the opportunity to prepare essays too ambitious, and perhaps too risky, for the average journal or review, but not long enough to constitute a book or monograph. It is clear the committee's hopes have been fulfilled in this respect.

A glance at the table of contents is enough to verify the absence of a closely integrated theme to this volume. Each topic was freely chosen by the author and developed independently of the others. It is not my desire to force the authors into a thematic straitjacket; yet the reader of these pages will find a set of common concerns. In brief, each author (with one possible exception) is concerned with the determinants of union power, and particularly with how society attempts to balance the often competing interests of organized labor and the general welfare through public policy.

In considering the subject matter of these papers, one might well reflect on the concerns of the New York State legislators of thirty years ago. The scars of the Depression were still very deep and there was great concern that the end of the war would bring high levels of unemployment once again. The CIO was less than a decade old, and, although significant organizing of the mass-production industries had occurred, 80 percent of the work force remained outside labor's ranks. The AFL had also entered a period of aggressive organizing, and bitter rivalries with the CIO existed in several industries. Strike activity had been suppressed during the war years, but it was clear that low strike levels did not necessarily indicate high levels of worker satisfaction with wages and working conditions. The principles enunciated in the Wagner Act had been vigorously applied by the NLRB but were under attack by many employer groups. New unions with beachheads in previously unorganized industries were concerned about their own institutional security and pushed for the union shop. If industrial strife was to be avoided in the coming postwar period, it was clear the nation would need to grapple with these problems: unemployment, union organizing rights, major union jurisdictional battles, methods of settling industrial disputes, the balance between union and employer power, union security, and many others.

Now note the extent to which solutions have been found for many of these sources of potential labor-management discord. If solutions have not been found, there has at least been progress in the development of accepted methods of handling the problems. On the other hand, assumptions once widely held are now open to question. Consider the following examples:

1. Few impartial observers in the mid-1940s supported direct government intervention in the internal affairs of trade unions. Although union democracy had always

been a "splendid invalid," unions were, after all, voluntary associations not subject to government regulation.

2. Few worried excessively about the ability of workers to *give up* their union membership or to *avoid* involvement in collective bargaining. The greater problem seemed to be the guarantee of the right of workers to join unions and participate in collective bargaining, if they so desired.

3. Few devoted much attention to the bargaining rights of public employees. Most government employees lacked even the right to organize, and the thought that large numbers of public servants might strike summoned up visions of anarchy and revolution.

4. Few perceived a "crisis of the work ethic." On the contrary, it was American industriousness and productivity that many credited as the source of victories over the Axis powers. Alienation from work was a luxury few could afford during the Depression, and few tolerated during the war. In the postwar years, more foresaw a problem with the quanity of jobs than the quality of jobs.

All of these questions, and others, are addressed in the essays that follow. The new concerns of industrial relations scholars are indicative of the dynamic nature of the field and of the wisdom of those legislators who created an educational institution that would help seek solutions to new problems that might arise. If new concerns indicate a measure of success in dealing with old problems, at least some credit must go to the senior scholars who have toiled for many years to increase our understanding of this complex field.

In the opening essay, Sidney Fine addresses directly a theme sounded in several of the papers: the difficult task of balancing the interests of labor, the interests of employers, and the "public interest." Specifically, Fine describes Michigan Governor Frank Murphy's effort to pass a state labor relations act in 1937. Murphy, of course, gained a national reputation shortly after he assumed the governorship for his handling of the sit-down strike at General Motors in Flint. The historic strike was settled on February 11, 1937, but was followed by a rash of sit-down strikes in Michigan and throughout the nation. Public disenchantment with labor's use of this weapon grew steadily throughout the early spring of 1937: many in the middle class saw the sit-down as a genuine threat to private property, the embryo of the revolution.

Pressure on Murphy from employers, newspapers, and "law-and-order" groups rose with the growing level of labor strife. As a self-acknowledged friend of labor, Murphy was viewed by many as an appeaser — a governor unwilling to enforce the law against his allies, the unions. In fact, however, Murphy on several occasions exerted pressure on union leaders to cease their questionable tactics.

The Wagner Act had been law for nearly two years. Five

states had adopted "baby" Wagner Acts in 1937. In the midst of the tumult over the sit-downs, Murphy presented his own proposal for a comprehensive labor relations statute to the state legislature on April 29, 1937. The most remarkable and surprising aspect of the governor's bill was its highly restrictive, "antiunion" character. Although it incorporated many Wagner Act provisions, including the right of workers to organize and bargain collectively, it also included a number of sections that foreshadowed those included in the Taft-Hartley and Landrum-Griffin Acts. Fine provides the following comparison: "Whereas the purpose of the NLRA and the baby Wagner Acts in the states was to enhance the bargaining power of organized labor, the major purpose of the Michigan bill, so clearly a product of the 1937 law-and-order crisis, was, as the measure stated, 'to remove some of the causes' of labor disputes and to 'provide facilities for their prompt settlement.' "

Accordingly Murphy's bill included a number of novel provisions. For example, it included a list of unfair *employee* practices; it set up a mechanism for the mediation of labor disputes; it permitted the governor to use factfinding and invoke a cooling-off period in intractable disputes; in the event of a strike that threatened the public order, it empowered the governor to seize and run the establishment, if such an action was consistent with the interests of the public and the parties; and it provided for public disclosure and state examination of union books and records.

Why Murphy's bill did not become Murphy's law is clearly explained by Fine. Ironically, in July, Murphy vetoed a revised version of his own bill. Fine attributes Murphy's action to the pressures put on him by the "labor-libertarian alliance," principally the UAW and the ACLU.

Fine believes Murphy suffered this embarrassment partly because of a desire to satisfy some ephemeral "public interest." Throughout the essay, Fine is skeptical of the ability of the policy maker to distinguish the public interest from the particular interests of individuals and groups. Fine does not point up the parallels between the Michigan experience and the contemporary period, perhaps because they are too obvious. One can surmise, however, that he approves of Murphy's beliefs about law and justice: "Unlike the advocates of law and order, who presumably favored the rigid and prompt enforcement of all the laws, Murphy contended that since the law often lagged behind the times and human needs government, in the interest of the public good, must sometimes refrain from 'a blind and rigorous enforcement' of the laws."

Murphy's bill suggested some internal regulation of unions ten years before the Taft-Hartley Act made the first steps in that direction. In this volume's second essay, Harry Wellington suggests that further controls are needed to protect the individual against the power his union may exert over him. Wellington uses as his starting point columnist William Buckley's victory in a suit brought against the

American Federation of Television and Radio Artists. United States District Judge Charles Brieant ruled that the possibility of AFTRA using discipline against him, in combination with its union-shop provision, "could place a direct threat of prior restraint" upon Buckley. But Wellington believes that the major premise of Brieant's decision is "almost surely incorrect." Under current law, Buckley need not subject himself to union discipline and may, in fact, "immunize himself from the union's jurisdiction without any diminution of his employment rights."

It is well known that, since the *Allis-Chalmers* case, valid union discipline does not contravene the Taft-Hartley Act and that union fines are subject to judicial enforcement. At the same time, however, under a union shop or agency shop, a member's employment and job rights are insulated from union interference, except in the case of the member's failure to meet his minimal obligation to pay union dues and fees. "The [Supreme] Court [has] thus described a grand dichotomy divided into internal union sanctions that could be enforced even in a court of law and impermissible job discriminations that could not be imposed at all." "Valid" union discipline is discipline that does not run counter to public policy. But the NLRB has considerable discretion in determining "public policy" exceptions. As long as this is true, Wellington reasons, "few members will know the extent to which they may be disciplined."

As Wellington points out, current public policy leaves a number of troublesome questions unanswered. For example, although the Landrum-Griffin Act requires unions to meet certain minimum procedural requirements in disciplining members, the courts have so far allowed unions wide latitude on most procedural questions. The guarantee of a full and fair hearing has been stunted by denying an accused union member the right to counsel and the right to a specific statement of the charges against him. Moreover, the NLRB has refused to consider questions concerning either the amount or the manner in which a union fine has been imposed. In *NLRB* v. *Boeing* (1973) the Supreme Court supported the NLRB, ruling that the enforcing courts and not the board must determine the reasonableness of fines. Wellington believes *Boeing* "will probably lead the unions to impose still larger, and hence still more coercive, fines."

There is one clear route a worker may take to escape discipline by his union: he may resign his union membership. Two recent Supreme Court decisions, *Granite State* and *Booster Lodge,* make it clear that the union member has an inherent right to resign. Of course there are practical limitations on this right. The resigner gives up his voice in union affairs, although the union will continue to represent him in collective bargaining. In a hiring hall industry, the lack of a union card may force him to give up his trade completely. The resigner also gives up his right to any benefits provided solely by the union, such as union-sponsored group insurance plans. Of course he also loses his right to strike benefits, and, if he works during a strike, crossing the picket line can be unpleasant.

Section 8(a)(3)(B) of the NLRA makes it clear that a union-shop worker who has his union membership "denied or terminated" for any reason other than nonpayment of dues and fees retains the right to his job. Wellington believes this provision must be interpreted as protecting the resigner, in addition to those denied membership because of a union-initiated action. But if "membership" under the law requires only the periodic payment of dues, union-shop provisions in collective bargaining contracts fail to acknowledge that fact. Wellington urges that unions not be allowed to discipline members unless they are fully informed that their legal obligation is merely to pay dues. Further, he suggests that the board prohibit "any union-security clause that did not explicitly limit the worker's obligation to mere dues paying." A new member might be given a "Miranda warning" by his union: he need not assume full membership in the union, but merely tender dues; if he does join and does not resign he will be subject to union discipline.

Wellington acknowledges that his proposals may seem antiunion to some. In deciding on the proper balance between union power and competing interests, Wellington obviously assigns the highest priority to individual rights. He concludes, "I am concerned to have laws that protect the dissenter from his government, his employer, and his union."

In the following essay, Harry Edwards considers the balance between the power of public sector unions and the public interest. How can the public servant's interest in having a voice in determining his working conditions be reconciled with the people's right to determine the allocation of public resources? No labor question has proved move vexing for policy makers over the past decade. Often the "easiest" solution has been to transfer wholesale principles of law developed in the private sector. But Edwards suggests that solution may frequently be inappropriate.

To examine the application of private sector principles to the public sector, Edwards restricts his study to two doctrinal areas: the bargaining rights of supervisors and the duty to bargain. Further, he concentrates on the law as it has developed in six states, each state having a somewhat different approach.

The Taft-Hartley Act excluded supervisors from the coverage of the law. This exclusion meant that employers could prevent supervisors from joining unions and that supervisors had no bargaining rights under the law. Further, unions are prevented from disciplining supervisors for performing their job duties. In fact, supervisors in the private sector are prevented from participating actively in the internal affairs of their union — they must be "passive members." This reflects the ever-present fear of unlawful

employer interference and domination when supervisors are allowed to join rank-and-file unions. Also, the law permits employers to refuse to recognize any separate union of supervisors.

These private sector principles have not generally been applied in the public sector. Historically there has been a strong community of interest between supervisors and the rank and file in many public sector occupations. The line between a supervisor and an employee is often blurred in the public sector hierarchy. Frequently public managers really do not manage, partly because civil service commissions have assumed the responsibility for personnel problems.

There is also the issue of whether it is constitutionally permissible to deny supervisors the bargaining rights enjoyed by other public employees. For example, in contrast to federal law, New York State prohibits public managers from becoming members in employee unions. In *Shelofsky* v. *Helsby* (1972) the New York Court of Appeals upheld the constitutionality of the exclusion of managerial personnel from union membership. The court relied on private sector precedents to deny bargaining rights to managers. But Edwards suggests that the New York rule may be too broad because the result to be achieved can be accomplished by limiting managerial participation in union affairs, rather than by denying managers membership.

Edwards points to the variety of approaches to the supervisor question adopted in the states he surveys. New York, for example, distinguishes between supervisors and managers, granting bargaining rights to the former and denying them to the latter. In Pennsylvania, "first-level" supervisors must form separate units. The employer's obligation with such units is only to "meet and discuss" employment conditions, while with rank-and-file employees he has a positive duty to bargain. The Michigan statute takes an approach comparable to the one used under the Wagner Act before the Taft-Hartley Amendments. Edwards finds that the private sector model has generally been rejected to allow for an expansion of union interests in the public sector and concludes, "If the developing law in the public sector continues to accommodate union demands for bargaining rights for supervisors, management may well lose its 'arms and legs' in executing labor policies."

Edwards also examines the duty to bargain in the public sector. Statutes concerned with public employees' bargaining rights either require collective negotiations or merely oblige the employer to "meet and confer" with his employees. Those states requiring negotiations have generally followed the private sector model. However, there has been a greater effort to define statutorily the scope of bargaining in the public sector. Moreover, several states appear to limit the *scope* of bargaining by limiting the *process* of bargaining. The strike proscription present in most statutes indirectly limits the scope of bargaining. The necessity for legislative ratification is another procedural requirement that has the practical effect of narrowing the scope of bargaining (and incidentally promotes the phenomenon of the "end run" in public sector bargaining). Also, preexisting civil service laws occasionally take precedence over public sector bargaining statutes and further narrow the scope of bargaining.

States have followed different routes in applying their public sector bargaining statutes. Edwards presents an interesting contrast between Pennsylvania and Michigan. In *State College Education Association* v. *PLRB* (1973), the Pennsylvania court so narrowly defined the scope of bargaining that, if literally enforced, few if any subjects would be mandatory subjects of bargaining. In Michigan, the MERC decided in the *Westwood Community Schools* case (1972) to reject the distinction made in the private sector between mandatory and permissive subjects of bargaining. Since Michigan public employees have no right to strike, the MERC reasoned that a wide scope of bargaining could not lead to the increased use of economic weapons. Thus in Pennsylvania, where strikes are permitted, the scope of bargaining has been narrowed; while in Michigan, where strikes are prohibited, the scope has been widened. Edwards argues that if a ban on strikes is not really enforced, a wide scope of bargaining could give public sector unions an advantage not enjoyed by their private sector counterparts.

Thus, in the attempt to balance the interests of public employees and the interests of the public, legislators and courts have in recent years often favored the former, perhaps out of a "sense of guilt" for the historic restrictions placed on civil servants.

The final three essays in this volume deal with international and comparative labor problems. This is entirely fitting since several of the retiring members of the collective bargaining department have done significant research on foreign labor movements. First, George Hildebrand examines industrial relations on British railroads. American railroads, particularly in the Northeast, have faced a continuing crisis. Many observers have suggested that nationalization represents the most realistic solution to their problems. British railroads, of course, have been nationalized since 1948. Yet nationalization has neither eliminated British Railways' operating deficits nor solved its manifold labor problems.

Hildebrand divides the period since nationalization into four segments. From 1948 to 1954 there were no basic changes in the structure of the railroads. As a result, employment levels and job structure remained fairly stable. But from 1955 to 1962 British Railways converted to the diesel and made other efforts at modernization. As a result, the job structure was modified and employment levels fell. "Single manning" on the diesels was agreed to by the parties. In 1962 Lord Beeching became chairman of

the British Railways Board and ushered in a period of extreme physical retrenchment and rationalization. As a result the period between 1963 and 1968 saw drastic changes in British Railways' job structure and skill requirements. In 1968 Parliament passed a Transport Act that used a somewhat different approach to attack the railway problem, although it still hoped to achieve the goal of a self-sustaining public enterprise. From 1969 to 1973, there continued a futile search for profitability, while employment continued to decline and further changes in job structure were made.

Thus, the environment in which labor relations has been conducted has consisted of cash deficits, dependence on the British Treasury, inflation, recession, and secular decline. It can be no surprise then that union-management relations have been dominated by political considerations, instability, and considerable stress. Hildebrand identifies three broad issues on which the strain has been particularly severe: reductions in force and redundancy, technological change and productivity, and general pay increases.

Over the decade 1963-1973 the work force on British Railways was reduced by more than 50 percent. Although the redundancy issue has been a severe problem, the railway unions and British Railways management have probably had more success in coping with the issue than their American counterparts. For example, dropping firemen from diesel locomotives was not the crisis issue in Britain that it was in the United States. This is largely because a single union had jurisdiction over both engineers and firemen in Britain, whereas a separate brotherhood represented firemen in the United States and thus depended on the continued employment of firemen for its institutional survival.

Initially British Railways hoped to handle redundancy through natural attrition; later it became clear that supplemental measures would be necessary. As a result, British Railways adopted "the quite revolutionary notion that an employee who is severed from the payroll because of a reduction in force deserves some reimbursement for the loss of his equity in the job." Accordingly, redundancy is now handled through a combination of lump-sum severance allowances, early retirement benefits, and allowances to promote mobility.

The productivity problem has proved somewhat more intractable. However, a major breakthrough occurred in 1968. Under the spur of Britain's incomes policy, the British Railways Board began to insist that wage gains would be granted only in exchange for union concessions that would lead to increased productivity. The unions' rejection of the board's proposals led them to ban overtime and to "work to rule." "Transportation chaos followed," Hildebrand reports. In a dramatic step, the board's negotiating team flew to the annual general meeting of the National Union of Railwaymen (NUR) at Penzance. Hard bargaining was resumed and continued later at Windsor. The talks culminated in productivity agreements patterned on the board's earlier proposals. There followed a significant rationalization of the wage and job structure.

The negotiation of general pay increases led to the most recent labor crisis on British Railways. Enginemen (i.e., engineers) feel that they should be on top in "pay, prestige, and power," but that their position "has been eroding for years as regards relative pay." In 1973 the enginemen rejected a proposal by British Railways for a major restructuring of pay. "There followed some nine ghastly weeks of disrupted or suspended train services," and a dispute still unsettled at this writing. On the whole, Hildebrand believes that British rail unions have not exerted extraordinary wage pressure over the period of nationalization. The railways are no longer a top-paying industry and have trouble recruiting and retaining personnel, a sign of a low pay structure.

In contrast to the United States, British Railways has not had as much difficulty with restrictive work rules, has escaped undue wage pressures, and, until 1973-1974, did not experience a chronic strike problem. The interminable peril of the British Railways has served to inhibit the exercise of unacceptable union power.

In the next essay, John Windmuller examines the distribution of authority in national trade union centers. National trade union centers, confederations, or central bodies (such as the AFL-CIO) exist in most Western countries, but there are large differences in the amount of authority a national center exerts over its affiliates. For example, it is generally acknowledged that the AFL-CIO has little authority in relation to its member unions, while, at the other extreme, the Austrian ÖGB exerts almost total authority over its individual unions. Windmuller seeks to achieve two goals: first, to identify the "salient characteristics by which the internal authority of a confederation over its affiliates may be assessed," and second, to discover the determinants of the distribution of this internal authority. His research design involves a comparative examination of fourteen national centers in eleven Western industrial democracies.

Windmuller uses three "attributes of authority" to gauge the degree of centralization or autonomy within a national labor movement. The first is the share of total dues income accruing to the confederation. Clearly, the greater the share of resources captured by the central authority, the greater its authority. In actuality the variation in income shares among national centers is quite substantial; the range is from 2 percent to 80 percent. On one end of the scale are Australia, Great Britain, and the United States; on the other are Belgium and Austria.

The second attribute Windmuller uses is the degree of confederal control over the internal affairs of member unions. Clearly the British TUC and the AFL-CIO exert minimal control over the affairs of their constituent unions. Expulsion of an offending union is the ultimate discipline permitted both bodies. But in Austria and Sweden the national centers exercise sweeping powers of supervision over their affiliated unions.

The third attribute of authority used by Windmuller is the extent to which the central body is involved in industrial rule making or collective bargaining. In countries where centralized bargaining occurs at the national level, the authority of the central body is very great. Such is the case in Austria and the Scandinavian countries. In Belgium and France, the national centers settle important issues of social policy, but bargaining over wages and working conditions is the function of individual unions. In the Netherlands, a considerable degree of decentralization has occurred over the past several years. Still, the Dutch confederations retain more influence over bargaining than do the West German, British, and North American central bodies.

The analysis of the three attributes of authority permits Windmuller to rank each labor movement according to the degree of confederal authority. The next task is to identify those factors that may explain the relative rankings. Several "independent variables" are specified. For example, one important factor seems to be whether the national unions existed before the creation of the confederation. If they did, the power of the confederation tends to be low. This is not a complete explanation, however, because some confederations created as weak organizations eventually became very strong. Another determinant seems to be the size of the country. Weak central bodies seem to be found in countries "large in space or population or both." A strong personality can also create a strong body. For example, the AFL declined in authority after William Green succeeded Samuel Gompers. Membership concentration is yet another factor. Where membership is dispersed rather evenly among affiliates, the central body tends to be strong. But where membership is concentrated in one, two, or a few national unions, the central body remains weak. In addition, in countries with a strong craft tradition centralizing forces are often resisted. Strong central bodies exist in countries where the labor movement has always been committed to industrial unionism.

Still another factor mentioned by Windmuller is the relation between government intervention in the economy and confederal authority. Economic controls and other forms of government intervention foster the centralization of trade union authority. In particular the imposition of wage controls is associated with an increase in confederal authority. As Windmuller notes, "to the extent that expanding government intervention is the consequence of wage-push or cost-push inflation, the centralizing tendencies that emanate from it are really the cumulative result of individual unions' efforts to raise wages faster than productivity. In that sense, paradoxically enough, the constituent unions of national centers are actually fashioning their own centrally controlled restraints."

In the concluding essay, Irving Bernstein considers the current "crisis of the work ethic." In so doing, he traverses terrain usually unknown to industrial relations scholars. Most notably he investigates the sciences of ethology and zoology to show that all animal species are compelled to work to satisfy their primal drives: hunger, sex, fear, and aggression. "It seems evident that all animals, including man, expend energy in a gainful manner to satisfy these fundamental instincts. That is, by this definition, all animals work. Work, therefore, is a natural condition of every animal species, including man." But Bernstein implies that industrialism has imposed on man a coercive work discipline that he had not encountered in his long prior history. Adjusting to this discipline is a continuing problem and the cause of considerable alienation, especially in developing economies.

In contrast to the other animals, man's need to work "goes beyond that of the instinctual forces that drive other animals." Important social needs are fulfilled for man through his work. Bernstein quotes Freud: "No other technique for the conduct of life attaches the individual so firmly to reality as laying emphasis on work; for his work at least gives him a secure place in a portion of reality, in the human community."

Bernstein reminds us of the critical role time plays in the definition of the employment relation. He cites a number of collective bargaining agreements to demonstrate the complex and often subtle ways in which time is used to regulate the life of the worker. It is interesting to note that precision clocks were not built until just before the Industrial Revolution. In fact, for industrialism to succeed, it was necessary for the intervals of the day to be measured accurately. The close tie between man's work and the clock is a development that has occurred only over the past 200 years and is not characteristic of the work routines of other species. Bernstein believes "that the regular work rhythm demanded by industrial discipline is a basic, if not the prime, source of alienation from work. Although work is a natural condition for man, work locked into the clock and the calendar is unnatural."

Bernstein then examines "the comparative propensity to work" of national and religious ethnic groups. As he notes, attributing different propensities to work to dif-

ferent ethnic groups is not a popular exercise in academic circles. Undeterred, he proceeds to rank ethnic groups according to their "historic propensity to work" and to seek factors that explain these differential propensities. Bernstein identifies three central determinants: climate, religion, and family. Ethnic groups with a strong work ethic have generally lived in a temperate climate. They have followed a religion supportive of the work ethic. In addition, they have enjoyed a strong family life, although this factor appears to be a necessary rather than a sufficient condition. In the twentieth century, all three factors have lost considerable force. Technology has permitted man to overcome problems of climate, religion appears on the wane in all cultures, and the family as an institution is also eroding. "Insofar as the work ethic is concerned, we are in a period of tension between traditional institutions and the forces of change. . . . Where the forces of change have taken over decisively, where the backs of religion and family have been broken, one of the results has been alienation."

Bernstein thinks the best hope for overcoming alienation is to improve working conditions through collective bargaining and social legislation. In particular, he recommends measures that help attenuate the bond between the worker and the clock: reducing working hours and working years and rearranging work schedules.

These brief discussions of the papers contained in this volume can do no more than suggest some of the authors' major themes. Omitted is each paper's rich detail, careful development, and sophisticated analysis. The close reader will find many rewarding insights in the following pages. It is hoped the ILR School's regard for its senior colleagues is amply reflected in the excellence of these papers.

I, as editor, would like to thank the other members of the organizing committee for their advice and assistance: Donald Cullen, Robert Ferguson, Kurt Hanslowe, and James Morris. Mary Jo Powell, Frances Benson, and Charlotte Gold provided invaluable help in the preparation of this volume. Finally, a debt of appreciation is owed Dean Robert McKersie for his support of this project.

DAVID B. LIPSKY
Associate Professor
New York State School of
Industrial and Labor Relations

CHAPTER I

Frank Murphy, Law and Order, and Labor Relations in Michigan, 1937

by Sidney Fine, *Andrew D. White Professor of History,*
The University of Michigan, Ann Arbor

"Oh, Michigan!," *The New York Times* editorialized on March 13, 1937. "Isn't that uneasy place between the lakes the place where all the trouble that afflicts the nation starts?" As the *Times* saw it, the governor of the state, Frank Murphy, appeared to be "a man of peace" but with "a strong prejudice against enforcing the law." The New York newspaper wondered if Murphy, somehow, could be "induced to withdraw and let JOHN LEWIS [*sic*] take over Michigan as a kind of mandated territory. . . . Then the State could isolate itself as a social laboratory devoted exclusively to Mr. Lewis's experiments."[1]

MICHIGAN SIT-DOWN STRIKES

It was the wave of sit-down strikes in Michigan in the early months of 1937 that riveted the nation's attention on the Wolverine State, and it was the reaction to these strikes of the state's new governor that heightened the widespread concern about law and order that the increasing use of the novel labor weapon had induced. Responding to the public clamor, the 1937 equivalent to the fear of crime in the streets that prevailed in the 1960s and the early 1970s, Governor Murphy sought to reassure the anxious that the law would be enforced in Michigan and order would be preserved. Appropriate state legislation, Murphy proclaimed, could contribute materially to the peaceful adjustment of labor disputes, and with this in view he submitted to the state legislature a labor relations bill that he hoped would become the prototype for the nation as a whole. Although Murphy was the very model of a prolabor governor, his bill did not conform to the pattern of the National Labor Relations Act (NLRA or Wagner Act), pointing rather in the direction of the Taft-Hartley and Landrum-Griffin statutes of a later era. The Murphy administration failed to secure the enactment of its labor relations bill, but the abortive effort nevertheless revealed a good deal about the tides of popular opinion concerning the exercise of labor power, the clash between abstract conceptions of the public interest and the influence of concrete private interests, and the play of personal ambition.

In a paper entitled "Politics and the Laborer" that he prepared as a college junior in 1911, Murphy wrote with regard to his choice of topic:

> I love the subject. I want to make it my life's work. If I can only feel, when my day is done, that I have accomplished something towards uplifting the poor, uneducated, unfortunate, ten hour a day, laborer from the political chaos that he now exists in, I will be satisfied that I have been worth while.

As a criminal court judge from 1924 to 1930, mayor of Detroit from 1930 to 1933, and governor-general and high commissioner of the Philippines from 1933 to 1936, Murphy consistently championed the cause of organized labor and consistently enjoyed the labor movement's support. "I am heart and soul in the Labor Movement," he declared in an interview with the *Detroit Labor News* while he was campaigning for the governorship of Michigan in September 1936. "I have yet to go contrary to the expressed will of Organized Labor in matters that affect it and as expressed by its official chosen representatives, and you all know that I shall never do so."[2] This assertion was put to a severe test when Murphy became Michigan's governor at the beginning of 1937.

The General Motors Strike

The great General Motors (GM) sit-down strike was already underway when Murphy took his oath of office. Murphy sent National Guardsmen to Flint following the famous Battle of the Running Bulls on January 11, 1937, but he used the troops to preserve the status quo rather than to drive the workers from the plants that they occupied. When Judge Paul Gadola issued a writ on February 5 ordering the sheriff of Genesee County "to attach the bodies" of the Fisher Body sit-downers, their

---

[1] *The New York Times,* March 13, 1937.

[2] Murphy, "Politics and the Laborer," [1911] manuscript, Frank Murphy Papers, Michigan Historical Collections, University of Michigan, Ann Arbor, Michigan; Frank Martel to Fred Pettinga, August 11, 1936, Wayne County AFL-CIO Papers, box 7, Archives of Labor History and Urban Affairs, Wayne State University, Detroit, Michigan; *Detroit Labor News,* September 11, 1936.

"confederates" who were picketing, and local and international officers of the United Automobile Workers (UAW) for failure to comply with the injunction that the judge had granted three days earlier, Murphy counseled the sheriff to delay the enforcement of the court's order. The governor acted as he did because he believed that the enforcement of the writ would destroy the chances for the peaceful resolution of the dispute that appeared imminent and would also lead to the shedding of blood, a result that Murphy wished to avoid at almost any cost. The governor privately advised John L. Lewis on the night of February 9 that "the time has come for all concerned to comply fully with the decision and order of the Court and take necessary steps to restore possession of the occupied plants to their rightful owners"; but this fact was not made public until January 1939 and, in any event, the governor's law-and-order letter, as recent research has revealed, did not contribute materially to the settlement of the strike on February 11.

Murphy's peacemaking role in the GM strike was lavishly and widely praised in the nation, and a Murphy associate was undoubtedly correct in his later judgment that, "in terms of public esteem and prestige," the GM sit-down was "the high point in Frank Murphy's entire career." There was, to be sure, some criticism of the governor's action and his ranging of the power of the state on the side of the strikers, but the consensus was that, if a price had been paid in law and order to achieve a peaceful settlement, the results gained had justified the expenditure.[3]

The Detroit Sit-Downs

The settlement of the GM strike was quickly followed by an "epidemic" of sit-down strikes in Detroit. "Sitting down," a *Detroit News* reporter soon observed, "has replaced baseball as the national pastime, and sitter-downers clutter up the landscape in every direction." There were thirty-four sit-down strikes in Detroit between February 12 and the end of the month and seventy-eight such strikes, as well as fifteen conventional strikes, in March. Detroit alone accounted for almost half of all the sit-down strikes in the nation in February and March, making it the undisputed sit-down strike capital of the United States.[4]

Initially the Detroit sit-downs occurred mostly in businesses with which the general public had little direct contact; but on February 27, 1937, one hundred women sat down in the downtown store of F. W. Woolworth and Company, the first sit-down in Detroit in a mercantile establishment and the beginning of a rash of strikes among Detroit's nonunionized service employees. At the beginning of March about one hundred fifty workers who were sitting down in the Newton Packing Company plant decided to ignore an injunction directing them to permit the removal of $170,000 in food products from the plant and were consequently declared in contempt of court. On March 8 employees of the eight Chrysler Corporation plants in the Detroit area began "the largest and most effectively organized sit-down strike on record," and this action precipitated a new "tidal wave" of sit-downs and outside strikes. Four hundred workers staged a sit-down in the Crowley-Milner Company department store on March 10, and Detroit's four largest downtown hotels were closed by strikes on March 16. At the Book-Cadillac Hotel, employees locked themselves in the dining room, while organizers carrying meat cleavers rushed the rear entrance of the building and seized the establishment.[5]

The seeming challenge to property rights represented by the sit-down strikes heightened the traditional middle-class concern about trade union behavior; and the manner in which the Detroit daily press, hostile to unionism and sympathetic to the employer, generally treated the issue did nothing to lessen the mounting anxiety. "Perhaps this IS the revolution," some of the fearful thought as the strike wave spread, and *Time* magazine, disdaining the use of "perhaps," was quite certain that Detroiters had been "getting an idea of what a revolution feels like." It was not revolution, however, that the strikers were seeking but collective bargaining and improved working conditions. What was taking place was an uprising of the unorganized in an open-shop city, and the *Detroit News* correspondent W. K. Kelsey was quite correct in his judgment that the strikers had "no more idea of 'revolution' than pussy cats." In so far as the strikers resorted to the sit-down tactic, it was because the weapon seemed to be effective and because, it must also be said, it had become "a

---

[3] For a detailed treatment of the GM strike, see Sidney Fine, *Sit-Down: The General Motors Strike of 1936-1937* (Ann Arbor: University of Michigan Press, 1969).

[4] There is a list of the sit-down and conventional strikes in Detroit in U.S. Congress, House, Special Committee on Un-American Activities, *Investigation of Un-American Propaganda Activities in the United States*, 75th Cong., 3rd Sess., 1938, 2:1609-21. The totals for the nation are given in "Number of Sit-Down Strikes in 1937," *Monthly Labor Review* 47 (August 1938):361. According to the latter, 217 sit-down strikes occurred in the United States in February and

March, but this number does not include sit-downs lasting less than one day. Of the 112 Detroit sit-downs in February and March, perhaps 17 lasted less than one day. The quotation is taken from the *Detroit News*, March 14, 1937.

[5] For the sit-down epidemic in Detroit in the early months of 1937, see *Detroit News*, February 16-March 19, 1937; *The New York Times*, March 7, 10, 17, 1937; Burnham Finney, "Worse Than the Plague," *American Machinist* 81 (April 7, 1937):286-87; *Business Week*, March 27, 1937, pp. 13-14; *Time* 29 (March 29, 1937):11-13; Carlos A. Schwantes, "...The 1937 Non-Automotive Strikes in Detroit," *Michigan History* 56 (Fall 1972):179-99; and Carol A. Westenhoefer, "Non-Automotive Sit-Down Strikes in Detroit," manuscript (in my possession, 1964).

fashion, a fad, the thing to do." They were making use of the technique of "creative disorder," seeking change and entry into the "system" by disorderly but essentially nonviolent means. It was a technique that had been successfully applied in Flint and had been tolerated by the state's chief executive because the ends sought were sanctioned by law, so why should not the same method be applied in Detroit to achieve the same goals?[6]

For those who viewed the Detroit sit-downs with foreboding, it was, indeed, the Flint precedent that came to be seen as the cause of the city's strike troubles. It was the "tacit blessing" given the GM sit-down by the "vacillating state administration," *Automotive Industries* declared, that had opened the door "to any and all groups." The Flint experience had taught "lawless strikers everywhere" that they could "safely defy the law" without fear of counteraction by Governor Murphy. "They should have turned the machine guns on them in Flint" was the way one Detroiter put it in explaining the city's strike wave. The Detroit sit-downs deprived Murphy of a good deal of the luster of his Flint achievement, and to an overwrought *Time* magazine it appeared that he was on the way to becoming "the Kerensky of the New Deal."[7]

Murphy's original reaction to the Detroit sit-downs was to dispatch his commissioner of labor and industry, George A. Krogstad, to the city to mediate those strikes in which this procedure was agreeable to the disputants, which was the extent to which the state could legally involve itself in these labor disputes. Krogstad worked "night and day" on the settlement of Detroit's labor troubles, and he achieved some success; but he soon called for help.[8] The governor's assistance was also invoked on

March 12 by the Detroit Board of Commerce, which urged him to convene a conference of law-enforcement officials for the purpose of devising a "militant program" to cope with the "intolerable situation" endangering Detroit's "international civic reputation."

Of greater importance in affecting Murphy's judgment than the plea of the Detroit Board of Commerce was a memorandum prepared by Michigan's Attorney General Raymond W. Starr. Starr contended that organized labor had "misconstrued" Murphy's role in Flint and had concluded that he would "not — under any circumstances — interfere or permit interference by lawful force with. . . Union activities in taking possession of factories, stores, etc." and would tolerate labor's "disregard" of the law and of court orders. It was consequently "opportune — if not necessary —" for Murphy to make it evident that "the integrity of judicial orders and the law must be upheld." Starr thought that "a proper first step" would be for the governor to meet with labor leaders to clarify his position, but it was eventually decided that Murphy would get together in Lansing on March 15 with the prosecuting attorneys of five southern Michigan counties and then would meet in Detroit on March 17 with representatives of labor, management, and the general public.[9]

In his remarks to the law-enforcement officials, Murphy stated that the use of force by employer or employee to achieve reasonable objectives was "wholly unnecessary under a democratic regime." Both labor and management, he asserted, were obliged to obey the law, and it was essential that they respect the authority of the courts "if we are to have orderly government and an orderly peaceful society." He urged employers and employees to cooperate with local law-enforcement officials so that it would be unnecessary for them to take "extreme measures" in discharging their obligation to preserve "public authority" and protect the "rights of private property."

The law-enforcement officials agreed to support the governor; and, reflecting the anxieties of the moment, Duncan McRea, the prosecuting attorney of Wayne County and the official at the meeting most directly in the eye of the strike hurricane, went so far as to suggest that martial law should be declared if the strike situation worsened. The law officers, however, do not appear to have come to any decision regarding the legality of the sit-down strike, a very clouded matter in Michigan's criminal law at that time. In Michigan forcible entry and detainer was not a statutory offense for which a penalty had been expressly provided, although it would be argued later that, since it was an indictable offense under the

[6] Daniel Bell, "Industrial Conflict and Public Opinion," in Arthur Kornhauser *et al.*, eds., *Industrial Conflict* (New York: McGraw-Hill, 1954), pp. 242-43; Dwight W. Chapman, "Industrial Conflict in Detroit," in George W. Hartmann and Theodore Newcomb, eds., *Industrial Conflict* (New York: Cordon Co., 1939), pp. 63-65; Mary Heaton Vorse, "Detroit Has the Jitters," *New Republic* 90 (April 7, 1937):256; *Time* 29 (March 29, 1937): 12; *Detroit News,* March 19, 21, April 5, 1937. See Arthur I. Waskow, *From Race Riot to Sit-In, 1919 and the 1960's* (New York: Anchor Books, 1966), pp. 204, 228-30, 278-79, 297-98, for a discussion of the technique of "creative disorder."

[7] *Automotive Industries* 76 (March 20, 1937):452; Vorse, "Detroit," p. 256; *Time* 29 (March 29, 1937): 12; *Detroit Saturday Night,* February 13, 1937; *Detroit News,* March 14, 1937; *The New York Times,* March 16, 21, 1937; [*New York Herald Tribune,* March 23, 1937] clipping in Edward G. Kemp Papers, box 10, Burton Historical Collection, Detroit, Michigan (unless otherwise noted, all references to Kemp Papers are to this collection); "Six Months after the Strikes," *Survey Graphic* 26 (November 1937):562-64.

[8] *Public Acts of the Legislature of. . . Michigan. . . 1915* (Lansing, 1915), pp. 387-92; *Detroit News,* February 26,

1937, August 11, 1938; *Detroit Labor News,* March 5, 1937; Norman H. Hill to Murphy, March 2, 1937, Murphy Papers.

[9] Harvey Campbell to Murphy, March 12, 1937, Murphy to Kemp, March 12, 1937, and Kemp note on same, Murphy Papers; Starr to Kemp, March 12, 1937, Kemp Papers, box 10; *Detroit News,* March 14, 1937.

common law, sit-downers were guilty of a felony according to the terms of a Michigan statute that made it felonious to commit a common-law offense for which no statute had specified a punishment. With specific regard to the Detroit sit-downs, McRea had ruled that employers could seek redress against sit-downers in the civil courts, but that the police could not interfere with a peacefully conducted sit-down.[10]

Murphy's hopes of bringing together a representative group of persons for the Detroit law-and-order conference were frustrated when the UAW's General Executive Board decided to forbid any of its members to participate in the proceedings. UAW President Homer Martin, thereupon, informed Murphy that there could be no solution to the wave of sit-downs as long as employers refused to engage in collective bargaining. The sit-downs, Martin noted, had been characterized by "peacefulness and absence of violence," and the real issue was not whether they were legal but whether the workers had a right to better their conditions of employment. Since public opinion had turned against the strikers, the UAW decision was a foolish one, at least from a public relations standpoint, and many persons no doubt agreed with the Michigan Manufacturers' Association that the action demonstrated that unionists believed they were "a law unto themselves." Unlike the UAW, the Detroit and Wayne County Federation of Labor (DWCFL) and the Michigan Federation of Labor (MFL) were represented at the governor's conference.[11]

Murphy told the twenty-three members who gathered for what was described as "the first meeting of Governor Murphy's Law and Order Commission" that he had always counseled negotiation and the peaceful settlement of disputes, but that there was a "limit" to this policy. It should not be assumed, he said, that the state government would "forsake its responsibility to maintain order and protect citizens in the full exercise of their legal rights." Public officials and the populace at large, he noted, had become "gravely disturbed" by the numerous disputes and "a disposition in some quarters to ignore the law and violate the security and freedom of individuals and corporations in the exercise of their personal and property rights." Behavior of this sort discredited labor organizations; impaired public confidence in liberal, democratic government; and impeded social progress. Although it was important to protect human rights, personal liberty

would be of little value if the integrity of courts were not preserved and property rights went unprotected.

He was aware, the governor stated, that there was "fault on both sides" and that labor was responding to unjust conditions and the refusal of "backward employers" to recognize the right of collective bargaining, but it would be necessary, nevertheless, to find some way "to prevent these disorderly and unlawful methods of pursuing lawful and worthy objectives." Although Murphy recommended the establishment of dispute-adjustment machinery within individual industries and in the local communities to meet the immediate situation, he made it clear at the same time that appropriate state legislation would be required to make "wholly unnecessary" the kind of labor difficulties that Michigan was experiencing. The conferees at the meeting endorsed the governor's suggestions for dealing with the strike problem, but the only immediate action taken by Murphy was to appoint an Emergency Mediation Committee, consisting of three liberal clergymen, to assist in the settlement of the minor Detroit strikes while he turned his attention to the key Chrysler dispute.[12]

The different perspectives from which the law-and-order issue was being viewed in Michigan are indicated by the contrasting reactions to Murphy's law-and-order remarks of Maurice Sugar, the UAW's counsel, and Edward G. Kemp, the governor's legal advisor and closest friend. It was the employers who were "the real criminals" and law breakers, Sugar protested to Murphy, not the workers. The employers had been "sitting down on the law" ever since the NLRA had been passed, whereas the workers were "liberty loving Americans rebelling against submission to the dictates of the criminal elements in the community." Why, Sugar asked, had Murphy called for law and order only after the sit-downs had occurred and not at an earlier time to protest employer defiance of the law? Kemp, by contrast, was afraid that Murphy, in his zeal "to assist labor groups or avoid losing the good will and confidence of their leaders and organizers," had placed too much emphasis in his Lansing and Detroit talks on the peaceful settlement of disputes and labor's freedom to organize and its right to strike. These, he thought, were "secondary" or "collateral" matters compared to the state's primary obligation to have the law respected and enforced and to give employers some "practical alternative" to negotiating with groups or individuals, some of them "Communistic," who had "taken forcible possession of their business establishments and been allowed to keep them in defiance of the law."[13]

The turning point in the Detroit strike crisis actually

[10] *Detroit News*, December 20, 1936, February 26, 28, March 16, 1937; Samuel D. Pepper to John S. Bersey, March 17, 1937, Samuel D. Pepper Papers, privately held; Fine, *Sit-Down*, pp. 176-77.

[11] UAW General Executive Board Minutes, March 15, 1937, Henry Kraus Papers, box 7, Archives of Labor History and Urban Affairs; Murphy to Hill, March 16, 1937, Martin to Murphy, March 17, 1937, Murphy Papers; *Michigan Manufacturer and Financial Record* 59 (March 20, 1937):3, hereafter cited as MMFR.

[12] Statement by Governor Murphy, March 17, 1937, and Minutes of March 17, 1937, meeting, Murphy Papers; *Detroit News*, March 17-19, 1937.

[13] Sugar to Murphy, March 22, 1937, Kemp Papers, box 10; Kemp to Murphy, [March 20, 1937], Murphy Papers.

occurred while the governor's law-and-order conference was in session. Word came to the conferees that "professional 'sit-downers'" had raided the Frank and Seder department store, instigated a sit-down strike, ejected customers and company executives, and prevented employees, most of whom apparently opposed the strike, from leaving the establishment. Mayor Frank Couzens, who was attending the governor's conference, ordered the police "to clear out all persons" who did not belong in the store. Murphy himself left the conference to go to the Frank and Seder store and was urging the employees to leave the building just as the police arrived, an incident that was distorted before Martin Dies' House Special Committee on Un-American Activities during the course of the 1938 gubernatorial campaign in Michigan.

The Frank and Seder dispute was quickly resolved, but the press and the forces of law and order could now claim that it was "outsiders" who were responsible for the Detroit strikes. Detroit, the executive secretary of the Detroit Board of Commerce warned, was "swarming" with "imported organizers, agitators and labor racketeers.' Even Murphy, who had objected to the seizure of plants in Flint by outsiders, declared that, although a "legitimate strike" required "respect and a neutral attitude" on the part of government officials, "a raid is not a strike but a modified form of banditry and must be treated as such. Such matters are not going to be handled by red tape and technicalities and will be straightened out once and for all."[14]

For the next several days the Detroit newspapers contained pictures and accounts of persons with police records who were alleged to be responsible for some of the sit-down strikes in the city, and the *Detroit News* stated flatly that the sit-downs could now be placed in "the gangster racket class." Mayor Couzens ordered the police not to interfere with "peaceful" sit-downs if the strikers were employees, but to take "proper action" where "total strangers" had "lawlessly" invaded stores and plants. Couzens' directive led to a series of police raids against establishments that had been closed by sit-down strikes, including some in which no outsiders were present. On March 19, 1937, the police ejected the strikers occupying six downtown shoe stores and the Dossin Food Products Company. Two days later police and sheriff's deputies evicted and arrested sixty-four Newton Packing Company strikers who, as we have seen, had defied a court order. On the same day, about three hundred police, without benefit of any court order and without any real evidence of the presence of outsiders, evicted 150 to 200 kicking, screaming, biting, hair-pulling, and club-wielding women from the Bernard Schwarz Company cigar plant, while near the plant forty mounted police battled five hundred

strike sympathizers who threw missile-laden snowballs at the officers. There were two more police raids the next day, in one of which nineteen sit-downers were evicted from one of the city's welfare stations.[15]

Protesting the "brutal eviction" of sit-downers and "ruthless clubbing" by the police, the UAW called a mass meeting for March 23 to register its disapproval of the tactics being employed by the Detroit city government against some of the sit-down strikes. When the Common Council, on the grounds that it would paralyze traffic, rejected the union's application for a permit to hold the demonstration at 5:00 P.M. in Cadillac Square in downtown Detroit, flannel-mouthed UAW Vice-president Ed Hall retorted, "We don't give a good whoop in hell about the permit; we'll be there anyhow." Cooler heads prevailed, however; and an agreement was worked out with the city for the union to hold the rally at 5:45 P.M. at the east end of the square, with the understanding that the meeting would be "peaceful and orderly" and that the police would be present to direct traffic and to prevent "any unlawful or outside interference."

A crowd of approximately fifty thousand attended the March 23 demonstration and resolved not only to support the Chrysler strikers but also to stage two sit-down strikes for every police eviction. Headlining its story, "UAWA Threatens Detroit Overturn," *The New York Times* reported Frank Martel, the president of the DWCFL, as proclaiming at the rally, "From this time on the constitutional rights of this community are going to be respected in the City Hall, the police station and the courts, or we'll turn them wrong-side up." Martel, however, was simply indulging in rabble-rousing and symbolic rhetoric, and neither he nor his listeners had a coup d'état in mind. Although the "tone of the city" was reported to have been "very uneasy" following the rally, the peaceful and orderly character of the demonstration served to puncture the "balloon of panic" that had been inflating in anticipation of the event. Four days after the Cadillac Square rally Murphy's Emergency Mediation Committee reported to the governor that it had successfully adjusted most of the strikes in Detroit, and it requested that its services be terminated.[16]

[14] *Detroit News*, March 18, 19, 1937, October 21, 22, 1938; *The New York Times*, March 21, 1937; *Investigation of Un-American Propaganda*, 2:1630-31.

[15] Couzens to M. Udale, March 25, 1937, Couzens to Martin W. Rolnick, March 27, 1937, Mayor's Office Records, Burton Historical Collection; *Detroit News*, March 19-22, 1937; *Detroit Free Press*, March 21, 1937; *The New York Times*, March 24, 1937.

[16] *United Automobile Worker*, March 23, 1937; *Detroit News*, March 21, 23, 24, 1937; *Detroit Free Press*, March 25, 1937; copy of agreement, March 22, 1937, Mayor's Office Records; *The New York Times*, March 24, 1937; Vorse, "Detroit," pp. 257-58; Frederic Seidenburg *et al.* to Murphy, March 27, 1937, Murphy Papers. *Detroit Labor News* of March 26, 1937, reported Martel as having said that the people would "wipe aside" (not "overturn") public officials who disregarded labor's rights.

Murphy, in the meantime, was devoting his attention to the settlement of the Detroit area's most important industrial dispute, the Chrysler sit-down strike. Cautioning both sides to be mindful of their obligation to preserve law and order, Murphy initially indicated a disinclination to intervene unless there was "no other way of working out the problem," but he in the end played almost as large a part in the settlement of the Chrysler strike as he had in the GM sit-down. When the Chrysler Corporation obtained an injunction from Judge Allan Campbell of the Wayne County Circuit Court on March 15 ordering the sit-downers to evacuate the company's plants by 9:30 A.M. on March 17, the day of Murphy's law-and-order conference, the issue of obedience to the law was thrust into the forefront of the dispute. Murphy by this time had privately informed Adolph Germer, the Congress of Industrial Organizations' (CIO) man in Michigan, that "he deplored the sit-down strikes — taking possession of other people's property," and he stated with regard to the injunction that "the law should be obeyed and there should be no disobedience of court orders."

Undoubtedly because of the pressure that Murphy was exerting both publicly and privately and the increasing public opposition to the sit-down tactic, the UAW and CIO leadership was prepared to evacuate the Chrysler plants in return for a promise by the company not to operate the factories while negotiations for a settlement proceeded; but, since the UAW, John L. Lewis, Frances Perkins, and Murphy were unable to work out such an arrangement with the management, the union decided to ignore Judge Campbell's injunction and to retain possession of the Chrysler plants. On March 19 the judge therefore ordered the arrest of the approximately six thousand workers sitting in the eight Chrysler plants in the Detroit area. The responsibility for executing the order fell on Sheriff Thomas C. Wilcox, but Wilcox did not have the manpower to enforce the writ, leading his chief deputy to state, "it will be up to the Governor."

Murphy, while expressing his preference for "peace without bloodshed," let it be known that the state would proceed "with vigor" if the sheriff decided that he could not cope with the situation and requested the governor's assistance; and, privately, Murphy even considered the possibility of imposing martial law. There is no documentary evidence that Wilcox ever formally requested the governor's assistance, but the sheriff could hardly have been unaware that Murphy preferred to negotiate the men out of the Chrysler plants rather than to "shoot them out." It may be that the governor privately discouraged Wilcox from invoking the aid of the state just as he had discouraged the Genesee County sheriff from doing so in the GM strike.[17]

The decision reached by Murphy, following the advice of James Dewey, the federal conciliator who was assisting the governor in the dispute, was to demand that the union comply with the court order and evacuate the Chrysler plants, but at the same time to request that Walter Chrysler and Lewis confer with the governor as to the means of carrying out the evacuation. This decision, in Kemp's view, involved "a serious compromise on the fundamental issue of law and order," but to have insisted on evacuation without a conference would have antagonized organized labor, which Murphy preferred not to do.

On March 23 Murphy wired Lewis and Chrysler that if the sheriff, as expected, requested its assistance, the state would

> employ all necessary and available means. . . to uphold public authority. . . and protect property rights. . . . In view of the large interests at stake, however, and [the] desirability of ascertaining whether adjustment is possible before taking extreme and costly measures with possible unfortunate consequences,

the governor requested the two men to confer with him the next day in an effort to find a "prompt satisfactory solution without unwarranted delay in [the] enforcement of [the] court's order." Both Lewis and Chrysler accepted Murphy's invitation, although Lewis protested that he was being asked to confer "under duress" and Chrysler replied that the court order was "not a proper subject for negotiation" and that the corporation would "not enter into any trade to get the men out of the plants."[18]

After more than eight hours of negotiation with Murphy on March 24, Lewis and Chrysler agreed to truce terms. The UAW was "immediately" to evacuate the Chrysler plants that it occupied, while the company committed itself not to operate these plants or to remove any dies or machinery pending negotiations with the union on its demand for exclusive bargaining rights. The state police were to guard the gates of the factories to guarantee the observance of the agreement. This arrangement was identical with a Murphy proposal that Lewis had rejected following the breakdown of the January 15, 1937, truce in the GM strike; but the mood of the country had changed since that time, and the presence in Murphy's office of the state's adjutant general, the commissioner of the Michigan

[17] *Detroit News*, March 9, 11, 15-17, 19-21, 1937; *The New York Times*, March 16, 20, 21, 1937; *Detroit Times*, March 21, 1937, clipping in Murphy Scrapbooks (hereafter

MSB), and Murphy to Kemp, March 22, 1937, Murphy Papers; Adolph Germer Diary, March 12, 15, 16, 18, 1937, Adolph Germer Papers, State Historical Society of Wisconsin, Madison; Germer to John Brophy, March 18, 1937, CIO File (notes on this file in possession of Irving Bernstein); *Dodge Main News*, March 21, 1937, Joe Brown Collection, Archives of Labor History and Urban Affairs; J. Woodford Howard, "Frank Murphy and the Sit-Down Strikes of 1937," *Labor History* 1 (Spring 1960):120.

[18] Kemp Memorandum, March 22, 1937, Murphy to Lewis and Chrysler, March 23, 1937, Lewis to Murphy, March 23, 1937, Chrysler to Murphy, March 23, 1937, Murphy Papers.

State Police, and the colonel who had commanded the National Guard in Flint during the GM strike no doubt helped to persuade the CIO chief that the governor was determined that the Chrysler plants be evacuated forthwith. The sit-downers marched out of the plants on March 25, eight days after the injunction deadline had expired. Murphy had accomplished his objective, but there was some truth to the comment in *News-Week* that the governor had "still put peace first, law second."[19]

Murphy took charge of the negotiations that followed the end of the sit-down phase of the Chrysler strike and was instrumental in fashioning the April 6 agreement that brought the strike to a close. The UAW did not officially receive the exclusive bargaining rights that it had publicly proclaimed it was seeking, but it was accorded the kind of preferential status in Chrysler Corporation that it had privately been willing to accept from the outset and that gave it the substance, if not the form, of what it sought. It may also be that Chrysler provided Lewis with private assurances that the corporation would act on the presumption that the UAW represented all Chrysler plant workers.[20]

Three days after the Chrysler settlement had been achieved Dewey met with the UAW's General Executive Board and reported Martin as saying that "the sit-down strategy was no longer necessary; that it had served its purpose; had been effective; that it was now necessary to abandon this practice which had attracted so much public attention; that public opinion was against it; and that it was unsafe to use it further." On April 12 the United States Supreme Court, in *NLRB* vs. *Jones and Laughlin*, upheld the NLRA, which made it far easier for unions to gain recognition by using less drastic tactics than the sit-down. The dwindling number of sit-down strikes (there were only fifteen such strikes in Detroit and only fifty-two in the nation in April) somewhat lessened the urgency of the public concern about labor strife and law and order, but it did not end the acrimonious debate on the subject between Murphy and his opponents that had begun shortly after the conclusion of the GM sit-down and that had been especially intense in March and early April. Murphy's

numerous critics accused him of being simply "a labor advocate" who had "practicaly [sic] turned over the management" of Detroit to "a rabble mob" and had "practicaly [sic] abdicated" his office. They complained that the "coddling of a minority class as against the entire public welfare" had "gone about far enough" and that the time had come for action. "Words Won't Win This War, Mr. Murphy — Where Are Your Troops?" the *Detroit Saturday Night* asked in a headline of March 20.[21]

The concern about law and order as it pertained to the sit-down strikes was by no means confined to Michigan. When the Chrysler sit-downers defied Judge Campbell's injunction, "millions," according to *News-Week*, "sensed a threat against every man's right to keep what he owns, and against the courts' power to protect that right." An executive of the First Machinery Corporation of New York City wrote Murphy: "The insurrection against constituted authority is no longer a local concern within the confines of your State. It threatens the safety and security of private property everywhere in our land."

Occurring at the same time as President Franklin D. Roosevelt was pressing his controversial plan to reorganize the Supreme Court, the wave of sit-downs aroused fears among some that the very foundations of the Republic were being undermined. "Armed insurrection — defiance of law, order, and duly elected authority — is spreading like wildfire," a group of Boston civic leaders wired the United States Senate late in March.

> If minority groups can seize premises illegally, hold indefinitely, refuse admittance to owners or managers, resist by violence and threaten bloodshed all attempts to dislodge them, and intimidate properly constituted authority to the point of impotence, then freedom and liberty are at an end, government becomes a mockery, superseded by anarchy, mob rule and ruthless dictatorship.

A Gallup poll released on March 21 indicated that 67 percent of the respondents believed that the states should make the sit-down strike illegal.[22]

Concerned because of an alleged "collapse of

[19] Murphy to UAW, March 24, 1937, Murphy Papers; Germer Diary, March 24, 1937, Germer Papers; *Detroit News*, March 24-26, 1937; *The New York Times*, March 25, 1937; Fine, *Sit-Down*, pp. 254-55; *News-Week* 9 (April 3, 1937):7; "The Sitdown Hysteria," *Nation* 144 (April 3, 1937):368.

[20] The negotiations are best followed in the Murphy Papers, which also contain a copy of the April 6 agreement. See also Doris McLaughlin, ". . .The Chrysler Strike of 1937," manuscript (in my possession, undated), p. 55; *Detroit Times*, April 7, 1937, MSB; and *Detroit News*, April 7, 1937. Those who have characterized the strike as a defeat for the UAW have been unaware of the union's realistic goals in the dispute and have underestimated the significance of the terms of the settlement.

[21] "Following Information from Dewey," April 9, 1937, Conciliation Service File 182-2259, Records of the Federal Mediation and Conciliation Service, record group 280, National Archives and Records Service, Washington, D.C.; *Investigation of Un-American Propaganda* 2:1614, 1620; "Number of Sit-Down Strikes in 1937," p. 361; *Business Week*, April 3, 1937, p. 15; P. D. Jones to Murphy, March 18, 1937, G. H. Hoffman to Murphy, March 20, 1937, Elizabeth Baylis to Murphy, April 8, 1937, Citizens of Michigan Petition [April 12, 1937], Murphy Papers; *MMFR* 59 (March 13, 1937):12; *Detroit Saturday Night*, March 20, 1937.

[22] *News-Week* 9 (March 27, 1937):9; F. Howard Mason to Murphy, March 24, 1937, Murphy Papers; Fine, *Sit-Down*, pp. 322-23; George Gallup, *The Gallup Poll: Public Opinion, 1935-1971* (New York: Random, 1972), p. 52.

government" in Detroit and Michigan, a group of Detroiters headed by former Mayor Philip Breitmeyer formed an organization known as Citizens of Michigan and circulated petitions requesting that Murphy and law-enforcement officials "demand respect for law and the courts and unflinchingly enforce the laws of the State." On April 7 the Michigan senate passed two bills making it a felony for anyone to participate in a sit-down strike and for an employer to negotiate with workers who were unlawfully in possession of his plant.

There had been some criticism of Murphy in the United States Congress even while the GM strike was underway, especially by Clare Hoffman, an archconservative Republican congressman from Michigan, and the criticism mounted once the sit-downs hit Detroit with full force in March. Hoffman accused Murphy on March 19 of sowing "the seeds of rebellion and anarchy" in Flint; and Michigan's Senator Arthur Vandenberg declared in the United States Senate on the same day that "America could disintegrate in another swift and reckless 60 days" if the "illegal contagion" were not stemmed. Republican Dewey Short of Missouri charged in the House of Representatives that Michigan had once been a "State of law and order" but had become a "State of anarchy"; and he explained that this would not have occurred had Murphy possessed "a bone instead of a rubber band for a spine." The Senate on April 7 passed a concurrent resolution declaring the sit-down "illegal and contrary to sound public policy"; but, at the insistence of administration forces, the resolution also condemned the unfair labor practices that the NLRA declared illegal.[23]

For Frank Murphy, "the actor in the center of the stage" in 1937 was "the American workingman" and the labor movement was "the greatest cause" of the age. Murphy believed that the laboring man's contentment was essential to the preservation of democracy and that the very "stability" of the nation depended on labor. As we have seen, Murphy had long been devoted to the cause of the workingman, but politics, not surprisingly, commingled with idealism to influence his prolabor stance. He had sensed for some time that labor would be a "growing" political force in the nation, he believed that this development would result in "fundamentally important changes in the location of political control and... in the policies of government," and he liked to portray himself as playing a key role in "directing and controlling" this new source of political power.

During the 1936 gubernatorial campaign and in postelection remarks Murphy had stated that, although strikes were "unfortunate," the right to strike was "an inherent right" and labor's advances could be traced to the exercise of this right. To those who thought that the strike wave of 1937 portended a revolutionary intent on labor's part, Murphy correctly replied that the strikers were simply seeking improved working conditions, a greater measure of economic security, and a "larger participation" in the decisions affecting their jobs. The strikes, he insisted, were not the result of what had occurred in Flint, but were rather "a normal reaction" to the economic insecurity workingmen had experienced in the years of depression, the "humiliation" of unemployment and the dole, and the refusal of employers to engage in collective bargaining. If employers had observed the terms of the NLRA and recognized the right of workers to organize and to bargain (Detroit, he noted in this connection, was "the most avowed open shop city in the U.S."), it would have "taken the edge off a great deal of the trouble in Michigan" and would have obviated the need for the sit-downs. Labor, of course, had been guilty of excesses, but Murphy attributed these to its "coming so suddenly into a new sense of power" and the inclination of the masses "to push beyond the legal structure of a country where the law provided no redress or help for them."

Although Walter Lippmann criticized the Roosevelt administration and Murphy during the course of the Chrysler strike for according the sit-down "a kind of bewildered approval," the governor stated publicly during the strike that there was "no disputing" the illegality of the tactic, and he had taken the same position with the union negotiators in the GM strike. "We stand for law enforcement," Murphy declared of his administration. "We believe in the protection of property rights. We believe in intelligent obedience to duly constituted authority." At the same time, however, Murphy preferred that the legal aspects of the sit-down be worked out in a "more judicial atmosphere," when labor and management were not locked in mortal combat. Unlike the advocates of law and order, who presumably favored the rigid and prompt enforcement of all the laws, Murphy contended that since the law often lagged behind the times and human needs government, in the interest of the public good, must sometimes refrain from "a blind and rigorous enforcement" of the laws; and he noted that "an apparent concern for the minute details of legality" had all "too often" been employed "to disguise or justify a denial of the basic rights of working people."

The sit-down strikes in particular, Murphy thought, were "complicated with so many other situations in which human beings feel they are the victims of injustice" that the issue could not be resolved by "blind adherence to a legalistic formula" or by "the exact kind of justice that looks neither to the right nor the left and takes no heed of realities." "We must love justice rather than its form," Murphy concluded, providing a significant clue as to the kind of justice he would be when he later served on the United States Supreme Court.

23 Breitmeyer to Hill, undated, Murphy Papers; *Detroit News*, March 20, 26, April 8, June 24, 1937; Fine, *Sit-Down*, pp. 334-36; *Journal of the Senate of the State of Michigan, 1937 Regular Session* (Lansing, 1937), 1:483-85.

It is evident that Murphy's reluctance to resort to violence to enforce the law stemmed from his profound abhorrence of bloodshed and his unwillingness to be cast in the role of a strikebreaker. "When they want that done," he said with regard to shooting workers out of the plants, "they will have to get another man for Governor of Michigan." He also believed that the use of force by government in a strike only made matters worse. The use of force in the GM and other strikes would not have taught the workingman to respect government, he contended, but would rather have made government for him "a horrible, oppressive thing" and would have created animosities that it would have taken many years to remove. Those who believed that the machine guns should have been turned on the strikers in Flint or Detroit mistakenly assumed, Murphy asserted, that government should demonstrate the error of his ways to the workingman by "clubbing him into temporary submission"; but the lesson, the governor thought, need not be "written in blood." In his remarks on the law and law and order, Murphy, of course, was rationalizing his own behavior in the GM and other strikes, but that does not mean that what he said was necessarily inaccurate.

MURPHY'S LEGISLATIVE PROGRAM

Because of the deleterious impact of labor disputes on the economy, government, Murphy asserted, could not pursue a policy of laissez-faire in dealing with labor disputes in major industries. It was the responsibility of government in such controversies to assert the supremacy of "the public interest" over and above the private interests of the parties involved. Murphy thus reminded Lewis and Chrysler, he wrote a friend, that "their final word did not end the controversy; that there was a third party — the people of the State represented by the Governor to whom due consideration must be shown."[24]

It was not sufficient, however, in Murphy's view, for the state government simply to play some kind of role in bringing ongoing labor disputes to an end; it should also seek to remove the causes for industrial warfare and to forestall threatened strikes and lockouts. This meant the enactment of "progressive and enlightened laws" designed to prevent "unhealthy conditions and unfair practices" that engendered labor unrest and also the passage of a comprehensive labor relations statute. Murphy appreciated that the strike is "only an index of the status of industrial relations" and that the problem of labor-management relations is "essentially . . . a problem of the daily adjustment of a person to his occupational environment." To improve the quality of that "environment" and to provide "a larger measure of social justice" in accordance with the spirit of the New Deal and his own campaign pledges, Murphy urged the state legislature to enact a variety of labor and social insurance laws.

Murphy was unable to secure some of his legislative objectives — the legislature's failure to enact wages-and-hours legislation for women and children was his most important defeat — but his administration was responsible for legislation to include occupational diseases in the workmen's compensation system, the adoption of one of the most progressive state unemployment insurance laws in the nation, major improvements in the state's old-age assistance program, a substantial increase in the inspection powers of the commissioner of labor and industry, and various statutes that met the demands of particular trade unions in the state. Murphy also provided the labor movement with far greater representation in the state government than any of his predecessors had.[25]

Murphy was even more eager that the state adopt legislation to deal with labor disputes and labor relations than that it enact measures of the ameliorative sort. "Something must be written on Labor," he noted to one

[24] The description of Murphy's views is based on *Selected Addresses of Frank Murphy. . . January 1, 1937, to September 30, 1938* (Lansing, 1938), pp. 7-9, 12-17, 20-23, 25, 27, 30-31, 35-38, 45, 47, 56; Murphy statement, March 17, 1937, Murphy speech, March 29, 1937, Murphy to Arthur H. Vandenberg, March 15, 1937, Murphy to Joseph R. Hayden, April 8, 1937, Murphy to B. E. Hutchinson, June 24, 1937, Murphy Papers; Murphy to Kemp, March 23, 1937, Kemp Papers, box 10; Hayden to Murphy, February 7, 1938, Joseph R. Hayden Papers, Michigan Historical Collections; Murphy to Martel, November 10, 1938, Wayne County AFL-CIO Papers, box 11; Murphy, "First Quarterly Accounting," July 10, 1937, MSB; Murphy, "New Era," *American Hungarian* 1 (July 1, 1937), MSB; *New York American*, April 1, 1937, MSB; (Lansing) *State Journal*, April 29, 1937, MSB; unidentified New York newspaper, June 30 [1937], MSB; [*Detroit Times*, October 22, 1936], MSB; *Detroit Labor News*, November 6, December 25, 1936, March 11, 1938; *Detroit News*, March 20, 25, 26, 30, April 14, 1937, February 22, 1938; *The New York Times*, March 26, April 1, 1937; *Detroit Free Press*, March 25, 1937; Fine, *Sit-Down*, pp. 152, 234, 239, 247, 294; Murphy, "The Shaping of Labor Policy," *Survey Graphic* 26 (August 1937):411-13, 450; and Georges Schreiber, "Roosevelt's Successor?," *Common Sense* 6 (June 1937):9.

[25] *Message of Frank Murphy. . . ,* January 7, 1937, pp. 3-5, Murphy to Frank Fitzgerald, December 15, 19, 1936, DWCFL to Central Labor Union. . . , January 9, 1939, Murphy to John J. O'Brien, January 21, 1938, Murphy Papers; Murphy to Kemp, March 31, 1937, Kemp Papers, box 8; Murphy to Kemp, October 22, 1937, Kemp Papers, box 16; William Haber to Kemp, August 5, 1937, Murphy to Mary Anderson, July 22, 1938, Kemp Papers, box 11; Martel to Joseph Cummings, September 29, 1938, Wayne County AFL-CIO Papers, box 11; *Selected Addresses*, pp. 24, 27-30, 35; Murphy, "Shaping of Labor Policy," pp. 450-51; *Detroit News*, December 23, 1936, April 11, 18, 30, May 28, June 26, July 30, 1937; *Detroit Labor News*, June 18, July 9, 30, December 31, 1937, January 26, February 11, 1938; "State Labor Legislation, 1937," *Monthly Labor Review* 46 (January 1938):143.

of his aides with regard to the preparation of the governor's inaugural message to the legislature.

> We want a new co-operation between labor and industry in Michigan. We want a labor board which will help make soluble all differences between labor and industry in our national industrial centers. The State of Michigan must play a significant part in minimizing disturbances costly to the interest of the public.

The rash of strikes in Michigan in the early months of his governorship induced Murphy to think increasingly of securing legislation that would enhance the state's ability to cope with labor disputes. Unduly influenced by the National Recovery Administration's plan for establishing committees within codified industries to deal with labor complaints and labor disputes, Murphy favored the voluntary establishment of similar agencies in the state's various industries; and, since the state lacked any appropriate agency to conciliate or mediate disputes, Murphy realized that there was a need for a state mediation board. It would be necessary, he thought, not only to bring the parties together but also to place some "reasonable restraint" upon the ability of labor and management to strike and to lock out, without, however, "unreasonably interfering" with freedom of contract and the right to strike "peaceably" and without providing for compulsory arbitration.

Murphy firmly believed that workers must have the right to organize and to bargain collectively and must be protected against unfair practices by their employers, but, once again, the strike experience of Michigan in the early weeks of 1937 and the reaction of the public to what was happening in industrial relations convinced him that the time had come for the state to hold labor, as well as management, to account. "Without suggesting undue restrictions on [the] freedom of labor to organize and act in its own interest," he averred, "we may properly consider *whether such organizations should be subject to some degree of regulation. . . .*" It was "axiomatic," Murphy was to say, that "responsible leaders of responsible labor organizations should be accountable for the acts of such organizations."[26]

In advocating restraints upon the right to strike and upon the behavior of labor organizations, Murphy was clearly responding to what seemed to be overwhelming public opinion in favor of such action. This message was conveyed in the governor's mail and in Michigan press editorial opinion,[27] and it was confirmed by public opinion polls. Polls released in March, April, and May of 1937 revealed that 65 percent of those with opinions thought that state and local governments should use force to remove sit-down strikers; an astonishing 89 percent that employers and employees should be compelled by law to settle their differences before striking; 69 percent that unions should be regulated by government; and 86 percent that unions be required to incorporate. It may also have appeared to Murphy that organized labor was itself prepared to accept at least some restrictions on its activities. After all, the UAW in the agreements that ended the GM and Chrysler strikes had accepted language committing the union not to "intimidate" or "coerce" the employees of the respective companies, which was precisely the sort of restriction on unions that critics of the NLRA as a one-sided piece of legislation favored. Also, since organized labor in the state knew that it had a friend in the governor's chair in Lansing, would it not give its support to a labor relations statute that he deemed to be in the public interest?[28]

Ambitious as he was for the presidency,[29] Murphy also wanted to attract favorable national attention and to repair whatever damage his reputation may have suffered as the result of Michigan's well-publicized labor troubles by presenting "the first well-balanced program" of labor relations legislation in the nation. In devising labor relations statutes other states were following the pattern of the NLRA — five states adopted "baby" Wagner Acts in 1937 — and so it could be assumed that a different sort of statute that was responsive to the recent exercise of labor power would not go unnoticed. This assumption was particularly pertinent for a labor relations measure emanating from Michigan, which Murphy characterized as "the laboratory in which the problems of labor . . . are being worked out" and which he now hoped to make "the proving ground of new Labor relations legislation in the United States."[30]

---

[26] Murphy to Kemp, November 24, 1936, March 23, 1937, Kemp Papers, box 10; Kemp to Murphy, March 12, 1937, Murphy to Robert J. Caldwell, July 6, 1937, Murphy statement, March 17, 1937, Murphy Papers; *Detroit News*, December 21, 1936, March 26, 30, April 11, 30, 1937; Fine, *The Automobile under the Blue Eagle* (Ann Arbor: University of Michigan Press, 1963), pp. 453-54n; Murphy, "Shaping of Labor Policy," p. 412; Murphy, "New Era," p. 1; *Selected Addresses*, pp. 24-25, 38.

[27] See, for example, *Detroit News*, March 21, April 29, 1937, and *MMFR* 59 (April 10, 1937):8.

[28] Hadley Cantril, ed., *Public Opinion, 1935-1946* (Princeton, N.J.: Princeton University Press, 1951), pp. 14, 872; Gallup, *Gallup Poll*, pp. 55, 58; *Detroit News*, December 21, 1936; Murphy statement, March 17, 1937, Murphy Papers. There are copies of the GM and Chrysler agreements in the Murphy Papers.

[29] Marguerite Murphy to Frank Murphy [June 1920], Murphy Papers; Harold Murphy to Ruth [Treglown], December 7, 1938, Harold Murphy Papers, Michigan Historical Collections.

[30] Kemp to Murphy, January 27, 1937, E. Blythe Stason to Kemp, March 18, April 13, 1937, Murphy Papers; (Lansing) *State Journal*, April 14, 1937, clipping in Murphy Papers; *Detroit Labor News*, April 2, 23, 1937; *Detroit News*, April 18, 1937.

The Kemp and Stason Draft

The kind of labor relations bill that Murphy ultimately presented to the state legislature was also influenced by the views of the two principal authors of the bill, Ed Kemp and University of Michigan law professor E. Blythe Stason, an accomplished legislative draftsman whom Murphy had originally hoped to appoint as chairman or a member of the state's public utilities commission.[31] Both men were "cautious conservatives," and both viewed with dismay the developments in the labor field during the early months of Murphy's governorship. Kemp, who was disturbed about the allegedly "coercive methods" being used to organize workers, advised Murphy during the Chrysler strike, "We can no longer entertain illusions about a situation in which Communists and racketeers by ruthless and lawless methods are building up an organization. . . that may undermine and threaten the security of our present order and democratic institutions." A fervid imagination led Kemp to fear that Michigan, under its "new New Deal," was "apparently" heading in the direction of "workers' soviets" and the possibility, as a consequence, of "a break-down or dictatorship."

Kemp hoped that Michigan would enact "a more intelligent and. . . more equitable" labor relations statute than the NLRA. He was prepared to protect the right to organize, but only if this could be accomplished "*voluntarily*"; and he believed that majority rule in the choice of employee representatives, let alone the closed shop, violated minority rights and was "prejudicial to individual freedom." If, on the other hand, it were argued that the closed shop and exclusive bargaining rights were justified in the public interest, the corollary, Kemp insisted, was that unions then assumed a "public character" and should be subjected to public regulation to protect the public interest and individual rights.

Kemp favored the incorporation of unions, the regulation of union elections and finances, and the licensing of organizers; and he was disposed to place severe restraints on the right to strike. Government, he argued, must have the "facilities and authority to control strikes and not leave it to the whim or discretion of union organizers who are not charged with any public responsibility and have private interest to serve." Like Kemp, Stason thought it essential for a labor relations statute to impose obligations on employees and employee organizations as well as on employers and to require unions to behave responsibly; and he, too, favored a large role for the state in the conciliation, mediation, and arbitration of labor disputes.[32]

The drafting of a labor relations statute for Michigan was not undertaken until the latter half of March. A committee on legislation, which Stason served as secretary, had been formed at the March 17 law-and-order conference and had endorsed legislation "providing a comprehensive program concerning labor relations and labor disputes," but the committee disbanded without recommending the specific content for such legislation. Stason, however, promptly began to familiarize himself with the subject, and Murphy advised Kemp to work with the law professor and to devote as much of his own time as was possible to the formulation of labor legislation for the state. Murphy erred in not including someone with a trade union point of view among the bill's draftsmen, and this mistake was to cause him a good deal of trouble in the weeks ahead.[33]

In preparing their draft of a labor relations bill, Stason and Kemp examined the relevant labor statutes of the United States and other countries. They were particularly influenced by the British experience with the Whitley Councils, the Canadian Industrial Disputes Investigation Act, and the railway labor legislation of the United States. Kemp was impressed with the Whitley Councils, joint employer-employee agencies that had been established primarily in the weakly organized industries in Great Britain, because he believed that they had served "to keep watch on conditions and head off disputes." The Canadian statute, which had been copied by Colorado, provided for a thirty-day strike notice and factfinding and conciliation in the interim. It had a "very enthusiastic" supporter in University of Michigan economics professor William Haber, who briefly assisted Kemp and Stason and who believed that "the public can't stay out of a strike situation." Intent on finding a mechanism to forestall strikes, Kemp and Stason also looked approvingly on the adjustment boards in the railroad industry (these boards interpreted the provisions of existing contracts) and the machinery for compulsory mediation, factfinding, and possible arbitration provided by the Railway Labor Act of 1926 and the 1934 amendments to the statute.[34]

University, Princeton, N.J.; Kemp to Murphy, January 27, March 20, 23, 1937, Stason to Murphy, March 24, 1937, and enclosed "Outline. . . , " Stason to Kemp, April 13, 1937, Murphy Papers; Kemp to Murphy [March 19, 1937], Kemp Papers, box 10; Kemp drafts and notes, undated, in Kemp Papers, box 10, and in Murphy Papers, box 21.

[33] Minutes of March 17, 1937, meeting, Stason to Murphy, March 18, 24, 1937, Stason to Kemp, March 18, 31, 1937, Murphy to Kemp, March 25, 1937, Kemp to Murphy, March 30, 1937, Murphy Papers; Murphy to Kemp, March 23, 1937, Kemp Papers, box 10; *Detroit News*, March 30, 1937.

[34] Undated Kemp notes in Murphy Papers, box 21, and Kemp Papers, box 10; Stason to Murphy, March 18, 1937, Stason to Murphy, March 24, 1937, and enclosed "Outline... ," Kemp to Murphy, March 30, 1937, Murphy Papers; Haber

[31] Murphy to Hayden, November 20, 1936, Hayden to Murphy, December 2, 1936, Murphy to Stason, December 7, 1936, Murphy Papers.

[32] Roger N. Baldwin to Sugar, October 1, 1937, American Civil Liberties Union (ACLU) Archives, vol. 1048, Princeton

Murphy rejected some of the more stringent restraints on unions and union behavior that Kemp and Stason thought should be included in the state's labor relations law. Forecasting the course that labor relations statutes at the state and federal levels would eventually follow, Kemp and Stason proposed the fairly detailed regulation of the internal affairs of labor unions. They would have required unions to register with a state agency as a condition of their being permitted to engage in collective bargaining and to solicit members. They recommended that no union be permitted to register unless its officers were selected and its policies determined by a majority vote of its members and that no person be permitted to serve as a union officer or agent who had ever been associated with an organization or movement seeking the violent overthrow of the government, who had engaged in violence or extortion, or who had committed an unlawful act to accomplish union purposes. Had their wishes been followed, unions in the state would have been required to issue annual financial reports to their members and would have been subject to suit in their registered names. Kemp and Stason would have prohibited the closed shop, sit-down strikes, and jurisdictional, sympathy, and political strikes. They would also have provided for minority representation and individual bargaining and would have required that employee representatives for bargaining purposes be selected by secret ballot.[35]

Following the Supreme Court's *Jones and Laughlin* decision, Stason advised Kemp that there was now talk in Washington of the enactment of a better-balanced labor relations statute than the NLRA and that if Murphy wished to gain credit for a state measure of this type, he would have to act quickly. Murphy may also have been prompted to act when he did by the possibility that the Michigan legislature would pass labor relations legislation of its own devising if he did not soon submit his bill. As we have seen, the state senate passed two anti-sit-down strike bills on April 7, and on April 15 the House Committee on Labor favorably reported a measure that followed the pattern of the NLRA. Administration forces succeeded in sending the bill back to committee, but the friends of

organized labor in the house were becoming restless over the governor's delay.[36]

House Bill 571

When Murphy submitted his labor relations bill to the Michigan legislature on April 29, he gave the impression of haste in its preparation by describing the bill as a "tentative measure" that provided "a suitable working base or framework" for legislation that might be required and by stating that some questions of a "controversial nature" had been reserved for further study.[37] It is doubtful, however, that the draftsmen of the bill thought of the measure as "tentative" since they had been working on it for more than a month. It may be that what Murphy really meant by his puzzling language was that he was not fully committed to the measure and was prepared to shift ground if serious opposition developed.

Unlike the Findings and Policy Statement of the NLRA, the Statement of Premise and Purpose of what became Michigan House Bill 571 emphasized the harmful effects of labor disputes, contending that they had "operated to the great detriment of the parties thereto, and in some cases. . . endangered the welfare and the safety of the public. Such disputes," it was stated, "threaten and cause serious damage to both public and private property, and menace the peace and order of the state." Both the NLRA and the Michigan bill asserted that denial by employers of the right of employees to organize and bargain and refusal by employers to engage in collective bargaining led to industrial disputes, the Michigan bill adding that these disputes were "inimical to the public welfare and safety"; but, unlike the NLRA, House Bill 571, which applied only to "large" employers, made no reference to the dangers flowing from the inequality of bargaining power between employer and employee and stated that the measure was designed to serve "the public interest" as well as the interest of employers and employees. Whereas the purpose of the NLRA and the baby Wagner Acts in the states was to enhance the bargaining power of organized labor, the major purpose of the Michigan bill, so clearly a product of the 1937 law-and-order crisis, was, as the measure stated, "to remove some of the causes" of labor disputes and to "provide facilities for their prompt settlement."

House Bill 571 provided for the establishment of a three-man board of industrial relations to be appointed by the governor. It asserted the right of employees to organize

to Murphy, January 31, 1937, and document dated May 3, 1937, Kemp Papers, box 10; *Detroit News*, March 30, April 9, 1937; *Ann Arbor News*, May 21, 1937; Howard S. Kaltenborn, *Governmental Adjustment of Labor Disputes* (Chicago: The Foundation Press, 1943), pp. 37-60, 193n, 195-96; Charles C. Killingsworth, *State Labor Relations Acts* (Chicago: University of Chicago Press, 1948), pp. 219-20; G. D. H. Cole, *A Short History of the British Working-Class Movement, 1789-1947* (London: Allen and Unwin, 1948), pp. 368-69.

[35] Stason to Kemp, March 31, 1937, and enclosed bill, Stason to Kemp, April 9, 1937, and enclosed draft, Murphy Papers; Kemp draft of industrial relations bill, April 22, 1937, Kemp Papers, Michigan Historical Collections.

[36] Stason to Murphy, March 24, 1937, Stason to Kemp, April 13, 1937, Murphy Papers; *Detroit News*, March 17, 26, 31, April 7, 9, 16, 1937; Michigan, Legislature, Senate, *Senate Journal, 1937*, 1:483-85; *Journal of the House of Representatives of the State of Michigan, 1937 Regular Session* (Lansing, 1937), 1:209-10, 670.

[37] *Detroit News*, April 30, 1937.

and to bargain through representatives of their own choosing and stated that it was "unfair" and "unlawful" for employers to (a) interfere with employees in the exercise of this right by espionage, circulation of blacklists, or "any other acts of repression and intimidation"; (b) interfere with the formation or administration of a labor organization, although employer were permitted to provide facilities for shop councils or similar bodies; (c) discriminate against employees because of their membership or nonmembership in a labor organization or for signing complaints or providing information in accordance with the terms of the statute; (d) refuse to bargain unless for a "just cause" as approved by the board; (e) violate the terms of a labor contract "knowingly and intentionally"; and (f) alter the terms of a contract when there was a dispute or declare a lockout either without first submitting the matter to the board or during a period not exceeding thirty days[38] while the matter was pending before the board or a special board of mediation.

House Bill 571 also contained a list of "unfair" employee practices. It made it "unlawful" for employees to (a) "interfere with, injure, restrain, or attempt to intimidate or to coerce" any employee with respect to his affiliation or nonaffiliation with a labor organization, the selection of representatives, or his engaging in lawful employment; (b) strike without exhausting "every method of voluntary agreement and negotiation" specified in the measure and without giving an unspecified number of days notice to the employer and the board or during a period not exceeding thirty days while the issue was pending before the board or a special board of mediation; (c) refuse to bargain; (d) "prevent, obstruct, or interfere with" an employer, employee, or labor organization that was complying with the act; and (e) violate the terms of a contract. In addition, every labor organization had to file a statement with the board providing the names of its officials, the international organization with which it was affiliated, and the "resident agent" upon whom summons could be served; and the union's books and records were subject to examination by the board.

The bill specified that employee representatives were to be selected "without interference, influence, or coercion by any person or organization." If there was a controversy regarding who represented the employees, the board, "on request of any party in interest" or on its own motion, was to investigate and by an election or by "any other suitable method" might "ascertain and determine the choice of representatives on a basis that shall be just and fair to all employees." It was also the responsibility of the board to determine whether the appropriate unit for bargaining

purposes was the employer unit, the craft, the plant, or some other unit.

The board was empowered to investigate and determine if the public interest was likely to be "adversely and materially" affected by an existing or threatened dispute; use its good offices or that of any special board of mediation or other agency to aid in adjusting the dispute; "encourage or induce" the parties to submit the dispute to arbitration and to assist in creating the arbitration tribunal; report to the governor, with recommendations, the facts in any dispute that it could not adjust; and hear and adjudge complaints concerning existing labor contracts and "issue appropriate orders and undertake proceedings to enforce the same." It was also to supervise the selection of representatives, investigate charges of the violation of the act, and issue "cease and desist" orders against the offending employer, employee, or labor organization; conduct investigations to protect employers or employees against "racketeering, extortion, and other unfair labor practices"; assist in the organization of industrial councils composed of employers and employees in the same industry or unit to consider questions and grievances concerning working conditions and working rules; and establish special boards of mediation possessing all the powers of the board of industrial relations itself. Provision was made for the enforcement and judicial review of board orders.

The bill provided that when the board reported to the governor that it could not adjust a dispute, he could appoint a special committee to investigate the controversy and to report to him. If the governor decided that the dispute, because it involved "a major industry or an essential public service or for other substantial reason," was of such a nature that a strike or lockout would cause "grave injury, hardship, or inconvenience to the public," it became illegal for any person or organization to order, advise, or encourage a strike or lockout until the governor had had "reasonable opportunity" to consult with the parties to the dispute and the state administrative board (the elected executive officers of the state). If either party to the dispute violated this section, the governor was to take such action as he deemed necessary under the laws of the state and nation for "the due protection of the public peace, welfare, and safety." When, despite the act, a strike or lockout occurred and local police authorities were unable to maintain public order or to protect the owners and operators of the property in the peaceful exercise of their rights, the governor, if in his judgment the public interest so required, could place the establishment in the charge of the commissioner of the Michigan State Police pending further mediation efforts. During the interim the establishment was to remain closed or was to be permitted to operate under regulations approved by the governor as consistent with the interests of the public and the affected parties.

---

[38] The number of days was left blank in the bill as submitted, but Kemp suggested the thirty-day limitation to the legislature. See the document dated May 3, 1937, Kemp Papers, box 10.

Michigan did not have a statute resembling the Norris-La Guardia Act, and even peaceful picketing had been declared illegal by the state's courts. House Bill 571, however, specified that, except as provided in the act, no court was to issue a restraining order or a temporary or permanent injunction in a case growing out of a labor dispute to prohibit a person "interested in such dispute," singly or in concert with others, from striking; becoming or remaining a union member; paying or withholding strike benefits; giving publicity to the facts of a dispute by picketing or any other method not involving "fraud or violence, coercion or intimidation"; or assembling peacefully to promote his interest in the dispute. Nothing in the measure, however, was to be construed

> to permit patrolling or attendance by any persons, whether on behalf of a labor organization or otherwise, at or near a place of business or employment affected by a labor dispute, or the residence of any person employed therein or other place where such person may be, in such manner as to be calculated to intimidate any such person, or to obstruct approach thereto or egress therefrom, or to lead to a breach of the peace. . . .[39]

House Bill 571 was a far cry from the NLRA and the five state laws modeled on the Wagner Act even though it incorporated many of the provisions contained in these prolabor statutes. It added contract violations and premature lockouts to the list of unfair labor practices of employers, but it weakened the ban on company unions by specifically authorizing shop councils or similar bodies. By requiring the board, in effect, to hold an election for employee representatives at the employer's request, it authorized a procedure that the NLRB at the time did not permit lest it enable the employer to force a premature test of a union's strength and to challenge the majority status of the union at the end of each contract term. House Bill 571 also left open the question of whether the board should apply the majority-rule criterion to the selection of employee representatives, even though the *Jones and Laughlin* decision, as Stason realized, seemed to foreclose the issue at least for interstate employers.

By including a list of employee unfair practices to balance the proscribed unfair labor practices of employers, House Bill 571 departed from the model of the "protective" labor relations statutes like the NLRA and anticipated both the "restrictive" state labor laws of 1939 and later and the federal Taft-Hartley Act of 1947. All that survived of the Kemp and Stason proposals to regulate the internal affairs of unions was the bill's provision regarding the examination of union books and records, but in this mild form House Bill 571 also pointed in the

direction of future state and federal labor relations statutes.[40]

Advocates of statutes such as the Wagner Act insisted that it was necessary to include restraints on employer behavior in such laws because organized labor, as the weaker of the two parties, needed protection against the "abusive use of economic power" and unfair tactics by management in order to attain the goal of equal bargaining power. On the other hand, they contended that it was unnecessary and unwise to specify employee unfair practices since most such practices were prohibited by statutes already on the books and since there was a "very real danger" that the courts would extend the impact of these provisions beyond what the enacting legislatures intended (making refusal to bargain an unfair employee practice could thus be construed as a curb on the right to strike, and almost any type of union effort at persuasion might be considered coercive). Not all the proscribed employee unfair practices in the Murphy bill, however, were specifically prohibited by existing Michigan legislation, and men like Kemp and Stason were convinced that labor had the upper hand in the state and that events had demonstrated that employers, nonunion workers, and the general public required protection against abuses of union power, a point of view that influenced all the restrictive labor laws that were to come.[41]

The concept of an undefined public interest distinguishable from the interests of employers and employees, a concept present in the restrictive laws, was most evident in the bill's elaborate provisions regarding the adjustment of strikes and threatened strikes, provisions that clearly reflect the influence on the bill's draftsmen of the Canadian Industrial Disputes Investigation Act, the Railway Labor Act, the Whitley Councils, the NRA experience, and the truce terms in the Chrysler sit-down strike. The NLRB and the labor relations boards in the states, except Wisconsin, with statutes similar to the Wagner Act were forbidden to engage in conciliation, mediation, and arbitration; but this limitation on their activity was included in these statutes partly because other agencies were assigned this role in these jurisdictions. The experience of other states demonstrated that the framers

---

[39] Michigan, Legislature, House, "House Bill No. 571," House Bills 400-599, Regular Session, 1937-1938 (University of Michigan Law Library, Ann Arbor, Michigan); *Detroit News*, January 3, 1937.

[40] Harry A. Millis and Emily Clark Brown, *From the Wagner Act to Taft-Hartley* (Chicago: University of Chicago Press, 1950), pp. 161-62; Stason to Kemp, April 13, 1937, Murphy Papers; Killingsworth, *State Labor Relations Acts*, pp. 1-2, 42-107; Sanford Cohen, *State Labor Legislation, 1937-1939* (Columbus: Ohio State University Press, 1948), pp. 36, 43.

[41] Nathan Greene to A. L. Wirin, June 12, 1937, and enclosed "Analysis of proposed Michigan labor law . . . ," ACLU Archives, vol. 1048; Polier, "An Analysis of the Michigan Industrial Relations Bill" [July 2, 1937], ACLU Archives, vol. 1049; V. A. Zimmer to Murphy, December 9, 1937, Kemp Papers, box 11; Killingsworth, *State Labor Relations Acts*, p. 42; *Detroit News*, June 17, 1937.

of the Michigan statute probably placed too much faith in the effectiveness of cooling-off periods and factfinding; and it would seem that the mediation of disputes is best entrusted to an agency that specializes in that task rather than to a body like the proposed Michigan board that must perform additional tasks that may impair its standing as a disinterested neutral with the conflicting parties.[42]

Reaction to House Bill 571

The press and Michigan employers found more to praise than to criticize in House Bill 571 (the *Detroit News* thought it "an admirably thorough and balanced effort"), but they expressed concern about the seizure powers that the measure vested in the governor. The "aroma" of this provision, the *Detroit Free Press* editorialized, was "communistic rather than democratic."[43] The strongest opposition to the bill came from organized labor in Michigan, particularly from the UAW. The DWCFL did not take a public stand on the matter since it did not wish to embarrass Murphy, but Martel wired the governor that his organization thought the bill "so hostile to the interests of labor both organized and unorganized and so dangerous to the peace of the community" that it would not even seek to have the bill amended. The UAW protested the terms of the bill both publicly and privately, and UAW attorney Sugar submitted to Murphy a detailed, point-by-point refutation of the measure. UAW spokesmen warned that passage of the bill, which Martin denounced as "one of the most dangerous pieces of legislation to labor ever proposed in any state," would destroy Murphy's reputation as a liberal governor.

The UAW complained about House Bill 571's failure to endorse majority rule and about the limitation of the measure to large employers. It objected to the filing provisions of the bill and feared that the authority granted to the board to investigate union records was the "opening wedge" leading to incorporation of unions in the state, a traditional union bugaboo. It thought that the bill's language regarding shop councils might be construed as a legalization of company unions, and it did not think that contract violations should be made a crime. It favored an antiinjunction section in the bill that conformed more closely to the terms of the Norris-La Guardia Act. Above all, the UAW protested the provisions of House Bill 571 that dealt with unfair employee practices and that imposed restraints on the right to strike. "The entire section" dealing with the proscribed employee practices, Sugar

wrote, was "objectionable to labor" and could be construed so as to curb its activities. He observed:

> If we assume a virtually complete organization of workers so that there would be a balance, relatively speaking, between capital and labor in the field of labor relations, one might conceive of the application of some of these provisions to labor. But in this period of growing organizations where labor is yet relatively weak, the application of any of these provisions would furnish the employers with very effective weapons to destroy the labor movement and to hinder its growth.

As for the bill's provisions relating to strikes, Martin alleged that even the "slightest restraint" on labor's exercise of the right to strike marked "a long stride in the direction of destruction of labor unions and the introduction of fascism in this country." The UAW objected to the bill's requirement of a strike notice, it protested that the provisions for compulsory mediation would lead to compulsory arbitration, it opposed the creation of special boards of mediation and gubernatorial factfinding committees, it objected to the governor's power to delay strikes in major industries, and it pointed out that the authority given him with regard to struck plants placed in charge of the commissioner of the state police would permit him to authorize the operation of such a plant with strikebreakers. What the UAW would have preferred for Michigan was a statute similar to the Wagner Act that also included some mediation provisions and the terms of the Norris-La Guardia Act.[44]

Objections to the house bill were also voiced to Murphy by the American Civil Liberties Union (ACLU), which had been alerted to the measure by the Conference for the Protection of Civil Rights, a left-leaning Michigan civil-rights group. The ACLU wired Murphy, with whom it maintained close ties, that it was "distressed" that "a great state under a liberal governor" was preparing to enact legislation that would infringe so important a civil liberty as the right to strike. Its advice was that Michigan, instead, should simply enact a statute similar to the Norris-La Guardia Act.[45]

Reacting to the criticism of his bill, Murphy began a series of conferences regarding the measure with representatives of the MFL and DWCFL, the UAW, and industrialists in the state and also with members of the legislature. He was especially eager to conciliate his friends

[42] Killingsworth, *State Labor Relations Acts*, pp. 215, 221-22, 230, 258; Kaltenborn, *Labor Disputes*, pp. 70, 177-78, 200; document dated May 3, 1937, Kemp Papers, box 10.

[43] *MMFR* 59 (May 8, 1937): 8; *Detroit News*, May 1, 3, 1937; *Detroit Free Press*, May 1, 1937; *Ann Arbor News*, May 1, 1937; *Flint Journal*, May 9, 1937, MSB.

[44] Martel to Murphy, May 4, 1937, Robert Travis to Murphy, May 1, 1937, document dictated by Sugar, May 11, 1937, and Sugar draft of labor relations bill, undated, Kemp Papers, box 10; *Detroit News*, May 3, 4, 6, 13, 1937; *United Automobile Worker*, May 8, 1937; *Ann Arbor News*, May 11, 12, 1937.

[45] A. G. Mezerik to unnamed correspondent, undated, ACLU to Murphy, May 6, 1937, ACLU Archives, vol. 1049; *ACLU Bulletin*, May 4, 1937, ACLU Archives, vol. 1048; Fine, *Sit-Down*, p. 218.

and supporters in the labor movement, less willing to
accommodate suggestions of the manufacturers. This
conclusion is strongly supported by a document in the
Kemp Papers indicating the precise changes in the bill
recommended by Martel, Sugar, and one of the employer
representatives and noting those suggestions the governor
accepted and those he rejected. Martel and Sugar offered
Murphy pretty much the same advice, but, despite Martel's
objection, Murphy decided to retain the provision of the
bill granting the board of industrial relations the authority
to investigate racketeering since Sugar found the provision
"acceptable."[46]

Partly because he was a dedicated civil libertarian,
partly because he did not wish to impair his good standing
with his friends in the ACLU, Murphy was anxious to meet
the ACLU wishes for proper antiinjunction legislation in
Michigan. He was "convinced" that a separate
antiinjunction bill of the Norris-La Guardia type could not
be passed, but he was willing to attach a section to Bill 571
that would serve the same purpose. Roger Baldwin, the
ACLU's director, consequently had attorneys Isadore
Polier and Nathan Greene prepare the draft of "a
concentrated baby Norris-La Guardia Act," and Murphy
added it to the bill over Kemp's strong objections.[47]

Sixty of the one hundred members of the Michigan
House of Representatives were Democrats, and most of
them were ready to follow the governor's lead in the labor
relations field. On June 3, by a vote of sixty-three to
thirty-one, the house approved a substitute for the original
bill that the chairman of the Committee on Labor
described as "Gov. Murphy's bill." The limitation of the
bill to larger employers was dropped, as were the original
provisions regarding shop and industrial councils and those
subjecting union records to examination. The measure now
specifically provided that representatives of the majority in
a bargaining unit were to be "the exclusive
representatives," and the board was no longer required to
hold elections at the request of "any party in interest." To
please Martel, it was provided that the board did not have
to define the appropriate unit for bargaining if it decided
that the purposes of the bill would be "better promoted by
not acting." The measure still contained a list of unfair
employee practices, but contract violations were not
included among them. Of greater importance to organized

labor, the required strike notice was dropped from the bill,
and the governor was no longer authorized to place certain
struck establishments under the state police and to
determine whether they remained closed or open. In
addition to authorizing "all-union" (closed-shop)
agreements and prohibiting yellow-dog contracts, the
substitute bill also included the antiinjunction section
drafted by the ACLU. A hearing in open court that
involved the taking of testimony and opportunity for
cross-examination was now required before an injunction
could be granted, injunctions were to be denied to
plaintiffs with "unclean hands," and jury trials were
authorized in contempt cases.[48]

"Take a look at the Labor Relations Bill as I directed it
out of committee," Murphy wrote Baldwin the day the bill
passed the house. The governor asked the ACLU director
to pay special heed to the antiinjunction section of the bill
since "it's yours." Baldwin replied that "on quick reading"
the bill appeared "to be beyond criticism as an example of
progressive fair dealing in the most difficult field of
lawmaking," and he called for support of the measure by
the Conference for the Protection of Civil Rights.
Baldwin's initial opinion of the bill was not, however,
shared by the UAW, which claimed that the measure,
although an improvement over its predecessor, was still
"a most reactionary piece of labor legislation." The major
UAW objections centered on the continued inclusion in
the bill of unfair employee practices, the power still
retained by the governor to declare strikes illegal for a time
in "a major industry or an essential public service or for
other substantial reason," and a new provision in the bill
banning strikes of public employees who were engaged in
work "necessary for the public welfare and safety," which
Sugar thought would encourage "a psychology of
submission and slavery" among them.

After learning that Baldwin had written approvingly of
the new bill, Sugar, who was a sometimes attorney for the
ACLU and who had already sent a critical analysis of the
measure to ACLU headquarters, wrote the ACLU director,
"What in hell has happened to you!" A contrite Baldwin
replied that the "only answer" he could give was that he
had not read the bill with sufficient care, and the ACLU,
accepting Sugar's evaluation, now advised Murphy that the
substitute bill interfered with the right to strike and
nullified the guarantees of the Wagner Act. A few days
later the ACLU forwarded to Murphy an analysis of the
bill that Greene had prepared at its request in which the
labor lawyer, who professed to be "as much disturbed by
this Michigan bill as I have ever been disturbed by
anything," charged that the measure made "all organ-

[46] *Detroit News*, May 6, 11-13, 23, 26, 1937; *Ann Arbor
News*, May 8, 11, 12, 1937; document dated May 3, 1937,
Murphy to Travis, May 3, 1937, Kemp to Mrs. Alkouri,
undated, and attached copy of bill, Kemp Papers, box 10.

[47] Baldwin to Murphy, May 15, 1937, Minutes of ACLU
Board of Directors' Meeting, May 17, 1937, ACLU Archives,
vol. 1048; Polier to Murphy, May 16, 1937, Wirin to Greene,
May 17, 1937, Wirin to Polier, May 20, 1937, Baldwin to
Murphy, May [21], 1937, ACLU Archives, vol. 1049; Kemp
to Alkouri, undated, and attached copy of bill, Kemp Papers,
box 10.

[48] *Detroit News*, May 26, 29, June 3, 4, 1937; *Ann Arbor
News*, June 6, 1937; Polier to Murphy, May 16, 1937, ACLU
Archives, vol. 1049; Michigan, Legislature, House, *House
Journal, 1937*, 2:1285-95, 1379-80, 1397-99.

izational activity" by labor an unfair practice. From here on in the ACLU and UAW strategy regarding a Michigan labor relations bill was, for all practical purposes, coordinated, with Sugar, who had a foot in both camps, playing the key role. This cooperation is a little-known example of the functioning of the "libertarian-labor alliance" in the New Deal era and of the manner in which the ACLU identified itself with the goals of organized labor in those years.[49]

The UAW-ACLU criticisms of the house substitute bill were endorsed by Labor's Non-Partisan League (by that time the political arm of the CIO) and by John L. Lewis, who complained to Murphy that the measure would lead to "a ghastly ham-stringing of the organized labor movement" and would "put Michigan back a century in labor legislation." In view of the central position that Michigan occupied on the labor scene in 1937, organized labor feared that what happened in Michigan would become a precedent for other states and perhaps for the national government as well. The Supreme Court had just validated the NLRA, and organized labor, consequently, was not prepared to accept a state labor act that appeared to weaken the guarantees that it had received in the federal statute. Ten years later organized labor denounced the Taft-Hartley Act as a "slave labor law"; it is not surprising, under the circumstances, that a much less secure labor movement, just beginning to gather strength and just having won a great victory in the courts, should have reacted so strongly to the legislation being considered in Michigan in 1937. It could not know, after all, that the restrictive state labor relations acts would, in the end, prove to be "remarkably ineffective."[50]

Clearly troubled by the objections of organized labor and the ACLU to the house substitute bill, Murphy queried Kemp as to whether the sections of the measure about which they complained really did "nullify" the guarantees of the NLRA. Kemp conceded that, unlike the Wagner Act, the Michigan bill restricted the right to strike under certain circumstances, but he insisted that this "merely recognize[d] a century of industrial development" and was a "reasonable regulation for the public safety." As for the objections to the bill's inclusion of unfair employee practices, "Lewis and associates," Kemp asserted, "see only their own side, and are unable or unwilling to recognize and comprehend the desire of many workers to be free from interference and compulsion."[51]

If organized labor thought that the house substitute bill imposed far too many restraints on unions, industrialists and businessmen in Michigan complained about the extent to which Murphy's original bill had been amended to accommodate labor criticism. The Detroit Board of Commerce urged Detroit's six hundred "largest employers" to seek the enactment of the original bill since the amendments that the house had approved would make it "almost impossible for you to maintain a payroll in Michigan." The impossibility of devising a labor relations statute that would satisfy both the UAW and the Michigan Manufacturers' Association was becoming increasingly evident.[52]

There was little likelihood that the Michigan senate would approve the labor relations bill that the house had passed and even less likelihood that it would revise the measure to please organized labor. "The Senate," a *Detroit News* reporter observed, "never will approve a bill which would satisfy labor." The Democrats had a 17 to 13 majority in the senate, but since one Democratic senator was in jail, the party lacked the seventeen votes required to pass legislation in the upper house. A body made up almost entirely of businessmen, farmers, and professional persons and in which populous and industrialized Wayne County (Detroit) was underrepresented, the senate, furthermore, simply did not "speak the Murphy language." New Deal ideas had hardly penetrated the body, and, as Murphy observed, "the Republicans and one or two Democrats" in the senate were "almost entirely sympathetic with the employer's viewpoint."[53]

[49] Murphy to Baldwin, June 3, 1937, Baldwin to Murphy, June 4, 1937, Sugar to Baldwin, June 9, 1937, Baldwin to Sugar, June 10, 1937, ACLU to Murphy, June 15, 1937, Wirin to Sugar, June 15, 1937, ACLU Archives, vol. 1049; Baldwin to Mezerik, June 4, 1937, Wirin to Greene, June 7, 1937, Greene to Wirin, June 12, 1937, and enclosed "Analysis of proposed Michigan labor law," Wirin to Mezerik, June 15, 1937, Sugar Memo on Substitute for House Bill 571, June 7, 1937, ACLU Archives, vol. 1048; Baldwin and Arthur Garfield Hays to Murphy, June 9, 1937, Kemp Papers, box 9; *United Automobile Worker,* June 12, 1937; Jerold S. Auerbach, *Labor and Liberty: The La Follette Committee and the New Deal* (Indianapolis: Bobbs-Merrill, 1966), pp. 213-15 *et passim.*

[50] Lewis to Murphy, June 11, 1937, E. L. Oliver to All Michigan Members, June 14, 1937, Kemp Papers, box 9; *Detroit News,* June 15-17, 1937; *United Automobile Worker,* July 31, 1937; Killingsworth, *State Labor Relations Acts,* pp. 43-44, 260-64.

[51] Murphy note to Kemp on Baldwin and Hays to Murphy, June 9, 1937, Kemp Papers, box 9; Kemp to Murphy, June 10, 14, 1937, Kemp Papers, box 8; Murphy to Baldwin, June 16, 1937, ACLU Archives, vol. 1049.

[52] *MMFR* 59 (June 5, 1937): 7; Carl F. Clarke to Murphy, June 14, 1937, Campbell to Hill, undated, enclosing Campbell, "Help Influence Enactment of Governor Murphy's Original Labor Bill," June 7, 1937, Kemp Papers, box 10; *Detroit News,* June 15, 1937.

[53] *Detroit News,* June 20, 24, 1937; *Michigan Official Directory and Legislative Manual, 1937-1938* (n.p., n.d.), pp. 519-20; Richard Theodore Ortquist, Jr., "Depression Politics in Michigan, 1929-1933" (Ph.D. diss., University of Michigan, 1968), pp. 96-97; Josiah L. Sayre, "Some Aspects of the Legislative Process in Michigan, 1925-1937" (Ph.D. diss., University of Michigan, 1938), p. 10; Murphy to Polier, August 11, 1937, Kemp Papers, box 9.

By the time the senate turned its attention to labor relations legislation, the standing of organized labor in middle-class circles in Michigan had sunk to a new low, the position of the governor in the state had been weakened, and the issue of law and order had taken on an added urgency. Three events occurring in rapid succession — the Lansing Labor Holiday of June 7, a Consumers Power Strike on June 9, and a clash on the picket line outside the Newton Steel Plant in Monroe on June 10 — accounted for these developments, and they helped to shape the labor relations bill that emerged from the Michigan senate.

When UAW Local 182 defied an injunction against picketing the Capitol City Wrecking Company of Lansing, the sheriff of Ingham County responded at 2:00 A.M. on June 7 by arresting eight pickets, including the wife of the local's president, Lester Washburn. With Martin's permission, Washburn thereupon promptly proclaimed "a general labor holiday throughout the city to celebrate the brave act" of the sheriff and the prosecuting attorney and called on the city's numerous auto workers to absent themselves from their jobs that day. Several thousand UAW members and sympathizers, responding to Washburn's proclamation, took possession of the Lansing downtown that morning. They blocked traffic, forced the closing of stores and offices, jammed into the city-county building, where the pickets were being held, and listened to speeches of UAW leaders delivered from the steps of the state's capitol building.

Murphy was not in Lansing on the morning of June 7, but when he returned to the capitol in the afternoon, he summoned Washburn and told him to clear the streets in ten minutes, something that was not revealed at the time. Murphy then went out on the capitol steps and, in what many thought was "too much of 'a welcoming address,'" cautioned the crowd against "extreme or unnecessary acts," but told his audience that the capitol could not be put to "better use" than the exercise by citizens of their freedom of speech and freedom of assembly, that public officials had to "face and recognize new conditions," and that the demonstrators would suffer "no injustice" while he was governor.

Either Murphy's warning or the release of the pickets, which the governor helped to arrange, brought the holiday to a close in the downtown area. Some "overeager" unionists, however, then decided to close down East Lansing, the home of Michigan State College, but they were repulsed at the edge of the city by hundreds of college students, who threw eight of the demonstrators into the Red Cedar River. Headlines such as "CIO Seizes Michigan Capitol. . ." gave the Lansing Labor Holiday a rather frightening character, and U.S. Senator Arthur Vandenberg later wrote that the episode had "excited" his "critical attention" even more than the GM sit-down had.[54]

Two days later, on June 9, while Murphy was in Pittsburgh to deliver a commencement address at Duquesne University, UAW members staged an unauthorized strike against the Consumers Power Company that affected one-half million people in the Saginaw Valley. An indignant Murphy, who had warned after a UAW strike against the same company the previous month that the state government would not "tolerate" further strikes of this kind, called Martin and Robert Travis in Flint and told them to "Get those lights back on!" Similar instructions had been sent out by John L. Lewis, whom Murphy had also called, and after about fifteen hours the wildcat strike came to an end.[55]

As the lights went on in the Saginaw Valley, trouble erupted in Monroe, Michigan, the home of the Newton Steel Company, a Republic Steel subsidiary that the corporation had selected as the testing ground for a carefully orchestrated back-to-work movement designed to break the Little Steel strike. The weak Monroe local of the Steel Workers Organizing Committee (SWOC) struck Newton on May 28 and established a picket line on the single road leading to the plant. Until June 10 the line was maintained without any "serious disorder or untoward incident" since the company made no effort to operate the plant and the pickets did not interfere with company personnel wishing to enter the factory. The Steel Workers' Association, an "independent" local union formed just before the strike, nevertheless requested state and local authorities to remove the pickets so that those who wished to return to work could do so safely. Murphy ignored the request, but the mayor of the town, Daniel A. Knaggs, conducted a referendum of the employees to ascertain whether they wished to return to work. When the results of the referendum, which was boycotted by SWOC but in which about 60 percent of the workers participated, indicated that the overwhelming majority of those who voted wished to resume their employment, the company

54 Albert A. Blum and Ira Spar, "The Lansing Labor Holiday," *Michigan History* 49 (March 1965):1-11; *Detroit News,* June 7, 8, 13, 1937, October 25, 1938; *Detroit Free Press,* June 8, 1937; *Detroit Times,* June 8, 1937, clipping in Murphy Papers; Joseph H. Creighton to Murphy, May 11, 1938, Hill to Murphy, January 11, 1939 [1940], Vandenberg to Murphy, January 16, 1939, Murphy Papers; draft of statement in Murphy Papers, box 22; (Lansing) *Industrial News,* June 4, 11, 1937; *United Automobile Worker,* June 12, 1937; *The New York Times,* June 8, 1937; *MMFR 59 (June 12,* 1937):4; *Investigation of Un-American Propaganda,* 2:1695, 1704, and 3:2063-72; Burt Darling, *City in the Forest: The Story of Lansing* (New York: Stratford House, 1950), pp. 238-42.

55 *Detroit News,* May 19-21, June 5, 9, 10, 1937, June 7, 1938; *Pittsburgh Press,* June 9, 1937, MSB; *Pittsburgh Post-Gazette,* June 10, 1937, clipping in Murphy Papers; Interview with Wyndham Mortimer, December 9, 1964, pp. 22-26, Michigan Historical Collections.

announced that the plant would be reopened. Knaggs asked Murphy for National Guard or state police protection for the reopening of the plant, but the governor, believing that the state government could not "take sides," replied that the state government would not comply with such a request unless it was officially informed in writing by local authorities that they could not control the situation. Knaggs thereupon swore in 383 citizens as special police to augment the small force of city police and sheriff's deputies available to him. The arms for the special police were paid for by the company.

The return to work was scheduled for June 10. On the morning of that day a SWOC organizer was dragged from his car, beaten, and run out of town while the police looked on. Word of this transformed the 150 pickets into "an angry, unruly crowd." They had promised not to interfere with the return to work, but they now armed themselves with clubs and steel bars and blocked the highway. Murphy, who had previously sent George A. Krogstad to Monroe to mediate the dispute and had vainly tried to delay the reopening of the plant for a few days, sought to prevent a clash on the picket line. From Lansing, he told the pickets that, although they had a right to picket peacefully, they must not blockade the road, and he urged the police not to "go through that line." The pickets were willing to permit the reopening of the plant, but only if the city government disarmed and removed all vigilantes who were not Newton employees. City officials refused to accept these terms, and repeated calls from Lansing failed to break the deadlock. While veterans deputized by Knaggs policed the downtown with baseball bats, the special police moved against the pickets behind a barrage of nauseating gas, broke the line, and drove the pickets from the road. A cavalcade of autos then carried the workers into the plant.

On instructions from their locals, hundreds of auto workers from nearby Pontiac proceeded toward Monroe the next day in an apparent effort to reactivate the picket line, but Martin called off the invasion before very many auto workers had reached the city, where bat-wielding American Legionnaires awaited them. Knaggs would have liked Murphy to declare martial law and send the National Guard into Monroe, but this proved to be unnecessary since the UAW, at the governor's behest, remained away from the city and agreed instead to hold a rally of protest on June 13 in a state park three miles north of Monroe. Murphy dispatched National Guardsmen and state police to ensure that there would be no trouble, and the rally, attended by about twenty thousand persons, proceeded without incident. Two days later the picketing of the Newton plant was resumed, but under severely restricted conditions.

The Monroe affair received a tremendous amount of press coverage, and it helped to stimulate further the opposition to the CIO and to Governor Murphy. A prominent Michigan Republican thought that if the events in Monroe had occurred in a foreign land, an American reading about them would have thought that the affected nation was in "a state of revolution"; and Congressman Hoffman, alleging concern because of "Murphy's yellow streak and previous protection to law violators," offered to "raise an army" of Michigan citizens to "protect" Monroe. "Sowing the seeds of kindness in the vineyard of 1937 is not altogether an easy errand," Murphy ruefully noted.[56]

The events of June 7 to 10 substantially heightened the concern about the state of law and order in Michigan and led to the formation of law-and-order leagues in several Michigan cities, to support local law enforcement agencies it was alleged. "When the state's capitol is taken over, power lines are shut off and streets are barricaded...," the *Michigan Manufacturer and Financial Record* declared, "there is an approach to anarchy which honest citizens cannot stomach." Senator Vandenberg, who judged from his mail that "a virtual state of terror" had "taken possession" of the people of Michigan, concluded that the labor problem was ceasing to be "primarily a question of industrial relations" and was "rapidly approaching the naked question of sovereignty — who runs America? Is there a Government?" He thought that the question was especially pertinent with regard to Michigan, "where an amiable Governor has so far compromised with law and order that he has lost all chance to be effective except at a terrific price."[57] It was in this atmosphere, with the tide of opinion running heavily against organized labor and its friend in Lansing, that the Michigan senate began its

56 Donald G. Sofchalk, "The Little Steel Strike of 1937" (Ph.D. diss., Ohio State University, 1961), pp. 208-22; Sofchalk, "The Chicago Memorial Day Incident...," *Labor History* 6 (Winter 1965), 34; *Detroit News*, May 28, 30, June 3, 4, 8-16, 1937; [(Lansing) *State Journal*, June 2, 1937], MSB; Hill to Murphy, June 10, 1937, Murphy to F. J. Thieme, June 14, 1937, Robert Wohlforth to Murphy, August 6, 1938, and Murphy comments on enclosed transcript, Murphy Papers; U. S. Cong., Senate, Committee on Education and Labor, *Violations of Free Speech and the Rights of Labor, Report No. 6 (Industrial Munitions)*, 76th Cong., 1st Sess. 1939, part 3, pp. 148-55; U. S. Cong., Senate, Subcommittee of the Committee on Education and Labor, *Violations of Free Speech and the Rights of Labor, Hearings...*, 75th Cong., 3rd Sess. 1939, part 27, pp. 11364-65, part 28, pp. 11515-29, 11547-48, 11586, 11599-603, 11750-56, 11179-80, 12057-59, part 42, pp. 16302-9, 16314, 16323-26; Howard C. Lawrence to Vandenberg, June 14, 1937, Howard C. Lawrence Papers, Michigan Historical Collections.

57 *MMFR* 59 (June 12, 1937):3, and 60 (July 17, 1937):12; Vandenberg to Couzens, June 11, 1937, Couzens to Vandenberg, June 14, 1937, Arthur H. Vandenberg Papers, William L. Clements Library, Ann Arbor, Michigan; Vandenberg to Lawrence, June 16, 1937, Lawrence Papers; *Detroit News*, June 13, July 4, 1937; *The New York Times*, June 13, 1937; *Ann Arbor News*, June 16, 1937.

deliberation of the labor relations bill that the house had passed on June 3.

Subsequent Bills and Murphy's Veto

After conferring with Murphy, the Senate Committee on Labor reported out a labor relations bill on June 18 that preserved the conciliation, mediation, and arbitration provisions of the house bill, but made no reference to unfair practices by either employers or employees, limited the governor's power to halt strikes to disputes threatening an essential public service, and proscribed picketing that obstructed the approach to or egress from a business or that interfered with "the free and unimpeded use of public highways." The committee struck the employee unfair practices from the bill and limited the governor's powers in strikes to accommodate organized labor, and it then eliminated the unfair employer practices to preserve the idea of balance. The restrictions on picketing were almost certainly inserted at Murphy's behest, the governor's views on the subject having been influenced by the Monroe experience. Murphy by this time was seemingly prepared to accept a bill that focused primarily on conciliation, mediation, and arbitration, partly because of the overriding concern with strikes in Michigan, partly because it was presumed that the NLRA covered "most of the territory needing regulation of employment relations," at least for industries operating in interstate commerce.[58]

The bill reported by the committee did not, however, reflect the mood of the senate, which on June 23 approved a far different measure. Its author characterized the bill as seeking "law and order instead of disorder"; but Murphy's personal secretary described the measure as "very regulatory and suppressive," blaming this on "present public opinion." The senate bill restored the provisions of the original House Bill 571 regarding representation, the examination of union books, and picketing but also included a ban on stranger picketing as well as the restrictions imposed in the Senate Committee on Labor's bill. The new bill required a fifteen-day notice before a union could strike; and, if the dispute was not resolved in this time period, the board was to investigate and to publish a report within five days identifying the party that was "mainly responsible or blameworthy." Labor organizations were to be required to include provisions in their articles of association, constitution, or by-laws forbidding violation of the provisions of a labor contract, sit-down strikes, and strikes in violation of the act and providing for the expulsion of members who engaged in strikes in contravention of the terms of the statute.[59]

The house overwhelmingly rejected the senate bill, and a conference committee of the two chambers then wrote a new bill that hewed closely in many respects to the house substitute bill that had been approved on June 3. The conference committee bill, however, omitted the provisions specifying unfair employer and employee practices and permitting the governor to delay strikes in major industries and essential public services, limited the application of the act to employers of twenty or more workers, failed to include the restraints on the issuance of injunctions provided in the house substitute bill and in the Norris-La Guardia Act, and prohibited picketing that served to "obstruct or otherwise interfere with" the approach to or egress from an establishment or interfered with the unimpeded use of public highways and picketing "by a person who is neither employed therein nor a party to the dispute nor an official of a labor organization that is a party to the dispute." The bill in this form was approved on June 25 by a margin of 72 to 3 in the house and 29 to 0 in the senate. The measure was passed at 3:00 A.M., and for the next twenty-four hours the UAW counsel was unable to contact any member of the legislature since, he reported, "They were all drunk or in bed, or both."[60]

Business Week thought that businessmen in Michigan were privately "pretty well satisfied" with the industrial relations bill, but the organ of the Michigan Manufacturers' Association, which preferred the governor's original bill, concluded that the new measure was "not much of an improvement over conditions which prevailed previously." Business opposition, however, was far more muted than the opposition of organized labor and its friends. The UAW, the American Federation of Labor, the ACLU, and labor sympathizers all found the measure flawed beyond redemption and called upon Murphy to kill it with a veto. They were dissatisfied with the bill's failure to prohibit unfair labor practices by employers, the deficiencies in its antiinjunction provisions as compared to the Norris-La Guardia Act and the house substitute bill of June 3, and language in the bill, partly the result of hurried and careless drafting, that they feared would make it possible for a hostile board and unfriendly courts to circumscribe labor's rights. Above all, the labor and libertarian critics of the bill focused on its provisions regarding picketing and especially the ban on stranger picketing. Stranger picketing, they contended, was "the only realistic approach to unionism in modern industry," and to prohibit it, they feared, was to

---

[58] Michigan, Legislature, Senate, *Senate Journal, 1937* 2:1534-35; *Detroit News,* June 18, 1937; Murphy draft of picketing clause, and Kemp to Murphy, June 15, 1937, Kemp Papers, box 10.

[59] Michigan, Legislature, Senate, *Senate Journal, 1937,*

2:1657-64; *The New York Times,* June 16, 1937; *Detroit News,* June 24, 1937; Eleanor M. Bumgardner to Baldwin, June 23, 1937, ACLU Archives, vol. 1049.

[60] Michigan, Legislature, House, *House Journal, 1937,* 2:2054, 2060, 2092, 2123, 2165, 2171-79; Michigan, Legislature, Senate, *Senate Journal,* 1937, 2:1884; Sugar to Baldwin, July 6, 1937, ACLU Archives, vol. 1048.

deprive labor of its power to maintain and extend its organization.[61]

Murphy, initially, seemed disposed to sign the labor relations bill. He described it as a "progressive step" and as "a truly pioneering measure" that went beyond the NLRA and was "broader than any other [labor] law." Accenting the positive, he noted that the statute guaranteed collective bargaining, legalized picketing, restricted the use of injunctions, and authorized the investigation of racketeering and extortion. The restraints on picketing, he contended, were required to cope with "abuses" of a sort that had caused "a great deal of trouble." Above all, Murphy pointed to the measure's emphasis on conciliation, mediation, and arbitration as offering the means by which the state government could "impartially" assist in the resolution of labor disputes and the elimination of violence in the labor relations field.

Still bemused by the concept of the public interest, Murphy apparently viewed the opposition to the bill by both labor and management as proof of the reasonable character of the measure. Criticizing both the "Communist cliques" that he now alleged had "deliberately created" some of Michigan's labor disorders and the "hardboiled reactionaries" who, he charged, wanted to deal with labor problems by "shoot[ing] it out in a revolutionary sort of way," he said that his "objective" was "not to let the extremists on either side have their way"; and he insisted that it was the "extremists" who were opposing the bill. Murphy, finally, still wanted an industrial relations bill for Michigan that could be "heralded nationally," and he doubtlessly realized that the measure that was now before him was probably the best one that could be obtained from "the reactionary State Senate."[62]

The pressures exerted upon him by the labor-libertarian alliance began to have their effect on Murphy, however, and he "listened sympathetically" to their criticisms,

particularly with respect to stranger picketing. When the legislature reassembled for a brief adjournment session on July 29, the final day on which the governor could legally veto the June 25 measure, Murphy addressed a joint convention of the two chambers and noted that the bill contained features that would make it difficult to gain the "cooperation and support" of labor and industry that was essential if the measure were to be effectively implemented. It was, of course, the opposition of organized labor with which Murphy was particularly concerned, and it was for this reason that he requested that the bill be reconsidered and revised to permit picketing by members of a labor organization at a plant where any one of them was engaged in a dispute and, also, that the words "otherwise interfere" be eliminated, because of their ambiguity, from the language restricting picketing.

When the senate proved unwilling to follow the governor's advice, Maurice Sugar feared that Murphy would feel obliged to sign the unamended bill, and so the UAW counsel called for the "widest and most vigorous protest" by the labor-libertarian alliance before the day was out. The UAW, Lewis, Labor's Non-Partisan League, and the Conference for the Protection of Civil Rights all communicated with the governor that day requesting him to veto the bill, and they were not disappointed in the result. In a veto message that night, Murphy briefly noted what he regarded as some of the deficiencies of the June 25 bill and explained once again that, if industrial peace were to be achieved through industrial relations legislation, it was necessary to have the support of the interests primarily affected by this legislation.[63]

Speaking informally after submitting his veto message, the governor declared that he had not vetoed the measure because of the pressure of any group, but rather because of "conscience." It is clear, though, that Murphy had abandoned the amorphous concept of the "public interest" that had informed his defense first of House Bill 571 and then of the June 25 bill and was now assigning veto power over industrial relations legislation to organized labor and, presumably, to the employers as well. In this sense, he was embracing interest-group liberalism and its definition of the public interest in terms of "the organized interests in society," but this interpretation, to be sure, presents in theoretical terms a problem that Murphy obviously saw in practical political terms. He was, in the

[61] *Business Week*, July 3, 1937, p. 14; *MMFR* 60 (July 3, 1937): 3, 8; *Detroit News*, June 27, July 1, 29, 1937; *The New York Times*, July 1, 1937; *United Automobile Worker*, July 10, 1937; Sugar to Baldwin, June 29, 1937, Polier to Murphy, July 2, 1937, and enclosed "Analysis," Baldwin to Murphy, July 3, 1937, ACLU Archives, vol. 1049; Sugar to Baldwin, July 6, 1937, and enclosed Memo on Michigan Industrial Relations Act as Passed June 25, 1937, Baldwin to Sugar, July 7, 1937, and ACLU Release, July 12, 1937, ACLU Archives, vol. 1048; Arthur J. Hartley to Murphy, June 30, 1937, William Green to Murphy, July 20, 1937, Kemp Papers, box 9; Harold A. Cowell to Murphy, July 25, 1937, Sugar to Murphy, July 29, 1937, Kemp Papers, box 10; *Detroit Labor News*, July 23, 1937.

[62] *The New York Times*, June 29, 1937; Murphy to C. C. Chase, July 7, 1937, (Lansing) *State Journal*, July 2, 1937, clipping, Murphy Papers; Murphy, "Shaping of Labor Policy," pp. 411-13; *Detroit News*, July 2, 3, 1937; Polier to Murphy, July 2, 1937, ACLU Archives, vol. 1049; Sugar to Baldwin, July 6, 12, 1937, ACLU Archives, vol. 1048.

[63] Sugar to Baldwin, July 6, 12, 1937, Sugar to ACLU, July 29, 1937, ACLU Archives, vol. 1048; UAW Release, July 29, 1937, ACLU Archives, vol. 1049; Sugar to Murphy, July 29, 1937, Kemp Papers, box 10; Lewis to Murphy, July 29, 1937, Kemp Papers, box 9; Conference for Protection of Civil Rights to Murphy, July 29, 1937, Murphy Papers; *The New York Times*, July 28, 1937; *Detroit News*, July 30, 1937; Michigan, Legislature, House, *House Journal, 1937*, 2:2265-66, 2279-80.

final analysis, simply not willing to defy a group with whose interests he had identified his career even before it was as powerful as it had become in 1937. As he told the DWCFL after he vetoed the bill, "I have never yet done anything to hurt Labor. . . . and I never will." The *Detroit News* thought that Murphy's "mental processes" in all this were "a puzzle," and even the *Nation* remarked that the governor had gotten himself "tangled in as hopeless a web as ever troubled a well-meaning labor governor." The *Detroit Labor News*, however, thought that "a great governor" had been "doing a great job," and the ACLU informed Murphy "confidentially" that there were "very few governors — or any public officials for that matter — whose acts we so frequently endorse."[64]

Murphy, on July 15, had called a special session of the legislature to meet on July 30, just two hours after the close of the regular session, and one of the three matters that he now submitted to the extra session was the adoption of legislation to deal with labor disputes. A majority of the senators, regarding the antipicketing section of the vetoed bill as its "most important" feature, ignored the governor's wishes and repassed the June 25 measure. The house, however, promptly substituted a version of the bill acceptable to Murphy and the Michigan Federation of Labor that permitted picketing by persons who were employed in or residents of the municipality or township in which the dispute occurred, or in the adjoining community. Although the house bill was described by one authority on labor law as "no bill at all" and as having "all the ear marks of being the end result of a series of compromises as a consequence of which the baby is thrown out with the bath," the senate buried the measure in committee and then illegally voted to adjourn. Senator James Burns, who had insisted that the senate remain in session and pass the bill, thereupon strode to the desk of the anti-Murphy Democratic floor leader, William Palmer, jerked off his glasses, struck him twice in the face, and then rushed from the chamber. The special session actually continued until August 12, but the house and senate were unable to reconcile their differences on labor relations legislation.[65]

When the special session came to a close, Murphy remained "confident" that Michigan would "work out a satisfactory [industrial relations] law," and he sought the advice of organized labor, the ACLU, employers, and the United States Department of Labor in framing such a law. The governor considered the possibility of calling another special session to enact a labor relations measure; but legislative leaders were cool to the idea, and the times hardly seemed propitious for the enactment of the kind of measure that would have satisfied the labor-libertarian alliance. As the director of the Division of Labor Standards of the Department of Labor advised Murphy in December, it would have been difficult, in view of prevailing attitudes, to prevent the inclusion of a list of unfair employee practices in such a measure. The "serious division" between the AFL and the CIO had become "a real deterrent" to the successful administration of labor relations legislation, the director thought; and he feared that the troublesome and unresolved problem of the respective jurisdictions of state labor boards and the NLRB would make it possible, should Michigan enact a labor relations statute, for lawyers to produce "endless confusions and delays to the great advantage of the employer." The director suggested that Michigan, under the circumstances, should simply enact a state mediation statue, and, at Kemp's request, the federal official prepared drafts of such legislation. The Murphy administration, however, decided not to press the matter, probably because the recession of 1937-1938, which hit Michigan with devastating force, had begun to push other issues into the background.[66]

[64] *Detroit News*, July 30, August 8, 1937; *The New York Times*, July 30, 1937; Murphy to Lee Jaffe, August 13, 1937, Murphy Papers; Murphy to Lewis, August 12, September 3, 1937, Kemp Papers, box 9; Theodore J. Lowi, *The End of Liberalism* (New York: W. W. Norton, 1969), pp. 71, 75; Grant McConnell, *Private Power and American Democracy* (New York: Vintage Books, 1971), pp. 47, 158-60, 336, 365-68; *Detroit Labor News*, August 6, 1937; *Nation* 145 (August 7, 1937):142; Wirin to Murphy, August 9, 1937, ACLU Archives, vol. 1049.

[65] Michigan, Legislature, Senate, *Senate Journal, Extra Session of 1937* (Lansing, 1937), pp. 2, 4, 13-20, 29, 30, 33-40, 50; Michigan, Legislature, House, *House Journal, Extra Session of 1937* (Lansing [1937]), pp. 9, 17, 24, 43, 44, 48;

Detroit News, July 16, 31, August 1, 4-6, 8, November 7, 1937; *Detroit Free Press*, July 30, 31, 1937; *Ann Arbor News*, July 31, August 2, 1937; *MMFR* 60 (August 4, 1937): 8; *Detroit Labor News*, December 17, 1937; Polier to Murphy, October 1, 1937, ACLU Archives, vol. 1048; Conference of . . . the MFL . . . , December 12, 1937, Wayne County AFL-CIO Papers, box 8. The support of the AFL is partially explained by the inclusion in the bill of language satisfactory to craft unionists regarding the determination of the appropriate unit for collective bargaining. *The New York Times*, July 30, 1937.

[66] Murphy to Baldwin, August 11, 1937, Murphy to Polier, August 11, 1937, Murphy to H. Lynn Pierson, August 11, 1937, Murphy to Nicholas Kelley, August 11, 1937, Murphy to Lawrence Fisher, August 11, 1937, Murphy to Frances Perkins, August 11, 1937, Murphy to Green, August 12, 1937, Murphy to Lewis, August 12, 1937, Murphy to Hartley, August 12, 1937, Kemp Papers, box 9; Zimmer to Murphy, December 9, 1937, and enclosed memorandum, Kemp to Zimmer, January 4, 1938, Zimmer to Kemp, January 26, 1938, Kemp Papers, box 11; Wirin to Sugar, September 14, 1937, ACLU Archives, vol. 1049; Polier to Baldwin, October 1, 1937, [October 8, 1937], Baldwin to Sugar, October 11, 1937, Minutes of ACLU Board of Directors' Meeting, October 11, 1937, ACLU Archives, vol. 1048; *Detroit News*, September 26, 1937.

It was in 1939, after Frank Murphy had ceased to be Michigan's governor, that the state finally enacted a labor relations statute. The measure required a notice of at least five days before most strikes or lockouts could be called, during which time the labor mediation board created by the act could seek to adjust the dispute, and a thirty-day delay for strikes or lockouts in public utilities, hospitals, and other industries "affected with a public interest," while a three-man commission appointed by the governor sought to mediate the dispute and prepared a report on the matter for the state's chief executive. The act specified several unfair employer practices but did not require employers to engage in collective bargaining. It made participation in a sit-down strike a misdemeanor and made it unlawful for anyone "by force, coercion, intimidation or threats" to compel any person to join a labor organization or to cease working. As with the labor relations bills sponsored by Murphy, the emphasis of the 1939 Michigan act was on the mediation of disputes, and, as with House Bill 571, unfair practices by both employers and employees fell under the statute's ban. The unfair-practice provisions of the 1939 law, however, were little more than "an appendage" to the statute and were less detailed than the comparable sections of the Kemp-Stason measure. Also, House Bill 571, unlike the 1939 measure, did not proscribe sit-down strikes.[67]

The Michigan labor relations experience of 1937 demonstrates how quickly a reaction set in against the kind of prolabor sentiment that had led to the enactment of the NLRA. The sit-down strikes and the labor turbulence of the early months of 1937 adversely affected the public standing of organized labor, as polling data demonstrate,[68] and led to a spreading demand for law and order that influenced a governor known throughout the nation for his support of organized labor. Just as the sit-down strikes had focused national attention on Michigan at the beginning of 1937, so the attempt of the Murphy administration to devise legislation that would curb unions and restrain the use of the strike received important notice in the nation. It was deemed "a significant straw in the wind" that the reaction against the exercise of labor power had come, of all places, in Murphy's Michigan.[69] Michigan failed to pass a labor relations act in 1937 because of Murphy's veto, but the trend toward the enactment of state laws of the restrictive type that became so evident in 1939 and that was followed by the framing of similar legislation at the national level was foreshadowed by what had taken place in Michigan during the first year of Murphy's governorship.

[67] *Public and Local Acts of the Legislature. . . of Michigan . . .1939* (Lansing, 1939), pp. 336-40; Killingsworth, *State Labor Relations Acts*, pp. 132-33, 220.

[68] A Gallup poll released on July 4, 1937, revealed that among the 50 percent of those interviewed who indicated that their attitude toward labor unions had changed during the preceding six months, 71 percent were now less well disposed toward unions. Gallup, *Gallup Poll*, p. 63.

[69] See, for example, *Detroit News*, May 2, July 1, 1937; *The New York Times*, June 29, 30, July 30, 1937; *Washington Post*, June 30, 1937, clipping in Murphy Papers; Murphy, "Shaping of Labor Policy," pp. 411-13, 450-52, 465-68; and "For and Against — Governor Murphy's Labor Policy," *Survey Graphic* 26 (September 1937):464-69.

CHAPTER II

Mr. Buckley and the Unions: Of Union Discipline and Member Dissidence

by Harry H. Wellington, *Edward J. Phelps Professor of Law,* Yale University

Somewhere between his estate in Connecticut and his *National Review* offices in Manhattan, it may have occurred to William F. Buckley, Jr., that it was incongruous for him to belong to both the New York Yacht Club and a common labor union. Since he also believed his membership in the latter constrained his not insubstantial wit and might force him to compromise his often unpopular views, Mr. Buckley wanted out. Indeed, he later testified that he had never wanted in: He had joined the union, the American Federation of Television and Radio Artists (AFTRA), only because he had been forced to do so, like many of his working-class brethren, under a union-security clause in his employment contract.[1]

Mr. Buckley has, at least for the moment, triumphed over organized labor. In January 1973, United States District Judge Charles Brieant held that Section 8(a)(3) of the National Labor Relations Act, and its permissive attitude toward union-security arrangements, was not intended "to provide any means whereby a union," through disciplinary action, "could place a direct threat of prior restraint upon" Buckley

. . . as a combined result of (a) compulsory membership; (b) the need to subscribe to terms and conditions of union discipline; (c) the need to refrain from speaking through a broadcast outlet judged unfair, or not organized; (d) the need to refrain from crossing a picket line; and (e) the need to heed any other union directions which would operate directly or indirectly as a prior restraint on freedom of speech.[2]

Mr. Buckley's victory has encouraged the well-heeled National Right to Work Legal Defense Foundation in its financing of similar suits by other disgruntled members of the involuntary rank and file.[3] An examination of the major premise of Judge Brieant's opinion, however, demonstrates that it is almost surely incorrect. This paper will examine the theoretical basis for the type of discipline feared by Mr. Buckley and will contend that as a matter of law his apprehensions are unfounded. It will then, however, suggest that neither Mr. Buckley nor Judge Brieant is alone in his confusion over the extent of a worker's obligation to his union, but rather that their misconceptions may result in part from ambiguous dicta that flaw the Supreme Court's major pronouncements on union discipline. Finally, it will argue that such misconceptions, together with the Court's apparent determination to leave many critical issues of union discipline to union trial boards or inferior state courts, require action by the National Labor Relations Board to insure that members and nonmembers alike appreciate their rights under the NLRA.

This paper deals with the law as of November 1973. I am very grateful to Mr. Peter T. Grossi, Jr., J.D. Yale, 1973, for his able assistance in the preparation of this paper.

[1] Evans v. American Federation of Television & Radio Artists, 354 F. Supp. 825, 834-35 (1973). The AFTRA union-security clause is representative of its genre:

It is agreed that during the term of this agreement we [the broadcasters] will maintain in our employment only such persons covered by this agreement as are members of the American Federation of Television and Radio Artists in good standing or as shall make application for membership on the thirtieth (30th) day following the beginning of employment hereunder or the date of execution of the agreement, whichever is the later, and thereafter maintain such membership as a condition of employment.

[2] *Ibid.,* p. 847.

[3] See *Time,* May 28, 1973, p. 76. The foundation, which is presently sponsoring more than fifty suits by dissident members, is itself being sued by ten unions contending that a significant portion of its $2,000,000 annual income comes from employers in violation of the Landrum-Griffin Act (*ibid.*). The unions appear to have a fairly strong case under Section 101(a)(4) of the act (29 U.S.C. Section 411 [1970]), which provides that "no interested employer or employer association shall directly or indirectly finance, encourage, or participate in" any suit by a union member. In the only reported decision applying the section, Farowitz v. Associated Musicians of N.Y., Local 802, 241 F. Supp. 895 (1965), the district court construed it rather narrowly, holding that employers were not sufficiently "interested" in the suit of a member expelled for attacking a union tax despite the fact that they had previously litigated against the tax themselves (pp. 898, 900).

BUCKLEY'S COMPLAINT

An initial difficulty with *Evans* v. *AFTRA* (plaintiff Buckley was joined by conservative columnist M. Stanton Evans) is that it is not immediately clear that union activity, no matter how discriminatory or proscribed by federal labor law, is regulated by the First Amendment. Judge Brieant apparently believed that the regulatory framework of the NLRA was sufficient to make such activity "governmental action." Citing the Supreme Court in *American Communications Association* v. *Douds*,[4] he reasoned that,

> ". . . when authority derives in part from Government's thumb on the scales, the exercise of that power by private persons becomes closely akin, in some respects, to its exercise by Government itself" and therefore justiciable.[5]

The well-worn arguments for and against extending constitutional mandates to the unions need not be rehearsed here.[6] For our purposes it need only be noted that the Court has never actually declared union activity "governmental." Rather, it has left us with the suggestion in *Railway Employees' Dept.* v. *Hanson* that only a total displacement of state law by federal labor law constitutes governmental action.[7] Though this doctrine was immediately criticized for its anamolous results,[8] the Court in *Machinists* v. *Street*[9] refused to go any further, producing an opinion that despite its "constitutional overtones"[10] was nothing more than statutory construction.[11] It must be remembered that both *Hanson* and *Street* arose under the Railway Labor Act, which not only permits, but also encourages, compulsory unionism by nullifying state laws to the contrary.[12] This circumstance has led some judges[13] to distinguish the lesser governmental involvement of the NLRA that merely permits union shops under Section 8(a)(3),[14] a permission that can be nullified by a state right-to-work law.[15]

In short, the facts that even *Hanson* appeared to accept this distinction between command and permission, that in the twelve years since *Street* the Court has made no attempt to extend the Constitution to unions, and that the Burger Court seems hardly eager to extend the doctrine of governmental action in general[16] suggest that the Court is not likely to hold internal union discipline, without additional reasons, to constitutional standards. Once a union seeks judicial enforcement of such discipline, however (as it may under *Allis-Chalmers*[17]), the case for governmental action seems far stronger. While the possibility of judicial enforcement of a collective agreement may not bring every action of the contracting parties under constitutional scrutiny,[18] *Shelley* v. *Kramer*[19] must mean that when a union sues to enforce a fine it has levied, the court decree *itself* constitutes state action.[20]

It therefore seems proper to conduct a constitutional inquiry into the chilling effect on free expression of this possibility. Nevertheless, a second, more fundamental question remains: Does Mr. Buckley have anything to fear? While the case is ripe for adjudication, in the sense that there was the "real possibility" that free expression would

---

[4] 339 U.S. 382, 401 (1950). See p. 402, however, where the Court cautioned, "We do not suggest that labor unions which utilize the facilities of the National Labor Relations Board become Government agencies or may be regarded as such."

[5] Evans v. American Federation of Television and Radio Artists, 354 F. Supp. 823, 837 (1973).

[6] See Freidmann, "Corporate Power, Government by Private Groups, and the Law," *Colorado Law Review* 57 (1957):155, 176; Malick, "Toward a New Constitutional Status for Labor Unions: A Proposal," *Rocky Mountain Law Review* 21 (1949): 260; Rauh, "Civil Rights and Civil Liberties and Labor Unions," *Labor Law Journal* 8 (1957): 874; Read, "Minority Rights and the Union Shop: A Basis for Constitutional Attack," *Minnesota Law Review* 49 (1964): 227; Wellington, "The Constitution, the Labor Union, and 'Governmental Action,'" *Yale Law Review* 70 (1961):345; and Wellington, "*Machinist v. Street:* Statutory Interpretation and the Avoidance of Constitutional Issues," *Supreme Court Review* 49 (1961):49, 72-73.

[7] 351 U.S. 225, 231-32 (1956).

[8] See Wellington, "The Constitution, the Labor Unions, and 'Governmental Action,'" pp. 345, 355-56.

[9] 367 U.S. 740 (1961).

[10] See Seay v. McDonnell Douglas Corp., 427 F.2d. 966, 1004 (9th Cir. 1970) (suggesting that *Street* involved the application of constitutional standards).

[11] See Wellington, "*Machinists v. Street,*" pp. 53-60.

[12] Railway Labor Act, §2 Eleventh, 45 U.S.C. §152 Eleventh (1970).

[13] See, for example, Reid v. McDonnell Douglas Corp., 443 F.2d. 408, 409-11 (10th Cir. 1971); Linscott v. Millers Falls Co., 440 F.2d 14, 19-20 (1st Cir. 1971) *cert. den.* 404 U.S. 872 (1971) (Judge Coffin concurring); but also see the court opinion, pp. 16-18.

[14] 29 U.S.C. §158 (a)(3)(1970).

[15] 29 U.S.C. §164 (b)(1965).

[16] See, for example, Moose Lodge No. 107 v. Irvis, 407 U.S. 163 (1972). Compare Columbia Broadcasting System, Inc. v. Democratic National Committee, 93 S.Ct. 2080 (1973).

[17] 388 U.S. 175 (1967).

[18] See Linscott v. Millers Falls Co., 440 F.2d. 14, 19-20 (1st Cir. 1971), *cert. den.* 404 U.S. 872 (1971) (Judge Coffin concurring).

[19] 334 U.S. 1(1948).

[20] "Once the courts enforce the [collective] agreement the sanction of government is, of course, put behind them. See *Shelley v. Kramer. . . .*" Railway Employees' Dept. v. Hanson, 351 U.S. 225, 232 n. 4. (1956).

be chilled,[21] Mr. Buckley's fears seem largely hypothetical: he need not have subjected himself to union discipline, and he may even now, under the Court's recent *Granite State* decision,[22] immunize himself from the union's jurisdiction without any diminution of his employment rights.[23]

THE EXTENT OF UNION DISCIPLINE

The Subject Matter of Permissible Discipline

In *Allis-Chalmers*[24] the Supreme Court declared that the literal ban of Section 8(b)(1)(A)[25] on union attempts to "restrain or coerce" employees did not prohibit valid union discipline. Relying on legislative history, the Court stated:

> Integral to . . . federal labor policy has been the power in the chosen union to protect itself against erosion of its status under that policy through reasonable discipline of members who violate rules and regulations governing membership.[26]

The Court held that in addition to suspending or expelling a recalcitrant member, a union could seek judicial enforcement of its fines as for any other contractual debt. In so doing, the Court ignored its previous decisions that had invoked Section 8(a)(3)[27] to insulate a worker's employment rights from union

interference, save from the minimal obligation to pay union dues or agency-shop fees under a union-security clause.[28] The Court thus described a grand dichotomy divided into internal union sanctions that could be enforced even in a court of law and impermissible job discriminations that could not be imposed at all. Such a distinction, however, leads to some rather troublesome problems under the Court's latest resignation decisions.

Despite *Allis-Chalmers* and the fact that unions have been permitted to discipline members for a wide range of transgressions,[29] certain substantive and procedural limitations should be noted, if not fully explained, before considering the Court's latest sorties in the field. The first concerns the board's remedial powers. In two companion cases, *H. B. Roberts*[30] and *Skura*,[31] the board held that a union could not fine a member for filing an unfair labor practice charge before he exhausted his internal union remedies. Distinguishing their own approval of the strikebreaking fines upheld in *Allis-Chalmers*, the board explained,

> There, unlike the instant case, the Board was dealing with a union rule which . . . did not run counter to other recognized public policies and, therefore, was not beyond the competence of the union to adopt and enforce. . . . By the rule under consideration here, however, [the union] attempted to regulate its

---

[21] Evans v. American Federation of Television & Radio Artists, 354 F. Supp. 823, 838, 842 (1973).

[22] 409 U.S. 213 (1972).

[23] Judge Brieant considered Mr. Buckley's general obligation to the union, but never explicitly dealt with the issue of whether he could meet that obligation by merely paying dues. See Evans v. American Federation of Television & Radio Artists, 354 F.Supp. 823, 834-36 (1973). Judge Brieant, however, apparently believed that Mr. Buckley was compelled to do more than merely tender dues, as he concluded his opinion by noting

> The pleadings and the prior conduct of the parties clearly indicate that what is at issue, and what has been litigated, is the question of the requirement of membership and subjection to union discipline of. . . [the plaintiffs]. More is involved in this controversy than mere payment of a modest dues bill. . . .

[24] NLRB v. Allis-Chalmers Mfg. Co., 388 U.S. 175 (1967).

[25] 29 U.S.C. §158 (b)(1)(A):

> It shall be an unfair labor practice for a labor organization or its agents—
> (1) to restrain or coerce (a) employees in the exercise of the rights guaranteed in [§7 of the NLRA]. . . .: *Provided,* That this paragraph shall not impair the right of a labor organization to prescribe its own rules with respect to the acquisition or retention or membership therein. . . .

[26] 388 U.S. 175, 181 (1967).

[27] But see *ibid.*, p. 197, n. 37.

[28] See Radio Officers Union v. NLRB, 347 U.S. 17 (1954); NLRB v. General Motors, 373 U.S. 734 (1963).

[29] While by no means complete, the following is a representative list of cases upholding union discipline for various "internal" offenses: NLRB v. Allis-Chalmers, 388 U.S. 175 (1967) (strikebreaking); Scofield v. NLRB, 394 U.S. 423 (1969) (exceeding production quotas); Local 167, Progressive Mine Workers v. NLRB, 422 F.2d 538 (7th Cir. 1970) *cert. den.* 399 U.S. 905 (1970) (dual unionism); Glasser v. NLRB, 395 F.2d 401 (2nd Cir. 1968) (working with nonunion employees); Reyes v. Laborers Union, Local 16, 464 F.2d 595 (10th Cir. 1972), *cert. den.* 93 Sup. Ct. 1542 (1973) (threatening union officials with violence); Rocket Freight Lines v. NLRB, 427 F.2d 202 (10th Cir. 1970), *cert. den.* 400 U.S. 942 (1970) (reporting to work after local but not international ratification of a new contract); Minneapolis Star & Tribune, 109 N.L.R.B. 727, 34 LRRM 1431 (1954) (failing to report for picket duty); Carpenters & Joiners, Locals 1913 and 25, 189 N.L.R.B. No. 81, 77 LRRM 1252 (1971) *enf.* 464 F.2d 1395 (9th Cir. 1972) (creating a disturbance in a hiring hall); Teamsters No. 70 (Grinnel Co.), 191 N.L.R.B. No. 43, 77 LRRM 1415 (1971) (splitting vacations to please an employer in violation of union rules); Local 5795, Communications Workers, 192 N.L.R.B. No. 85, 77 LRRM 1827 (1971) (reporting a coworker for drinking on the job in violation of a union rule against informing).

[30] H. B. Roberts, Business Manager of Local 925, I.U.O.E., 148 N.L.R.B. 674 (1964), *enf.* 350 F.2d 427 (D.C. Cir. 1965).

[31] Local 138, I.U.O.E. (Charles S. Skura), 148 N.L.R.B. 679 (1964).

members' access to the Board's processes. Considering the overriding public interest involved, it is our opinion that no private organization should be permitted to prevent or regulate access to the Board. . . .[32]

Four years later, in *NLRB* v. *Marine & Shipbuilding Workers,*[33] the Court upheld this concern for "overriding public interests." Justice William O. Douglas, writing for the Court, reasoned that since both the employer and the public have an interest in the adjudication of unfair labor practices, the processing of such charges is not a matter for union self-regulation.[34] The issue, however, is not as clear as *Marine Workers* suggests. In citing the employer's interest as one that would torpedo claims of union sovereignty,[35] Justice Douglas' opinion led to speculation as to why the employer's obvious interest in those willing to cross picket lines had not similarly protected the strikebreakers in *Allis-Chalmers.*

Such speculation is enhanced by the recent explication of the ban in Section 8(b)(1) (B) on union coercion against an employer "in the selection of his representatives for the purposes of collective bargaining or the adjustment of grievances."[36] While the section seems clearly directed at interference with the *selection* of such representatives, the board, again relying on legislative history, held in 1968 that it prohibits a union from *disciplining* member-supervisors as well.[37] In *Meatcutters Union Local*

81 v. *NLRB,*[38] the first judicial test of this doctrine, the District of Columbia circuit court held that the Supreme Court's previous approval of fines for work-rule violators in *Scofield* v. *NLRB*[39] did not sanction similar fines for member-supervisors who permitted such violations, because the supervisor's union-member contract was of "only secondary importance" to the more fundamental employer-supervisor relationship.[40] This distinction seems far from compelling. While supervisory personnel are obviously in a critical position during bargaining or grievance processing, one may well ask why the interests of the union, employer, and employee are different when ten workers independently break a production rule from what they are when one supervisor orders or allows them to do so.

The same anamoly is evident in *Electrical Workers (IBEW)* v. *NLRB,*[41] where the same circuit court initially agreed with the board that a union could not fine member-supervisors who had crossed picket lines to perform rank-and-file jobs. The majority's distinction of strikebreaking by normal members as an internal union affair from strikebreaking by member-supervisors as an external matter failed to impress Judge Wright:

> The majority ignores the fact that the very purpose of having a union is to affect external relations between employees and their employer. All union rules are therefore "external" since they are all designed to insure a strong and united front among union members when the union confronts its employer adversary. *Allis-Chalmers, Scofield,* and *Marine Workers* stand for the proposition that such rules may nonetheless be enforced "unless some impairment of a statutory labor policy can be shown."[42]

---

32 *Ibid.,* p. 682.

33 391 U.S. 418 (1968).

34 *Ibid.,* p. 425.

35 *Ibid.*

36 29 U.S.C. §158 (b)(1)(B) (1970).

37 San Francisco-Oakland Mailers' Union, 172 N.L.R.B. No. 252, 69 LRRM 1157 (1968). Noting that its public policy exception had been upheld in *Marine Workers* the board, in rather cavalier fashion, pp. 1158-59, rejected the union's defense based on *Allis-Chalmers*:

> The Supreme Court, in finding lawful the union action in *Allis-Chalmers,* relied in part on the proviso to Section 8 (b)(1)(A), providing that the right of a labor organization to prescribe its own rules with respect to the acquisition or retention of membership shall not be impaired. However, that proviso is limited to Section 8(b)(1)(A) of the Act only and is not a part of Section 8(b)(1)(B). In addition, only legitimate internal union affairs are protected under Allis-Chalmers. The primary relationship there affected was the one between the union and its members. . . . In contrast, in the present case, the relationship primarily affected is the one between the Union and the Employer, since the underlying question was the interpretation of the collective bargaining agreement [on the work rules]. . . .

It should be noted that this interpretation of *Allis-Chalmers* is simply incorrect. The Court in fact made very little use of the proviso, but rather based its decision on the legislative history behind the phrase "restrain or coerce" that triggers both §8(b)(1)(A) *and* §8(b)(1)(B). Compare 388 U.S. 175, 187 with 388 U.S. 175, 178-195. Moreover, both Justice Byron

White in his concurrence and Justice Hugo L. Black in his dissent stated without contradiction from the majority that the Court had not relied on the proviso (388 U.S. 175, 197-98, 200-01). Finally, the board itself later conceded that the Court had not based its opinion on the proviso (see Machinists, Lodge 405 [Boeing], 185 N.L.R.B. No. 23, 75 LRRM 1004, 1006 [1970]).

38 458 F.2d 794 (D.C. Cir. 1972).

39 394 U.S. 423 (1969). The Court held that the rule that required union members to bank piecework earnings beyond a fixed production ceiling (to be returned on days the worker did not meet the ceiling) was a valid union concern (*ibid.,* p. 424-25). Despite the antifeatherbedding provisions of §8(b)(6) (29 U.S.C. §158(b)(6) (1970)), the *Scofield* Court further found such a rule did not violate federal labor policy and could, therefore, result in judicially enforced fines (*ibid.,* p. 434-36). Only Justice Black, adhering to his literal reading of §8(b)(1)(A), dissented (*ibid.,* p. 436).

40 458 F.2d 794, 801 (D.C. Cir. 1972).

41 81 LRRM 2257 (D.C. Cir. 1972).

42 *Ibid.,* p. 2277 (Judge Wright, concurring in part, dissenting in part).

A few months later, the ninth circuit court, agreeing with this analysis, held that a union could discipline member-supervisors who crossed picket lines.[43] Yet another month later, Judge Wright persuaded a bare majority of his own circuit, on a rehearing of *Electrical Workers*, that Section 8(b)(1)(B) did not preclude such discipline.[44] The seventh circuit, however, subsequently held, in its own *Electrical Workers* case, to the contrary:

[M]anagement has "traditionally" relied upon supervisors, where practicable, to pitch in and perform rank-and-file work in an attempt both to strengthen its bargaining position and to preserve the enterprise from repercussion following a strike. Insofar as the supervisors work to give the employer added economic leverage, they are acting as members of the management team [and] are expected to act when the employer and union are at loggerheads in their most fundamental of disputes. Indeed, in a real sense they are representing the employer for the purpose of collective bargaining for "the use of economic pressure by the parties to a labor dispute * * * is part and parcel of the process of collective bargaining." NLRB v. Insurance Agents International Union, 361 U.S. 477, 495.[45]

It remains to be seen whether the Supreme Court, in resolving this conflict in the circuit courts, will ultimately accept Judge Wright's theory that only some overriding *public* interest, and not merely the employer's, removes an offense from the ambit of union discipline. What is clear is that the present state of the law with regard to supervisors is confused and, in at least one circuit court and the NLRB, in apparent conflict with the Court's earlier decisions. Moreover, it should be noted that even Judge Wright's restrictive public policy exception leaves room for expansion. For example, the board has already held that unions may not discipline members for failing to strike where such activity would breach a no-strike clause, on the grounds that the integrity of collective agreements is a public matter and thus beyond the disciplinary authority of the unions.[46]

Similar ambiguities surround the board's policy on members disciplined for filing decertification petitions. In *Tawas Tube Products*[47] the board held that Section 8(b)(1)(A) did not prohibit the expulsion of such members. Distinguishing the case from *Skura,* the board argued that in the decertification context the member was not asking the board to correct some unfair labor practice, but rather was "attacking the very existence" of the union; expulsion was, therefore, a properly "defensive" response.[48] Four years later, however, in *Blackhawk Tanning,*[49] the board refused to apply the same logic to permit the fining of a member who filed a decertification petition. The board admitted, as it had not done in *Tawas Tube,* that every decertification case involves an implicit balancing of "the public policy against permitting a union to penalize a member because he seeks the aid of the Board" with the "union's right to self-defense."[50] The board reasoned that since fines did not serve the same rudimentary elements of self-defense as expulsions, that is, did not excise the dissident fifth column within the union, they could only be regarded as punitive. Stripped of their self-defense rationale, the fines thus fell into the public policy snakepit of *Skura* and were held invalid under Section 8(b)(1)(A).[51]

Beyond its initial lack of candor, the board's attempt to juggle the interests of the unions, their members, and the public by limiting the form, but not the subject matter, of union discipline is itself troubling. As noted by critics of *Allis-Chalmers,* the relative coerciveness of a judicially enforced fine and an expulsion will vary with the strength of the union.[52] A weak union will have little power to discourage decertification by mere expulsions, since membership may mean nothing to its dissidents. By contrast, a worker attacking a strong union may be effectively blocked by the jeopardy to his job of the loss

fining workers for crossing a sister union's picket lines where the collective agreement contained the standard Teamster's clause prohibiting such conduct).

[47] 151 N.L.R.B. 46, 58 LRRM 1330 (1965).

[48] *Ibid.,* p. 1331.

[49] 178 N.L.R.B. 208, 72 LRRM 1049 (1969), *enf.* NLRB v. Molders, Local 125, 77 LRRM 2067 (7th Cir. 1971).

[50] *Ibid.,* p. 1050.

[51] *Ibid.* The board has similarly held that a member who files a certification petition for a rival union can be suspended, but not fined. Printing Specialties Union No. 481, 183 N.L.R.B. No. 125, 74 LRRM 1698 (1970). *Accord:* Tri-Rivers Marine Engineers Union (U.S. Steel), 189 N.L.R.B. No. 108, 77 LRRM 1027 (1971); Price v. NLRB, 373 F.2d 443 (9th Cir. 1967), *cert. den.* 392 U.S. 904 (1968).

[52] See, for example, Note, "Judicial Enforcement of Labor Union Fines in State Court," *North Carolina Law Review* 46 (1968): 441, 443.

[43] NLRB v. San Francisco Typographical Union No. 21, 71 L.C. Para. 13,712 (9th Cir. 1973).

[44] Electrical Workers v. NLRB, 42 U.S.L.W. 2045 (D.C. Cir. June 29, 1973) *(en blanc).*

[45] NLRB v. Electrical Workers, 42 U.S.L.W. 2046, 2047 (7th Cir., July 13, 1973).

[46] National Grinding Wheel, 176 N.L.R.B. 628, 71 LRRM 1311 (1969); Glaziers Union No. 1162, 177 N.L.R.B. 393, 73 LRRM 1125 (1969); Local 1197, Communications Workers, 202 N.L.R.B. No. 45, CCH Para. 25,116 (1973) (rejecting the defense that the employer had not invoked the clause against the workers). Compare Machinists Lodge 284 (Morton Salt), 190 N.L.R.B. No. 32, 77 LRRM 1100 (1971), *mod. sub. nom.* Morton Salt v. NLRB, 472 F.2d 416 (9th Cir. 1972) *pet. for cert. filed* 41 U.S.L.W. 3628 (May 5, 1973) (no violation in

of all union membership, at least until new representation elections are held.[53]

This crusade to protect the public interest has taken the board into union proceedings themselves. For example, in *August Bohl Contracting*[54] the board, and eventually the second circuit, cited the lack of due process in holding that a fine allegedly imposed for a physical assault on a union brother, an offense clearly subject to union discipline, was in reality intended to sanction the accused for filing unfair labor practice changes. Similarly, the board has found violations of Section 8(b)(1)(A) in discipline imposed for pretext charges where the actual offense was expression protected by the Labor-Management Reporting and Disclosure Act (Landrum-Griffin Act).[55] Again, the board

relied on the suspicious nature of the union proceedings, including, in one case, threats by union officials to "think of something" with which to charge the accused.[56]

Thus, while the member is subject to a wide range of union rules, the board and the courts retain the option of curtailing the subject matter of union discipline by expanding a rather nebulous public policy exception. Unfortunately, this interpretation also leaves the board with considerable discretion that may at times surprise labor lawyers and union members alike. Indeed, until the Court limits this discretion by explaining its public policy objections more fully, few members will know the extent to which they may be disciplined.

Procedural Limitations on Union Discipline

In their 1969 survey of the procedural limitations on union discipline, Etelson and Smith concluded,

> [A]lthough the Landrum-Griffin Act spawned numerous controversies over its scope, its procedural guarantees, and its remedial provisions, the past ten years have seen a satisfactory resolution of most issues. Time and further experience should lead to a practical resolution of the conflicts which remain. The courts are steadily moving toward a new and more desirable accommodation between the private institutional needs of labor unions and their public responsibility under federal labor policy.[57]

Today this prediction seems a bit too optimistic. If the tensions have been resolved, it has been largely because the courts have retreated under a banner of judicial abstention. Today members challenging disciplinary proceedings on procedural grounds generally have only the minimal protections of Section 101(a)(5) of the Landrum-Griffin Act:[58]

---

[53] Given the board's discretion in calling new elections, the expelled member may have to wait for some time before the union he favors can be elected. See, for example, Kearney & Tecker Corp. v. NLRB, 210 F.2d 852 (7th Cir.) *cert. den.* 348 U.S. 824 (1954) (allowing the old union to maintain its position for the last ten months of its contract before holding new elections).

[54] 193 N.L.R.B. No. 138, 78 LRRM 1479, *enf. sub. nom.* NLRB v. Teamsters Local 294, 470 F.2d 57 (2nd Cir. 1972). See also Philadelphia Moving Picture Mach. Op. U., Loc. No. 307 v. NLRB, 382 F.2d 598 (3rd Cir. 1967) (voiding the expulsion of a member on four charges where three were valid, but one was for filing an unfair labor practice); Automotive Salesmen's Assn. (Spitler-Demmer, Inc.), 184 N.L.R.B. No. 64, 74 LRRM 1576 (1970) (finding a violation of §8(b)(1)(A) in fining strikebreakers from $100 to $4,000 where the variance was attributed to the fact that the most heavily fined member had also filed a decertification petition).

[55] 29 U.S.C. §511(a)(2)(1964):

> Every member of any labor organization shall have the right to meet and assemble freely with other members; and to express any views, arguments, or opinions; and to express at meetings of the labor organization his views, upon candidates in an election of the labor organization or upon any business properly before the meeting, subject to the organization's established and reasonable rules pertaining to the conduct of meetings: *Provided,* That nothing herein shall be construed to impair the right of a labor organization to adopt and enforce reasonable rules as to the responsibility of every member toward the organization as an institution and to his refraining from conduct that would interfere with its performance of its legal or contractual obligations.

This section, which should be of obvious interest to Mr. Buckley, has been held to guarantee the union member the right to express himself, subject only to

> reasonable union rules relating to the conduct of union meetings; reasonable rules relating to individual responsibility to the union as an institution; and reasonable rules requiring members to refrain from conduct which would interfere with the union's performance of its legal or contractual obligations.

Fulton Lodge No. 2 of IAM v. Nix, 415 F.2d 212, 217 & n. 14

(5th Cir. 1969) *cert. den.* 406 U.S. 946 (1972) (citing numerous cases where the member's activity was protected). See also Salzhandler v. Caputo, 316 F.2d 445 (2nd Cir. 1963) *cert. den.* 375 U.S. 946 (1963). The importance that the Supreme Court gives this guarantee was demonstrated in the 1972 term when it upheld an award of attorney's fees to a member who had challenged his expulsion on free speech grounds. The Court held that the vindication of such rights constituted the "overriding public considerations" required to merit such an award (Hall v. Cole, 93 S.Ct. 1943 [1973]).

[56] Carpenter's Local 22, Graziano Construction Co., 195 N.L.R.B. No. 5, 79 LRRM 1194 (1972); but also see Burch v. Machinists, 433 F.2d 561 (5th Cir. 1970) (finding no pretext in terminating a union president for nonpayment of dues despite allegations that the international was "displeased" with him).

[57] Etelson and Smith, "Union Discipline under the Landrum-Griffin Act," *Harvard Law Review* 82 (1969):727, 771.

[58] Before he even reaches the courts, the member may be required to exhaust his internal union appeals for up to four months; see 29 U.S.C.C. §411(a)(4)(1964). Such appeals will

No member of any labor organization may be fined, suspended, or expelled, or otherwise disciplined except for nonpayment of dues . . . unless such member has been (A) served with written specific charges; (B) given a reasonable time to prepare his defense; (C) afforded a full and fair hearing.[59]

Even a cursory examination of the decisions applying this section suggests that a union tribunal is still hardly a forum for the vindication of individual rights. The Supreme Court has played a major role in preserving this union autonomy. In rejecting, in *Boilermakers v. Hardeman*,[60] the view of some lower courts that "penal provisions in union constitutions must be strictly construed,"[61] the Court concluded that there was nothing

in either the language or the legislative history of §101(a)(5) that could justify such a substitution of judicial for union authority to interpret the union's regulations in order to determine the scope of offenses warranting discipline of union members.[62]

Indeed, the Court went so far as to explain that since

a union may discipline its members for offenses not proscribed by written rules at all, it is surely a futile exercise for a court to construe the written rules in order

to determine whether particular conduct falls within or without their scope.[63]

The *Hardeman* Court did concede that when an accused is provided with a statement of charges, the courts should insure that he is not misled or prejudiced in preparing his defense.[64] Nevertheless, *Hardeman's* overly generous attitude toward vague or even unwritten union rules seems a clear invitation to even less specific indictments. Other courts have continued to reverse union convictions where specificity and notice were grossly inadequate;[65] but in so doing each has more or less sidestepped *Hardeman*, suggesting that the Court has, at least for the present, impeded the progess predicted by Etelson and Smith.

The other major safeguard of Section 101(a)(5), the right to a "full and fair hearing," is also not as significant as one might wish. While the courts have guaranteed to the accused some of the rudiments of due process (the right to be present, to call his own witnesses, and to cross-examine his accusers,[66] growth of the fair-hearing concept has undoubtedly been stunted by a reluctance to require counsel.[67] While it is undeniably true that the framers of the Landrum-Griffin Act never intended to require counsel, it is also true that in the past fourteen years both the stakes involved in union discipline and the very meaning of due process have changed. Unions may now impose substantial fines and enforce them judicially, a penalty that is often far harsher than the expulsion contemplated in 1959. As we shall see, such fines today often exceed $1,000, an amount typically the line between a misdemeanor and felony.[68]

At the same time that union discipline has become more severe, the level at which we guarantee the right to counsel, even at public expense, has been reduced.[69] Not

---

normally be based on union procedural safeguards that vary substantially. Compare *Constitution of the International, U.A.W.*, Art. 31 (1972) (guaranteeing specific charges, a timely trial, the right to counsel, a randomly selected trial committee, and fixed penalties) with *Book of Laws of the International Typographical Union*, Bylaws Art. V, § 19 (1973) ("The evidence of rats shall not be received in the trial of union men for any cause whatever, as they are under the ban of the union .... "); and *Constitution of the International Union, United Steelworkers of America*, Art. XIII, §3 (1972) (leaving all trial procedures to the discretion of the local).

Unfortunately for the members of more enlightened unions, there is some authority suggesting that the unions need not adhere to their own procedures so long as they meet the minimal standards of §101(a)(5); see, for example, Buresch v. International Broth. of Electrical Workers, Local No. 24, 343 F.Supp. 183 (D.Md. 1971) *aff'd* 460 F.2d 1405 (4th Cir. 1972). Such a position seems clearly wrong given the court's reliance on the fiction of the union-member contract. Surely if the member is held to have consented to union discipline by accepting membership, that consent must be based on the union fulfilling its half of the bargain by imposing discipline only in accordance with its own rules.

[59]   29 U.S.C. §411(a)(5)(1964).

[60]   401 U.S. 233 (1971).

[61]   *Ibid.*, p. 242 (citing Boilermakers v. Braswell, 388 F.2d 193, 198 [5th Cir. 1968], *cert. den.* 391 U.S. 935 [1968] and Allen v. Theatrical Employees, 338 F.2d 309, 316 [5th Cir. 1964]). See also Gleason v. Restaurant Employees Union, 422 F.2d 342 (2nd Cir. 1970).

[62]   401 U.S. 233, 242-43 (1971).

[63]   *Ibid.*, pp. 244-45.

[64]   *Ibid.*, p. 245.

[65]   See, for example, Smith v. Musicians, 80 LRRM 3063 (S.D.N.Y. 1972).

[66]   See Etelson and Smith, pp. 745-46 and cases collected there.

[67]   See Buresch v. International Broth. of Elec. Workers, Local 24, 343 F.Supp. 183, 191-92 (D.Md. 1971), *aff'd* 460 F.2d 1405 (4th Cir. 1972); Cornelio v. Metropolitan District Council of Philadelphia, *et al.*, 243 F.Supp. 126 (E.D.Pa. 1965), *aff'd* 358 F.2d 728 (3rd Cir. 1966), *cert. den.* 386 U.S. 975 (1967); Smith v. General Truck Drivers, 181 F.Supp. 14, 17 (S.D.Cal. 1960).

[68]   See, for example, *A. L. I. Model Penal Code* §603 (Prop. Final Draft No. 1, 1961). See also 18 U.S.C.§1 (1964) (defining "petty offense" as one for which the penalty does not exceed six months imprisonment or a fine of $500) and 18 U.S.C. §3006A(b) (1964) (requiring counsel in all cases other than "petty offenses").

[69]   After more than a decade of development, a unanimous Court in Argesinger v. Hamlin, 407 U.S. 25 (1972), held that

that the right to counsel in union proceedings is of constitutional dimensions; but, if the courts are to consider the prevailing level of due process in society in applying Section 101(a)(5),[70] they should reconsider the relative severity of a few days in jail as opposed to a judicially enforced fine of perhaps $1,000 coupled with expulsion from the union which may control the accused's opportunity to make a living. Moreover, it would seem that if the Supreme Court is interested in avoiding the complex questions of fundamental fairness in union proceedings, it might well adopt its approach in the coerced confession cases[71] and avoid many difficult factual determinations by simply requiring counsel as an adequate prophylactic.

This brief review is not intended to suggest that members are completely at the mercy of their unions. It does seem, however, that in failing to require specific indictments or counsel in cases of even major proportions, the courts have failed to appreciate that what is involved in their review of union discipline is not some role-playing game between the courts and union tribunals, but rather a more fundamental balancing of the individual rights of the member and the institutional imperatives of his union.

Penalties and Enforcement: The Issue of Reasonableness

Though union constitutions and bylaws typically provide for a wide range of penalties (suspensions, expulsions, reprimands, and disbarments from office[72]) the sanction that has recently received the greatest attention is the monetary fine. It is, of course, well known that the Court in *Allis-Chalmers* approved of the judicial

counsel must be provided where any imprisonment might result. While Justice Douglas, writing for the Court, was careful to note that it was not considering "the requirements of the Sixth Amendment as regards the right of counsel where loss of liberty is not involved" (*ibid.*, p. 37), Justice Lewis F. Powell, Jr., may well have been writing for a Court of the future when he stated, without contradiction by the Court,

It would be illogical . . . to hold that no discretion [as to the need for counsel] may ever be exercised where a nominal jail sentence is contemplated and at the same time endorse the legitimacy of discretion in "non-jail" petty offense cases which may result in far more serious consequences than a few hours or days of incarceration.

[70] See, for example, Gleason v. Chain Service Restaurant, 300 F.Supp. 1241, 1251 (S.D.N.Y. 1969), *aff'd* 422 F.2d 342 (2nd Cir. 1970).

[71] Compare Miranda v. Arizona, 384 U.S. 436 (1966) with Townsend v. Sain, 372 U.S. 293 (1963).

[72] See, for example, *Constitution of the International Brotherhood of Teamsters, Chauffeurs, Warehousemen and Helpers of America*, Art. XIX §9(a) (1971); *Constitution of the International Union, U.A.W.*, Art. 31 §10 (1972); and *Constitution of the International Union, United Steelworkers of America*, Art. XII, §2 (1972).

enforcement of such fines.[73] What was not clear until very recently was the extent to which that enforcement, and its immunity from Section 8(b)(1)(A) of the NLRA, depended on the fine's reasonableness and the accused's full membership in the union. In three decisions last term, *Granite State, Booster Lodge*, and *Boeing*, the Court resolved these two questions by striking a rather curious balance that leaves the member but one option, resignation.[74]

The *Allis-Chalmers* Court had conceded that,

There may be concern that court enforcement may permit the collection of unreasonably large fines. However, even were there evidence that Congress shared this concern, this would not justify reading the Act also to bar court enforcement of reasonable fines.[75]

Similarly, in his majority-creating concurrence, Justice Byron White based his assent on the reasoning that since Section 8(b)(1)(A) had not been intended to prohibit expulsions, it should not be construed to limit the lesser penalty of a reasonable fine.[76] Thus, in *Allis-Chalmers*, the reasonableness of the fine was apparently related to its amount and severity for the sanctioned member.

In *Scofield* the Court broadened this definition to include the manner in which the fine was imposed and apparently made reasonableness a prerequisite for judicial enforcement:

§8(b)(1) leaves a union free to enforce a properly adopted rule which reflects a legitimate union interest, impairs no policy Congress has imbedded in the labor laws, and is reasonably enforced. . . .

In the case at hand, there is no showing in the record that the fines were unreasonable or the mere fiat of a union leader. . . .[77]

Scofield led to speculation that the Court would invalidate fines that were either unreasonably large in relation to the damage done to the union (as suggested by the Court's contract theory), unreasonably large in relation to the financial status of the member (as suggested by the anticoercion policy of Section 8(b)(1)(A)), or imposed under vague or arbitrary procedures (as suggested by the guarantees of Section 101(a)(5) of the Landrum-Griffin Act).[78]

[73] 388 U.S. 175 (1967).

[74] 409 U.S. 213 (1972); 93 S.Ct. 1961 (1973); and 93 S.Ct. 1952 (1973). For a discussion of these cases and some of the problems addressed in this paper, see Note, "Union Power to Discipline Members Who Resign," *Harvard Law Review* 86 (1973):1536.

[75] 388 U.S. 175, 192-93.

[76] *Ibid.*, p. 198 (Justice White concurring).

[77] 394 U.S. 423, 430 (1969).

[78] See, for example, Gould, "Some Limitations Upon Union Discipline under the National Labor Relations Act: The Radiations of Allis-Chalmers, 1970," *Duke Law Journal*, 1970,

At about this time the NLRB trial examiners began to inquire into a series of fines substantially larger than the $50 to $100 deemed reasonable in *Scofield*. The examiners generally considered the size of the fine in relation to the wages derived from the forbidden activity; and a number were found to be unreasonable and therefore violations of Section 8(b)(1)(A).[79] When these cases reached the board, however, the examiners learned that their reliance on *Allis-Chalmers* and *Scofield* had been misplaced. In *Machinists Local 504 (Arrow Development)*, the board held that it had no authority to inquire into the reasonableness of union fines.[80] In refusing to consider either the amount or the manner in which the fine had been imposed, the board held that Congress had never intended it to have such authority under Section 8(b)(1)(A).[81] Reading the reasonableness language of *Allis-Chalmers* and *Scofield* as directed to the enforcing courts, the board concluded that such determinations were "of an equitable nature rather than of the character of restraint or coercion with which [Section 8(b)(1)] treats."[82]

In dissent, Member Frank W. McCulloch insisted that the Court's repeated use of reasonable constituted a necessary gloss on its approval of judicially enforced fines.[83] In defining reasonable as not more than the

amount derived from the forbidden activity, McCulloch reasoned that to allow more excessive penalties would permit the union to go beyond the regulation of its internal affairs and encroach on the job rights of the accused.[84] He further contended that, while the lines delimiting reasonable fines would obviously be difficult to draw, the need for a uniform labor policy required that the board, and not fifty state courts, do the drawing.[85]

Such arguments, however, have never commanded a majority on the board, and in the three years since *Arrow Development* it has steadfastly refused to consider the reasonableness issue,[86] despite the fact that its position fared badly in the courts of appeals. In *Local 405, Machinists* v. *NLRB (Boeing)*,[87] the District of Columbia circuit court held that the board was obligated to void unreasonably large fines. Noting the need for a uniform labor policy that provided a quick remedy for fined members unwilling to await state court determinations, the court of appeals held that fines going beyond the "vindication of a legitimate union interest" were outside the proviso in Section 8(b)(1)(A).[88] The court ordered the board to consider the size of fines in relation to

> . . . the compensation received by the strikebreakers, the level of strike benefits made available to the striking employees, the individual needs of the person being disciplined, the detrimental effect of the strikebreaking upon the effectiveness of the strike effort, the length of time of the work stoppage, the strength of the particular union involved, the availability of other less harsh union remedies, and many other considerations. . . .[89]

Similarly, in *Morton Salt* v. *NLRB*, the ninth circuit held that the board's abstention was incorrect; both

pp. 1067, 1123-27; Rapore, "Protected Rights and Union Sanctions under 8(b)(1)(A) of the National Labor Relations Act," *Labor Law Journal* 21 (1970):728, 736-37; Silard, "Labor Board Regulation of Union Discipline after Allis-Chalmers, Marine Workers and Scofield," *George Washington Law Review* 38 (1969):187, 193-94.

[79] See, for example, Machinists, Lodge 405 (Boeing Co.), 185 N.L.R.B. No. 23, 75 LRRM 1004 (1970) ($450 fine for strikebreaking producing $200 to $300 ruled excessive); Machinists Local 504 (Arrow Development), 185 N.L.R.B. No. 22, 75 LRRM 1008 (1970) ($500 fine for strikebreaking netting $511, excessive); Local 205, Lithographers, 186 N.L.R.B. No. 69, 75 LRRM 1356 (1970) (fines of $250 upheld since they were less than the amount earned); Rubber Workers, Local 510 (Uniroyal Inc.), 186 N.L.R.B. No. 106, 75 LRRM 1420 (1970) (fine of $525 for $425 of strikework, excessive); Carpenters Union (Swallow & Sons), 186 N.L.R.B. No. 119, 75 LRRM 1421 (1970) (fine of $300 for four hours of strikebreaking, excessive); American Newspaper Guild (Washington Post Co.), 186 N.L.R.B. No. 133, 75 LRRM 1438 (1970) (fines held unreasonable on procedural grounds [vagueness]); Communications Workers, Local 2100 (C&P Tel. Co.), 186 N.L.R.B. No. 132, 75 LRRM 1441 (1970) ($242 fine for crossing a sister union's picket lines, excessive); Printing Pressmen's Union (Herald-News), 190 N.L.R.B. No. 38, 77 LRRM 1199 (1971) ($2,000 fine for one day of strikebreaking, excessive).

[80] 185 N.L.R.B. No. 22, 75 LRRM 1008 (1970).

[81] *Ibid.*, p. 1009-10.

[82] *Ibid.*, p. 1010.

[83] *Ibid.*, p. 1011-12.

[84] *Ibid.*, p. 1013. Member McCulloch analogized the excess fine over earnings to a continuing penalty on protected work after the strike was over.

[85] *Ibid.*, p. 1014.

[86] The board has refused to consider the reasonableness of the following: Communications Workers, Local 6222 (S.W. Bell Tel.) 186 N.L.R.B. No. 50, 75 LRRM 1324 ($200 fine for four hours strikebreaking); Newspaper Guild, Local 69, 186 N.L.R.B. No. 78, 76 LRRM 1219 (1970) (strikebreaking fine of approximately $2,000, entire earnings less the strike benefits the member would have received); Printing Pressmen's Union (Herald-News), 190 N.L.R.B. No. 38, 77 LRRM 1199 (1971) ($2,000 fine for one day of strikebreaking); Machinists, Lodge No. 284 (Morton Salt), 190 N.L.R.B. No. 32, 77 LRRM 1100 (1971) ($1,000 fine for crossing a sister union's picket lines); Printing Pressmen, Local 7 (North Shore Pub.), 192 N.L.R.B. No. 122, 78 LRRM 1047 (1971) ($250 and $750 fines for strikebreakers earning $50 and $155). See also cases cited, all reversed by the board, in note 79 above.

[87] 459 F.2d 1143 (D.C. Cir. 1972).

[88] *Ibid.*, p. 1156-57.

[89] *Ibid.*, p. 1159.

Allis-Chalmers and the need for a uniform labor policy were advanced as reasons.[90]

The board ultimately prevailed. In reversing *Boeing*, the Supreme Court largely restated the board's opinion in *Arrow Development*.[91] Conceding that reliance on the repeated use of reasonable in *Allis-Chalmers* and *Scofield* was not totally illogical, the Court nevertheless branded such language dicta and quickly moved to broader issues.[92] Stating that the "multiplicity of factors" cited by the circuit court was a question for the enforcing courts and not the board, the Court held, "Issues as to the reasonableness or unreasonableness of such fines must be decided upon the basis of the law of contracts, voluntary associations, or such other principles of law as may be applied. . . ."[93] Justice William Rehnquist, writing for the Court, further contended that,

> state courts applying state law are quite willing to determine whether disciplinary fines are reasonable in amount. Indeed, the expertise required for a determination of reasonableness may well be more evident in a judicial forum that is called upon to assess reasonableness in varying factual contexts than it is in a specialized agency. In assessing the reasonableness of disciplinary fines, for example, state courts are often able to draw on their experience in areas of the law apart from labor relations.[94]

A review of the seven state cases cited by the Court however, is not reassuring. In two, the fines were upheld without any discussion of their reasonableness.[95] In two others, the issue was given less than a paragraph, as the fines were summarily upheld as liquidated damages under the *Allis-Chalmers* contract theory.[96] In yet another, cited by the Court as involving the reduction of a fine, the amount of the fine was actually upheld as reasonable (in one sentence the nature of the offense, the profit to the transgressor, and "current economic conditions" were cited), but one of the three counts of the union indictment was found to be invalid and the total fine was therefore reduced by one-third.[97] Finally in the oldest case cited by the Court, a fine of $300 was reduced to $100 solely because the larger amount would have made an intraunion appeal difficult.[98]

Thus, the only decision cited by the Court that involved the reduction of a fine on grounds of reasonableness was that of the Los Angeles Municipal Court in *Farnum* v. *Kurtz*.[99] There the court, in reducing a fine for circulating a "nasty letter" about union officials, cited no contract and precious little labor law and concluded that the union had not been damaged by as much as the larger amount.[100] The court then added,

> Moreover, this Court has had the duty and obligation of passing judgment in thousands of cases where defendants were found guilty of misdemeanors. In the vast majority of such cases the first offender is always dealt with kindly, compassionately, and understandingly, not only by this individual judge but by practically all judges. The first offender in misdemeanor cases is usually regarded as a student who should be taught that society requires its laws be obeyed, not as a hardened criminal.
>
> Based upon the facts herein and the Court's experiences aforesaid, the fine assessed is much too large and unreasonable.[101]

Whatever else may be said for this melange of contract, criminal, and labor law, it is clear that state courts have not yet developed anything approaching a consistent view on the reasonableness of union fines. Indeed, it is surprising that the Supreme Court even expects them to do

[90]   472 F.2d 416 (9th Cir. 1972). See also David O'Reilly v. NLRB, 82 LRRM 2066 (9th Cir. 1972) *pet. for cert. filed* 41 U.S.L.W. 3509 (March 6, 1973) (reversing the board in *Arrow Development* on the basis of *Morton Salt*). Compare U.O.P. Norplex v. NLRB, 445 F.2d. 155, 158 (7th Cir. 1971) (stating that reasonableness was an issue for the state courts in the related context of determining whether the enforcement of fines could be the subject of mandatory bargaining).

[91]   NLRB v. Boeing, 93 S. Ct. 1952 (1973).

[92]   *Ibid.*, p. 1955-56.

[93]   *Ibid.*, p. 1956-57.

[94]   *Ibid.*, p. 1958.

[95]   Local 248, U.A.W. v. Natzke, 36 Wis. 2d 237, 153 N.W.2d 602 (1967); Jost v. Communications Workers of America, Local 9408, 13 Cal. App. 3d Supp. 7, 91 Cal. Rptr. 722 (Cal. Super. Ct. 1970).

[96]   Auto Workers Local No. 283 v. Scofield, 50 Wisc. 2d 117, 134, 183 N.W. 2d 103, 112 (1971); Walsh v. Communications Workers of America, Local 2336, 259 Md. 608, 614-15, 271 A.2d 148, 151 (1970).

[97]   New Jersey Newspaper Guild Local No. 173 v. Rakos, 110 N.J. Super. 77, 91, 264 A.2d 453, 461 (N.J. Super. Ct. App. Div. 1970).

[98]   McCauley v. Federation of Musicians, 26 LRRM 2304, 2305-06 (Pa. Ct. of Com. Pleas, 1950).

[99]   70 LRRM 2035 (Los Angeles Mun. Ct. 1968).

[100]   At one point in his decision that the letter-writing member was not protected because he had sent copies to U.S. Attorney-General Nicholas Katzenbach, Governor Edmund O. Brown, and the Los Angeles newspapers, Judge Grillo suggested "with all due respect" that Senator John McClelland was confused when he stated that §101(a)(2) protected speech outside of the union as well as within it (*ibid.*, p. 2040). The California Superior Court, Appellate Division, subsequently held that Judge Grillo's "inside/outside" distinction was "utterly without merit" and reversed the judgment enforcing the fine entirely, Farnum v. Kurtz, 81 Cal. Rptr. 924, 926, 2 Cal. App. 3d Supp. 1, Supp. 4 (Cal. Sup. Ct. App. Div. 1969).

[101]   70 LRRM 2035, 2041.

so. The contracts involved are almost always a figment of judicial imagination;[102] the criminal law is seldom specific and is applied in the first instance by tribunals that have few of the safeguards of a criminal court;[103] and the labor law at issue is now, thanks to *Boeing*, one enormous vacuum created by both administrative and judicial abstention.[104]

---

[102] One state supreme court has turned the contract theory back on a union and refused to enforce union fines unless the union constitution specifically warned members that they ran such a risk, United Glass Workers Local 188 v. Seitz, 65 Wash. 2d 640, 642, 399 P.2d 74, 75 (1965). As a general rule, union constitutions fail to explain either the prohibitions or penalties the union may enforce.

[103] See text above at note 67.

[104] Beyond providing no substantive guidance for the state courts in determining the reasonableness of union fines, *Boeing* also creates a number of procedural ambiguities. For example, as fines increase, it will become increasingly likely that defendant members will be entitled to, and will demand, jury trials. When this happens, the state courts' present emphasis on the damages of the union suggests that the question of whether the fine was reasonable compensation for the union's loss will be decided by a jury. Indeed, one state court has already so held, Ballas v. McKiernan, 63 Misc. 2d 432, 435, 312 N.Y.S. 2d 204, 208, 74 LRRM 2647, 2649 (N.Y. City Civil Court, 1970) *rev. on other grounds*, 83 L.R.R.M. 2013 (N.Y. Sup.Ct. App. Div., 1973). Thus, the *Boeing* Court's faith in the experience of state judges may, in reality, come to rest on less-experienced state juries.

Similarly, given the state courts' analogy of union fines to liquidated damage clauses (see, for example, Walsh v. Communications Workers, Local 2336, 259 Md. 614-15, 271 A.2d 148, 161 [1970]; Auto Workers, Local 283 v. Scofield, 50 Wisc. 2d 117, 134, 183 N.W. 2d 103, 112 [1971]), the courts will also be faced with the question of whether the union or its fined member carries the burden of proof on reasonableness. Normally, the defendant must prove that the amount in the liquidated damages clause now appears to be unreasonable in light of the actual damages flowing from the breach. See, for example, Norwalk Door Closer Co. v. Eagle Lock and Screw Co., 153 Conn. 681, 686-87, 220 A.2d 263, 267 (citing support from various jurisdictions). With a union fine, though, no fixed amount is established before the breach; rather, the union is allowed to complete an *implied, unwritten* clause to the effect that, "I, loyal union member, promise to pay the union $_____in the event I am found guilty of breaking union rules prohibiting (or requiring) the act of _____." Given such an interpretation, the burden would seem to be initially on the union to prove that its completion was reasonable. As the plaintiff collecting a debt, the union would have the burden of proving that the debt was thus validly due.

That such questions, apparently not yet considered by the state courts, can be pushed to such absurdities suggests the more fundamental folly of allowing the state courts to enforce imaginary contracts without the limitations to be derived from somewhat more substantial labor law.

There is more wrong with *Boeing* than the Court's undue faith in the state courts. First, it should be noted that near the end of the opinion, Justice Rehnquist turns the doctrine of preemption on its head:

Since state courts will have jurisdiction to determine reasonableness in the enforcement context in any event, the Board's independent determination of reasonableness in an unfair labor practice context might well yield a conflict when the two forums are called upon to review the same fine.[105]

This argument assumes its conclusion, that is, that an unreasonably large fine is not a violation of Section 8(b)(1)(A). For if the board and the Court were willing to brand such fines coercive, the board's jurisdiction over the initial imposition of the fine would preclude any subsequent enforcement by state courts.[106]

Thus, despite all the dicta on the role of the state courts, the central question remains the legality of an unreasonably large fine under Section 8(b)(1)(A). Here the dissent seems to have the better of it:

As member McCulloch of the Board, dissenting, said, the excess of the fines over wages collected during this period is in actual effect an assessment after the strike is over. If after the strike the union had caused Boeing to suspend a member without pay after the strike because he had worked during the strike, there could be no question but that the union violated §8(b)(1)(A). Yet the assessment of fines greater than the wages earned during the strike has precisely that effect. Thus, in assessing an unreasonable fine the union . . . goes beyond the permissible bonds of regulating its internal affairs.[107]

While such reasoning is hardly flawless (for example, what if the union could prove damages greater than the wages earned?) and would fail completely in the rarer cases where discipline is imposed for noneconomic conduct, the prima facie rule that a union can do no more than insure that transgressors are denied the fruits of their offenses seems far more promising than the cursory examinations thus far provided by the state courts. Similarly, it seems absurd to assume that the state courts, with little or no experience in labor relations, will develop more consistent and rational standards than would the NLRB, which is frequently called on to determine the reasonableness of labor-related activity.[108]

---

[105] 93 S.Ct. 1952, 1958 (1973).

[106] See Motor Coach Employees v. Lockridge, 403 U.S. 274 (1971); Local 100, Plumbers v. Borden, 373 U.S. 690 (1963).

[107] 93 S.Ct. at 1960-61 (Justice Douglas).

[108] The board determinations most akin are those involving excessive initiation fees. Section 8(b)(5) requires the board to consider the reasonableness of such fees, 29 U.S.C. §158(b)(5)(1970).

Finally, if the post-*Allis-Chalmers* era is any guide, the Court's hands-off approach in *Boeing* will probably lead the unions to impose still larger, and hence still more coercive, fines. By abstaining on the issue of reasonableness, the Court leaves an excessively fined member with only the far less effective remedy of defending himself in the state courts when, and if, the union seeks judicial enforcement. By refusing to consider the claims of such workers under Section 8(b)(1)(A), the Court has undoubtedly made it less likely that the union will even need to sue to collect its fines from all save the most well-informed and litigious members.[109]

Jurisdiction over the Member

At the same time the board and the Court were retreating from the problem of unreasonably large fines, they were developing the proposition that *any* fine for activity occurring after a member has severed his relationship with the union is not only unenforceable, but a violation of Section 8(b)(1)(A) as well. While the practical limitations of this doctrine are not yet clear, it does hold promise for dissidents such as Mr. Buckley who find that the advantages of union membership are outweighed by the potential liability for breaking union rules.

The major premise of the resignation theory, that a union has no power to discipline a nonmember, is hardly novel.[110] In *Allis-Chalmers* the Court took great pains to note that the fined workers had voluntarily accepted "full union membership."

> Each executed the pledge of allegiance to the UAW and took the oath of full membership. Moreover, the record. . . discloses that two disciplined employees testified that they had fully participated in the proceedings leading to the strike. . . . [the employer] offered no evidence. . . that any of the fined employees

enjoyed other than full membership. We will not presume the contrary.[111]

Similarly, in *Scofield* the Court found no evidence that the disciplined members had been forced to accept full membership, noting that they had always been "free to leave the union and escape the rule"[112] under which they had been fined.

A year later the extent of this freedom was first tested before the board. In *Booster Lodge*,[113] the board, adhering to the same union-member contract fiction that had permitted the fines in *Allis-Chalmers*,[114] had little difficulty in holding that once that contract was terminated, the union's authority to discipline under the proviso to Section 8(b)(1)(A) expired:

> In joining a union, the individual member becomes a party to a contract-constitution. Without waiving his Section 7 right to refrain from concerted activities, he consents to the possible imposition of union discipline upon his exercise of that right. But the contract between the member and the union becomes a nullity upon his resignation. Both the member's duty of fidelity to the union and the union's corresponding right to discipline him for breach of that duty are extinguished.[115]

Again, as with the decision on the issue of reasonableness, the board's ruling on the extent of union jurisdiction did not meet with approval in the courts of appeals. In the first resignation case to reach the court, *NLRB* v. *Textile Workers, Local 1029 (Granite State)*,[116] the first circuit, while accepting the board's contract theory, stated that it had been too wooden in its exegesis of the unwritten bond between union and member. Stressing that the members fined in *Granite State* had voted for both the strike and the penalty for strikebreaking, the court reasoned that the contract doctrine of mutual reliance required members to refrain from crossing picket lines they themselves had helped erect:

> We can imagine a case involving three hypothetical employees whom we shall call Jones, Smith and Parks. Initially Jones is anxious to strike but Smith and Parks hesitate, finally acquiescing on the condition that all agree to stick it out for the duration of the strike. We suggest that this kind of mutual reliance is implicit in all strike votes; many employees would hesitate to forego several weeks or months of pay if they knew their

---

[109] The board does have one final string in its bow should it ultimately decide to consider the reasonableness issue. The board might resurrect the union's duty of fair representation in order to challenge fines that vary among individuals charged with the same offense or among groups of individuals charged with offenses differing from others' offenses only in that they were committed more frequently by certain factions within the union yet were deemed by the courts to be similar to others' actions in their deleterious impact on the union. See Note, "Fair Representation and Union Discipline," *Yale Law Journal* 79 (1970):730. Given both the weakness of the doctrine of fair representation and the emphasis of the board and the Court on the capability of the state courts in dealing with unreasonable fines, this possibility seems rather remote.

[110] See, e.g., Allis-Chalmers Mfg. v. NLRB, 358 F.2d 656, 662 (7th Cir. 1966) (Judge Hastings, dissenting): "Here the strikebreaking employees had a choice. They could reject full union membership, and thus remain outside and beyond the reach of union discipline."

[111] 388 U.S. 175, 196 (1967).

[112] 394 U.S. 423, 430 (1969).

[113] 186 N.L.R.B. No. 23, 75 LRRM 1004 (1970).

[114] See 388 U.S. 175, 192 (1967); but also see, 388 U.S. 175, 207-08 (Justice Black dissenting); Summers, "Legal Limitations on Union Discipline," *Harvard Law Review* 64 (1951): 1049, 1055-56.

[115] 75 LRRM 1004, 1006 (1970).

[116] 446 F.2d 369 (1st Cir. 1971).

cohorts were free to cross the picket lines at any time by merely resigning from the union.[117]

The court, noting the importance given strike solidarity in *Allis-Chalmers,* then held that the board was confused in its reliance on the worker's Section 7 right to refrain from concerted activity:

> The plain meaning of the word "refrain" is "to keep oneself from doing, feeling, or indulging in something." ... this definition suggests that, although §7 gives an employee the right to refuse to undertake and involve himself in union activities, it does not give him the right to abandon these activities in midcourse once he has undertaken them voluntarily.[118]

Similarly, the court concluded that there was nothing in the legislative history of either Section 7 or Section 8(b)(1)(A) limiting "union-employee agreements and obligations that have been undertaken voluntarily and without coercion."[119]

Six months later, the District of Columbia circuit reviewed the original *Booster Lodge* decision.[120] Though the court affirmed the board's holding that *innocent* members could resign at any time and thus immunize themselves from union discipline, it generally approved of the mutual reliance tack taken in *Granite State:*

> In *Granite State,* the Board conceded that all the fined employees had voted for the strike . . . . [In *Booster Lodge* there was no such stipulation.] Furthermore, all of those disciplined in *Granite State* had been expressly warned of possible punishment for strikebreaking, while the employees with whom we are herein concerned received no such pre-strikebreaking notification. Because of these distinguishing facts, we refuse to apply the rationale of *Granite State* to the instant factual situation. The strong equities which weighed in favor of the union there are clearly not present here.[121]

Despite the first circuit's hypotheticals, the District of Columbia circuit court's apparent acquiescence, and the unions' emphasis on the mutual reliance theory in their briefs,[122] the doctrine commanded very little support, for

the Supreme Court reversed it in *Granite State.*[123] The Court, on the basis of *Allis-Chalmers, Scofield,* and Section 7, endorsed the board's original view that

> When a member lawfully resigns from a union and thereafter engages in conduct which the union rule proscribed, the union commits an unfair labor practice when it seeks enforcement of fines for that conduct. That is to say, when there is a lawful dissolution of a union-member relation, the union has no more control over the former member than it has over the man in the street.[124]

Addressing itself to the question of mutual reliance, the Court said,

> We give that factor little weight. The first two members resigned from the Union from one to two months after the strike began. The others did so from seven to 12 months after its commencement. And the strike was still in progress 18 months after its inception. Events occurring after the calling of a strike may have unsettling effects, leading a member to change his mind. The likely duration of the strike may increase the specter of hardship to his family; the ease with which the employer replaces the strikers may make the strike seem less provident. . . . [W]e conclude that the vitality of §7 requires that the member be free to refrain in November from the actions he endorsed in May and that his §7 rights are not lost by a union's plea for solidarity or by its pressures for conformity and submission to its regime.[125]

---

[117] *Ibid.,* p. 372.

[118] *Ibid.,* p. 373.

[119] *Ibid.*

[120] Lodge 405, Machinist v. NLRB, 459 F.2d 1143 (D.C. Cir. 1972).

[121] *Ibid.,* p. 1153.

[122] See, Brief for Respondent, NLRB v. Granite State Joint Board, 409 U.S. 213 (1973) at 10-18; Brief for International Association of Machinists as *Amicus Curiae,* NLRB v. Granite State Joint Board, 409 U.S. 213 (1972) at 18-20, 24-27, 38-42. In the union's version of "mutual reliance," the actual assent of the member is irrelevant:

> The essence of the solidarity indispensable to effective strike action is that a member is bound by the institutional decision to strike whether or not he was individually

opposed to that group decision. A member is required to refrain from strikebreaking despite his dissent from the decision to strike.

[123] 409 U.S. 213 (1972).

[124] *Ibid.,* p. 217. It may be argued that in stressing the "enforcement of fines" rather than the act of fining, this passage avoids the issue of whether a union may fine a resigner where the fine is enforced only by expulsion. The board in *Booster Lodge* made it clear that any discipline of resigners "including," but apparently not limited to, "attempts to collect the illegal fines through court proceedings" violated §8(b)(1)(A), 75 LRRM 1004, 1006-07 (1970). In Local 1255, I.A.M. v. NLRB, 456 F.2d 1214 (5th Cir. 1972), *den. enf. to* 188 N.L.R.B. No. 135, 76 LRRM 1456 (1971), however, the fifth circuit held that where a fine was enforceable solely by expulsion, even postresignation fines were valid (*ibid.,* p. 1217).

This suggestion that a union can expel a member who has already resigned seems rather strange and may lead to confusion among both union members and the courts should the member seek reinstatement. It would seem far better to stress the *Granite State* Court's "man in the street" language and hold that once the member resigns the union cannot discipline him in any way. The possibility of members jumping in and out of a union merely to avoid strikebreaking penalties should not arise since such activity would incur additional initiation fees and substantial social pressure upon reinstatement.

[125] 409 U.S. 213, 217-18 (1972).

Only Justice Harry Blackmun, arguing that the Court was exalting "the formality of resignation over the substance of the various interests and national labor policies that are at stake," dissented on the basis of the mutual reliance theory.[126]

A few months later, in a short per curiam affirmance of *Booster Lodge,* the entire Court, with Justice Blackmun now concurring on the facts, rejected the Machinists' rather lame contention that the antistrikebreaking clause in its constitution was more effective in limiting the member's right to resign than the strike and penalty vote had been in *Granite State.*[127] While *Granite State* and *Booster Lodge* make it clear that there is an inherent right to resign, a closer examination of what those decisions said, and left unsaid, about that right suggests some rather unsettling possibilities for its practical application.

PRACTICAL LIMITATIONS ON THE RIGHT TO RESIGN

Before examining the real, potential, or simply imagined limitations on the right to resign, it should be noted that even an absolute right to resign would not completely protect the dissident who wants to leave his union. In many industries, especially those governed by hiring halls and similar referral arrangements, the worker is well aware that, despite his legal rights, his livelihood, or at least bearable working conditions, depends on union membership. In such industries the right to resign will undoubtedly go unexercised, save by a few rather rugged individualists. Just as we must note the social pressures in favor of unions today, we must also remember that it was not that long ago that the same type of pressures were exerted *against* the few who dared to exercise their right to join a labor organization. Thus, although Leonard Woodcock and Frank Fitzsimmons need not fear mass resignations tomorrow, an effective and well-known right to resign would enhance the worker's options and act as at least a subtle brake on union power. Were this not true after all it is unlikely that unions as powerful as the Auto Workers and Machinists would have litigated the issue of resignation so strenuously.

Union Limitations on the Right to Resign

The first question concerning the right to resign is the extent to which a union can limit it in its constitution, bylaws, or collective agreements. In permitting the resignations in the cases discussed above, the board and the lower courts have been careful to note that the union constitutions involved contained no explicit limitations on

the right to resign.[128] In *Granite State,* the Supreme Court clearly reserved the question of how far a union may go in developing such restrictions: "We do not now decide to what extent the contractual relationship between union and member may curtail the freedom to resign."[129] Similarly, in *Booster Lodge* the Court again noted the absence of any explicit limitations and cautioned that it was leaving "open the question of the extent to which contractual restriction on a member's right to resign may be limited by the [NLRA]."[130]

Despite such statements, both *Granite State* and *Booster Lodge* do suggest some boundaries for future consideration. The *Granite State* Court, in a footnote to the passage just cited, rejected the union's contention that the right to resign was limited by the practice of only accepting resignations during an annual ten-day "escape period." The Court did not, however, hold that such a practice was invalid per se, but rather merely affirmed the court of appeals finding that in *Granite State* the employees were not aware of it.[131] In *Booster Lodge,* the Court further encouraged speculation that there could be valid restrictions on the right to resign by noting, again in a footnote, that, "Since the collective bargaining agreement expired prior to the times of the resignations, the maintenance-of-membership clause therein was no impediment to resigning."[132] Since this strange little dictum cannot mean that a dissident can be discharged for resigning so long as he continues to tender his dues,[133] the Court must have been suggesting that a maintenance-of-membership clause can, under so far unknown conditions, limit the right to resign. Such a doctrine seems an inordinate price to pay for a casual judicial footnote.

Despite the Court's confusing dicta, neither the board nor any post-*Allis-Chalmers* court has yet found a valid

[126] *Ibid.,* p. 221.

[127] Booster Lodge No. 405, I.A.M. v. NLRB, 93 S.Ct. 1961 (1973).

[128] For board decisions, see, for example, Machinists Lodge, 405 (Boeing), 185 N.L.R.B. No. 23, 75 LRRM 1004, 1006, n. 11 (1970); Lithographers, Local 205 (General Gravure), 186 N.L.R.B. No. 69, 75 LRRM 1356, 1356-57, n. 3 (1970); Chemical Workers, Local 143 (American Cyanamid), 188 N.L.R.B. No. 100, 76 LRRM 1385, 1387, n. 3 (1971); Machinists Local 1255 (Mason & Hanger-Silas Mason Co.), 188 N.L.R.B. No. 135, 76 LRRM 1456 (1971) *enf. den. on other grounds,* 456 F.2d 1214 (5th Cir. 1972); Machinists Union (G.E.), 194 N.L.R.B. No. 163, 79 LRRM 1208, 1210 (1972). A lower court decision of interest is Local 405, Machinists v. NLRB, 459 F.2d 1143, 1153 (D.C. Cir. 1972); compare NLRB v. Textile Workers, Local 1029, 446 F.2d 369, 372 (1st Cir. 1971).

[129] 409 U.S. 213, 217 (1972).

[130] 93 S.Ct. 1961, 1964 (1973).

[131] 409 U.S. 213, 217, n. 5 (1972).

[132] 93 S.Ct. 1961, 1964, n. 8 (1973).

[133] See note 168 below.

restriction on the right to resign. Though one or two cases have required some rather tortured constructions of resignation provisions,[134] by and large the record has been fairly easy to maintain since few unions had ever considered a member's right to resign. Though union constitutions and bylaws typically provide for the transfer of membership from one local to another, for the honorable withdrawal of a worker leaving the trade, and for the termination of a member who is delinquent in his dues, the vast majority are silent on the right to resign.[135] A survey of the constitutions and bylaws of thirteen of the nation's largest unions[136] with a combined membership of some 10 million reveals that only two mention member resignation. The Teamsters' constitution provides only that a member may not resign until he has paid any outstanding dues or assessments.[137] The somewhat more elaborate provisions of the Auto Workers require the member to tender his resignation by registered mail during the last ten days of the year.[138]

Thus, for the moment at least, the board and the courts appear safe in their reliance on cases reaching back to the common law of voluntary associations to the effect that without some explicit limitation in a union's rules a member is free to resign subject only to any outstanding financial obligations.[139] It seems only a matter of time, however, before unions revise their constitutions to restrict the new right to resign and its corresponding immunity from union discipline.

When they do, the courts will find that there is very little law on the extent to which a union may limit the right to resign. Though the freedom-to-resign cases stretch back to pre-Taft-Hartley days, it was not until 1961 that the board was asked to rule on a union resignation provision. In *Local 889, U.A.W. (John Paulding)*,[140] the board held that the union could not seek the discharge of a worker who had "resigned," though not in accordance with the UAW's ten-day provision, before the effective date of a new maintenance-of-membership clause. The board did not hold that the resignation provision was invalid as a limitation on the member's right to resign; rather the trial examiner stated, and the board affirmed, that

> the union would be privileged to finally determine whether the employees still were members of the Union under its own rules and regulations and what their rights and obligations were under the membership contract. But we are not here concerned with the rights and obligations which the employees had or may have under the membership contract. We are solely concerned in these proceedings with their rights and obligations under the [NLRA] and under the collective-bargaining contract under which their discharge was being demanded by the Union.[141]

From such language, it would appear that the board was holding only that the ineffective resigner could not be discharged for the nonpayment of dues accruing during the hiatus between the two maintenance-of-membership clauses. In its petition for enforcement, however, the board went somewhat further and asked the first circuit to declare that the ten-day escape clause was invalid and that, therefore, the resigners had no continuing obligation to pay future dues as well.[142] The court, however, refused to

---

[134] See, for example, NLRB v. Mechanical Workers, Local 444, 427 F.2d 883, 885 (1st Cir. 1970); Newspaper Guild Local 69 (Hearst Corp.), 186 N.L.R.B. No. 78, 76 LRRM 1219, 1220-21 (1970); Christian Labor Ass'n (Erhardt Construction), 187 N.L.R.B. No. 99, 76 LRRM 1121, 1122-23 (1971).

[135] For transfers, see *Constitution of the International Brotherhood of Teamsters, Chauffeurs, Warehousemen and Helpers*, Art. XVIII (1971); *Constitution of the International Union, U.A.W.*, Art. 17 (1972); *Constitution of the International Union, United Steelworkers*, Art. XV (1972). *Book of Laws of the International Typographical Union*, Art. XIV (1973) covers leaving the trade and delinquent dues are found in *Constitution of the Communications Workers of America*, Art. V. §4 (1971).

[136] Teamsters, United Auto Workers, Machinists, Steelworkers, Carpenters and Joiners, Communications Workers, Amalgamated Meatcutters, Ladies Garment Workers, Laborers, Retail Clerks, Electrical Workers (I.B.E.W.), Typographical Workers, and Mine Workers.

[137] *Constitution of the International Brotherhood of Teamsters, Chauffeurs, Warehousemen and Helpers of America*, Art. II, §2(h)(1971):

No member may resign from his membership in the International Union or any subordinate body before he has paid all dues, assessments, fines and other obligations owing to the International Union and all its subordinate bodies, and no resignation shall become effective until such payment.

[138] *Constitution of the International Union, U.A.W.*, Art. 6, §§17-18 (1972):

A member may resign or terminate his membership only if he is in good standing, is not in arrears or delinquent in the payment of any dues or other financial obligation to the International Union or to his Local Union and there are no charges filed and pending against him. Such resignation or termination shall be effective only if by written

communication, signed by the member, and sent by registered or certified mail, return receipt requested, to the Financial Secretary of the Local Union within ten (10) day period prior to the end of the fiscal year of the Local Union as fixed by this Constitution, whereupon it shall become effective sixty (60) days after the end of such fiscal year....

[139] See, for example, Communications Workers of America v. NLRB, 215 F.2d 835, 383-39 (2nd Cir. 1954); Colonie Fibre Co. v. NLRB, 163 F.2d 65, 67-68 (2nd Cir. 1947).

[140] 130 N.L.R.B. 1035 (1961).

[141] *Ibid.*, p. 1043.

[142] See NLRB v. U.A.W., 297 F.2d 272, 276 (1st Cir. 1961).

rule on the resignation provision and merely enforced the board's original order that the employees could not be discharged for the nonpayment of past dues.[143]

The board, in a reconsideration of the case, then held the ten-day provision invalid insofar as it could lead to discharges for the nonpayment of dues under the new maintenance-of-membership clause.[144] Again the board stressed that it was invalidating the provision only as it interfered with the employee-employer relationship;[145] the union was apparently still free to consider the ineffective resigners members for internal purposes such as union discipline.

Then, after more than two years of litigation, the first circuit let the ax fall. In setting aside the board's second order, the court upheld the ten-day restriction.[146] Reasoning that Section 7 did not protect a member from "reasonable internal regulation of the organization with which he chooses to cast his lot," the court found that the ten-day rule was reasonably related to the legitimate union purpose of fiscal certainty.[147] The court further noted that the book of rules given to all members put them on notice that they could resign only under such conditions.[148]

It should be emphasized that all four *Paulding* opinions occurred long before *Allis-Chalmers, Scofield,* and the new resignation decisions. Perhaps with this in mind, the board last year again invalidated the Automobile Workers' ten-day clause in a case involving resignations for strikebreaking.[149] The board found that the provision was so restrictive, "as to amount, in effect, to a denial to members of a voluntary method of severing their relationship with the Union."[150] Now able to cite *Scofield* to the effect that union discipline is valid only where members are "free to leave the union," the board held that the ten-day escape period did not satisfy this condition. Nevertheless, the Board has reserved the broader question of whether any restriction could be consistent with the newly proclaimed right to resign.[151]

What type of restriction would be valid? First, the Teamsters' requirement that a member meet any outstanding financial obligation should pass muster. Indeed, such a provision may not even be necessary, since even the freedom-to-resign cases condition the right to resign on the member's being paid-up.[152]

Second, those restrictions that seek to insure that the resignation is intentional should also prove valid to a point. The board has already adopted the general rule that an effective resignation should be in writing, though it has permitted resignations in the form of surrendered membership cards.[153] More exotic forms of verification, such as witnesses, certain "magic words," or "counseling" by union officials to determine the reasons for the resignation, would appear to be either unnecessary given the informal agreement between a union and its members *or* coercive in that they would provide an opportunity for union officials to pressure the member to stay within the fold.

Third, restrictions related to notifying the union that the member has resigned should also be limited to the requirement of a written statement. While the union may occasionally need a very brief period in which to update its records, any more restrictive notice requirement should be invalidated as an unnecessary limitation on the right to resign. Unfortunately, the board has complicated the simplicity of its written-notification rule by holding that a resignation does not take effect until the union is actually notified.[154] The member who is not up to facing union

---

[143] *Ibid.*

[144] 137 N.L.R.B. 901, 904-05 (1962).

[145] *Ibid.*

[146] 320 F.2d 12 (1st Cir. 1963).

[147] *Ibid.*, p. 15-16.

[148] *Ibid.*

[149] Automobile Workers (G.E.), 197 N.L.R.B. No. 93, 80 LRRM 1411 (1972).

[150] *Ibid.*, p. 1412.

[151] *Ibid.* It should also be noted that the first circuit's approval of union restrictions on the right to resign may have diminished over the past ten years. See NLRB v. Mechanical Workers, 427 F.2d 883, 885, n. 5 (1970).

[152] See, for example, Communications Workers v. NLRB, 215 F.2d 835, 838 (1954).

[153] For resignations in writing, see, for example, Machinists Lodge 405 (Boeing), 185 N.L.R.B. No. 23, 75 LRRM 1004 (1970); Newspaper Guild, Local 69 (Hearst Corp.), 186 N.L.R.B. No. 78, 76 LRRM 1219, 1220 (1970); Electrical Workers (U.E.), Local 1012 (G.E.), 187 N.L.R.B. No. 46, 76 LRRM 1038 (1970); Christian Labor Ass'n (Erhardt Construction Co.), 187 N.L.R.B. No. 99, 76 LRRM 1121, 1122 (1971); Machinists Union (Union Carbide), 196 N.L.R.B. No. 114, 80 LRRM 1079, 1080 (1972). Surrendered membership cards are discussed in Communications Workers, Local 6135 (S.W. Bell Tel.), 188 N.L.R.B. No. 144, 76 LRRM 1635, 1636 (1970).

Despite repeated union attempts to argue the inconsistency of a resigner's actions, in only one case has the board held that a member failed to resign. The member had merely revoked his dues-checkoff authorization and told a union official that he was "thinking about getting out of the union." See Machinists Union (G.E.), 194 N.L.R.B. No. 163, 79 LRRM 1208, 1210 (1972).

[154] See, for example, Electrical Workers (U.E.) Local 1012 (G.E.), 187 N.L.R.B. No. 46, 76 LRRM 1038 (1970); Communications Workers, Local 6135 (S.W. Bell Tel.), 188 N.L.R.B. No. 144, 74 LRRM 1635, 1636 (1971); Book Binders Union Local 60, 203 N.L.R.B. No. 104, CCH Para. 25,369 (1973).

officials should, therefore, be warned that his resignation will not be effective until the end of the business day on which his mailed resignation is received.[155]

Since strikes are often called on rather short notice and because the board's position on the "reasonableness" issue may result in a member being fined a staggering amount for even a few hours of strikebreaking, such a rule delaying immunity for a few days after the member has irrevocably decided to resign will undoubtedly prove a trap for the unwary.[156] Nor is it necessary. A union gains very little by receiving actual notice of the member's resignation. The board must, of course, insure that members cannot cross picket lines and subsequently resign in order to immunize themselves from union discipline. When the strikebreaking occurs on Day 1, however, and the union receives the member's letter of resignation on Day 2 or Day 3, it seems reasonable to assume that the worker irrevocably entrusted his resignation to the mails before he broke the union's rules. In this regard, the courts should be especially sensitive to the fact that, since few workers even know they have a right to resign, any procedural complexity is very likely to become a needless snare for the uninformed.

Finally, the courts will undoubtedly be confronted with provisions prohibiting resignation completely or limiting it to certain stated times. The board is clearly correct in its ruling that under Section 7, *Scofield,* and the resignation cases such provisions are invalid. If the resignation doctrine is to have any real import, the right to resign cannot be confined to those few periods when the member is least likely to be disenchanted with his union.[157] Indeed, Section 7 requires that a member be free to leave even at those times of greatest stress. To hold otherwise is to resurrect the doctrine of mutual reliance and liken the

union member, as the union urged in *Granite State,* to a "volunteer for military service" who "is under strict discipline for the duration."[158]

Such pleas did not move the *Granite State* Court, and they should not sway future courts explicating the right to resign. It is difficult to believe that most union officials are so far removed from their rank and file that they cannot predict how many deserters they will encounter as a strike lingers on. Moreover, to the extent union officials do have honest doubts about their capacity to wage protracted economic war, a source of concern if one accepts the underlying rationale of *Allis-Chalmers,*[159] they could poll their membership in a secret ballot.[160]

Thus, in considering any future restrictions on the right to resign, the courts should follow the spirit, if not the occasional dicta, of both the discipline and resignation decisions and hold that a union may do no more than require that resigners fulfill past financial obligations and tender their resignations in some relatively unambiguous manner. The discipline decisions demand no less, and the decisions involving even broad union-security clauses require no more.

The Real and Imagined Effects of Resignation

As Mr. Buckley and his equally disaffected union brethren contemplate the rewards of resignation, it will undoubtedly occur to them that such benefits will not be realized without some corresponding costs. It is clear that

[155] See, for example, Book Binders Union Local 60, 203 N.L.R.B. No. 104, CCH Para. 25, 369 (1973); Machinists Local 1255 (Mason & Hanger-Silas Mason Corp.), 188 N.L.R.B. No. 135, 76 LRRM 1456 (1971) *enf. den. on other grounds,* 456 F.2d 1214 (5th Cir. 1972); Electrical Workers (U.E.), Local 1012 (G.E.), 187 N.L.R.B. No. 46, 76 LRRM 1038 (1970).

[156] See, for example, Printing Pressmen's Union (Herald-News, 190 N.L.R.B. No. 38, 77 LRRM 1199 (1971) ($2,000 fine for one day of strikebreaking).

Timing will also be critical to members of transportation unions facing rather quick decisions about whether or not to cross the picket lines of sister unions. See Machinists Lodge No. 284 (Morton Salt), 190 N.L.R.B. No. 32, 77 LRRM 1100 (1971).

[157] For example, Professor Gould has noted that, while auto strikes are normally called in September, the U.A.W. member has to make his resignation decision between December 21 and 31, hardly a period known for sober reflection. See Gould, "Some Limitations Upon Union Discipline under the National Labor Relations Act: The Radiations of Allis-Chalmers," pp. 1067, 1105.

[158] Brief for Respondent, NLRB v. Granite State Joint Board, 409 U.S. 213 (1972) at 15.

[159] See 388 U.S. 175, 181-82 (1967).

[160] It is not persuasive for union leaders, who have conducted strike votes in a nonconfidential manner, to argue that free resignation will defeat their carefully developed consensus. Indeed, the *Granite State* Court was probably impressed by the fact that the strike vote in that case, which was touted by the first circuit as an expression of unanimous resolve (see 446 F.2d 369, 370-73 [1971], in reality stood for very little because it was not conducted in a confidential manner: "Radziewicz, the first employee to resign, testified that he attended the strike authorization meeting and 'stood up' in favor of the strike because 'they all stood up.'" Brief for Petitioner, NLRB v. Granite State Joint Board, 409 U.S. 213 [1972] at 20, n. 16).

If the union were allowed to sample rank-and-file opinion, including a periodic check on the members' inclination to resign, all strike votes and such opinion sampling would have to be conducted in some confidential manner. Unfortunately, while many unions now require such secrecy, many others — including such major ones as the Bricklayers, Carpenters, Electrical Workers (both the IBEW and IUE), Operating Engineers, Garment Workers, Longshoremen, Maritime Workers, Steelworkers, and Textile Workers (TWU) — do not. See Brief for I.A.M., *Amicus Curiae,* NLRB v. Granite State Joint Board, 409 U.S. 213 (1972) at 16a-17a.

resignation does have its disadvantages, most notably the loss of whatever influence the member once had in the union that will still, despite his resignation, represent him in bargaining with his employer. Moreover, beyond such internal union benefits, the worker may also be misled, as Mr. Buckley apparently was, into thinking that his job will be terminated along with his union membership. While this fear is largely imagined, such a concern is, unfortunately, supported by the unduly narrow Court pronouncements on the right to resign.

Resignation and Union Rights. In choosing between working for internal reform as a union member and resigning so as to free himself from the policies he finds distasteful, the dissident must remember that, unless he ultimately defeats the union in a decertification election, it will continue to hold substantial economic power over him as exclusive bargaining agent. In resigning, the member gives up his right to vote for union officials, to express himself at union meetings, and even to take part in determining the amount or use of union dues he may be forced to pay under a union-security arrangement.[161]

The resigner also surrenders any influence in the collective bargaining process. He will have no part in determining the union's demands or its bargaining team and will have no vote in either declaring a strike or ratifying the contract it produces.[162] While he will be able to cross picket lines with immunity from union discipline, this "right to work" may not prove very meaningful given both the rather unpleasant nature of strikebreaking and the fact that in most heavily unionized industries a strike will shut down operations. The nonmember will then have to endure a strike he has had no part in calling without the strike benefits provided to union members.

The dissident should also consider the effect of a resignation on his use of the collective agreement's grievance procedures. First, no matter how impartial the union is in its role as grievance processor, the nonmember with an interest not shared by most members may find that interest has been previously bartered away so effectively that he simply has no grounds for invoking the procedure.

Second, the nonmember, especially one who has challenged the union, may have a difficult time invoking

the "duty of fair representation" to force union grievance committee members to process even valid complaints. Though a nonmember is not completely at the mercy of such officials, the deference shown to union "discretion" in processing such claims must be a factor in a dissident's decision to resign.[163]

Third, the union may not deprive the resigner of payments such as insurance or pensions that accrue from the operation of the collective agreement. The board and the courts have repeatedly held that a union violates Section 8(b)(1)(A) in denying, or even threatening to deny, such "terms of employment" to nonmembers.[164] The union still can, however, and undoubtedly will, deny resigners union benefits, including pensions, insurance, strike benefits, medical facilities, recreation centers, and dependents' scholarships.[165] The former member has financed these benefits in the past and may be forced to fund them in the future through continuing dues.[166]

---

[161] The member's right to participate in union government, including, but not limited to the rights enumerated in the text, are guaranteed by the Landrum-Griffin Act. See 29 U.S.C. §411(a)(1-3)(1964). Section 3(o) of that act, however, defines "member," the term used in all the guarantee provisions, as one who has "fulfilled the requirements for membership. . . and who neither has voluntarily withdrawn from membership nor has been expelled or suspended from membership. . . ."

[162] See NLRB v. General Motors, 373 U.S. 734, 737 (1963). See also 29 U.S.C. §411(a)(1).

[163] The employee may, under the proviso to §9(a) (29 U.S.C. §159[a] [1970]), present his grievances directly to the employer; see NLRB v. Union Pacific Stages, 99 F.2d 153 (9th Cir. 1938). In attempting to invoke the final appeal to arbitration as provided in most collective agreements, the employee must rely on the union's duty of fair representation, a breach of which is difficult to prove. See Vaca v. Sipes, 386 U.S. 171, 190-93 (1967) (merely proving the employee's claim is meritorious is not sufficient to show a breach of duty of fair representation when the union subsequently chooses not to seek arbitration).

[164] Local 167, Progressive Mine Workers v. NLRB, 422 F.2d 538, (7th Cir. 1970) *cert. den.* 399 U.S. 905 (1970) (pension benefits); Clothing Workers Union (Jaymar Ruby), 151 N.L.R.B. 555, 58 LRRM 1439 (1965) (insurance benefits); Teamsters Local 729 (Penn Truck Co.) 167 N.L.R.B. 147, 66 LRRM 1009 (1967) (insurance benefits).

[165] See, for example, NLRB v. Automobile Workers, 222 F.2d 95 (7th Cir. 1955) (insurance benefits held to be union related).

[166] Since the union shop was permitted out of a concern that nonmembers would be given a "free ride" in the collective bargaining process, the board had at one time held that the mere dues-payer could refuse to pay dues levied for nonbargaining purposes (Teamsters Local 959 [RCA Service], 167 N.L.R.B. 1042, 66 LRRM 1203, 1205 [1967]). See also NLRB v. Food Fair Stores, 307 F.2d (3rd Cir. 1962) (special assessments for particular purposes are not dues that may be demanded under a union-security clause).

More recently, however, the board has all but overruled *RCA Service* in holding that there was no basis for distinguishing between dues used for collective bargaining and those used for other "institutional expenses of the Union" (Detroit Mailers Union [Detroit Newspaper Publishers Ass'n], 192 N.L.R.B. No. 107, 78 LRRM 1053, 1054 [1971]). The board held that so long as the dues were "periodic and uniformly required and are not devoted to a purpose that would make their mandatory exaction otherwise inimical to

Though this is not the place for a detailed account of such benefits, American unions in 1970 had a net worth of some $2.3 billion, or more than $1,200 per member.[167] While the value of this substantial capital aggregation obviously varies from member to member, it can hardly be ignored in a cost-benefit analysis of continued union membership.

Resignation and Employment Rights. Let us now assume that a member, such as Mr. Buckley, is so alienated that he is willing to forego all union benefits and is prepared to take his chances as a nonunion employee. Does he have any further reason to fear that the union will seek his discharge under a union-security clause? The short, and, we would hope, correct, answer is that so long as he continues to tender his dues, a resigner fulfills the "financial core" to which union membership, under even the broadest of union-security clauses, has been "whittled" by Section 8(a)(3) of the NLRA and the Supreme Court's *General Motors* decision.[168] Yet some doubt remains; and neither the board nor the Court has done anything to dispel it, despite their recent emphasis on the right to resign.

At the outset, it should be noted that unlike the union-security clause in *General Motors*,[169] most maintenance-of-membership and union-shop clauses fail to warn the worker that his union obligation is limited to mere dues paying.[170] This absence is not surprising since fifteen years ago the board suggested a model

union-security clause that also failed to contain such a warning:

It shall be a condition of employment that all employees of the Employer covered by this agreement who are members of the Union in good standing on the effective date of this agreement shall remain members in good standing and those who are not members on the effective date of this agreement shall, on the thirtieth day (or such longer period as the parties may specify) following the effective date of this agreement, become and remain members in good standing in the Union. It shall also be a condition of employment that all employees covered by this agreement and hired on or after its effective date shall, on the thirtieth day following the beginning of such employment (or such longer period as the parties may specify) become and remain members in good standing in the Union.[171]

Faced with such a clause, it is hardly surprising that Mr. Buckley and other dissidents fear that mere dues paying will not suffice. There is, of course, the judicial gloss of *General Motors,* for those conversant with ten-year-old decisions, but even that case may not be completely relevant in applying Section 8(a)(3) to resigners. For that section, at least literally, requires some union act making the employee a nonmember:

It shall be an unfair labor practice for an employer — ... (3) by discrimination in regard to hire or tenure of employment or any term or condition of employment to encourage or discourage membership in any labor oraganization: *Provided,* That nothing in this subchapter ... shall preclude an employer from making an agreement with a labor organization... to require as a condition of employment membership therein on or after the thirtieth day following the beginning of such employment. . . . *Provided further,* That no employer shall justify any discrimination against an employee for nonmembership in a labor organization (A) if he has reasonable grounds for believing that such membership was not available to the employee on the same terms and conditions generally applicable to other members, or (B) if he has reasonable grounds for believing that membership was denied or terminated for reasons other than the failure of the employee to tender periodic dues and the initiation fees uniformly required as a condition of acquiring or retaining membership. . . .[172]

Thus far, the board and the courts have had no difficulty in limiting the worker's obligation to mere dues paying on the grounds that any further requirement (such as passing union tests, securing the endorsement of union members, attending initiation ceremonies, or even swearing

---

public policy," as in *Machinists* v. *Street,* they could be required under a union-security clause and §8(a)(3). See also Reid v. Auto Workers, Local 1093, 83 L.R.R.M. 2406 (10th Cir. 1973) (union does not violate its duty of fair representation by spending union dues and agency shop fees on political campaigns).

This change is of no small significance. For example, in 1970 the International Typographical Union reported that only 13 percent of its dues were used for internal staff, bargaining representatives, and legal expenses. The remainder went to union pensions, strike benefits, training centers, public relations bureaus, and the union journal (*Book of Laws of the I.T.U.,* Back Cover [1973]).

[167] See U.S. Bureau of the Census, *Statistical Abstract of the United States,* 1972 (Washington: GPO, 1972), p. 243.

[168] See NLRB v. General Motors, 373 U.S. 734, 742 (1963).

[169] See *ibid.,* p. 735, n. 3.

[170] See, for example, U.S. Steel Corp. United Steelworkers, *Collective Agreement,* §5,A (1971), CCH Lab. Law Rptr. Para. 59,908; *National Master Freight Agreement, (Teamsters-Trucking Employers, Inc.),* Art. 3 §1(b)(1970), CCH Lab. Law Rptr. Para. 59,944. See Ford Motor Co.-United Auto Workers, *Collective Agreement,* Art. II,§1 (1970), CCH Lab. Law Rptr. Para. 59,923 (explicitly stating that required membership is limited to dues paying).

[171] Keystone Coat, Apron & Towel Supply, 121 N.L.R.B. 880, 885, 43 LRRM 1251 (1958).

[172] 29 U.S.C. §158(a)(3)(1970).

allegiance to the union[173] constitutes something beyond "the periodic dues and the initiation fees uniformly required. . . ." Again, it is not entirely clear that these decisions are applicable to the resigner. His membership has not, after all, been "denied or terminated" by the union at all. It was the *resigner and not the union* who terminated the union-member contract. One can imagine the president of AFTRA testifying that he watched helplessly as Mr. Buckley severed his relationship with the union and that AFTRA was now only exerting its rights in reporting Mr. Buckley to CBS so that the network might live up to *its* contractual agreements by firing the ill-advised commentator.[174]

_____

[173] For union tests, see A. Nabakowski Co., 148 N.L.R.B. 876 (1964), *enf. sub. nom.* N.L.R.B. v. Sheet Metal Workers Int. Ass'n Local No. 65, 359 F.2d 46 (6th Cir. 1966). The endorsement of union members is covered in Bricklayers Union No. 4, 160 N.L.R.B. 1837, 63 LRRM 1204 (1966). See United Brotherhood of Carpenters (Brunswick-Balke-Callender), 115 N.L.R.B. 518 (1956) for initiation ceremonies and Union Starch & Refining Co., 87 N.L.R.B. 779, *enf'd.* 186 F.2d 1008, 1011-12 (7th Cir.) *cert. den.* 342 U.S. 815 (1951); Boilermakers, Local 749 v. NLRB, 192 N.L.R.B. No. 58, 77 LRRM 1839 (1971), *enf'd.* 466 F.2d 343 (D.C. Cir. 1972), *cert. den.* 41 U.S.L.W. 3447 (1973) for swearing allegiance to the union. See also NLRB v. Zoe Chemical 406 F.2d 574 (2nd Cir. 1969) on failure to sign an application card.

[174] Alternatively, though less persuasively, the union might rely on dicta in both *General Motors* and *Allis-Chalmers* suggesting that a union may waive all other membership rituals and declare the mere dues-payer a full member subject to union discipline like any other member. See NLRB v. General Motors, 373 U.S. 734, 743-44 (1963):

> [o]f course, if the union chooses to extend membership even though the employee will meet only the minimum financial burden, and refuses to support or "join" the union in any other affirmative way, the employee may have to become a "member" under a union shop contract, in the sense that the union may be able to place him on its roles.

Also see NLRB v. Allis-Chalmers Mfg., 388 U.S. 175, 197 (1967) ("Whether those prohibitions [of §8(b)(1)(A)] would apply if the locals had imposed fines on members whose membership was in fact limited to the obligation of paying monthly dues is a question not before us and upon which we intimate no view").

It seems absurd to argue that a union may redefine its membership to include those who grudgingly pay dues, but have expressed a clear intent to limit their participation to the bare minimum. Indeed, the *General Motors* Court noted with approval that the board had permitted union-shop provisions that protected conscientious objectors from becoming full union members even though they had regularly tendered their dues (373 U.S. 734, 744, n. 11[1963]); and the *Allis-Chalmers* Court, despite its refusal to consider the question of disciplinary powers over mere dues-payers, cited *General Motors* for the proposition that §8(a)(3) "whittled down" the obligation of such "members" to its "financial core" (388

In attempting to justify such a discharge, AFTRA and CBS could cite not only their literal reading of Section 8(a)(3), but also the ambiguous footnote in *Booster Lodge* stating that since the maintenance-of-membership clause there had expired it was "no impediment to resigning."[175] It may, of course, be that the Court was merely embellishing its freedom-to-resign argument; but, if that is true, it went about it in a rather strange way. The Court should have simply stated that a resigner is protected by Section 8(a)(3) so long as he tenders his dues, even though he has not been "terminated" by his union.

Surely, there is ample support for such a construction of Section 8(a)(3). In *Radio Officers,* the Court found that the legislative history of the section "clearly indicates that Congress intended to prevent utilization of union security agreements for any purpose other than to compel payment of union dues and fees."[176] While the Court found that Section 8(a)(3) did express a congressional intent to avoid the "free-rider" problem by allowing unions to exact dues from nonmembers, "No other discrimination aimed at encouraging employees to join, retain membership, or stay in good standing in a union is condoned."[177] Similarly, the *General Motors* Court noted that in explaining Section 8(a)(3), Senator Robert A. Taft compared it to Canadian law, which provided that if an employee "pays dues without joining the union, he has the right to be employed."[178]

In fairness to the advocates of the literal reading of Section 8(a)(3), it should be noted that there does not appear to have been any legislative consideration of the applicability of the section to a resigner.[179] Even Senator

_____

U.S. 175, 197, n. 37 [1967]).

Despite such language and the clear intent of the resignation decisions, the question is still considered open even by courts fully aware of the right to refrain from all but financial membership. See, for example, Boilermakers, Local 749 v. NLRB, 466 F.2d 343, 345, n. 3 (D.C. Cir. 1972), *cert. den.* 41 U.S.L.W. 3447 (1973) ("We decide nothing, and intimate no opinion, as to the extent of a union's power to discipline an employee who, though refusing formal membership, pays union dues and fees"). In view of such uncertainty, the Court would be well advised to resolve the issue, preferably by clearly limiting the liability of the mere dues-payer to the "financial core."

[175] 93 S.Ct. 1961, 1964, n. 8 (1973). See also *ibid.,* p. 1962, n.1.

[176] Radio Officers Union v. NLRB, 347 U.S. 17, 41 (1954).

[177] *Ibid.,* p. 41-42.

[178] NLRB v. General Motors, 373 U.S. 734, 743, n. 9 (1963).

[179] See generally U.S. National Labor Relations Board, *Legislative History of the Labor Management Relations Act, 1947,* 2 vols. (Washington: GPO, 1948).

Taft's comment regarded an employee who had sought membership, but had been denied it by the union.[180] Nevertheless, in their consideration of those who refused to become union members for nonfinancial reasons, the courts have repeatedly emphasized that Section 8(a)(3) requires no more than dues paying.[181]

Similarly, the resignation decisions make little sense if the Court is viewed as having added an unspoken, "Of course, if you resign, you will be fired." To suggest that in its *Booster Lodge* footnote the Court is engaging in such a hidden-ball game is to accuse it of the worst form of legalism, since two board members had previously suggested, albeit in dicta, that resignation would not justify discharge: "There is nothing to prevent a union member from resigning from the union (he may be required to pay dues as a condition of continued employment if the union contract contains a union-security agreement). . . ."[182]

Finally, as a matter of federal labor policy, the conclusion that a worker may not be discharged for resigning is consistent with the overriding intent of both Section 8(a)(3) and Section 8(b)(1)(A) to separate employment rights from union rights.[183] Just as union discipline cannot be enforced by either actual or threatened job discrimination,[184] it seems clear that no union-security clause, no matter how broad, can justify the discharge of a former member who has resigned to escape union discipline, so long as he meets his minimal financial obligations.

Notice Problems in the Right to Resign

Given that Mr. Buckley was apparently misled as to his right to resign without losing his job, there is little reason to believe that the average worker, confronted with a similarly overly inclusive union-security clause, a silent union constitution, and the same ambiguous Supreme Court dicta, will fully appreciate his right to immunize himself from union discipline.[185] Today, as in 1967 when Justice Black first noted the problems inherent in the "full membership" concept, "Few employees forced to become members of the union by virtue of the union security clause will be aware that they must somehow limit their membership to avoid the union's court enforced fines."[186]

Clearly, the board and the courts must develop some theory to insure that only genuinely willing and informed members subject themselves to union discipline. Of course, the ideal solution, or at least the foundation of an ideal solution, would be for Congress to rewrite the proviso to Section 8(a)(3) to make explicit what is now only inferred from legislative intent, that while the union may discipline its members, a worker cannot be forced to become a member to that extent.[187] As such statutory tinkering is

---

[180] *Congressional Record* 93 (1947):5088-89; *Legal History of the LMRA*, vol. 2, p. 1422.

[181] See, for example, Boilermakers Local 749 v. NLRB, 466 F.2d 343 (D.C. Cir. 1972), *cert. den.* 41 U.S.L.W. 3447 (1973); NLRB v. Zoe Chemical, 406 F.2d 574, 579-80 (2nd Cir. 1969); NLRB v. Technicolor Motion Picture Corp., 248 F.2d 348, 351-52 (9th Cir. 1957); Union Starch & Refining v. NLRB, 186 F.2d 1008, 1011-13 (7th Cir.), *cert. den.* 342 U.S. 815 (1951).

[182] Molders, Local 125 (Blackhawk Tanning Co.), 178 N.L.R.B. No. 25, 72 LRRM 1049, 1-53 (1969) (Members Fanning and Jenkins dissenting).

[183] See Radio Workers Union v. NLRB, 347 U.S. 17, 40 (1954); Motor Coach Employees v. Lockridge, 403 U.S. 274, 284 (1971).

[184] Radio Officers Union v. NLRB, 347 U.S. 17, 39-42 (1954) (union may not penalize dues delinquency by a loss of seniority); NLRB v. Brotherhood of Painters, 242 F.2d 477 (10th Cir. 1957) (union may not enforce rules on reporting piecework by seeking the discharge of a worker); Local 167, PMW v. NLRB, 422 F.2d 538 (7th Cir. 1970), *cert. den.* 399 U.S. 905 (1970) (union may not deny job-related pension benefits after expelling a member for dual unionism); NLRB v. Pulp Workers (Fibreboard Paper Products), 431 F.2d 1206 (9th Cir. 1970) (union may not threaten a worker with an otherwise valid discharge for the nonpayment of dues in order to make him pay a fine); NLRB v. Longshoremen (Rice Growers Ass'n of California), 431 F.2d 872 (9th Cir. 1970) (union may not condition discharge on the payment of a fine); Teamsters, Local 729 (PennTruck), 167 N.L.R.B. 147, 66

LRRM 1009 (1967) (union may not threaten a worker with the loss of job-related insurance benefits in order to make him pay a fine); Local 43, Printing Pressmen, 202 N.L.R.B. No. 37, CCH Para. 25, 128 (1973) (union may not remove a worker from overtime lists for breaking union rules).

[185] See Gould, "Some Limitations Upon Union Discipline under the National Labor Relations Act: The Radiations of Allis-Chalmers," pp. 1067, 1096. Professor Gould also suggests that this lack of knowledge may lead "unscrupulous management" to attempt to break unions by providing resignation information on a sub rosa basis (p. 1108). This fear, and its premise that the employer will prove to be the employee's advisor of last resort, seems overstated. It is difficult to imagine a large corporation risking the wrath of a firmly entrenched union by advising prospective members that they need not assume the burdens of full membership or that they may resign at any time. Where the employer does have something to gain by such counseling, his actions may constitute an unfair labor practice under §8(a)(1). Compare NLRB v. Elias Bros. Big Boy, Inc., 325 F.2d 360 (6th Cir. 1963) with Martin Theatres of Georgia, Inc., 126 N.L.R.B. 1054, 45 LRRM 1441 (1960).

[186] 388 U.S. 175, 215 (Justice Black dissenting).

[187] Wording such as the following might be used: Nothing in this subchapter shall preclude an employer from making an agreement with a labor organization to require as a condition of employment that each employee, on or after

always difficult, the board and the courts should begin now, with what they have, to develop a duty on the part of the union to differentiate between truly committed members and mere dues-payers.

The Duty to Disclose under Existing Law. Beyond the fact that the right to resign will go largely unexercised unless workers are better informed, authority in the related area of discharges for the nonpayment of dues suggests that a union violates Section 8(b)(1)(A) when it fails to advise prospective members of their minimal obligations under a union-security clause. In *I.U.E., Frigidaire Local 801* v. *NLRB*,[188] then Judge Warren E. Burger employed the union's duty to deal fairly with its members in holding that it was a violation of both Section 8(b)(1)(A) and Section 8(b)(2)[189] to seek the discharge of a dues delinquent who had not been properly advised of his financial obligation under the union-security clause in his contract. Arguing that employees have no choice but to comply with such a clause, Judge Burger stated,

> the union which can require his membership or command his discharge is therefore charged with an obligation of fair dealing which includes the duty to inform the employee of his rights and obligations so that the employee may take all necessary steps to protect his job.[190]

Drawing on the law of agency, he continued:

> A union may not treat as adversaries either its members or those potential members whose continued employment is dependent on union membership. . . .The union is the agent for employees and as such "is subject to a duty to use reasonable efforts to give his principal information which is relevant to affairs entrusted to him and which, as the agent has notice, the principal would desire to have. . . ."[191]

_____

the thirtieth day following the beginning of such employment, shall tender and shall continue to tender the periodic dues and reasonable initiation fees uniformly required as a condition of acquiring or retaining membership in said labor organization.

[188] 307 F.2d 679 (D.C. Cir. 1962), *cert. den.* 371 U.S. 936 (1962).

[189] 29 U.S.C. §158(b)(2)(1970):

It shall be an unfair labor practice for a labor organization . . . to cause or attempt to cause an employer to discriminate against an employee in violation of [§8(a)(3)] or to discriminate against an employee with respect to whom membership in such organization has been denied or terminated on some ground other than the failure to tender the periodic dues and the initiation fees uniformly required as a condition of acquiring or retaining membership. . . .

[190] 307 F.2d 679, 683 (D.C. Cir. 1962), *cert. den.* 371 U.S. 936 (1962).

[191] *Ibid.* (citing *Restatement [Second], Agency* §381 [1958]).

In applying this doctrine to the resignation context, the board and the courts should consider both the probable lack of knowledge on the part of the employee and the likely consequences of an ill-advised act.[192] On the first count, the case for requiring disclosure of the limited nature of mandatory union membership seems far stronger than that for the obligation to pay dues. A poll of prospective employees would undoubtedly reveal that the vast majority in union- or agency-shop industries are aware that they must tender dues in order to keep their jobs; moreover, those who are blissfully ignorant are very likely to be informed by fellow workers or union officials long before the expiration of the thirty-day grace period in Section 8(a)(3).[193] By contrast, very few workers realize that they need not assume the burdens of full membership in order to work, and they are not likely to be so advised by fellow workers or union officials interpreting an overly inclusive union-security clause.

As to the potential harm of an ill-advised act, discharge is, of course, the most severe penalty a union can exact; but a substantial fine, one from which a misinformed member cannot escape even by finding a new job, is hardly a laughing matter. It should be remembered that both Section 8(a)(3) and Section 8(b)(1)(A) resulted from the same congressional desire to insure that the worker's Section 7 right to refrain from union activity would not be infringed.[194]

In sum, there seems to be good reason to hold that a union violates Section 8(b)(1)(A) when it disciplines a member who was not previously informed of his right to limit his membership to mere dues paying. When the union has further obfuscated that right by adopting an overly inclusive security clause and then seeks to extend its disciplinary sanctions beyond the internal union punishments of suspension or expulsion, the case of a Section 8(b)(1)(A) violation seems compelling.

Nevertheless, such is *not* the law. Rather the *Allis-Chalmers* Court held that, despite the existence of a union-security clause, there was no evidence that the fined

_____

[192] In addition to the District of Columbia circuit, the second and third circuit courts have held that a union has a duty to disclose to members information on dues and discharge, NLRB v. Local 182, Teamsters, 401 F.2d 509 (2nd Cir. 1968) app. dis., *cert. den.* 394 U.S. 213 (1969); NLRB v. Hotel Employees, Local 586, 320 F.2d 254 (3rd Cir. 1963).

[193] See 29 U.S.C. §158(a)(3)(1970).

[194] It should also be noted that under §105 of the Landrum-Griffin Act (29 U.S.C. §415 [1964]), the unions have an affirmative obligation to inform members of their rights with regard to free speech, union elections, and the like. It seems bizarre to contend that federal labor policy requires the explanation of a member's rights under Landrum-Griffin, but does not require that the worker be told that he has a §7 right to refrain from becoming a member in the first place.

members contemplated anything less than full membership.[195] Citing *Machinists* v. *Street,* the Court declared that full membership should be assumed if there was no clear evidence to the contrary. Such a view, which is implicitly endorsed each time the board or a court upholds a union fine without first determining that the accused knew the extent of his minimal obligation, suggests that the unions have no duty to inform members of their Section 7 right to refrain from "full union membership." Given such a stance, at least for the present, the board and the courts must look elsewhere for a duty to disclose.

Since the courts are inclined to rely on the fiction of contract in enforcing union discipline,[196] the body of contract law seems a fair place to begin in developing the union's duty to inform prospective members that they need not accept the "full contract." Indeed, the Supreme Court has itself suggested that contract theory may be relevant in this regard. In *Granite State* the Court based its opinion on the premise that "the power of the union over the members is certainly no greater than the union-member contract."[197] Similarly in *Machinists* v. *Gonzales* the Court, noting that the "contractual conception of the relation between a member and his union widely prevails in this country,"[198] upheld the authority of state courts to interpret provisions of the union's constitution and bylaws as a limitation on the union's right to expel a member.

It does not seem too great a leap from such an interpretation of explicit provisions to the proposition that a court should not enforce union discipline unless the union-member "contract," — that is, the union's constitutions and bylaws, warned members that such discipline was possible *and* the member nevertheless accepted that possibility in the finest tradition of "offer-and-acceptance." One state supreme court has, in fact, already adopted this approach. In *United Glass Workers' Local No. 188* v. *Seitz,* the Washington Supreme Court refused to enforce a union fine after finding no explicit warning of such enforcement in the union's constitution or bylaws.[199] The *Seitz* approach has not, unfortunately, been followed in the few state decisions enforcing union fines;[200] but, if it were, it would be devastating. Of the constitutions and bylaws of thirteen

major unions studied, only two contained any warning that they would seek judicial enforcement of their fines.[201]

While *Seitz* has not been followed, its approach seems valid so long as the courts insist on the fiction of a union-member contract. Moreover, it seems proper to ask whether, in this day of increasing consumerism, the union-member contract can withstand scrutiny on "contract of adhesion" grounds.[202] When we now require auto dealers to put warranty disclaimers in conspicuous print and loan companies to emphasize their annual effective interest rate, it seems bizarre to permit unions to obfuscate the potential liability of prospective members. Indeed, the case for declaring the union-member relationship a contract of adhesion seems far stronger than that for the auto dealer or loan company, for only in the union is there an apparent legal compulsion, the overly inclusive security clause, to sign the contract. Thus, while it may be difficult to assess the "voluntariness" of every union-member contract, it seems absurd to enforce fines as the product of that contract where there is good reason to believe the member was misled into accepting the contract and was never warned, in even the finest of print, that it contained the possibility of judicially enforced fines.

Moving beyond Existing Law. While conditioning judicial enforcement on such a demonstration of voluntariness would undoubtedly be desirable, it would not go nearly far enough in guaranteeing the employee's right to refrain from union membership, except for mere dues paying. First, the preemption doctrine would limit state courts to

---

[195] 388 U.S. 175, 196 (1967).

[196] See, for example, *ibid.,* p. 192; Scofield v. NLRB, 394 U.S. 423, 426, n. 3 (1969); NLRB v. Boeing Co., 93 S.Ct. 1952, 1957 (1973).

[197] 409 U.S. 213, 217 (1972).

[198] 356 U.S. 617, 618 (1958).

[199] 65 Wash. 2d 640, 399 P.2d 74 (1965).

[200] See, for example, Local 248 U.A.W. v. Natzke, 36 Wisc. 2d 237, 251-52, 153 NW 2d 602, 610 (1967).

[201] *Constitution of the International Brotherhood of Teamsters, Chauffeurs, Warehousemen, and Helpers of America,* Art. XXVI, §1(1971):
The provisions of this Constitution relating to the payment of dues, assessments, fines or penalties, etc., shall not be construed as incorporating into any union-security contract those requirements for good standing membership which may be in violation of applicable law. . . . However, all such financial obligations imposed by this Constitution and Local Union Bylaws . . . shall be legal obligations of the member upon whom imposed and enforceable in a court of law.
International Association of Machinists and Aerospace Workers, *Rules of Order for Local Lodges,* Art. F., §1:
. . . initiation fees, reinstatement fees, dues and fines shall constitute a legal liability by a member to the [local union]. Cost of litigation arising from charges against a member by reasons of such liabilities shall constitute a legal debt payable by such member.

[202] See Kessler, "Contracts of Adhesion: Some Thoughts about Freedom of Contract," *Columbia Law Review* 43 (1943):629; Wilson, "Freedom of Contract and Adhesion Contracts," *International and Comparative Law Quarterly* 14 (1965):175.

denying enforcement of fines already imposed.[203] They would have no power to stop a union from initially imposing the fines or from threatening the worker's employment rights. Since it is clear that even an unenforceable fine may be coercive,[204] it is the board that must develop a solution.

The board could prohibit, as a violation of Section 8(b)(1)(A), any union-security clause that did not explicitly limit the worker's obligation to mere dues paying. The fact that so few workers are aware of the *General Motors* gloss on more extensive clauses and that a number of major collective agreements function quite adequately with clauses limited to the minimum financial obligation[205] suggests that such a decision would help insure the workers' right to refrain from membership without unduly hindering the union's right to organize. Ample precedent in board and court rulings supports this approach. For example, illegal preferential hiring plans were not "saved" by clauses that noted their probable invalidity, since the average worker would not appreciate such legalisms.[206] In declaring such a plan, by its own terms a nullity, an unfair labor practice, the second circuit explained,

> [T]he existence of such an agreement without more tends to encourage membership in a labor organization. The individual employee is forced to risk discharge if he defies the contract by refusing to become a member of the union. It is no answer to say that the Act gives him a

remedy in the event he is discharged. The Act requires that the employee shall have freedom of choice, and any form of interference with that choice is forbidden.

The court concluded,

> [T]he question is not only whether under principles of contract law the addendum [to the effect that any clause in violation of Taft-Hartley would not be enforced] would contractually negative the illegal union-security clauses, but whether it would have the effect of preventing the coercion that would otherwise follow. . . .[207]

A union-security clause that requires membership without any further warning that it cannot under *General Motors* demand more than mere dues paying also unfairly encourages membership. It is, therefore, no answer that a dissident who risks discharge would be protected by Section 8(a)(3). The union can too easily rewrite its security clause to permit such obviously coercive language to stand.

Similarly, the board should use both the fiduciary duty developed by the District of Columbia circuit[208] and the basic policy against union coercion in Sections 7 and 8(b)(1)(A) to declare it an unfair labor practice for a union official, who by now should know better, to tell a worker that he must "join the union" without simultaneously informing him that he has the right to limit that membership to dues paying, that if he does join he may resign at any time, and that if he joins and does not resign he will be subject to union discipline. Perhaps such a "Miranda warning" is too much to police in every instance; but the board could go a long way toward encouraging compliance by holding that discipline involving more than suspension or expulsion violates Section 8(b)(1)(A) unless the union can demonstrate, by an oath of allegiance,[209] a conspicuous warning in its constitution or bylaws, or some other evidence concerning the making of the union-member contract, that the member was aware that he did not need to assume the obligations of full membership. The board would, in short, be reversing the *Allis-Chalmers* presumption of full, voluntary membership, a presumption that hardly seems realistic, especially where the worker has been confronted with a broad union-security clause.[210]

---

[203] Local 100, Plumbers v. Borden, 373 U.S. 690 (1963); Local 207 Bridge Workers v. Perko, 373 U.S. 701 (1963); Motor Coach Employees v. Lockridge, 403 U.S. 274 (1971).

[204] The levy of a fine is calculated to force an individual both to pay money and to engage in particular conduct against his will. This is true regardless of the ultimate collectibility of the fine. A man who is held up at gunpoint is coerced whether or not the gun is loaded. Machinists, Lodge 405 (Boeing Co.), 185 N.L.R.B. No. 23, 75 LRRM 1004, 1005 (1970). See also NLRB v. American Bakery and Confectionary Workers' Local Union 300, 411 F.2d 1122, 1126 (7th Cir. 1969).

[205] See, for example, Ford Motor Co. United Auto Workers, *Collective Agreement*, Art. II, §1 (1970), CCH Lab. Law Rptr. Para. 59,923; B. F. Goodrich Co.-United Rubber Workers, *Collective Agreement*, Art. VI, §1 (1970), CCH Lab. Law Rptr. Para. 59,917.

[206] See NLRB v. Local 1566, Longshoremen, 278 F.2d 883 (3rd Cir. 1960), *cert. den.* 364 U.S. 890 (1960), 366 U.S. 909 (1961), *enfg.* 122 N.L.R.B. 967 (1959); NLRB v. Broderick Wood Products, 261 F.2d 548 (10th Cir. 1958), *enfg.* 118 N.L.R.B. 38 (1957); NLRB v. E.F. Shuck Construction Co., 243 F.2d 519 (9th Cir. 1957), *enfg.* 114 N.L.R.B. 727 (1955); NLRB v. Gottfried Baking Co., 210 F.2d 772 (2nd Cir. 1954), *enfg. in part* 103 N.L.R.B. 227 (1953); Red Star Express of Auburn v. NLRB, 196 F.2d 78 (2nd Cir. 1952), *enfg.* 93 N.L.R.B. 127 (1951).

[207] Red Star Express of Auburn v. NLRB, 196 F.2d 78, 81 (2nd Cir. 1952).

[208] See text above at note 190.

[209] While such oaths of allegiance typically stress the member's duty to abide by union rules and regulations, apparently none presently includes a disclaimer of either actual or implicit coercion: for example, "I assume these obligations voluntarily with full knowledge that I need not do so in order to retain employment."

[210] When the *Allis-Chalmers* Court reversed the seventh circuit's finding that the disciplined workers' membership was

Finally, as a remedial matter, the board might even consider exercising its atrophied rule-making powers to require unions with such clauses to inform their members that they may resign from full membership without fear of job discrimination. The union could, of course, also cite the benefits of full membership, but the right to resign would have to be made clear.

Such proposals may strike some as drastic or perhaps antiunion. They are intended, however, to be proindividual. For while I believe in majority rule, I am concerned to have laws that protect the dissenter from his

---

coerced by a union-security clause, it was construing an agency-shop clause that explicitly limited the member's obligation "to the extent of paying monthly dues. . . ." See 388 U.S. 175, 196 (1967); see also Allis-Chalmers Mfg. v. NLRB, 358 F.2d 656, 662 (7th Cir. 1966) (Judge Hasting dissenting).

Both the board and future courts should, therefore, consider open the validity of a presumption of full membership where the union-security clause is not similarly limited.

government, his employer, and his union.

Moreover, the proposal may be what the unions need to keep their disciplinary powers intact. Union officials should be aware that Supreme Court opinions are now and then overturned and that at the age of six *Allis-Chalmers* hardly qualifies as hoary precedent. Indeed, a brief in one of the latest resignation cases, argued that the Court's wisest response would be to overrule *Allis-Chalmers* completely.[211] While the Court took the less drastic approach of limiting *Allis-Chalmers* to full members, the unions might do well to perceive a more general reluctance to enforce union fines,[212] a reluctance they could largely eliminate by assuring the Court that only truly committed members are ever disciplined.

---

[211] Brief of the Chamber of Commerce of the United States of America, *Amicus Curiae*, NLRB v. Granite State Joint Board, 409 U.S. 213 (1972) at 9, n. 7.

[212] See, for example, NLRB v. Granite State Joint Board, 409 U.S. 213, 215-17 (1972).

CHAPTER III

The Impact of Private Sector Principles in the Public Sector: Bargaining Rights for Supervisors and the Duty to Bargain

by Harry T. Edwards, *Professor of Law,*
University of Michigan Law School

Public sector "unionization" and collective bargaining represent the most important developments in labor relations since the post-Wagner Act period of the 1930s and 1940s. This development derives significance both from the sheer magnitude and success of public sector organizing efforts and from its major impact on the management of governmental affairs and public employees at all levels of government.

Shortly before the late Walter Reuther resigned from the AFL-CIO Executive Council, he repeatedly criticized a "general inertia in the whole labor movement" and complained that "the labor movement [was] vegetating."[1] If this inertia still exists, it appears to be limited to the private sector. Public employee unions have shown a remarkable rate of growth during the last decade at a time when labor unions in the private sector are expanding only slowly, if at all.[2] In August 1973, the Bureau of Labor Statistics reported that there were 4,514,000 union members in the public sector. Of this total, there were 1,381,000 persons employed at the federal level and 3,133,000 persons employed at state and local government levels. The BLS report also showed that approximately 33 percent of all public employees presently belong to unions or employee associations, whereas only about 24 percent of the employees in the total labor force do.[3] In 1963, a year after President John F. Kennedy promulgated Executive Order 10988, it was reported that approximately 21 percent of all executive branch employees (excluding postal employees) were represented by recognized unions in exclusive bargaining units. A recent survey showed, however, that, as of November 1972, nearly 55 percent of all executive branch employees

in the federal government were represented by unions holding exclusive recognition rights.[4]

In mid-1973, the membership totals for six major public sector unions were as follows: American Federation of Government Employees (AFGE), 293,000; American Federation of State, County and Municipal Employees (AFSCME), 615,000; American Federation of Teachers (AFT), 385,000; Assembly of Government Employees (AGE), 600,000; International Association of Fire Fighters (IAFF), 165,000; National Education Association (NEA) 1,400,000. In percentage of growth, AFT (250 percent), AFGE (176 percent) and AFSCME (140 percent) ranked first, second, and third among *all* unions (in both the public and private sectors) gaining more than 100,000 members between 1962 and 1972.[5]

During the past decade, dramatic changes have also occurred in relevant public sector law, as was true in the private sector in the 1940s. These changes have both contributed to and resulted from public sector unionization. There are now more than thirty-four states with laws providing some labor relations framework for dealing with organizations of government employees.[6] In 1971 alone, nineteen states adopted legislation to change their labor relations procedures for public employees. In 1972, new statutes were enacted in Wisconsin, Minnesota, and Alaska.

It is difficult, however, to assess the significance of the recent changes in public sector labor relations law. The proliferation of new and modified legislation surely gives some evidence of the increased growth of public sector unionism; on the other hand, it also suggests that federal, state, and municipal governments are experiencing certain difficulties in developing labor relations systems.[7] The

[1] Russell Smith, Leroy Merrifield, and Theodore St. Antoine, *Labor Relations Law* (Indianapolis: Bobbs-Merrill,1968), p. 54.

[2] See, generally, William Eaton, "Public Unions Surge, Private Ones Stall," *LMRS Newsletter* 3, no. 9 (September 1972).

[3] U.S. Department of Labor, Bureau of Labor Statistics, "Labor Union and Employee Association Membership, 1972," Release no. 73-390 (August 22, 1973).

[4] United States Civil Service Commission, Bulletin No. 711-27 (Washington, D.C.: GPO, 1973).

[5] "Labor Union and Employee Association Membership, 1972."

[6] Eaton, "Public Unions Surge."

[7] Harry Edwards, "The Emerging Duty to Bargain in the Public Sector," *Michigan Law Review* 77 (1973):885, 886-87.

underlying problem here is related to the recognized distinctions between the public and private sectors. Many legal scholars and politicians have concluded that, because of certain legal, economic, and political constraints unique to the public sector, private sector legal concepts developed pursuant to the National Labor Relations Act cannot be adopted wholesale in the public sector. This "enlightened skepticism," which has prompted the rejection of the private sector bargaining model in most public sector jurisdictions, has been ably defended by Yale Professors Harry Wellington and Ralph Winter who argue that

> Those skeptical of the value of collective bargaining in private employment will hardly press its extension. But even if one accepts collective bargaining in the private sector . . . the claims that support it there do not, in any self-evident way, make the case for its full transplant. The public sector is *not* the private, and its labor problems *are* different, very different indeed . . . . Collective bargaining in public employment, then, seems distinguishable from that in the private sector. To begin with, it imposes on society more than a potential misallocation of resources through restrictions on economic output, the principal cost imposed by private sector unions. Collective bargaining by public employees and the political process cannot be separated. The costs of such bargaining, therefore, cannot be fully measured without taking into account the impact on the allocation of political power in the typical municipality. If one assumes, as here, that municipal political processes should be structured to ensure "a high probability that an active and legitimate group in the population can make itself heard effectively at some crucial stage in the process of decision," then the issue is how powerful unions will be in the typical municipal political process if a full transplant of collective bargaining is carried out.[8]

Whether the public sector is indeed sufficiently different from the private sector to justify the assumption that private sector precedents should be avoided, or at least modified, is a question of great significance and is one that has been addressed at length by a number of scholars.[9] Nevertheless, the question may be too abstract

and untimely to provide any useful insights. Indeed, the answer to the question regarding the relevance of private sector precedents in the public sector may now be moot in light of the current growth of unionism in the public sector and the widespread enactment of legislation that provides a framework for collective bargaining among government employees. Although the body of law in the public sector is still in the formative stage, it is now substantial. As a consequence, it is not enough to ask whether the public sector is sufficiently different from the private sector to warrant the avoidance of private sector precepts; rather, it may be more important now to begin to examine the *extent* to which private sector principles have already been adopted in the public sector and to attempt to measure the *impact* of this adoption.

Many factors, including judicial, political, social, and economic forces, affect the development of law. All of these factors served, at various times, to move collective bargaining to the forefront of our national labor policy in the private sector. It is impossible to say which force was the most instrumental in effecting the development of the law in the private sector; however, it is probably fair to conclude that the primary justification for the creation of our system of collective bargaining was to give workers a meaningful voice in the establishment of policies and practices affecting their conditions of employment. This same justification has recently given impetus to the union movement in the public sector. If this is so, then the labor law that has developed in the private sector cannot be dismissed as irrelevant to the public sector. Insofar as the private sector scheme of bargaining has fulfilled this primary worker objective, it will be deemed relevant by those who seek to achieve the same objective in the public sector. The fact that an employer is labelled as "public" rather than "private" will initially appear to be an insignificant distinction to employees seeking an equal voice in the establishment of employment policies.

The workers' perception of the problem must, however, be considered in the light of public reactions to public sector unionism that have been at best cautious. The public's reticence is really not surprising when viewed in the context of prevailing social, legal, and political conditions in the United States. We have too long lived with the principle of sovereign authority, with the belief that public employee strikes cannot be permitted if the orderly function of society is to be preserved, and with the stated rule of law that public employment is a privilege, not a right. Indeed, even today, we are frequently referred

---

[8] Harry Wellington and Ralph Winter, *The Unions and the Cities* (Washington, D.C.: Brookings Institution, 1971), pp. 7-8, 29-30.

[9] See, generally, Arvid Anderson, "Strikes and Impasse Resolution in Public Employment," *Michigan Law Review* 67 (1969):943; Merton Bernstein, "Alternatives to the Strike in Public Labor Relations," *Harvard Law Review* 85 (1971):459; John Burton and Charles Krider, "The Role and Consequences of Strikes by Public Employees," *Yale Law Journal* 79 (1970):418; Harry Edwards, "The Developing Labor Relations Law in the Public Sector," *Duquesne Law Review* 10 (1972):357; Theodore Kheel, "Resolving Deadlocks without

Banning Strikes," *Monthly Labor Review,* July 1969, p. 62; Harry Wellington and Ralph Winter, "The Limits of Collective Bargaining in Public Employment," *Yale Law Journal* 78 (1969):1107; Clyde Summers, "Public Employee Bargaining: A Political Perspective," *Yale Law Journal* 83 (1974):1156.

to Justice Oliver W. Holmes' now famous admonition in *McAuliffe* v. *Mayor of New Bedford*:[10]

> [A policeman] may have a constitutional right to talk politics, but he has no constitutional right to be a policeman. . . . The servant cannot complain, as he takes . . . employment on the terms which are offered him.

Furthermore, even those who have recently supported bargaining rights for public employees have urged modifications to meet the exigencies of public service. Beyond the somewhat simplistic reference to "sovereign authority," the underlying concern of many has been, as noted by Wellington and Winter, that "collective bargaining by public employees and the political process cannot be separated." This concern was highlighted and reinforced in the landmark federal decision in *United Federation of Postal Clerks* v. *Blount* where the court observed that [11]

> In the private sphere, the strike is used to equalize bargaining power, but this has universally been held not to be appropriate when its object and purpose can only be to influence the essentially political decisions of Government in the allocation of resources.

These considerations make it clear that even if collective bargaining in the public sector is accepted, there are at least two major and competing interests that must be reconciled. On the one hand, there is the workers' interest in achieving an equal voice in the effectuation of employment conditions. It may be assumed that this interest can be well served by the adoption of many private sector principles in the public sector. On the other hand, there are the political considerations, detailed by Wellington and Winter and others, that militate against a wholesale transplant of private sector precepts.

Given these conflicting interests, it seems appropriate now to appraise the process of reconciliation which presumably has allowed for the development of a system of labor relations law and collective bargaining in the public sector. Has there been any rational process for the adoption (or rejection) of private sector principles in the developing labor relations law in the public sector? Have private sector principles been modified or rejected on the basis of the perceived differences between the two sectors or for other reasons? This paper will examine and appraise this process of reconciliation as manifested by the adoption, rejection, or modification of private sector principles in the public sector.

THE RESEARCH MODEL

Labor relations law in the public sector has drawn heavily on private sector precepts and models; however, it has also involved major departures in response to numerous problems peculiar to the public sector. These problems are not only substantive. In contrast to the preemptive federalization in the private sector, the most important body of public sector labor relations law is state and local. Thus, wide variations involving differing judgmental evaluations and determinations of public policy have resulted. Indeed, the states have proven to be laboratories for socio-political experimentation in the development of the law in this area.

There is obviously no sure way to measure the impact of the private sector on the development of labor relations law in the public sector. The National Labor Relations Act has usually provided a working model for most states that have adopted public sector legislation; however, there clearly has been no uniform adoption of private sector principles among the states that have thus far sought to provide bargaining rights for public employees. There are fifty states and at least as many bargaining models are currently in force in the public sector. This fact alone militates against a general survey of the developing labor relations law in the public sector. Rather, this paper will seek to examine the process of reconciliation with respect to two select problem areas that have raised important policy issues in both the public and private sectors and that have seemed difficult to resolve in both sectors. It is hoped that by so limiting the research effort some useful observations can be made about the extent and impact of this process of reconciliation, at least in connection with arguably difficult and important issues, where the consequences may be more critical.

To this end, particular attention will be devoted here to the developing labor relations law in the public sector related to bargaining rights for supervisors and the duty to bargain. The duty to bargain is at the heart of collective bargaining, which in turn is at the center of our national labor policy. Thus, it is probably the most important single area of concern in labor relations law in both the private and public sectors. The law relating to bargaining rights for supervisors is not nearly as important, on a relative scale, as the duty to bargin; however, it is both significant and interesting because it touches on several matters associated with the institution of collective bargaining. Included among these matters are questions related to the establishment of appropriate bargaining units, selection of bargaining representatives, unlawful domination of employee organizations by employers, and qualifying standards for recognized employee organizations.

It is hoped that this limited focus on two important policy questions will better reveal the developmental use and constructive importation of private sector precepts in the public sector.

THE STATES SURVEYED

The scope of review in this research has been limited to a sample group of states with somewhat diverse public

---

[10] 155 Mass. 216 (1892).

[11] 325 F. Supp. 879 (D.D.C.), *aff'd*, 404 U. S. 802 (1971).

sector policies. Accordingly, six states, which have adopted varying legislative and judicial approaches to deal with the problem of labor relations and collective bargaining in the public sector, have been selected for intensive study. These six states are Illinois, New York, Michigan, Pennsylvania, Kansas, and Missouri. The body of law in other jurisdictions has also been given careful consideration in the preparation of this paper; however, a special effort was made to unearth the process of reconciliation followed by the six sample states. Some of the considerations which prompted the selection of these six states follow.

Illinois was selected because public sector unionism has grown tremendously there even though there is no formal legislative scheme regulating public sector labor relations. The matter of appropriate legislation has been debated over the years;[12] but to date the only significant body of law has emanated from the judiciary and from a recently adopted governor's executive order covering state employees. The Illinois experience thus far surely supports the notion that "it has been characteristic of America that law works on social change initially through its courts rather than its legislatures."[13]

New York and Michigan were chosen because of their differing approaches to the problems of control and administration. Both states are highly industrialized and have a long and fertile history of labor relations in the private sector. There are also an abundance of highly skilled labor scholars, legal practitioners, and arbitrators in both states. New York and Michigan were among the pioneers in adopting public sector labor relations laws and both did so pursuant to recommendations made by special advisory committees, composed of outstanding labor relations specialists. It is significant, however, that the two states adopted significantly different statutory models to deal with public sector labor relations. New York created a special Public Employment Relations Board (PERB) to administer its act, whereas Michigan placed the responsibility for enforcement upon the already existing and experienced private sector Michigan Employment Relations Commission (MERC). The New York policy makers also struggled at length with questions concerning the strike proscription; and, following the recommendations of the Taylor Committee, the New York law specifies rigid sanctions aimed at both employees and unions defying the legislated strike ban. The Michigan law, on the other hand, gives relatively little attention to the problems associated with the enforcement of the strike

proscription. The Michigan Advisory Committee on Public Employee Relations, however, counseled against rigid sanctions to enforce the strike ban.[14] Therefore, although both state laws evolved from comparable private sector experiences and "liberal" leanings in favor of bargaining rights for public employees, the two laws nevertheless differ greatly in substantive details and in the scheme for administrative enforcement.

Pennsylvania was selected because it is one of the few states with a comprehensive public sector bargaining law allowing for strikes by certain public employees.

Kansas provides a view of one of the less-industrialized states with limited private sector experiences. Kansas has two public sector laws, a special act covering only teachers and another statute covering all other public employees except persons employed by the state. Both statutes follow the modified meet-and-confer bargaining model, discussed below. The Kansas law provides for a special public sector labor board to administer the statute; however, unlike the New York PERB (which is composed of three neutrals), the Kansas Public Employee Relations Board is composed of one member representing public employees, one member representing public employers, and three neutral members.

Finally, Missouri was selected because the state statute regulating public sector labor relations is at best a very conservative and minimal approach to the problem. Except for an apparently ineffectual state board of mediation, which is empowered to resolve issues concerning "appropriateness of bargaining units and majority representative status," the Missouri law provides for no detailed scheme of administrative enforcement. The obligation to bargain is defined as a duty to "meet, confer and discuss," and this statutory language has been defined very narrowly by the Missouri Supreme Court. It is also noteworthy that police officers and teachers, two employee groups traditionally in the forefront of the public sector union movement, are not covered by the Missouri statute.

BARGAINING RIGHTS FOR SUPERVISORS

The Experience in the Private Sector

The status of supervisory employees was one of the most hotly contested and perplexing problems to confront the National Labor Relations Board and the courts under the Wagner Act. It is ironic, therefore, that twenty-five years later the same problem has arisen at the same level of concern in the public sector.

[12] Theodore Clark, "Public Employee Labor Legislation: A Study of the Unsuccessful Attempt to Enact a Public Employee Bargaining Statute in Illinois," *Labor Law Journal* (March 1969).

[13] Harry Wellington, *Labor and the Legal Process* (New Haven: Yale University Press, 1968), p. 23.

[14] "Report to Governor George Romney by the Advisory Committee on Public Employee Relations," in *Collective Bargaining in the Public Service*, Daniel Kruger and Charles Schmidt, eds. (New York: Random, 1969), p. 100.

When the Wagner Act was passed in 1935, congress failed to indicate whether "employees" under the act included supervisory personnel. The Wagner Act merely defined an "employer" as "any person acting in the interest of an employer"; it did not otherwise explicitly exclude supervisors. As a consequence, in 1942, the NLRB first recognized an association of "minor supervisors" in the coal mines as an appropriate unit for collective bargaining under the NLRA.[15] Later during the same year, the NLRB decided that supervisory personnel could not be denied bargaining rights merely because they selected a bargaining representative that was an affiliate of the same parent union that represented the subordinate employees in the same company operation; in this latter case, the board recognized a separate appropriate unit of working and nonworking foremen.[16] Board member Reilly dissented in both cases and argued that

> Permitting representation of a unit of "full fledged foremen" by the same union which represents the production employees may raise an "unfortunate conflict of interest" and would permit the supervisors to "unduly interfere with the rights guaranteed the production employees under the Act."[17]

The board's position was severely criticized and a bill was introduced in congress to exclude supervisory employees from coverage under the NLRA.[18] In 1943, while the bill was pending in committee, the NLRB reversed itself and ruled that it would not thereafter find units of supervisors appropriate for the purposes of collective bargaining under the Wagner Act.[19] However, pursuant to considerable differences of opinion among members of the NLRB, the board reversed itself again in 1945 and certified the Foreman's Association of America as representative of a unit of foremen at Packard Motor Company. The board's order was subsequently enforced by the Supreme Court in 1947.[20] The Supreme Court was persuaded by the fact that the definition of employee under the Wagner Act did not expressly exclude supervisors and, therefore, that the NLRB had the discretionary authority to grant bargaining rights to such persons. The board position was solidified in 1946 when it ruled that District 50 of the United Mine Workers could represent mine foremen even though the UMW also represented the rank-and-file miners.[21]

Following a storm of protest, congress finally passed the Taft-Hartley Amendments to the Wagner Act in 1947.

These amendments included several provisions dealing with the status of supervisors under the NLRA. Section 2 of the amended act defined "employee" to exclude supervisors and Section 14(a) stated that employers were not compelled to consider supervisors as employees under any law related to collective bargaining. Another provision of Section 14(a), however, indicated that nothing in the law "shall prohibit any individual employed as a supervisor from becoming or remaining a member of a labor organization." The effect of these amendments was to allow employers to condition supervisors' employment upon nonmembership in a union or nonparticipation in union affairs, to allow employers to agree voluntarily to negotiate with unions concerning supervisors' conditions of employment, and to allow supervisors to join unions, even those that included or were dominated by rank-and-file personnel.[22]

The congressional debates that preceded the passage of the Taft-Hartley Amendments give some clue as to the gravity of the issue posed. The majority report of the House Committee on Labor and Education declared that the question concerning supervisors was "one of the most important and critical problems" before Congress.[23] In recommending that supervisors be excluded from coverage under the NLRA, the report stated that

> the evidence before the committee shows clearly that unionizing supervisors under the Labor Act is inconsistent with the purpose of the Act to increase output of goods that move in the stream of commerce, and thus to increase its flow. It is inconsistent with the policy of Congress to assure to workers freedom from domination or control by their supervisors in their organizing and bargaining activities. It is inconsistent with our policy to protect the rights of employers; they, as well as workers, are entitled to loyal representatives in the plants, but when the foremen unionized, even in a union that claims to be "independent" of the union of the rank and file, they are subject to influence and control by the rank and file union, and, instead of their bossing the rank and file, the rank and file bosses them. The evidence shows that rank and file unions have done much of the actual organizing of foremen, even when the foremen's union professes to be "independent." . . . Just as there are people on labor's side to say what

[15] Collieries Coal Company, 41 NLRB 961 (1942).

[16] Godchaux Sugars, Inc., 44 NLRB 874.

[17] Ibid.

[18] H.R. 2239, 78th Cong.

[19] Maryland Drydock Company, 49 NLRB 733 (1943).

[20] 330 U.S. 485 (1947).

[21] Jones & Laughlin Steel Corp., 66 NLRB 386 (1946).

[22] See, generally, Note, "The Role of Supervisors in Employee Unions," Chicago Law Review 40 (1972):185. In Beasley v. Food Fair of North Carolina, Inc., 94 S.Ct. 2023 (1974), the Court ruled that, since the NLRA excluded supervisors from the protections of the Act, and thus freed employers to discharge supervisors on account of union membership, supervisory employees could not sue under a state right-to-work law to recover damages for discharge because of union membership.

[23] H.R. Rep. No. 245, 80th Cong., 1st Sess. (1947), Legislative History of the LMRA, 1947 (Washington D.C.: GPO, 1948) 1:304.

workers want and have a right to expect, there must be in management and loyal to it persons not subject to influence or control of unions, not only to assign people to their work, to see that they keep at their work and do it well, to correct them when they are at fault, and to settle their complaints and grievances, but to determine how much work employees should do, what pay they should receive for it, and to carry on the whole of labor relations. . . . Supervisors are management people. They have demonstrated their ability to take care of themselves without depending upon the pressure of collective action. No one forced them to become supervisors. They abandoned the "collective security" of the rank and file voluntarily, because they believed the opportunities thus opened to them to be more valuable to them than such "security."[24]

These policy concerns obviously prevailed in the final congressional debates and supervisors have continuously been excluded from coverage under the NLRA since 1947. The status of a supervisor in the private sector is determined by the individual's duties, not his job title or classification. Section 2(11) of the NLRA expressly provides that a supervisor is any person

> having authority in the interest of the employer, to hire, transfer, suspend, lay off, recall, promote, discharge, assign, reward, or discipline other employees, or responsibly to direct them, or to adjust their grievances, or effectively to recommend such action, if . . . such authority is not of a merely routine or clerical nature, but requires the use of independent judgment.

Although supervisors are not forbidden from maintaining union membership under the NLRA, the act does prohibit employers from interfering with or dominating the creation or operation of a labor organization. Pursuant to this statutory proscription, the NLRB and the courts have found that it is unlawful for supervisors to retain membership in recognized unions and then also seek to vote in union elections or participate in union administration or bargaining, even in a minority capacity.[25] Thus, although supervisors are permitted to retain memberships in rank-and-file unions, they must remain passive in their roles as union members.

The NLRB and the courts have also ruled that a union violates the NLRA if it seeks to expel or fine a union member who is also a supervisor for reasons associated with the member's performance of supervisory duties in administering the collective bargaining contract.[26] In these cases the board has reasoned that, if a union is allowed to discipline a supervisor for performing duties related to

bargaining or contract administration on behalf of the employer, the bargaining process is undermined by depriving the employer of effective managerial representatives.

The private sector experience thus plainly recognizes that "supervisors play a central role in labor relations as the link between management and employees"[27] and, thus, that they should not be accorded bargaining rights under the NLRA. This judgment is based primarily on a recognition that "the conflicting demands on supervisors' loyalty and the consequent, potential conflicts between their interests and those of other employees become particularly problematic when supervisors retain membership in rank-and-file unions."[28] The existing law in the private sector plainly identifies and attempts to deal with three difficult problems in this area. First, it is assumed that "labor should not be allowed to choose its own watchdog,"[29] thus the concern about unions disciplining supervisory members. Second, it is assumed that problems of unlawful interference and domination are always present when supervisors are allowed to join rank-and-file unions, thus the concern about supervisors actively participating in the internal affairs of recognized rank-and-file unions. Third, it is assumed that "management, like labor, must have faithful agents"[30] whose interests are aligned with those of management; thus the law allows employers to decline to recognize any union of supervisors.

Some Problems Unique to the Public Sector

Although the entire struggle over the rights of supervisors under the NLRA was bitterly fought,[31] the private sector resolution of the issue has been curiously rejected in many public sector jurisdictions. Several historical facts have served to muddle the problem in the public sector.

First, some of the most active union adherents in the public sector have been teachers, social workers, fire fighters, and police officers. Long before the advent of a strong union movement in the public sector, a strong community of interest between supervisors and rank and file had existed in these occupations. Teachers, for example, whether supervisors or not, have traditionally been united by professional ties and have joined the National Education Association.

---

[24] *Ibid.,* pp. 305, 307-8.

[25] Charles Morris, ed. *The Developing Labor Law* (Washington, D.C.: Bureau of National Affairs, 1971) pp. 139-40.

[26] Dallas Mailers Union, 181 NLRB No. 49 (1970); NLRB v. Lithographers Locals 15-P and 272, 437 F. 2d 55 (6th Cir. 1971).

[27] Note, "The Role of Supervisors in Employee Unions."

[28] *Ibid.*

[29] Note, *University of Illinois Law Forum,* Spring 1955, pp. 129, 134.

[30] *Legislative History of the LMRA, 1947,* 1:307.

[31] See, generally, David Levinson, "Foremen's Unions and the Law," *Wisconsin Law Review* (1950):79.

Second, the appellation *supervisor* has tended to be pushed further down in the organizational hierarchy in public sector bureaucracies. Thus, the lines between supervisor and employee have frequently been blurred by meaningless titles.[32]

Third, many middle-management and supervisory officials in the public sector fail to act like managers, even when their public duties clearly specify supervisory responsibilities.[33] Part of the difficulty here may be attributed to the fact that many state and local civil service commissions have traditionally handled personnel problems in the public sector.

Finally, there is also a question of whether it is unconstitutional to deny supervisors bargaining rights that are accorded to other public employees.

The Constitutional Issues in the Public Sector

In *Orr* v. *Thorp*[34] a federal district court declared unconstitutional a Florida statute that authorized the dismissal of any administrator or supervisory person who joined a teacher union. The court found a Fourteenth Amendment denial of equal protection because the law applied only to employees working in the Palm Beach County School System; the court also found that the statute violated the "basic freedoms of expression and association protected by the First and Fourteenth Amendments" because it barred supervisory personnel from mere membership in a union organization.

Although *Orr* v. *Thorp* raises some thorny issues, it does not really dispose of, or even deal with, the more difficult constitutional questions concerning bargaining rights for supervisors. These more troublesome issues, which concern the constitutionality of a public sector statute that uniformly denies membership and recognitional rights to all public sector managers, were recently decided by the New York Court of Appeals in *Shelofsky* v. *Helsby*.[35] There the court, relying heavily on private sector precedent,[36] ruled that the exclusion of managerial personnel from collective bargaining rights under the New York Taylor Law was constitutionally permissible. On this point, the court made the following pertinent observations:

> In the *Budd* case, involving private employees, it was held the exclusion of supervisory personnel from collective bargaining rights did not infringe their First Amendment rights of freedom of assembly and was not an arbitrary classification violative of due process. The objective of the Taft-Hartley Act. . . was to assure the employer of a loyal and efficient cadre of supervisors and managers independent from the rank and file. That objective is equally applicable to the State, as an employer. . . . There has been no showing that exclusion of management personnel from association membership is an unreasonable limitation on State employees. Withholding the benefits of collective bargaining from management personnel has long been approved in private employment. Its carry-over into public employment is a reasonable means of promoting harmonious labor relations.

The New York policy of barring public sector managers from membership in employee unions may be a sound one; however, the reliance of the New York Court of Appeals on private sector precedent to overcome constitutional objections was misplaced. The NLRA does not, as does the New York law, prohibit mere membership in a labor organization. Indeed, Section 14(a) of the NLRA expressly states that nothing in the act shall prohibit any supervisor from becoming or remaining a member of a labor organization. Recognizing the obvious distinctions between the New York law and the NLRA, the New York PERB has ruled as follows: [37]

> That the 1971 Taylor Law does not parallel NLRA §14(a) is clear. It treats managerial and confidential employees more severely than the federal law treats supervisory employees. Section 214 of the State law. . . forbids managerial and confidential employees to "be a member of any employee organization which is or seeks to become . . . the certified or recognized representative of the public employees employed by the public employer of such managerial or confidential employee."

It may be argued that since the New York law recognizes a legitimate and compelling state interest and, because it carefully distinguishes between managers and supervisors, no constitutional infirmity should be found. On this point, the appellate court in New York observed that [38]

> It is common knowledge that the interest of employees and of management are frequently adverse. The government may rightfully require that those charged with the responsibility of implementing and administering collective bargaining agreements be free from any possible conflict of interest either because they are implementing or because they are unsympathetic to management's interest due to associational bias. The

---

[32] Charles Rehmus, "Labor Relations in the Public Service," Paper prepared for the Third World Congress, International Industrial Relations Association, London, England, September 3-7, 1973.

[33] U.S. Advisory Commission on Intergovernmental Relations, *Labor-Management Policies for State and Local Government* (Washington, D.C.: GPO, 1969), pp. 95-96.

[34] 308 F. Supp. 1369 (S. D. Fla. 1969).

[35] 39 App. Div. 2d 168, 332 N.Y.S. 2d 723 (1972), *aff'd.* 32 N.Y. 2d 54, 295 N.E. 2d 774 (1973).

[36] The New York court cited with approval the decision in NLRB v. Budd Mfg. Co., 169 F.2d 571 (6th Cir.), *cert. denied,* 335 U.S. 908.

[37] In the Matters of Copiague and Hempstead, 6 PERB 3002, 3005 (1973).

[38] 332 N.Y.S.2d, at 727.

State's police power may properly be exercised to this
end for the purpose of achieving stability in labor
relations, even though the result is to interfere with
some employees' personal rights to due process and
freedom of association. Furthermore, the classification
here involved [distinguishing between supervisors and
managers] is reasonable and avoids equal protection
criticisms.

Although the court's arguments are convincing, it still
cannot be persuasively asserted that the private sector
precedent is controlling on the issue of membership
exclusion. It is one thing to provide that supervisors and
managers shall be denied bargaining rights, but it is quite
another to proscribe "bare membership."[39] Indeed, it is
noteworthy in this regard that the *Budd* decision, cited by
the New York Court of Appeals in *Shelofsky,* suggested
that the NLRA exclusion of supervisors was constitutionally permissible in part because supervisors were not prohibited from joining unions. On this point the Sixth Circuit
noted that[40]

There is nothing in the [NLRA] which restricts freedom
of speech on the part of supervisory employees. . . .
[The] Act specifically reserves to them the right to join
a labor organization. The rights guaranteed by the First
Amendment are not interfered with.

Notwithstanding some of the tough constitutional
questions posed, the decision in *Shelofsky* may well be
upheld.[41] No serious due process or equal protection
questions should be raised by a state law which denies
bargaining rights to top-level managers. The statutory
designation of managers surely is not an arbitrary
classification and there is clearly a rational basis to support
the distinction between managers and nonmanagers;
therefore, it would seem that the private sector precedents
supporting the denial of bargaining rights for supervisors
should be controlling in the public sector, too. On the
other hand, a state law that prohibits managers from
joining any union that represents or seeks to represent the
employees of the affected manager's public employer
raises more serious constitutional concerns. The difficult
question here is whether the asserted state interest
(maintaining a loyal and efficient cadre of supervisors
independent from rank-and-file interests and pressures) is
sufficient to overcome the right of free association. Under
normal constitutional analysis, it must be determined
whether there is a strong governmental interest at stake,
whether the challenged rule or law actually serves to
protect or foster the public interest, and whether there are
any feasible alternative means to protect the public
interest adequately without impairing First Amendment
rights. If the private sector is any guide, then there can be
little doubt that the government, as an employer, has a
legitimate and strong interest in maintaining a loyal cadre
of managers who are willing and able to represent the
employer at the bargaining table. The private sector
experience also suggests that one very effective means to
achieving this end is to limit supervisors' participation in
rank-and-file unions. It still may be argued that the New
York rule is overly broad because, as in the private sector,
the result sought can be accomplished without barring
supervisors from mere membership in rank-and-file unions.
In the private sector, the board and courts only seek to
determine whether the presence of supervisors in
rank-and-file unions results in de facto interference with,
or domination of, employee organizations by employers;
the law does not otherwise command the exclusion of
supervisors from union membership.

The recent Supreme Court decisions in *United States
Civil Service Commission* v. *National Association of Letter
Carriers* and *Broadrick* v. *State of Oklahoma*[42] may give
some clue as to whether the New York membership
proscription will be declared constitutionally permissible.
In *Letter Carriers,* the Court ruled that the Hatch Act
prohibitions against federal employees taking an active
part in political management or in political campaigns were
not unconstitutional. In *Broadrick,* the Supreme Court
upheld the constitutionality of the Oklahoma State Merit
System Act that prohibited any state-classified employee
from being "an officer or member" of a "partisan political
club" or a candidate for "any paid public office." The law
also forbade the solicitation of contributions "for any
political organization, candidacy or other political
purpose" and the participation "in the management or
affairs of any political party or in any political campaign."
In both *Letter Carriers* and *Broadrick,* the Court rejected
arguments that the statutes were unconstitutionally vague
and that the statutory prohibitions were too broad.

The Supreme Court in *Letter Carriers* and *Broadrick*
plainly recognized that the statutes in question were
extremely broad in substantive coverage. Nevertheless, the
Court seemed prepared to allow such general prophylactic
legislation to stand because, as the Court noted in
Broadrick, "where conduct and not merely speech is
involved, we believe that the overbreadth of a statute must
not only be real, but substantial as well, judged in relation
to the statute's plainly legitimate sweep." Given this
rationale to support the Hatch Act, it may be that the
Court will have no difficulty with the New York law
covering managerial exclusions from union membership.
The New York law does not forbid managers from joining

[39] See Holder v. City of Columbia, 71 LC Para. 53, 128
(D.C.S.C. 1972); McLaughlin v. Tilendis, 398 F.2d 287 (7th Cir.
1968); Atkins v. City of Charlotte, 296 F. Supp. 1068
(W.D.N.C. 1969); Melton v. City of Atlanta, 324 F. Supp. 315
(N.D.Ga. 1971).

[40] NLRB v. Budd Mfg. Co., 169 F.2d 571 (6th Cir. 1948).

[41] The Supreme Court recently dismissed an appeal of the
Shelofsky decision. 42 L.W. 3176 (October 9, 1973).

[42] 93 S. Ct. 2280 (1973) and 93 S. Ct. 2908 (1973).

all unions and it does not cover *all* supervisors; thus, it may be sufficiently circumspect to pass muster. On the other hand, *Letter Carriers* and *Broadrick* can be read narrowly to cover political activities and not merely membership in a political party. On this point it could be argued that the cases are distinguishable from the New York case because the New York law forbids all *membership,* whether passive or active. Nevertheless, the New York law has a plainly legitimate purpose, to ensure managerial loyalty and avoid conflicts of interest in collective bargaining, and so it probably should be upheld.

The Various Approaches Followed in the Public Sector

If it may be assumed that it is constitutionally permissible to deny at least certain bargaining rights to public sector supervisors, then several approaches to the problem appear:

A. Definition of Class of Supervisors
  1. Distinguish between supervisors and policy makers, *or*
  2. Use functional definition of supervisor comparable to the NLRA definition.
B. Status of Supervisors under Applicable Law
  1. Deny membership and bargaining rights to all supervisors (or managers), *or*
  2. Deny bargaining rights to all supervisors (or managers), *or*
  3. Bar supervisors from joining rank-and-file unions, but allow them to gain bargaining rights in separate units with independent unions, *or*
  4. Allow supervisors to be represented by any union in separate bargaining units, *or*
  5. Allow supervisors to meet and confer, but not to bargain.
C. Regulation of Union Organizations
  1. Bar certification rights and statutory recognition to any union that allows supervisors to join a rank-and-file organization, or rank-and-file members to join a supervisors' organization, *or*
  2. Deal with the problem in unfair labor practice proceedings in connection with claims of unlawful domination or assistance by the employer or coercion by the union.

These approaches are plainly not all mutually exclusive and the list does not exhaust the full range of possibilities. The list does at least highlight some of the options that have been considered in various public sector jurisdictions.

Among the sample states surveyed, only Kansas has chosen the private sector model for supervisors' bargaining rights. Under the Kansas law, the statutory definition of a public employee clearly excludes supervisory personnel and the definition of a supervisor is essentially the same as that found in Section 2(11) of the NLRA. The Kansas act further provides, as does the NLRA, that supervisors may join any organization of their choice; however, the act makes it clear that "no public employer . . . shall be compelled to deem individuals defined. . . as supervisory employees as public employees [under the] act." The act also makes it a "prohibited practice" for a public employer to "dominate, interfere or assist in the formation, existence, or administration of any employee organization" and for a union to "interfere with, restrain or coerce a public employer. . . with respect to selecting a representative for the purposes of meeting and conferring or the adjustment of grievances." Thus, it is reasonable to assume that Kansas will follow the private sector model in all particulars when dealing with bargaining rights for supervisors under the act.

The Kansas Collective Negotiations Act for Teachers, however, expressly grants bargaining rights for "administrative employees," apparently including all professional supervisory personnel below the rank of "superintendent of schools or other chief executive officer employed by a board of education." Administrative bargaining units must be separate from teacher units; however, both groups are permitted to select an exclusive representative for bargaining purposes. The Kansas teachers' law in effect adopts the position of the National Education Association that has long favored bargaining rights for supervisors in recognition of preexisting professional associational ties among supervisors and rank-and-file personnel in teaching.[43]

The experience in Illinois is more difficult to assess because of the absence of a statute covering public sector bargaining. The report of the Governor's Advisory Commission on Labor-Management Policy for Public Employees, issued in 1967, recommended that "elected officials, the heads of departments and agencies, the members of boards and commissions, managerial employees, magistrates, [employer] negotiating representatives. . . and supervisors" be excluded from coverage under a state bargaining law.[44] In recommending the exclusion of supervisors, the commission sought "to avoid conflicts of interest in negotiations and in the administration of employee relations policies" and "to assure strong management direction."[45] A recently issued governor's executive order, which grants bargaining rights to some 60,000 employees working in the executive branch of the state government, expressly excludes supervisors and managerial employees.[46] Thus, the only formal and official statements issued to date in Illinois appear to adopt the private sector approach with respect to bargaining rights for supervisors.

[43] Advisory Commission on Intergovernmental Relations, *Labor Management Policies.*

[44] Clark, "Public Employee Labor Legislation."

[45] *Ibid.*

[46] GERR no. 522, at B-7.

In practice, however, many units with supervisors included have already been recognized in Illinois. For example, the collective agreement covering teachers in the City of Chicago includes all supervisory persons below the rank of principal. Several attorneys who are active in the practice of labor law in Illinois estimate that supervisors have been excluded from bargaining rights in many nonprofessional units, but that the experience has been mixed in units covering secondary school teachers and college faculty. It is likely, however, that the new executive order is likely to fortify the position of those employers determined to deny bargaining rights to supervisory personnel.

The situation in Missouri is hopelessly confused. The state statute is silent on the subject of supervisory inclusions in public sector bargaining units. The state board of mediation is given the power to determine appropriate units and, in at least one case, it has certified a unit consisting of rank-and-file fire fighters and their superior officers.[47] The attorney general of Missouri, however, has ruled that since a public employer in Missouri is not required to adopt any proposals or agreements pursuant to collective negotiations, the employer retains the full discretion to include or exclude supervisory personnel from appropriate units as it sees fit.[48] The opinion is troublesome because it seems to confuse the question of appropriate units with the legal obligation to bargain. Indeed, the attorney general's opinion appears to be patently inconsistent with the statute, which reserves judgments on appropriate units to the state board of mediation.

The Missouri law, which is otherwise a very conservative statute, is significant because it does not exclude supervisors from appropriate units. Only police officers, national guard personnel, and teachers are denied bargaining rights. It is indeed curious, given such a conservative statute, that supervisors and managers were not excluded. The simple answer may be that the bargaining rights granted were so sparse that it really did not matter whether supervisors were included.

The Pennsylvania statute provides yet another and different twist to the problem. The NLRA definition of supervisor is adopted by the Pennsylvania law, with no apparent distinction being made between supervisors and managers.[49] In a separate section of the statute, however, it is provided that the Pennsylvania Labor Relations Board "shall not permit employees at the first level of supervision to be included with any other units of public employees but shall permit them to form their own separate

homogenous [sic] units."[50] No provision is made for the establishment of bargaining units of supervisors above the first level of management, so it may be assumed that no such unit of supervisors or managers would be appropriate under Pennsylvania law. Indeed, this conclusion is reinforced by yet another section of the law that limits the process of bargaining for supervisors, as follows:

> Public employers shall not be required to bargain with units of *first level supervisors* or their representatives but shall be required to *meet and discuss* with first level supervisors or their representatives, on matters deemed to be bargainable for other public employees. . . .[51]

Thus, it appears that only first-level supervisors are accorded bargaining rights under Pennsylvania law and no limits are imposed on the rights of any supervisors or managers to join or retain membership in a labor organization. Public employers, however, are prohibited from "dominating or interfering with the formation, existence or administration of any employee organization," so it is likely that the NLRA rule limiting supervisors to passive membership in rank-and-file unions is applicable.

The interesting aspect of the Pennsylvania law is the provision that limits the process of bargaining to "meet and discuss" for first-level supervisors. Meet and discuss is defined to mean

> the obligation of a public employer upon request to meet at reasonable times and discuss recommendations submitted by representatives of public employees: Provided, that any decisions or determinations on matters so discussed shall remain with the public employer and be deemed final on any issue or issues raised.

Under this limitation, the public employer retains full discretion to act unilaterally on all supervisory proposals covering wages, hours, and terms and conditions of employment. Although public employees in Pennsylvania have a limited right to strike after mediation and factfinding procedures have been exhausted, the statute may be read to allow strikes only with respect to bargainable matters. Since public employers are only required to meet and discuss and not bargain with supervisors, it appears that supervisors have no right to strike under the act.

On balance, it can be argued that the Pennsylvania approach is probably the worst among those surveyed. If there is indeed a legitimate reason to distinguish between first-level supervisors and managers, so as to allow the former group to be recognized for bargaining purposes, then it makes little sense to further discriminate between first-level supervisors and other public employees. It would certainly seem likely that if the principle of meet and discuss were strictly enforced, so as effectively to limit the

[47] Francis Loevi, "The Development and Current Application of Missouri Public Sector Labor Law," *Missouri Law Review* 36 (1971):167, 187.

[48] *Ibid.*, p. 186.

[49] Pa. Stat. Ann. tit. 43, §1101.301(6) (Supp. 1972).

[50] Pa. Stat. Ann. tit. 43, §1101.604(5); but see note 67 below.

[51] Pa. Stat. Ann. tit. 43, §1101.704.

bargaining rights of first-level supervisors, the result would be to create dissension among the affected supervisors and force them to align more closely with rank-and-file interests. On the other hand, if the process of bargaining were essentially the same under both the meet and discuss and collective bargaining models and if supervisors were allowed to strike, too, then there would be no material distinction in fact between the rights of first-level supervisors and other public employees.

The Michigan approach clearly adopts the pre-Taft-Hartley private sector model. The Michigan law provides bargaining rights for public employees, and supervisors are not expressly excluded from coverage under the statute. Thus, MERC has ruled that public employees means all public employees, including supervisory personnel.[52] It is noteworthy that MERC adopted the rationale of the Supreme Court decision in Packard Motor Co. v. Labor Board[53] in deciding that separate units of supervisors were permissible under the Michigan law. In reaching this conclusion, MERC relied primarily on the fact that supervisors were not excluded from the definition of employee under the Michigan act; however, the commission also cited the following supporting rationale:

Supervisors in public employment are for the most part different than supervisors in the private sector, not only in the concept of employer loyalty but also in the performance of identifiable supervisory functions. Under a civil service system, the authority supervisors might have with regard to the hire, transfer, suspension, layoff, recall and promotion is subject to more stringent review than in private employment. Further, in civil service, employees performing normal supervisory duties have the same rights and protections as do rank and file employees with respect to tenure, job security and civil service grievance procedures, and normally their salary increments and increases have a distinct relationship to increments and increases granted to nonsupervisory personnel. These factors tend to create a community of interest with employees supervised rather than with management.[54]

This rationale, while superficially appealing, obviously ignores an important point. Public employers

are frequently not well organized for collective bargaining and never will be if they cannot create positions with effective responsibility for the administration of collective agreements. Such positions must necessarily be filled by persons who identify with, and are part of, management, not by those who are unionized, whether or not the union is exclusively supervisory.[55]

On this point, it has been aptly observed that

Allowing supervisors to organize and to present proposals perpetuates the vocational ambivalence that this group has long exhibited. The need at the present time is for management to identify members and to develop a healthy community of interest. This, in the long run, will benefit employees more than any short-term gains which might come from supervisors continuing to act as part-time advocates for the rank-and-file.[56]

Although supervisors have been allowed to bargain in separate appropriate units in Michigan, the MERC has ruled that "executive employees" should not be included in any appropriate unit. Executives are defined as "employees who formulate, determine and effectuate management policies."[57] This distinction between supervisors and executives is similar to the distinction adopted under the New York law between supervisors and managers. Before 1971, the New York PERB developed a concept of managerial and confidential employment. The Taylor Law, as originally enacted, contained no reference to managerial, confidential, or supervisory employees. Thus, before 1971, employee organizations had been recognized for units containing supervisory, managerial, and confidential employees and had been certified by PERB when the unit was not contested. When the unit was contested, the PERB declined to certify an organization for managerial and confidential employees, but it never decided whether they were entitled to representation under the Taylor Law.[58] On the other hand, supervisors, as distinguished from managerial and confidential employees, have always been accorded bargaining rights under the Taylor Law.[59] On this point, the New York PERB has ruled that

The Public Employees Fair Employment Act does not define supervisors or exclude supervisors from coverage thereunder as does the National Labor Relations Act in the private sector, or as does Executive Order 10988 in federal civil service, or as do some other state acts regulating public employment relations, such as Wisconsin. This omission is not a legislative oversight but rather reflects the recommendations of the Taylor Committee.[60]

PERB has, therefore, allowed supervisors to be included in rank-and-file bargaining units so long as there is a

[52] Hillsdale Community Schools, 1968 MERC Labor Op. 859.

[53] 330 U. S. 485 (1947).

[54] Ibid.

[55] Wellington and Winter, The Unions and the Cities, p. 114.

[56] Advisory Commission on Intergovernmental Relations, Labor Management Policies.

[57] Hillsdale Community Schools, 1968 MERC Labor Op. 859.

[58] See New York State Division of State Police, 1 PERB 3153 (1968); State of New York, 5 PERB 3001 (1972); in the Matters of Copiague and Hempstead, 6 PERB 3002 (1973).

[59] New York State Division of State Police, 1 PERB 3153 (1968).

[60] Ibid.

"community of interest" between the two groups and, further, so long as there is no apparent "conflict of interest" among the employees in the proposed unit.

In 1971, the Taylor Law was amended to deny bargaining and membership rights to persons designated as managerial or confidential employees. Under the amended act,

> employees may be designated as managerial only if they are persons (a) who formulate policy or (b) who may reasonably be required on behalf of the public employer to assist directly in the preparation for and conduct of collective negotiations or who have a major role in the administration of agreements or in personnel administration.

Thus far, PERB has construed this language narrowly to include only those persons who exercise significant discretion in determining the methods, means, and personnel by which state or agency policy is to be carried out or who play a significant and direct role in collective negotiation or contract administration. Most first-level and middle-level supervisors clearly are not covered by the statutory exclusion.[61]

The Problem of Unlawful Domination

Both the New York and Michigan approaches obviously reflect legislative policy determinations that lower-level supervisors should be recognized for purposes of collective bargaining. Unlike the private sector experience, this public sector determination has not been altered with time. The major difference between the two states is that New York has at least attempted to anticipate and deal with the serious problems of conflict of interest and domination by barring managers from joining rank-and-file unions. Although the New York approach may be declared unconstitutional, it is at least a realistic expression of legislative concern about allowing managers and rank-and-file persons to belong to the same union organization.

The potential significance of this problem was first seen in Michigan in *Michigan Nurses Association*.[62] A charge was filed by rank-and-file members of the Michigan Nurses Association who claimed that the MNA was an illegally dominated labor organization because many of the officers of the parent organization were supervisors working for various employers with whom the MNA was certified to bargain. The rank-and-file claimants thus sought to have MNA disestablished as bargaining agent and replaced by the Michigan Nurses Economic Security Organization, a rank-and-file collective bargaining division within MNA. The MERC first noted that if MNA was dominated then it followed that MNESO (a subsidiary organization within MNA) was also dominated and, therefore, both groups

would have to be disestablished. MERC then went on to hold that the mere fact that supervisors belonged to and held significant positions in the parent MNA organization was not, without more, evidence of unlawful domination. On this point, MERC ruled that so long as supervisors did not actually participate in or control *local* negotiations in rank-and-file bargaining units there was no taint of unlawful interference or domination.

Unfortunately, the problem of control and domination may have been viewed too narrowly by MERC. Other Michigan cases have made it clear that supervisors cannot lawfully hold positions on local rank-and-file bargaining committees. For example, in a 1966 decision involving the *School Board of the City of Grand Rapids*[63] it was observed that

> it is inconceivable that the actions of supervisors and executives on behalf of their employer can be separated from their activities and participation in the administration and functions of a labor organization. There is no magic moment at which the executives and supervisors could change hats or reverse their dual schizoid roles so as to remove this taint.

In the same opinion, the commission also held that

> executives and supervisors may belong to associations of public employees who are engaged in representing employees in the collective bargaining process, with the caveat that such executives and supervisors scrupulously avoid any participation in activities . . . which in any way relate to the representation of members in collective bargaining.

Although this last passage recognizes the problems inherent in allowing supervisors to infiltrate rank-and-file associations, the MERC rule is nevertheless too narrow in application. The *Michigan Nurses Association* case, and others like it, make it clear that MERC adopts the passive membership rule followed in the private sector, but only with regard to local union affairs. Thus, supervisors may apparently continue to dominate the parent organization so long as they do not actively participate in the collective bargaining function at the local level.

This resolution of the problem of domination may be somewhat naive. The facts in the *Michigan Nurses Association* case revealed that, although no supervisors participated in local bargaining in rank-and-file units, the executive board of the MNA included numerous top-ranking supervisors and managers; that the MNA director appointed professional labor negotiators to act for rank-and-file units; and that the MNESO budget was controlled by MNA. In effect, the facts of the case suggested that the policies of the parent MNA organization were promulgated to reflect, at least in part, the interests of persons who otherwise represented public employers. Furthermore, the activities of the parent association cannot be viewed in isolation, separate and distinct from

---

[61]   State of New York, 5 PERB 3001 (1972).

[62]   1972 MERC Lab. Op. 564.

[63]   1966 MERC Lab. Op. 282.

the local bargaining units. The officers of the parent organization may not bargain, but they are instrumental in controlling the philosophy of the organization, implementing organizational policies, directing legislative lobbying efforts for the association, and establishing budget priorities. All of these factors, having to do with the overall direction and control of the organization, may give some evidence of domination.

The same problem was highlighted in *City of Milwaukee*,[64] where it was contended that an employee organization should not be certified to represent rank-and-file personnel if there were a substantial number of supervisors among its members. Although the Wisconsin Employment Relations Commission (WERC) rejected this contention, it did give serious consideration to the problem raised. As to the questions of domination and conflict of interest, WERC ruled that

> Where supervisors are members of the rank and file employee organization, the fact that they are not included in the appropriate collective bargaining unit would not eliminate the possible conflict of interest. . . . Supervisors who are members of an employee organization, with rights and privileges extended to employee members, could exercise a voice and vote in the deliberations of the affairs of the employee organization. . . . The active participation by supervisory employees in the affairs of an employee organization could result in impeding and defeating the primary purpose of the employee organization — that of representing municipal employees in . . . negotiations. . . . Since supervisors are the agents of the municipal employer, a municipal employer, by permitting supervisory employees to participate actively. . . in the affairs of an organization representing employees . . . could . . . be found to have committed prohibitive practices. . . .

The decision in *City of Milwaukee* is somewhat more realistic than the MERC opinion in *Michigan Nurses Association*. Nevertheless, the decision by WERC to consider the problem only in the context of an unfair labor practice proceeding, when a charge of unlawful domination or interference has been raised, is a questionable resolution of the problem. For one thing, as seen in the *Michigan Nurses Association* case, the burden of proof in a domination case may, as a practical matter, be insurmountable in the absence of some evidence of active participation of supervisors in local bargaining. For another thing, given the preexisting professional ties between numerous groups of supervisory and rank-and-file persons in the public sector, it is not at all clear that the issue of domination will be raised with any frequency pursuant to unfair labor practice proceedings in the public sector. Indeed, the full impact of having supervisors within the membership ranks of rank-and-file unions may never be fully recognized by those persons most affected and,

therefore, the more subtle forms of domination, which occur in connection with policy making and budget allocation, will never be challenged.

The problem in *Michigan Nurses Association* is obviously a by-product of the historical professional ties among all nurses, without regard to supervisory status. Before the advent of collective bargaining, when all nurses were joined together professionally in the MNA, conflict of interest was not a serious concern. When the MNA decided to go into the business of collective bargaining, however, the problems of conflict of interest and domination became real. The MERC cited numerous private sector cases to support its decision in *Michigan Nurses Association,* but the cases are not salient. The problem seen in the public sector (i.e., supervisors and rank-and-file persons joining the same organizations in large numbers before the advent of collective bargaining) was never a real problem in the private sector. Supervisors and managers at Ford and General Motors do not now and never have held positions of consequence in the national United Automobile Workers organization. Even when supervisors in the auto industry do retain UAW memberships, they do so as inactive members and they certainly do not influence the policies of the union from within.

The other side of the problem is seen in cases where supervisors, such as principals, are certified in separate units, but are represented by unions otherwise representing rank-and-file personnel. In *Hillsdale Community Schools*[65] a public employer argued that the Michigan Education Association should not be certified as the bargaining representative for a unit of principals because the MEA also represented teachers. The employer argued that "where both the principals' and teachers' organizations are MEA affiliates . . . there is a conflict of interest where principals are the first step in the grievance procedure." The MERC rejected this contention, observed that "principals act merely as conduits rather than decision makers," and ruled that the principals were entitled to select any preferred bargaining agent. If principals truly "act merely as conduits," then it is not clear why they should even be relegated to separate bargaining units. Actually, the notion that principals are insignificant cogs in the management chain of command is absurd and the assertion is plainly belied by earlier MERC opinions. For instance, in *Board of Education, City of Hazel Park*[66] the commission was obviously impressed with the supervisory responsibilities of principals, which included control over all building administration, direction of all personnel in a school building, assignment of teachers, preparation of evaluation reports on all teachers, and supervision of

---

[64] Wisc. Employment Rel. Comm. Dec. No. 690 (1964).

[65] 1966 MERC Lab. Op. 859, *aff'd,* 24 Mich. App. 36 (1970).

[66] 1966 MERC Lab. Op. 233.

assistant principals and department heads. On the basis of this evidence, MERC ruled that the employer unlawfully interfered with the administration of a rank-and-file teacher association by allowing principals to participate in the activities of the local organization.

The findings in the *Hazel Park* case severely diminish the rationale that is cited to justify MERC's opinion in *Hillsdale Community Schools.* It is simply inconsistent to view first-line supervisors as being significant agents of the employer in a case involving a claim of unlawful interference and then to label these same supervisors as insignificant "conduits" in a representation proceeding.

An alternative approach to this problem is followed in Connecticut, where the state board of labor relations has refused to certify organizations to represent rank-and-file personnel when it has found that supervisors are active members or officers of the petitioning union or association.[67] Supervisors, however, are expressly excluded from coverage under the Connecticut state statute regulating collective bargaining in the public sector.

Some General Observations

Although several public sector jurisdictions have attempted to deny bargaining rights to supervisory personnel, many have intentionally rejected the private sector model. Both the New York and Michigan boards have expressed the view that principals (and other first-level supervisors) "act merely as conduits rather than as decision makers" and, therefore, they should not be denied bargaining rights.[68] This view ignores the realities

of collective bargaining. The jurisdictions that have rejected the private sector rules dealing with bargaining rights for supervisors do not appear to do so because the private sector model is unsatisfactory; rather, it appears that the private sector treatment of the problem has been rejected because of the apparent force of the workers' claim for wider bargaining rights.

Before the advent of public sector collective bargaining, first-line supervisors did not play a significant role in the management of the affairs of the public employer; in addition, the interests of supervisors and employees were often joined by professional or associational ties. These two factors have seemingly given force to union claims for bargaining rights for supervisors. To promote this worker interest, as against the employer's need for a loyal cadre of supervisors, we have witnessed the development of law that creates the artificial distinction between supervisors and executives. The distinction is artificial, not in an economic or political sense, but in terms of the requirements of collective bargaining.

The fact that first-line supervisors may have been relatively insignificant in the management hierarchy in the public sector before the advent of collective bargaining surely is not a justification for granting them bargaining rights now. Collective bargaining in the public sector has commanded a modification of traditional employment structures and policies; thus, it may also command the alteration of the traditional role of supervisors. As was aptly noted by Justice William O. Douglas in his dissent in *Packard Motor Co.* v. *Labor Board*:[69]

> The employer category [includes] all those who [act] for management not only in formulating but also in executing its labor policies. Foremost among the latter were foremen. Trade union history shows that foremen were the arms and legs of management in executing labor policies. In industrial conflicts they were allied with management.

If the developing law in the public sector continues to accommodate union demands for bargaining rights for supervisors, management may well lose its "arms and legs" in executing labor policies. It is curious on this score that the private sector model has been *rejected* to allow for an *expansion* of union interests. The force of history and the apparent political strength of various professional groups seems to be responsible for the development of the law in this area. These developments are probably unfortunate because they ignore the realistic needs of public employers in the adversary process of collective bargaining.

THE DUTY TO BARGAIN

The Bargaining Process

In private sector labor relations, the duty to bargain is defined by Section 8(d) of the NLRA as

---

[67] Connecticut State Board of Labor Relations, *Twenty-first Annual Report* (1967) pp. 8-9. The difficulty in allowing supervisors to retain memberships in rank-and-file unions was recently highlighted in Elwood City Area School Dist. v. Sec'y of Educ., GERR no. 525, at B-2 (Comm. Ct. of Pa., 1973). There an assistant principal was fired by the school board because he elected to retain membership in a teacher organization. The board claimed that the assistant principal was a first-level supervisor and that his teacher association membership precluded him from acting as a representative for the employer in bargaining relationships. Section 1101.1801 of the Pennsylvania statute, however, expressly states that

> No . . . member of the same . . . organization as the employee organization with which the public employer is bargaining . . . shall participate on behalf of the public employer in the collective bargaining process. . . . Any person who violates . . . this section shall be immediately removed . . . from his role . . . in collective bargaining....

Thus, the court ruled that, while the assistant principal could be removed from bargaining, he could not be fired.

[68] Hillsdale Community Schools, 1968 MERC Labor Op. 859; Board of Education, Union Free School District No. 7 and Depew Teachers Organization, Inc., 1 PERB 4045. See also Metropolitan Transit Authority, 48 L.R.R.M. 1296 (Mass. Labor Relations Board, 1961).

[69] 330 U. S. 485, 496 (1947).

the mutual obligation of the employer and the representative of the employees to meet at reasonable times and confer in good faith with respect to wages, hours, and other terms and conditions of employment, . . .but such obligation does not compel either party to agree to a proposal or require the making of a concession. . . .

The obligation to negotiate in good faith has been interpreted by the courts as requiring a duty to participate actively in deliberations with a sincere desire and intention to reach an agreement. Normally, this requirement would encompass give and take on both sides until some agreement is reached, but there is no legal duty to agree. In essence, the requirement of good faith bargaining in the private sector is simply that both parties manifest a type of attitude and conduct conducive to reaching an agreement.

Statutes concerned with public sector bargaining may be divided into two categories: those providing for "collective negotiations" and the so-called meet-and-confer statutes. In states such as Michigan and New York that have adopted the collective negotiations approach, the statutory definition of the duty to bargain is often identical or very similar to that found in the NLRA. As a consequence, the process of bargaining in these two states, and in numerous other public sector jurisdictions, closely resembles the practices followed in the private sector. For example, public employers are required to supply relevant information to the employees' bargaining agent, even when the information sought is in the public domain.[70] In addition, although unions and public employers may reserve the right to ratify a negotiated settlement, either by employee vote or legislative action, the negotiating agents for each side must still have sufficient authority to bargain in good faith.[71] In a recent Florida circuit court decision, it was found that the city had failed to negotiate in good faith because

the City Manager's function was not to negotiate with the Union on behalf of the Union, but rather to induce the Union to compromise some of its demands in the belief that they were reaching an agreement and then present these compromises to the City Council where further concessions from the Union were to be demanded. The refusal of the City to show any confidence in the preliminary agreement reached by its City Manager (its appointed negotiator) and its attempt to renegotiate the entire agreement and gain further

concessions from the Union . . . is not good faith bargaining.[72]

It has also been held that the parties to the bargaining process retain full discretion to designate their bargaining agents, that unilateral employer action upon a matter that is the subject of collective bargaining constitutes a failure and refusal to bargain in good faith,[73] that it is impermissible for an employer to bypass or denigrate the union by dealing directly with bargaining unit employees,[74] and that employers and unions in the public sector may lawfully participate in private negotiations without violating state "sunshine" or right-to-know laws.[75] All of these policies, which have to do with the bargaining process, have been adopted from the existing private sector case law. Indeed, numerous decisions rendered in New York, Michigan, Wisconsin, and Connecticut have relied specifically on private sector precedent in these areas of concern.

There is one unique aspect to the process of public sector bargaining. Frequently, the employer's bargaining agent in the public sector does not possess absolute authority to make a labor agreement. The Michigan Employment Relations Commission has even suggested that public employers *cannot* delegate the authority to agree to a bargaining agent.[76] Problems of unlawful delegation aside, it is generally true that legislative ratification of proposed settlements is normally required in the public sector. In addition, it has also been held that a legislative body may lawfully reject a proposed settlement or refuse to appropriate the money necessary to implement a settlement reached by bargaining agents.[77] As a consequence, it is not unusual for employee bargaining agents first to bargain with the designated employer agent and then to engage in additional bargaining with the members of a legislative body to ensure ratification of a proposed settlement.[78] In recognition of the problems inherent in such a process, MERC ruled in *City of Saginaw*[79] that "the bargaining representative of a

[70] Saginaw Township Board of Education, 1970 MERC Lab. Op. 127.

[71] International Association of Firefighters v. City of Homestead, Case No. 72-9285 (Florida Circuit Court, 1973). See also Board of Trustees of the Ulster County Community College and the Ulster County Legislature, 4 PERB 3749 (1971).

[72] International Association of Firefighters v. City of Homestead, Case No. 72-9285 (Florida Circuit Court, 1973).

[73] Town of Stratford, Decision No. 1069 (Conn. State Bd. of Labor Relations, 1972).

[74] West Hartford Education Association v. DeCourcy, 162 Conn. 566, 295 A.2d 526 (Conn. Sup. Ct. 1972).

[75] Bassett v. Braddock, 262 So.2d 425 (Fla. 1972).

[76] City of Saginaw, 1969 MERC Lab. Op. 293.

[77] N.Y. Civ. Serv. Law § 204-a(1) (McKinney 1973); see also City of Detroit, 1971 MERC Lab. Op. 237.

[78] See, for example, Board of Trustees of the Ulster County Community College and the Ulster County Legislature, 4 PERB 3749 (1971); City of Saginaw, 1969 MERC Lab. Op. 293.

[79] 1969 MERC Lab. Op. 293.

governmental body is under an obligation to keep the governmental body advised as to the progress of negotiations.'' The MERC also ruled that if the governmental body persisted in rejecting a union proposal "on principle," then it could be compelled to appear at the negotiating table "to bargain on the subject." Later in *City of Detroit*,[80] however, the MERC held that

> It is not required that Municipal Councils, Commissions and Boards bargain directly with the representatives of their employees. This may be done by administrative employees or other agents who are clothed with authority to participate in effective collective bargaining but reserving final approval to the governing body. Such is common practice in the private sector, and it is effective and workable.

The Wisconsin State Employment Labor Relations Act provides an example of how the legislature may not only legitimate public sector contracts, but also participate more directly in the bargaining process. It requires that agreements, once approved by the unions involved, be approved by a joint legislative committee. The committee then introduces bills in both houses to implement those portions of the agreement, such as wage adjustments and fringe benefits, that require legislative approval. If the committee rejects the agreement or the legislature rejects the resultant bills, the agreement is sent back to the parties for renegotiation. Thus, the parties must remain aware of the attitudes of both the legislative committee and the legislature itself.

Probably the most significant distinction between the public and private sectors is the long-standing and universally followed prohibition against public employee strikes. In most states and in the federal service, there is a common-law or legislated proscription of the right to strike in the public sector. Only Alaska, Hawaii, Montana, Pennsylvania, and Vermont have enacted legislation giving public employees a limited right to strike.

Labor leaders, of course, have argued that the absence of the strike weapon in the public sector reduces collective bargaining to collective begging; yet, the validity of such a conclusion is, at best, speculative. There are enough data to suggest that, in the public sector, there may be a de facto right to strike, despite the legal strike bans in force. The threat or exercise of this de facto right to strike appears to be no less effective than the legal right enjoyed by employees in the private sector. Moreover, it is possible that statutory impasse procedures, such as arbitration, factfinding, and legislative hearings, may be a source of great bargaining leverage for public unions. For example, many municipal employers in Michigan have claimed that the state's compulsory arbitration act for policemen and firemen has produced arbitrated settlements far in excess of what might have been produced by traditional

collective bargaining.[81] There obviously is no sure way to test this hypothesis, but the claim at least raises the question of how much, if any, bargaining power unions actually lose by virtue of the strike ban in the public sector.

In short, the process of bargaining is probably essentially the same in many important respects in both the public and private sectors, except in connection with the strike proscription and the process of legislative ratification. Several public sector jurisdictions, however, have apparently attempted to modify the private sector collective negotiations bargaining model by adopting meet-and-confer statutes; therefore, these statutes require some mention.

"Meet-and-confer negotiations" has generally been defined as the

> process of negotiating terms and conditions of employment intended to emphasize the differences between public and private employment conditions. Negotiations under "meet and confer" laws usually imply discussions leading to unilateral adoption of policy by legislative body rather than written contract, and take place with multiple employee representatives rather than an exclusive bargaining agent.[82]

This definition fairly describes what was originally intended by the meet-and-confer standard of bargaining. Implicit in the *pure* meet-and-confer approach is the assumption that the private sector bargaining model would be overly permissive if applied without qualification to the public sector. In other words, it is argued that public employers should retain broad managerial discretion in the operation of a governmental agency, subject only to the recall of the electorate. Thus, under the pure meet-and-confer bargaining model, the outcome of any public employer-employee discussions will depend more on management's determinations than on bilateral decisions by "equals" at the bargaining table.

Missouri and California are the best examples of states which have adopted the pure meet-and-confer bargaining model. In *Missey* v. *City of Cabool*,[83] the Missouri Supreme Court ruled that the state statute does

> not purport to give to public employees the right of collective bargaining guaranteed . . . to employees in private industry. . . . The act does not constitute a delegation . . . to the union of the legislative power of the public body, and therefore . . . the prior discretion in the legislative body to adopt, modify or reject outright the results of the discussions is untouched. . . . The act provides only a procedure for communication between the organization selected by public employees and their employer without requiring adoption of any agreement reached.

80 1970 MERC Lab. Op. 953.

81 "Police, Fire Arbitration Opposed by Cities," *LMRS Newsletter* 3, no 11 (November 1972).

82 GERR Reference File 91:02-03 (1970).

83 441 S. W. 2d 35 (Mo. 1969).

The Pennsylvania statute adopts an interesting variation on the meet-and-confer model. The Pennsylvania law provides that certain subjects, subsumed under the heading of "wages, hours and other terms and conditions of employment," are mandatory items of "collective negotiations," over which public employees can strike after impasse procedures have been exhausted. The statute also provides that

> Public employees shall not be required to bargain over matters of inherent managerial policy, which shall include but shall not be limited to such areas of discretion or policy as the functions and programs of the public employer, standards of services, its overall budget, utilization of technology, the organizational structure and selection and direction of personnel. Public employers, however, shall be *required to meet and discuss* on policy matters affecting wages, hours and terms and conditions of employment as well as the impact thereon upon request by public employee representatives [emphasis added].

Under the Pennsylvania law, the duty to meet and discuss is defined so as to ensure that "decisions or determinations on matters so discussed shall remain with the public employer." In addition, it appears that bargaining disagreements over matters in the meet-and-discuss category may not be appealed pursuant to statutory impasse procedures and, further, that public employees may not strike over such nonmandatory subjects.

At first glance, the Pennsylvania scheme appears to resemble closely and to adopt the private sector model, which distinguishes between "mandatory" and "permissive" subjects of bargaining and forbids bargaining to a point of impasse over permissive subjects. In *State College Education Association* v. *PLRB*,[84] however, the commonwealth court makes it clear that there are significant differences between the private sector model and the existing law in Pennsylvania. In *State College,* the court made the somewhat astounding finding that: "Any item of wages, hours, and other conditions of employment, if affected by a policy determination, is not a bargainable item." The court then went on to rule that a public employer was required to "meet and discuss," but not to "negotiate," over union demands for timely notice of teacher assignments, desks and lockers for each teacher, a cafeteria for teachers, rest periods for teachers, maximum workload for teachers, holidays, maximum class size, and various requests concerning teacher work assignments. The court ruled, in effect, that even though these matters may have concerned wages, hours, and conditions of work, they also affected policy and, therefore, were not negotiable. Many of these same matters would clearly be found to be mandatory subjects of bargaining under the NLRA and, indeed, they have been found to be mandatory subjects for bargaining in numerous other public sector jurisdictions. Thus, the category of "permissive" subjects is substantially greater in Pennsylvania than in the private sector; and, as a result, the employees' right to strike is narrowed accordingly. Public sector unions in Pennsylvania may now seek to avoid the impact of this ruling by camouflaging their real proposals, a difficult undertaking, however, because, if the decision in *State College* is literally enforced, very few, if any, subjects will be found to be mandatory subjects for bargaining.

The Pennsylvania law is plainly an odd statutory creation. Actually, most states have rejected the pure meet-and-confer bargaining model. In practice, most states have adopted either a *modified* meet-and-confer statute, which gives unions more bargaining power than the pure model, or a *modified* collective negotiations statute, which is more restrictive from the union's viewpoint than its private sector counterpart. For this reason alone, it is often difficult to distinguish between the meet-and-confer and collective negotiations concepts in the public sector.

A good example of this problem is seen in Kansas, where the duty to meet and confer encompasses more than a mere exhortation to the public employer to "consider" employees' proposals; it is a joint obligation to "meet and confer in order. . . *to endeavor to reach agreement* on conditions of employment." The supreme court in Kansas recently defined the required duty to bargain under the Kansas teacher bargaining law and clearly put to rest the claim that the statutory reference to meet and confer required something less than collective negotiations. On this point, the Kansas court observed that the "professional negotiation" required by the statute

> means not only meeting and conferring but doing so "in a good faith effort by both parties *to reach agreement.*" We think this is where the Board's determination not to be bound runs afoul of the act. If a board were merely required to "meet and confer," there would be no need for the legislative mandates of good faith and a mutual effort to reach agreement. "Agreement," in particular, is hardly necessary if the Board is to be free to ignore what is agreed upon. . . .
> The feature of the act which we think militates most strongly against the rigidity of the Board's position is the statutory provision that agreements when ratified by *both parties* are "binding." This is in contrast to the unilateral "implementary action" to make a "memorandum of agreement" effective, as contemplated by the "meet and confer" definitions of the [report by the Advisory Commission on Intergovernmental Relations]. . . . In reaching this conclusion we recognize the differences between collective negotiations by public employees and collective bargaining as it is established in the private sector, in particular by the National Labor Relations Act. . . . We do not, however, believe those differences prevent our reaching the conclusion that a public employer may negotiate and be bound by its agreements relating to terms and conditions of employment.

84 GERR no. 510, E-1 (1973).

The curious mixture of statutory schemes used to define the duty to bargain in the public sector probably just reflects the initial reluctance of state legislatures to adopt the private sector bargaining model in total. Some of this legislative reticence, however, is beginning to mellow. Minnesota and Alaska recently shunned meet-and-confer language in newly adopted statutes, and the word "negotiate" was recently substituted for the word "confer" in the South Dakota statute. The *State College* decision in Pennsylvania is a noteworthy exception to this trend. Even in Pennsylvania, however, it is not clear yet that the *process* of bargaining is actually different with respect to mandatory (collective negotiation) as opposed to permissive (meet-and-discuss) subjects. The *State College* opinion probably reflects an unstated belief by the judiciary that the scope of mandatory bargaining should be narrowed so as to avoid adversary confrontations and strikes over important public policy issues. Unfortunately, the decision is grossly overdrawn in this respect.

The trend in state legislation away from the initial flirtation with meet and confer is not yet complete. Some state legislatures continue to cling to the notion that there ought to be *some* differences between the public and private sectors with respect to the nature of the duty to bargain. It is not clear, however, that legislative attempts to preserve the remnants of a limited bargaining model will have any practical effect on the behavior of the parties at the bargaining table.

The Scope of Bargaining

The issues concerning the *process* of collective bargaining in the public sector raise important and sometimes troublesome questions, especially in connection with questions having to do with the strike proscription, impasse procedures, and processes for legislative ratification. While these issues are not insignificant, more important are the questions related to the range of legally permissible subjects about which the parties may meet and confer or negotiate in the public sector. If, as suggested above, there is no real difference in the technique of bargaining in most meet-and-confer and most collective negotiations states (because the parties negotiate as "equals" only under the latter approach), we are still not told much about the effective scope of bargaining in the states that have opted for the collective negotiations approach. A state statutory requirement that the parties negotiate as "equals" will be insignificant if the statute also narrowly limits the scope of bargaining. To promise the government employee equality at the bargaining table while at the same time excluding most items relating to wages, hours, and working conditions from the mandatory subjects of bargaining would make collective bargaining for the public sector an illusory gain indeed.

In the private sector, the scope of bargaining is derived from the words "wages, hours, and other terms and conditions of employment" found in Section 8(d) of the NLRA. Subjects covered by this phrase are deemed to be mandatory, and the employer must bargain over them. Other matters are either permissive or illegal subjects of bargaining. Bargaining with respect to permissive subjects is discretionary for both parties, and neither is required to bargain in good faith to the point at which agreement or impasse is reached. The parties are not explicitly forbidden from discussing matters that are illegal subjects of bargaining, but a contract provision embodying an illegal subject is, of course, unenforceable.

In the private sector, the line between mandatory and permissive subjects of bargaining is drawn on an ad hoc basis as the NLRB and the courts subject the distinction to constant redefinition and refinement. In the public sector, more is attempted by statute, generally in the form of specific restrictions on the subject matter of bargaining. It is clear that in defining the scope of bargaining, many public sector jurisdictions have attempted to consider the impact of collective bargaining on the allocation of political power. As noted by Wellington and Winter, "the issue is how powerful unions will be in the typical municipal political process if a full transplant of collective bargaining is carried out."[85] This concern is expressly stated in the "declaration of policy" in the Kansas Public Employer-Employee Relations Act, as follows:

[T]here neither is, nor can be, an analogy of status between public employees and private employees, in fact or law, because of inherent differences in the employment relationship arising out of the unique fact that the public employer was established by and for the benefit of all the people and its authority derives not from contract nor the profit motive inherent in the principle of free enterprise, but from the constitution, statutes, civil service rules, regulations and resolutions; and. . . the difference between public and private employment is further reflected in the constraints that bar any abdication or bargaining away by public employers of their continuing legislative discretion....[86]

Given these expressed concerns, which have been recognized in one form or another in almost every public sector jurisdiction, it is interesting to observe the disparate attempts that have been made to "regulate" the scope of bargaining in the public sector. Indeed, several states appear to attempt to regulate the *scope* of bargaining by limiting the *process* of collective bargaining. For the sake of convenience, some of these various attempts to regulate the scope of bargaining may be listed under the following general headings:

1. Strike Proscription. Although the prohibition against public employee strikes does not directly limit the list of

---

[85] Wellington and Winter, *The Unions and the Cities*, pp. 29-30.

[86] Kansas Stat. Ann. §§ 75-4321 (4) and (5).

bargainable subjects, it does reject the private sector notion that "the use of economic pressure by parties to a labor dispute . . . is part and parcel of the process of collective bargaining."[87] This rejection may be significant if it is assumed that an employer is less likely to capitulate on an important substantive issue if the strike threat is removed.

2. Legislative Ratification. As with the strike proscription, the process of legislative ratification may also be an indirect means of limiting the scope of bargaining. For example, New York's Taylor Law requires that each negotiated contract must contain the following notice:[88]

> It is agreed by and between the parties that any provision of this agreement requiring legislative action to permit its implementation by admendment of law or by providing the additional funds therefor, shall not become effective until the appropriate legislative body has given approval.

This process of legislative ratification, or budget allocation, obviously may involve judgments on certain substantive items contained in a collective bargaining agreement. The legislative body may be prohibited from attempting to "renegotiate" an entirely new agreement; however, it is not prohibited from refusing to allocate the funds necessary to implement an agreement fully.[89] The net impact of these actions may be the same in some cases and the refusal to appropriate may effectively limit the scope of matters covered by the collective agreement.

3. Preexisting Legislation and Civil Service Laws. Some statutory provisions restrict the scope of bargaining by giving precedence to existing state law or municipal ordinance over a collective bargaining agreement. For example, the Pennsylvania law states that

> The parties to the collective bargaining process shall not effect or implement a provision in a collective bargaining agreement if the implementation of that provision would be in violation of, or inconsistent with, or in conflict with any statute or statutes enacted by the General Assembly of the Commonwealth of Pennsylvania or the provisions of municipal home rule charters.

4. Statutory Management-Rights Clauses. Several states have attempted to limit the scope of bargaining by stating, in general terms, that the public employer shall not be required to bargain with respect to the "mission of the agency" or matters of "inherent managerial policy."

5. Statutory Exclusions. Some statutes expressly exclude certain matters from the range of permissible subjects, while other statutes expressly list the matters that may be discussed. For example, the Kansas statute (covering public employees other than teachers) explicitly limits the scope of bargaining to salaries, wages, hours of work, vacations, sick and injury leave, holidays, retirement

and insurance benefits, wearing apparel, overtime pay, shift differential and jury duty pay, and grievance procedures.

6. Meet-and-Confer Bargaining. The pure meet-and-confer bargaining model implicitly limits the scope of bargaining because the employees' bargaining agent can do no more than make suggestions that the public employer is free to ignore. In other words, the scope of "bargaining" is no more or less than what the public employer chooses to make it.

These various methods that have been used to "regulate" the scope of bargaining plainly are not mutually exclusive. Many jurisdictions have adopted two or more of these approaches; this fact alone makes it clear that there has been no uniform adoption of the private sector model in the public sector. Even though these various attempts have been made to "regulate" the scope of bargaining in the public sector, in recognition of the differences between the public and private sectors, it is not clear that the scope of permissible bargaining has been more narrowly defined in the public sector. Indeed, it may be contended that in certain public sector jurisdictions the private sector model has been rejected in favor of a *wider* scope of bargaining.

The experience in Michigan furnishes a good example of this development. The Michigan statute, like the NLRA, defines the duty to bargain as "the mutual obligation [of the **parties**] to meet at reasonable times and confer in good faith with respect to wages, hours, and other terms and conditions of employment, or the negotiation of an agreement. . . and the execution of a written contract. ..." In *Westwood Community Schools*[90] MERC construed this language and apparently rejected the mandatory-permissive distinction used in the private sector. Rather, the commission observed that

> A balancing approach to bargaining may be more suited to the realities of the public sector than the dichotomized scheme — mandatory and non-mandatory — used in the private sector. [The private sector] scheme prohibits the use of economic weapons to compel agreement to discuss non-mandatory subjects of bargaining, but strikes are permissible once the point of impasse concerning mandatory subjects of bargaining is reached. Economic force is illegal in the public sector. ... In Michigan, in the public sector, economic battle is to be replaced by invocation of the impasse resolution procedures of mediation and fact finding.
>
> An expansion of the subjects about which the public employer ought to bargain, unlike the private sector, should not result in a corresponding increase in the use of economic force to resolve impasses. In the absence of legal public sector strikes, our only proper concern in the area of subjects of bargaining is whether the employer's management functions are being unduly restrained. All bargaining has some limiting effect on an employer.

[87] NLRB v. Insurance Agents, 361 U.S. 477 (1960).

[88] N.Y. Civ. Serv. Law §204-a(1) (McKinney 1973).

[89] See City of Detroit, 1971 MERC Lab. Op. 237.

[90] 7 MERC Lab. Op. 313 (1972).

Therefore, we will not order bargaining in those cases where the subjects are demonstrably within the core of entrepreneurial control. Although such subjects may affect interests of employees, we do not believe that such interests outweigh the right to manage.

MERC then went on to find that a school board was required to bargain over the school calendar. On this point, MERC concluded that "the rather substantial interest which the school teachers have in planning their summer activities outweigh any claim of interference with the right to manage the school district."

The Michigan commission's juxtaposition of the duty to bargain and the strike proscription implies that the scope of bargaining ought to be *broader* in the public sector than in the private sector. According to this interpretation, since public employees are ostensibly prevented from using the strike or the threat of a strike to gain leverage at the bargaining table, there is no point in severely restricting the subjects that may be brought up in negotiations. The public employer cannot be penalized by work stoppages for taking a hard-line bargaining position and it is not compelled to agree with any position taken by the employees' union on any subject. Therefore, if the strike proscription is in effect *and is enforced,* the agenda at the bargaining table should be open to virtually any subject.

The same rationale was used by the Connecticut Supreme Court in *West Hartford Education Association* v. *De Courcy*[91] where it was held that class size, teacher work loads, and the length of the school calendar were all mandatory subjects of bargaining. In reaching this result, the Connecticut court ruled that the disputed subjects were not at the "core of entrepreneurial control" (i.e., they were not "fundamental to the existence, direction and operation of the enterprise"); cited private sector precedent to the effect that "while not determinative, it is appropriate to look to industrial practices in appraising the propriety of including a particular subject within the scope of mandatory bargaining"; and suggested that the absence of the strike weapon favored a broad interpretation of the duty to bargain. It may be argued of course that the disputed subjects in *De Courcy* would be found to be mandatory subjects even under the NLRA; however, it is nevertheless noteworthy that the decisions in Michigan and Connecticut, and other jurisdictions as well, indicate that the scope of bargaining in the public sector is *at least* as wide as the duty to bargain in the private sector.

The *Westwood* decision is significant because it suggests that the scope of bargaining may include any subject that "is likely to lead to controversy and industrial conflict." It could be argued that such language may include a number of subjects not within the literal definition of "wages, hours, and terms and conditions of employment," at least as that term has been construed in the private sector. Therefore, the *Westwood* test may in fact foreshadow a

movement to free public sector bargaining from the confines of the traditional mandatory-permissive distinction followed in the private sector. The difficulty with the *Westwood* test, however, is that it relies not only on the existence, but also on the effectiveness of the strike proscription. In those states, such as Pennsylvania, where strikes are legal, the *Westwood* test would seem inapplicable. Indeed, it is interesting to note the contrasting opinion on the scope of mandatory bargaining rendered by the Commonwealth Court of Pennsylvania in the *State College* decision. In those states where strikes are illegal but the proscription is not enforced the application of the *Westwood* test would seem to give public unions an unfair advantage at the negotiating table, perhaps enabling them to coerce agreement on subjects that in the private sector might not be mandatory subjects of bargaining. The recent six-week teacher strike in Detroit highlights this problem.

The Michigan situation is further complicated by the fact that public employers are not relieved from the duty to bargain even when faced with an unlawful work stoppage. In *Saginaw Township Board of Education*[92] MERC cited the Supreme Court's decision in *NLRB* v. *Insurance Agents International Union*[93] and ruled that an employer was lawfully bound to continue bargaining with a union even while the employees were engaged in prohibited strike action. The reliance on private sector precedent in *Saginaw* was plainly misplaced. In *Insurance Agents*, the Supreme Court ruled that there was no inconsistency between the application of economic pressure and good faith collective bargaining under the NLRA; consequently, the Court ruled that even when employees engaged in certain economic action that might be viewed as "unprotected," the employer's duty to bargain was not altered. The same rationale simply is not applicable to the public sector. Most public sector jurisdictions forbid strike action; thus, the strike proscription reflects a policy determination that concerted economic action taken by public employees against employers is inconsistent with the duty to bargain as defined in the public sector. Most public sector jurisdictions are not neutral on the strike issue; rather, the economic strike is positively and explicitly forbidden. In this context, it is truly naive to assume that the duty to bargain and the right to strike may be treated as independent problems. Strike action is taken to bring pressure to bear on the bargaining agents who are negotiating at the bargaining table. Such economic pressure is expressly tolerated in the context of private sector bargaining. So long as the strike is banned in the public sector, however, it is not clear why an employer should be required to continue negotiating (and submit to

_____
91 162 Conn. 566 (1972).

_____
92 1970 MERC Lab. Op. 127.
93 361 U. S. 477 (1969).

proscribed pressures) in the face of unlawful economic action by the union. The Wisconsin Commission recognized this problem in *City of Milwaukee*[94] when it was held that "We do not believe that labor organizations... engaging in a strike, should at the same time be entitled to the benefits of fact finding or other rights granted to them by statute." The commission then went on to hold that it would "decline to process any fact finding petition filed by a labor organization which is engaged in a strike."

The New York approach with respect to the scope of the duty to bargain varies somewhat from that in Michigan. The decisions rendered by the New York PERB clearly reject any expanded interpretation of the scope of bargaining comparable to that suggested in *Westwood*. The New York PERB, however, does appear to adhere closely to private sector precedent in defining the scope of mandatory bargaining. In *City of New Rochelle*[95] PERB upheld the right of a school board to make budget cuts resulting in the termination of the services of teachers. PERB noted that such budget cuts "obviously" affect terms and conditions of employment, but concluded that "the decision to curtail services and eliminate jobs is not a mandatory subject of negotiations, although the employer is obligated to negotiate on the impact of such decision on the terms and conditions of employment of the employees affected." The board was evidently relying on the Supreme Court's decision in *Fibreboard Paper Products Corp.* v. *NLRB.*[96]

Later, in *West Irondequoit Bd. of Education*[97] PERB ruled that class size was not a mandatory subject of bargaining. In reaching this decision, PERB made it clear that teachers' traditional interest in matters affecting educational policy, was not an adequate justification for expanding the scope of bargaining beyond that in the private sector. In particular, PERB ruled that

> The determination as to the manner and means by which education service be rendered and the extent of such service is the duty and obligation of the public employer. A public employer should not be required to delegate this responsibility.

It is interesting, however, that the same New York PERB, in *City of White Plains*,[98] ruled that a "demand that a minimum number of Fire Fighters be on duty at all times with each engine and each truck constitute[d] a mandatory subject of negotiations." The decision in *West Irondequoit* was distinguished on the ground that "the teachers' interest was limited to workload, [whereas] the interests of the Fire Fighters . . . also involved safety."

It is not really surprising to see that states like New York, Michigan, and Connecticut have followed private sector precepts in defining the scope of the duty to bargaining. Each of these states has adopted statutory language very similar to that found in the NLRA. Thus, it really may be more interesting to observe the developments in some of the public sector jurisdictions that have enacted statutory provisions at variance with the private sector model.

A good example of such a jurisdiction is Kansas. The Professional Negotiations Act of 1970, which provides for bargaining rights for teachers, defines the scope of the duty to bargain as "meeting, conferring, consulting and discussing in a good faith effort by both parties to reach agreement with respect to the *terms and conditions of professional service.*" The Supreme Court of Kansas recently ruled that this language required school boards to bargain about more than just salaries, work load, and fringe benefits.[99] In particular, the court also ruled that the statutory reference to "conditions of professional service" included subjects such as probationary period, transfers, teacher appraisals, disciplinary procedures, and resignations. The Kansas court specifically cited the Connecticut Supreme Court decision in *West Hartford Education Association* v. *De Courcy*[100] as a useful precedent; however, it declined to follow the Connecticut court's conclusion that class size was a mandatory subject of bargaining.

In defining the scope of bargaining, the Kansas court came close to adopting the impact test frequently followed in the private sector. On this score, the court observed that

> It does little good . . . to speak of negotiability in terms of "policy" versus something which is not "policy." Salaries are a matter of policy, and so are vacation and sick leaves. Yet we cannot doubt the authority of the Board to negotiate and bind itself on these questions. The key, as we see it, is how direct the impact of an issue is on the well-being of the individual teacher as opposed to its effect on the operation of the school system as a whole. . . . The similar **phraseology of the N.L.R.A.** has had a similar history of judicial definition. See *Fibreboard Corp.* v. *Labor Board*, 379 U.S. 203, and especially the concurring opinion of Stewart, J.

The court then went on to hold that matters such as class size, curriculum and materials, payroll mechanics, certification, use of paraprofessionals, and duties of substitute teachers were not mandatory subjects.

As an aside, it is interesting to note that the scope of the duty to bargain under the Kansas Public Employer-Employee Relations Act is much more narrowly

94 Dec. no. 6575 B (1963).

95 4 PERB 3704 (1971).

96 379 U. S. 203 (1964).

97 4 PERB 3725 (1971), *aff'd on rehearing*, 4 PERB 3753 (1971).

98 5 PERB, Para. 3008 (1972).

99 National Education Association of Shawnee Mission, Inc. v. Board of Education of Shawnee Mission Unified School District, GERR no. 521, at E-1 (1973).

100 162 Conn. 566 (1972).

defined and explicitly limited to discussions over salaries, hours of work, vacations, sick leave, holidays, retirement, insurance, wearing apparel, overtime pay, shift premium, jury duty pay, and grievance procedures.[101] Obviously, the Kansas legislature gave favored treatment to teachers in recognition of their traditional interest in matters affecting educational policy.

The Governor's Executive Order in Illinois is another example of public sector bargaining scheme that rejects the private sector model. Although the order requires negotiations in "good faith with respect to wages, hours and other terms and conditions of employment," it further provides that the state is not required to negotiate on the merit principle, agency policies, programs and statutory functions, budget matters, decisions on standards, scope and delivery of service, use of technology, the state retirement system, and anything required or prohibited by law. It might be assumed that this sweeping reservation of management rights might restrict the scope of bargaining; but the Federal Labor Relations Council, which is charged with the enforcement of Executive Order 11491 (regulating bargaining in the federal service), has construed a similar management rights provision very narrowly. In *Department of the Army Corps of Engineers*[102] the council ruled that even though federal agency officials retained the exclusive right to act "to maintain the efficiency of the Government operations," pursuant to the management rights provision in Section 12(b) of Executive Order 11491, the obligation to bargain over "matters affecting working conditions" was not narrowly reduced. The agency had refused to discuss a union proposal designed to curtail the use of swing shifts, contending that swing-shift scheduling minimized overtime and other premium costs to the employer and that, therefore, the union's proposal would impair the agency's ability to maintain efficiency and economy. The FLRC properly recognized that if the management rights provision was construed literally it would effectively nullify the duty to bargain. In rejecting the employer's argument on this point, the FLRC ruled that the Executive Order required:

> Consideration and balancing of all the factors involved, including the well-being of employees, rather than an arbitrary determination based only on the anticipation of increased cost. Other factors such as the potential for improved performance, increased productivity, responsiveness to directions, reduced turnover, fewer grievances, contribution of money-saving ideas, improved health and safety, and the like, are valid considerations. . . . The [management rights section] may not properly be invoked to deny negotiations unless there is a substantial demonstration by the agency that increased costs or reduced effectiveness in operations are inescapable and significant and are not offset by compensating benefits.

A similar ruling was handed down in *United States Merchant Marine Academy*[103] where the FLRC ruled that "an agency may [not] unilaterally limit the scope of its bargaining obligation on otherwise negotiable matters . . . merely by issuing regulations from higher levels." If these federal precedents are followed in Illinois, then the scope of bargaining will probably be defined as widely as is permitted in the private sector, notwithstanding the management rights provision.

Based on the evidence to date, it is not at all clear that a statutory management rights clause effectively narrows the scope of bargaining. The Nevada Local Government Employee Relations Act[104] sets forth an elaborate management rights provision that seems to remove numerous subjects from the scope of bargaining, but the Nevada Local Government Employee-Management Relations Board in *Washoe County School District*[105] ruled that proposals concerning class size, student discipline, school calendar, and teacher work load were negotiable matters. The board stated in this regard that

> Although it has been urged upon this Board . . . that the provisions of [the management rights section] limit the areas of negotiability on matters relating to wages, hours, and conditions of employment if said matters also involve any items [listed in the management rights section], the Board rejects this view as untenable. It is presumed the Legislature in enacting [the law] did not enact a nullity. . . . It is the opinion of the Board, therefore, that any matter significantly related to wages, hours, and working conditions is negotiable, whether or not said matters also relate to questions of management prerogative.

This decision directly conflicts with the decision of the Commonwealth Court of Pennsylvania in the *State College* opinion. Indeed, it appears that the Pennsylvania view concerning the weight to be given statutory management rights clauses is a distinctly minority position. Both the Hawaii Public Employment Relations Board and the Los Angeles County Employee Relations Commission[106] have also defined the scope of bargaining widely, following the same rationale as used in *Washoe County*, notwithstanding the presence of statutory management rights clauses.

Another question that has frequently arisen in the public sector is whether the scope of negotiations should be narrowed pursuant to existing state statutes or municipal ordinances. This subject has been masterfully

101 Kansas Stat. Ann. §§ 75-4322 (s).

102 FLRC no. 71A-36 (1972).

103 FLRC no. 71A-15 (1972).

104 Nevada Rev. Stat. §288.150 (1).

105 Item no. 3 (1971).

106 Hawaii State Teachers Association, GERR no. 480, at E-1 (1972); Los Angeles County Employees Ass'n, Local 600 v. County of Los Angeles, 71 LC Para. 53,129 (Calif. Ct. of App., 1973).

treated in an article by Hanslowe and Oberer,[107] who framed the question as follows:

> The general problem . . . is the relationship of the Taylor Law . . . to other laws of the State of New York and to the agencies which administer them, with regard to the determination of the scope of negotiations under the Taylor Law. . . . A question within the foregoing question is: What impact, if any, does the Taylor Law have on the pre-existing authority of public employers to determine "terms and conditions of employment" of their employees? In other words, is the scope of negotiations under the Taylor Law coterminous with or greater than the scope of the unilateral power held by the particular public employer under pre-existing law....?

Several public sector jurisdictions have resolved this issue by giving precedence to existing state law that conflicts with the duty to bargain. For example, the Massachusetts municipal employee bargaining statute provides: "In the event that any part or provision of any such agreement is in conflict with any law, ordinance, or by-law, such law, ordinance, or by-law shall prevail so long as such conflict remains. . . ."[108] Where the matter is not clearly resolved by statute, the duty to bargain has been seen to prevail in at least two important decisions handed down in Michigan and New York. In Michigan, where the public employee bargaining statute makes no mention of precedence, the state supreme court has ruled that those provisions of local civil service laws covering mandatory subjects of bargaining are superseded *pro tanto* by the Michigan Public Employees Relations Act.[109] In 1972 the New York court of appeals, in a landmark decision, *Board of Education* v. *Associated Teachers of Huntington*,[110] ruled that, in light of the Taylor Act, a school board had authority to enter into a collective bargaining agreement granting benefits to teachers, even though there was no *specific* statutory authorization to do so. In reaching this result, the court stated that

> . . . under the Taylor Law, the obligation to bargain as to all terms and conditions of employment is a broad and unqualified one, and there is no reason why the mandatory provision of that act should be limited, in any way, except in cases where some other applicable statutory provision *explicitly and definitely* prohibits the public employer from making an agreement as to a particular term or condition of employment.

It is certainly likely that these rulings will influence other states where the statutes do not contain a rule of precedence.

Thus, it may be concluded that, even though the scope of the duty to bargain has been defined differently in many public sector jurisdictions, private sector principles have nevertheless been widely recognized and adopted. It is significant to note that private sector precepts have also had a significant impact on the developing law in connection with the duration and enforcement of the duty to bargain.[111]

Some General Observations

The trend in public sector labor relations toward the private sector model suggests the need for criteria to identify situations in which private sector principles must legitimately be modified before they are applied to the public sector. There are two primary distinctions between the two sectors: the strike proscription and the nature of the political process, including budgetary considerations. The strike proscription arguably (although not necessarily) denies to government employees a powerful economic weapon available to other employees. To compensate for the loss of this weapon, some tribunals have made adjustments in duty-to-bargain requirements, including extending the duration of the duty to include the impasse procedures that function in part as strike substitutes. Additionally, the absence of the strike weapon may entitle employees to the maintenance of the status quo while a new contract is being negotiated. Another adjustment may come about if the *Westwood Community Schools* tests, or at least the rationale for these tests, are adopted generally in place of the mandatory or permissive distinction used in the private sector. So long as state legislatures believe that strikes in the public sector ought to be proscribed there may in fact be no reason to adhere strictly to the mandatory or permissive distinction. The real issue in the public sector concerns the appropriateness of the subjects for bargaining and not disruptions of industrial peace caused by refusals to bargain, a key rationale for the strict lines between mandatory and permissive subjects in the private sector. If strikes are legalized, however, the mandatory or permissive distinction would appear to be applicable to the public sector.

The difficulty with widening the scope of bargaining in the public sector, in consideration of the strike proscription, is that there still appears to be an unabated de facto right to strike in the public sector. Public employees have continued to strike despite strike bans and this fact poses some serious policy issues regarding the appropriate standard for the scope of the duty to bargain.

[107] Kurt Hanslowe and Walter Oberer, "Determining the Scope of Negotiations Under Public Employment Relations Statutes, *Industrial and Labor Relations Review* 24 (1971):432.

[108] Mass. Ann. Laws chap. 149, §1781 (Supp. 1972).

[109] Civil Serv. Commn. v. Wayne County Bd. of Supervisors, 384 Mich. 363, 184 N.W.2d 201 (1971).

[110] 30 N.Y.2d 122, 282 N.E.2d 109, 331 N.Y.S.2d 17 (1972).

[111] See, generally, Harry Edwards, "The Emerging Duty to Bargain in the Public Sector," *Michigan Law Review* 71 (1973):885.

The following scenario, recently played out in connection with the six-week teacher strike in Detroit, aptly highlights the problem.

After many weeks of futile bargaining during the 1973 teacher negotiations in Detroit, the employees struck and blocked the scheduled opening of all public schools in the city. Under Michigan law, the school board was required to continue bargaining even in the face of the strike. Several weeks passed before a court injunction was finally issued to halt the admittedly unlawful strike. Even after the injunction was issued, however, the teachers refused to return to work until a settlement had been reached. The trial judge awarded damages and fined the union for contempt, but the teachers, not surprisingly, persisted in their refusal to return to work until negotiations had been concluded. After the strike was more than five weeks old, it became clear that there were three issues blocking settlement: salaries, a teacher demand for maximum class sizes, and a school board demand, referred to as "teacher accountability," to revise the system of teacher evaluations. As public pressure to end the strike mounted, the parties finally agreed to the following reported settlement: the issues of salaries and class size were submitted to binding arbitration for impartial resolution, the school board waived its claims for damages resulting from the unlawful strike, and the school board withdrew its proposal on teacher accountability.

The results of the Detroit strike are indeed anomalous. First, it may be observed that, although the strike was unlawful from its inception and subsequently enjoined by court order, there was no effective sanction to block the proscribed activity. The teachers ignored the injunction; the board agreed to withdraw its claim for damages, and the union plainly was not threatened by fines imposed for contempt. Second, under the terms of the final settlement the parties agreed to have an impartial arbitrator decide

the issues of salaries and class size. There were, however, no statutory criteria in Michigan to govern the contemplated arbitration proceeding. Third, the impartial arbitrator was allowed to decide an issue, class size, that might not have been considered to be a mandatory subject of bargaining in the first place if public sector strikes had been legalized and if the NLRA mandatory or permissive test was employed to define the scope of bargaining. Thus, the teachers arguably gained more by virtue of a de facto right to strike than they might have gained with the traditional private sector bargaining model and a lawful right to strike. If nothing else, the Michigan situation certainly indicates that public sector jurisdictions cannot afford to be ambivalent about the strike proscription.

CONCLUSION

It is difficult to generalize from the data at hand, but it probably is fair to conclude that, at least in those states which have adopted a comprehensive statutory scheme to regulate public employee bargaining, the employee (union) interest has thus far fared well in the process of reconciliation in the public sector. It may be that the long history of strong opposition to public sector unionism is now perceived to be unfair and unwarranted by legislators, judges, and other public officials. It also may be that state officials are reacting against the possibility of federal legislation which might control all collective bargaining in the public sector. Whether prompted by a sense of guilt or a practical political problem, however, it would certainly appear that many legislators, judges, and other public officials have been willing to be *relatively* generous in establishing and enforcing bargaining rights for public employees. In any event, it surely may be seen that a number of significant public employee interests have survived well, both because of and without regard to prevailing private sector principles.

CHAPTER IV

Industrial Relations under Continuous Strain:
British Railways since Nationalization

by George H. Hildebrand, *Maxwell M. Upson Professor of Economics and Industrial Relations,* Cornell University

This paper constitutes a brief and provisional account of industrial relations on British Railways during twenty-five years of nationalization. Where relevant, it also considers larger aspects of railway policy because of their decisive bearing upon the character of labor-management relations and the morale of railway personnel.

AN OVERALL VIEW OF THE PERIOD OF NATIONALIZATION, 1948-1973

With the failure of the giant Penn Central system in June 1970, the United States began to confront a railroad problem unlike any that it had encountered throughout the entire history of this industry. In essence, the basic question now is, Can the six bankrupt northeastern companies be restored as self-sustaining, private profit-making, and tax-paying enterprises? Even if the government accorded full freedom to reduce routes, branches, and services, would it be possible successfully to undertake a classical income-based reorganization, in which the creditors take over and manage the property? Or do we now confront a fundamentally different kind of railroad problem, for which no amount of surgery, slimming down, or infusion of new managerial talent is likely to yield a solvent commercial undertaking? And if we do face a novel situation, how should the nation address itself to it: turn some 26,791 route miles (54,701 track miles) over to the junkman; let government take over the system intact, with all its employees, pouring in the funds needed to preserve and renew it; or attempt with government aid to merge the properties into a single company, cut drastically to a central core in hopes of finding profitability? Or should we search for other means of preserving some service, with less dependence upon public funds?

This paper is concerned, not with these issues of national policy, but rather with the way in which similar questions have been approached in the United Kingdom over the past quarter century. For it has to be said at the outset that, since the nationalization statute of 1947, British Railways and its managers and employees have had to wrestle with all of the major issues now emerging in the American Northeast: renewal of the traditional system without basic change, modernization and rationalization in search of what the British call the "commercially viable railway," or, as the question is currently put, a shift to a "socially necessary railway" whose extent and character are to be determined on grounds of social costs and benefits, rather than purely commercial profitability.

In 1948, the British Transport Executive took over control of the four main private systems that had been put together from some 125 older companies by parliamentary fiat between 1921 and 1923; the four were the Southern, the Great Western, the London and North Eastern, and the London, Midland and Scottish. The result was a composite system of almost exactly 20,000 route miles with over 600,000 employees. For the first few years, the Railway Executive as a component of BTE, concentrated its efforts upon restoration of plant and equipment that had been badly run down during the war. Little was done to the extent of the system, the structure of its services, or the physical character of its rolling stock and motive power.[1] With the fifties, truck competition began to make serious inroads into rail freight. Faced with a lengthening string of growing annual deficits, BR management decided that a massive infusion of new capital was required. This decision led to the Modernization Plan of 1956, which called for a cumulative investment of £1,400 million (about $4 billion at the time). Perhaps Joy's harsh criticism, that the basic error of the plan was a decision "to rebuild the existing railway," is an exaggeration.[2] After all, a major program for conversion to diesel power was begun in 1955. In the

---

[1] A stern critic of British Rail, Dr. Stewart Joy, says that during the 1948 to 1951 period BR bought twelve types of steam power, while doing nothing serious about diesels until the mid-fifties. Stewart Joy, *The Train That Ran Away: A Business History of British Railways, 1948-1968* (London: Ian Allan, 1973), pp. 37-38.

[2] *Ibid.,* p. 44. For more temperate accounts, see A. W. J. Thomson and L. C. Hunter, *The Nationalized Transport Industries* (London: Heinemann, 1973), pp. 124-213; and Richard Pryke, *Public Enterprise in Practice* (New York: St. Martin's Press, 1971), pp. 233-55.

main, however, investment policy did emphasize renewal of the existing system, rather than a searching scrutiny of all activities. In any event, the policy did not produce overall profitability.

By 1960, growing parliamentary disquiet with the perennial deficit led to investigation by the Select Committee on Nationalized Industries. At about the same time, the minister of transport sought the help of an advisory group headed by Sir Ivan Stedeford regarding what to "do" about the railways. Among its members was Dr. Richard Beeching, later Lord Beeching, then technical director of Imperial Chemical Industries.[3] Eventually, the Macmillan government brought forth a white paper announcing its intention to replace the BTE with a system of separate boards, one of which, British Railways Board, was to take over "the running of the railways as a single entity." With the Transport Act of 1962, the board came into being, with Dr. Beeching as its first chairman. So began the "Beeching period" on BR. In the same measure, various nonrail operations were "hived off" from the system.

Early in 1963, the Beeching Report finally appeared. Its goal was to attack the deficit by an attack upon its supposed sources. Thus profitability was made the official goal for BR. Local passenger[4] and way freight trains were to be sharply curtailed; "horse and cart" freight stations were to be closed; weak branches and rural lines were to be cut out; "single-wagon" and less-than-carload traffic was to be largely given up; steam power was to be phased out; rolling stock was to be largely reduced; and a number of main workshops were to be closed.[5] On the positive side, the plan called for concentration upon "liner services" (container) traffic, long-distance "unit" (through-block) freight services, fast "intercity" passenger trains, and full conversion to diesel or electric power.

Despite these drastic measures of rationalization, BR still was unable to pay its way or even to reduce its level of deficits. In fact, the Treasury had to continue to make cash advances simply to cover operating losses. In short, Beeching, who left BR in 1965 but bequeathed it the Reshaping Plan, had failed in his search for a commercially viable railway by means of retrenchment and rationalization.

Through the Transport Act of 1968, the Labor government attacked the railway problem in a somewhat different way, although, somewhat surprisingly, the goal of a self-sustaining public enterprise was retained. Freight services were to be made either commercially profitable or to be given up. Likewise, the intercity passenger services

were expected to pay their own way. In addition, a special class of "grant-aid" passenger services was created, embracing commuter services in the great conurbations, and passenger trains on certain secondary routes and branch lines. The basic idea was that if national or local government deemed passenger service to be "socially necessary," then it had the duty to make up any attendant losses, including avoidable long-run costs. In these ways, then, BR gained full freedom to design and manage a commercial freight and passenger service,[6] together with purportedly full reimbursement for losses imposed under required grant-aid operations. More than this, a massive write-off of BR debts was authorized. But, curiously enough, no significant new investment funds were provided, perhaps on the assumption that newly adjusted cash flow would meet this need. This, however, was not to be the case. In consequence, the deficit problem was still really not resolved.[7]

Although the period of physical retrenchment had ended with Beeching, to leave in being a stronger but greatly reduced system of 11,500 miles, the period of 1969-1973 saw no lasting relief from the deficit problem. In result, BR remained dependent upon Treasury assistance.[8] There was a vicious circle in all this: because the railways were continuing to lose money, they could not obtain enough investment funds to attempt any major breakthroughs in technology and operations. And because they thereby acquired the obloquy of a problem industry, a stodgy and chronic consumer of red ink, they were denied the fresh capital essential to a new start toward a better future. The irony in this has been that at this very time the track, vehicle, and signalling research developing at the Railway Technical Center in Derby was already promising substantial payoffs in speed and efficiency.

To put matters another way, continuing deficits have led to an official negativism within the Conservative government, a suspicion that probably BR could never be made to pay,[9] which has led in turn directly to the notion

---

[3] Michael R. Bonavia, *The Organisation of British Railways* (London: Ian Allan, 1971), p. 79.

[4] Local passenger trains are called "stopping trains" in England.

[5] Pryke, *Public Enterprise in Practice,* pp. 249-50.

[6] Common carriage obligations on freight had already been abolished in 1952.

[7] The 1968 act is discussed in Bonavia, *The Organisation of British Railways,* pp. 128-32.

[8] From 1969 to 1972, BR earned a declining operating profit including depreciation and amortization, but before interest. Beginning with 1971, recourse was made to external sources for loans and special grants, £59 million in 1971, and £38.7 million in 1972. In short, internal sources of capital were proving insufficient. British Railways Board, *Report and Accounts 1972,* p. 62.

[9] Railroads everywhere suffer from a peculiar bias in popular opinion, that they must pay for themselves and accordingly survive or perish by the dictates of profit-and-loss accounting. No one ever has applied such rigorous commerical logic to highway and air transport, much of which also has

that perhaps the best course for Britain would be either to do away with rail transport altogether, except possibly the commuter lines, or to cut the system back to between 3,000 and 5,000 miles, paving over the rest for trucks and motor cars.[10]

In June 1972, this defeatism found expression in a "remit" from the Conservative minister of transport, Mr. John Peyton, to British Railways Board, asking the board to respond to three key questions:

1. What implications could be drawn from the "failure" of earlier railway legislation and policies?
2. Is a commercially "viable" or self-sustaining railway attainable by appropriate changes in network and services?
3. What sort of railway system is socially "necessary" irrespective of profitability, in the view of the board?[11]

The short answer provided by the board to each of these fundamental questions was that:

1. Although the act of 1968 "was a notable step forward," inflation, industrial unrest, and a stop-and-go economy made it impossible for BR to become self-sustaining, making essential flexible external sources of financial support.
2. In "conventional commercial terms there is no viable railway network and . . . any significantly smaller network would require greater financial support than the present-day railway."
3. What constitutes a "necessary railway" depends directly upon what is determined to be "necessary national transport policy." At bottom, this is a political decision that must rest upon "social and environmental factors as well as economic. . ."[12]

These matters are now prominent in national debate. With emerging concern for newly recognized problems such as congestion, pollution, land use, preservation of landscapes, and oil shortages, there has occurred a dramatic shift in public opinion in favor of the railways. Already it is apparent that no drastic official mutilation of the system is likely. On the contrary, the Channel Tunnel

now seems likely at last and opens up entirely new possibilities for rail passenger and freight services. More than this, the Tunnel has become the symbol to those who hope for a switch to a new and brighter future, after half a century of demoralizing retrenchments. At the same time, furthermore, actions by both the late Heath government and the new (March 1974) Wilson government make it clear that the present system will be kept intact. More important, funds for long-term modernization now seem assured, more or less on the scale the board has recently proposed (about £ 198.5 million yearly from 1973 to 1981).

SOME IMPLICATIONS OF THE PERIOD FOR INDUSTRIAL RELATIONS

The history of British Railways over the past twenty-five years may be broken up into four stages. In the first, 1948 to 1954, policy centered upon renewal of plant and equipment, on the assumption that no basic changes were needed in markets and technology. In consequence, the job structure and the employment roster remained quite stable. The second stage, 1955 to 1962, encompassed the beginning of conversion to diesel traction in earnest, and freight and passenger traffic started moving to the roads in substantial amount during this period. With 1956 an extensive modernization plan was undertaken, but it was conceived more in terms of the status quo than of major change. Job structure began to be modified with "single manning" on diesels, but otherwise remained static. Employment dropped continuously and substantially, but more through withdrawal of train services and reduced traffic, especially in coal, than from changes in technology and improvements of efficiency.

The third stage, 1963-1968, was the period of Beeching, which ended in the pathbreaking Transport Act of 1968. It was marked by elimination of steam power, virtual withdrawal from local and single-wagon freight business, closures of local stations and depots, concentration upon longer-distance container and unit trains, introduction of the intercity passenger services, elimination of many workshops, and abandonment of over 4,000 route miles of line. Job structure and skill requirements underwent drastic change, while employment fell sharply and continuously. Clearly, this was the period in which a new railway was taking shape.

With the fourth stage, 1969 to 1973, the search for profitability shared the stage with continuing rationalization of methods, on the trains, in the office, at the stations, and in the shops. Job structure continued to change, while employment fell still further.

What are the principal factors in the social-economic environment for industrial relations on the railways over this period?

The first factor has to be BR's perennial shortage of cash because of its continuing inability to make its way as

never "paid" in the railroad sense. The reasons for this double standard are fascinating, but cannot be considered at this point.

[10] Late in 1972, *The Economist,* long an uncompromising adversary of the railways, looked with favor upon proposals to convert rail lines to road or to busways. It considers the "social and environmental value" of railways to be "grossly" overestimated. *The Economist,* October 14, 1972, p. 106; December 16, 1972, pp. 95-96; and December 23, 1972, p. 62.

[11] British Railways Board, *Review of Railway Policy: Summary of Report to the Government* (June 1973), *passim.*

[12] Richard Marsh, presently chairman of British Railways Board (since 1970), was minister of transport when the act of 1968 became law. His change of view regarding commercial profitability is therefore highly significant.

a profitable public enterprise. Two results have flowed from this: a dependence upon the government in all decisive matters, and what one BR executive aptly described as "a permanent posture of declinature" so far as fundamental initiatives were concerned, whether the issue be badly needed increases in pay or introduction of a large-scale program for high-speed passenger trains. In truth, although BR was intended to be an independent and in basic respects an autonomous public corporation, the fact that it has been perpetually hard up for cash has converted it to an intermediary institution lying between the cabinet on the one side and the unions and the public on the other. Politics, more than market forces, accordingly have dominated its labor relations. Further, financial assistance has been both sporadic and erratic, whether for capital investments or to pay for improved wages and working conditions. It is not easy to develop and to adhere to long-run policies when their fulfillment depends ultimately upon external sources of finance.

A second factor in the environment of BR labor relations has been inflation throughout the period. BR has hardly been a beneficiary here. It has not been easy to adjust rates and fares to higher costs, both because of periodic episodes of direct price control and because of high price elasticities of demand for virtually all types of freight and passenger services. In turn, 63 percent of costs are for labor, which means severe vulnerability to wage inflation as against other industries.

Third, BR's postwar profile has been that of a cyclical industry in secular decline — no doubt one of the worst conceivable settings in which to conduct labor relations. Railroads, of course, have always been cyclical industries, at least until the business cycle supposedly had been abolished. But recessions and erratic movements associated with stop-go credit policies have remained. Given the traditional sluggishness of their costs, the railways have suffered severely with each downswing in gross revenues.

Then there is the secular side: the contraction both of a network and of a panoply of services that even as late as 1948 still retained many Victorian characteristics: horse-and-cart spacing of often tiny freight depots, horse-and-carriage-oriented passenger stations, high density of light branch line operations, short-haul movements of freight in small lots, and a continuing competition among certain main-line routes.

Motorization—appropriation of traffic by auto and truck—began deeply to undermine this elaborate traditional railway infrastructure almost as soon as nationalization itself got under way. The "greenfields" branches, the little depots and stations, the "stopping trains," and the peddler freights all began to go, building up in the course of their passing a mass of statistical data that pointed to the railroad as a declining industry. As a concurrent effect, motorization drastically rearranged BR's marketing opportunities, in essence toward longer-distance, high-density main-line operations conducted in volume and at much higher speeds.[13]

A final factor in the environment of BR's industrial relations has to do with the special character of its trade unions. There are three principal organizations. In size, the National Union of Railwaymen (NUR) is by far the largest. It is an industrial or "all-grades" union whose membership involves train service employees other than engine drivers,[14] station, platform, and freight depot personnel, signalmen, maintenance of way forces, and some shop craftsmen.

By contrast, the Associated Society of Locomotive Enginemen and Firemen (ASLEF) has its base in a single occupation — the engine driver and his "secondman." In consequence, ASLEF is craft-minded, strategically placed, and possessed of a propensity for going it alone. Proportionately, ASLEF has suffered the greatest losses in membership in the continuing postwar cutback in the railway labor force. Given the aristocratic position that the footplate man once enjoyed, in pay, in rank, and in prestige throughout British industry, his falling behind in the past quarter century has been a decidedly negative factor for the quality of labor relations on BR. Undoubtedly, too, the apparently bleak future of the industry has not helped to maintain that former pride of place that was the key to the drivers' job satisfaction.

The third organization is Transport Salaried Staffs' Association (TSSA), which speaks for the white-collar group — lower management, supervisors, technicians, and the clerical grades.[15] TSSA people cover a wide range of activities, such as selling tickets, all types of record keeping, operating the new computerized car identification system (TOPS), and manning the technical staff connected with the research center at Derby.

The distribution of the BR work force among these three principal unions accounts for a certain degree of instability in labor matters, simply because relationships among the organizations are more competitive than cooperative. In fact, the situation has been made even more complex by BR's chronically cash-poor position. Under law its managers are enjoined to run their own show, including labor matters, and to make the whole

---

[13] The parallel secular decline of the British coal industry also contributed heavily to the fall of traffic and revenues.

[14] NUR does represent a small number of these "footplate men." The British union system does not include the principle of exclusive jurisdiction; thus more than one union may represent the same occupational group.

[15] A fourth group of unions, the Confederation of Shipbuilding and Engineering Unions (CSEU), serves (along with NUR) employees in the railway workshops. The National Union of Seamen is also involved with BR's Shipping Division, while TSSA negotiates for staffs of British Transport Hotels. (Hotels and shipping are not part of this study.)

venture pay its way. But the lack of adequate operating margins, an inadequate cash flow over most of the time, has denied management adequate room for constructive bargaining initiatives it has wanted to undertake, and at the same time has left it more or less a captive of the cabinet. In turn, the attitude of the cabinet toward the railways for the most part has been negative, irritation at BR's permanent financial dependency, a grudging view of assistance to be tendered, and a barely concealed skepticism about the ruling question of whether British Railways had any future at all.

Put together, these factors have made railway industrial relations exceedingly difficult over these years. Only two favorable events have offset the general setting of pessimism: the decision in late 1973 to go ahead at last with the Channel Tunnel and the well-publicized test runs of the high-speed passenger trains, also in 1973.[16] If, further, the present review of railway policy should culminate in a double decision—to keep the present system essentially intact and to provide investment finance for modernization and development on the order of at least $425 million a year over the next nine years, then BR could look forward to an assured and expanding future for the first time in almost two generations.[17] This change of outlook would be of large importance for the character of labor relations as well.

POINTS OF STRAIN: REDUCTIONS IN FORCE AND REDUNDANCY

The adverse combination of service cutbacks, line abandonments, and labor-saving innovations reduced the number of total staff on BR from 476,545 persons at the start of 1963 to 229,756 on January 1, 1973.[18] Thus in a single decade, the railway work force was cut by 51.8 percent. How was this enormous reduction in force brought about?

Data gathered on a somewhat different basis by the Personnel Department show that during the decade 1963 to 1973 the work force was reduced by 213,525 persons. Of this reduction, 64.0 percent were "declared redundant," 33.1 percent either resigned or were discharged, and 2.9 percent were separated for reasons such as ill health.[19] In addition, 66,810 employees were placed in other positions, to some extent in other locations.

As the program to convert from steam to diesel traction got under way in 1955, BR recognized that it would have to reduce forces. From the outset it adopted a two-pronged strategy: to engage in what is technically called "consultation," that is, to review problems and plans with the union before taking a decision; and to rely upon the voluntary actions of the affected personnel to achieve the desired cut in numbers, that is, offering the employee a choice between, say, relocation or retraining or a severance from the payroll with appropriate compensation. Adoption of the compensation principle by the railways came some seven years before its statutory extension to all industry in 1965. Also, it rested upon the quite revolutionary notion that an employee who is severed from the payroll because of a reduction in force deserves some reimbursement for the loss of his equity in the job, a payment that should be geared in some way to his age and length of service.

At the beginning, BR hoped to manage the contraction of its forces by attrition or "natural wastage." In short, the quit rate together with direct control over the rate of accessions were expected to bring members down to the desired level at the desired speed. Initially, therefore, the strategy was to assure the unions and their members that transfers would be offered to all whose jobs were to be declared redundant. With the closure of a substantial amount of trackage in East Anglia in 1958, however, the transfer method proved inadequate. In consequence, severance payments were unilaterally introduced. By the following year, the problem had spread to the shops,

[16] The Tunnel project includes a new high-speed line from the Dover portal to White City (Shepherd's Bush) in West London.

The high-speed train is an intermediate type, capable of a maximum speed of 150 m.p.h. using conventional track and cars. The so-called "advanced passenger train" (APT) calls for much higher speeds on existing track. It is still in the experimental stage and is not expected to be introduced before 1984. By contrast, the interim high-speed train will enter service to the West of England in 1975.

[17] The minister of transport has already given strong indication that he favors keeping the system intact, but the question of investment capital remains unresolved.

[18] Figures apply to rail business only, plus those employed in British Railways Engineering Ltd. (locomotive and car manufacturing). On January 1, 1963, BRE accounted for 59,627 employees (12.5 percent of total railway employment), as against 33,001 employees (14.3 percent) exactly ten years later. (Data kindly provided by BR.)

Employment figures before 1963 lack comparability because they include activities then part of BR, for example,

hotels, but since made technically separate. Furthermore, 1963 is a good base because this was the year that Beeching's Reshaping Plan got under way.

[19] BR practice is to abolish the job, which thereby becomes "redundant." The employee as such is not considered redundant. When his job is declared redundant, however, he may be offered either a transfer to another vacancy or "the Golden Handshake," that is, redundancy payments either in the form of early retirement with special compensating benefits or of severance without retirement but with special benefits. By comparison, if an employee wishes to leave a post that has not been declared redundant, he is deemed a voluntary quit and receives no payment.

where the payments were fixed at two-thirds of base pay, less unemployment benefits, for a number of weeks tied to length of service.[20]

If we backtrack for a moment to 1957, we find still another attack on the redundancy problem: a "single-manning" agreement for diesel locomotives, under which ASLEF allowed ultimate elimination of the secondman (fireman) in exchange for a guarantee that those presently on the rosters would be guaranteed continued employment and for a differential pay increase over the other unions.[21]

It should also be pointed out that BR's redundancy strategy was by no means confined to severance payments. It also included a minimum period of notice, retraining where appropriate to a transfer, guarantee against reduction of earnings upon transfer ("red-circle" rates), and relocation allowances.

In 1965, BR attempted to "buy up" ASLEF's restriction against single manning during deep-night hours by offering a special wage deal. This effort proved abortive, but it did prove possible to reach agreements with the various unions about redundancy payments. In essence these arrangements provided that a man leaving service because of redundancy would get both a lump-sum payment and continuing benefits for up to fifty-two weeks, if still unemployed, less his unemployment benefit, a yield of two-thirds of normal income.[22] A year later (1966), a dispute emerged with ASLEF over whether its redundancy agreement, which was related to the effects of enlarged single manning, also covered redundancy invoked because of the introduction of incentive pay schemes to increase productivity.[23] This matter was resolved only to be replaced by an NUR redundancy dispute, also in 1966.

The issue was whether BR was to be allowed to permit "outsiders" to pick up and deliver containers carried on rail flatcars. NUR resisted both because it feared a loss of work and because it was ideologically opposed to private enterprise. On his side, Beeching was anxious to start these "liner services," to obtain new business and revenues for BR. Accordingly, management offered a no-redundancy guarantee to NUR. It was initially refused, but the new transport minister, Barbara Castle, succeeded in getting NUR acceptance, early in 1967.[24]

Since that time, the pragmatic and pluralistic approach of BR to the problem of surplus labor has been retained. Lump-sum payments have replaced the earlier arrangement. These are weighted for age, if the employee is older than fifty years, and for length of service. Early retirement is now provided at up to three years before the minimum pensionable age (sixty, sixty-two, or sixty-five years), at benefit levels up to the equivalent of full pension, without deductions for other earned income. Severance payments for nonretirees now range from £500 to £2000, depending upon age, length of service, and wage or salary level. Mobility allowances have been used selectively by management at £300. A Redundancy Welfare Fund has been created to cover the gap between earlier ages of retirement and sixty-five, the age when a worker becomes entitled to the regular state pension. The objectives are to make interim income equal to one-half the retiree's final rate and to cover ages sixty to sixty-five for those with at least thirty years of service.[25]

Through 1970, BR estimates that it has spent between £40 and £50 million ($98 to $122.5 million) on redundancy payments. Considering the savings on labor and the relative ease with which BR has accomplished a drastic reduction of force, this was money well spent.

If, last, we ask the question, How was it possible to effect a force cut of this size? the answer partially suggests itself. BR from early on recognized the wisdom of compensating the losers as the easiest means of achieving the reductions required, free of bitter disputes, strikes, and serious personal hardships. In this, the railways were ahead of their time. It must also be recognized that BR saw redundancy as a complex matter, calling for diverse and imaginative solutions. Accordingly, it used redeployment to retain the more productive and adaptable younger men. It resorted to the Golden Handshake to get rid of the others, aided by almost continuous boom conditions. As for the older employees, it offered a relatively painless early retirement. By following a flexible and humane strategy, BR was able to accomplish a major adaptation of

---

[20] Charles McLeod, *All Change: Railway Industrial Relations in the Sixties,* with a Foreword by the Rt. Hon. Ray Gunter (London: Gower Press, 1970), pp. 56-59.

[21] ASLEF also extracted an additional restriction: no single manning during the "deep-night" (early morning) hours. It took another decade to get this provision relaxed.

One wonders why the "fireman off" issue in the United States proved so much more difficult to resolve. Perhaps the answer is twofold: The Brotherhood of Locomotive Firemen and Enginemen in the United States was mainly a firemen's union and thus looked to that occupation for institutional survival, whereas ASLEF controlled both sides of the cab; and, as a perennially cash-poor enterprise, BR was in no shape to pay for excess manning, and ASLEF, well knowing it, was willing to accept humane attrition in exchange for more money for its surviving members.

[22] The general government scheme provided only for a lump-sum payment at that time.

[23] This led to recall of a special Court of Inquiry headed by Jack Scamp (now Sir Jack Scamp), which handled the deep-night-hours issue in 1965. McLeod, *All Change,* pp. 78-82.

---

[24] McLeod, *All Change,* pp. 95-100.

[25] Later it was found that although such claimants were entitled to public ("national") assistance for the transition period, they were being carried wholly at BR's expense. This has been changed.

a tradition-minded work force to meet the new conditions now relentlessly imposed upon a very old industry.[26]

ANOTHER POINT OF STRAIN: TECHNOLOGICAL CHANGE AND PRODUCTIVITY DEALS

The late Sumner Slichter distinguished four different modes of union response to innovations and technological change. They ranged from outright obstruction through competition (lowered unit labor costs through wage cuts or higher productivity), accommodation (acceptance of the machine at the price of job protection and a share in the savings), and full cooperation in a version of joint management and shared responsibility for profits. On British Railways since the war, the policy of the unions exhibits a mixture of obstruction and accommodation, according to the union and the particular issue.

Of the three principal unions, TSSA has followed a policy closest to accommodation. It has accepted without resistance both the computer for record keeping, retrieval, and now for control of freight operations and the ticket-printing machines at the stations. Also, its technicians have been central to the research program at Derby, from which the two versions of high-speed trains have emerged. In fact, this involvement of TSSA people has helped to put the organization on the side of change rather than against it. After all, self-interest is involved. Moreover, TSSA has not been asleep as regards cushioning to absorb the disruptive effects of innovations. From the fifties it has actively developed a broad-gauge sequence of redundancy agreements, to cover minimum notice periods, relocation costs with red-circle guarantees, retraining, lump-sum severance pay for younger employees, and early retirement for the older ones. At the present time, TSSA confronts perhaps its largest problem in this field: the elimination of about 4,500 middle- and lower-management jobs as BR eliminates its former layer of administrative divisions in each of its five geographic divisions.[27]

With ASLEF the record reflects obstructionism and intransigence on occasion. Since the fifties, its membership has fallen from 75,000 to 29,000 as the combined effect of technological change and retrenchment. The Beeching cutbacks in system and services between 1963 and 1966 sharply reduced the number of road and shunting locomotives to be manned, as well as the size of the "shed" staff in locomotive depots. Starting from 1955, the conversion from steam to diesel began eliminating the need for a fireman, a changeover that was complete by 1965. Main-line electrification to Birmingham, Manchester, Liverpool, and now Glasgow (early 1974) has meant still faster trains, with fewer locomotives required.

With the first single-manning agreement in 1957, ASLEF did not refuse outright to man the new locomotives. Instead it hedged in the removal of the secondman with various protections and limitations, most prominently for operations in the deep-night hours. Another decade was required to get these restrictions mostly lifted, so that today about 75 percent of all trains, passenger and freight, are single manned.[28] These gains were purchased by BR through a combination of diverse redundancy protections, differential pay adjustments (relative to general increases to all unions), and tacit acceptance of attrition rather than a once-and-for-all displacement.[29]

At the present time, ASLEF has been obstructing trial runs of the new high-speed trains. Initially, it refused to move these trains at all and then limited them to 100 m.p.h. Later this was modified, but during the first half of 1973 the organization has been resorting to "industrial action" in the form of one-day strikes. ASLEF's goal seems not to be to prevent high-speed passenger operations, for these could well be the salvation of the railways. Rather, ASLEF apparently wants double manning on trains scheduled at over 100 m.p.h., as is the Continental and Japanese practice. BR is not necessarily opposed to this arrangement. ASLEF, however, seems to be using its restrictions on the high-speed trials as a lever to extract a special pay increase from BR, along with upward revision of the mileage bonus system.

---

[26] Much of the credit goes to Sir Leonard F. Neal, who then was board member for industrial relations, and who later became chairman of the new Commission on Industrial Relations, introduced by the Heath government in 1971. For example, it was Neal who decided to look at the age structure of BR's footplate staff, finding that it was bimodal and that consequently a different means of achieving a reduction in numbers would have to be sought rather than the conventional method of encouraging only the older men to leave. Neal used the established devices of lump-sum settlements and early retirement to induce separations at both age modes.

[27] The five regions are also being rearranged to become eight "territories," chiefly by splitting up the former Eastern Region based at York.

[28] On the Southern Region (formerly Southern Railway), where suburban commuter operations have been conducted from the twenties with multiple-unit electric trains, single manning has been accepted throughout by ASLEF.

Curiously, the safety argument that was put forward so vigorously by the BLF&E in the United States for both passenger and freight trains seems not to have had any importance in the British single-manning negotiations.

[29] The night-hours restriction was given up in the Windsor negotiations in 1968 in exchange for a general increase of 3 percent. Windsor was a "pay-and-efficiency" negotiation involving NUR and ASLEF, in July and August of 1968. It was arranged at the initiative of L. F. Neal, after his party had flown to Penzance at the beginning of July to get NUR to withdraw an overtime ban and work-to-rule strike. These events are considered on p. 83.

NUR's problems with innovation have been made somewhat more complex because of the much greater size and diversity of its membership. In addition to representing the guards on the trains,[30] NUR includes the signalmen, the track and bridge gangs, freight station and passenger platform personnel, and a significant portion of the manual group in the shops. As single manning progressed, it led to a claim that the guards had to do more work and accept greater responsibility. As power signalling and sophisticated electronic control of train movements have come in, the work of signalmen has been upgraded as well as concentrated in fewer boxes, mostly on the dense main lines. Track, depot, and station personnel have been given power equipment, and "pay-and efficiency" (productivity-raising) deals have been negotiated. Within the shop crafts, the main changes have involved closure and concentration programs, accompanied by further mechanization.

In the freightliners dispute considered earlier, which erupted first late in 1965, the posture of NUR was rather subtle. It was opposed neither to containers nor to liner trains composed of containers on flatcars. Rather it claimed all of the pick-up and delivery work as a matter of a "demarcation" (jurisdictional) right. This opposition was overcome finally at cabinet level, in the Wilson government.

In 1965 the Court of Inquiry headed by Sir Jack Scamp awarded the engine drivers forty minutes' added pay per day, scaled up to two hours for runs of 140 miles, in exchange for major single-manning concessions by ASLEF.[31] NUR eventually responded by demanding a special bonus for guards, claiming that single manning had imposed new duties and responsibilities. Early in 1967, BR offered twenty minutes. NUR rejected this proposal, insisting upon forty minutes (to match ASLEF). Upon BR's demurrer, NUR ordered its guards not to perform any secondman duties. This refusal led to an agreement to undertake a productivity study, whereupon NUR withdrew its ban. BR then produced estimates to show that the forty-minute bonus would cost between £600-£800,000 per year and that this expense could largely be met by three NUR concessions: greater flexibility in the assignment of guards; elimination of brake vans from trains fully equipped with automatic air brakes; and assumption of ticket collectors' duties by guards on passenger trains.[32] In early fall, 1967, NUR rejected these ideas and renewed its ban on secondman duties.

This impasse led to appointment of another special Court of Inquiry, this time headed by the late Professor Donald J. Robertson, of Glasgow University.[33] In its findings, this second court agreed with the board that twenty minutes' additional pay was ample for any extra duties. It then proposed various alternatives, none of which was acceptable to NUR. The ban was therefore continued, whereupon BR began sending men home for refusal to carry out their assignments. This action made much of the work force idle, inducing BR to threaten massive layoffs, known as "suspension of the guaranteed week" in the industry. The ensuing threat of a breakdown in railway service led immediately to ministerial intervention. Negotiations were duly resumed, but again reached impasse over NUR's continuing demand for forty minutes, coupled with its refusal to budge on the key BR counterdemands. With a second intervention by the minister of labour, settlement was reached at a figure of thirty minutes, with withdrawal of the brake vans.[34]

With the six months' pay freeze in late 1966, both ASLEF and NUR found their scheduled 3.5 percent increases frozen. At the same time, the government began reminding all employers that further wage increases would have to be linked to increased labor productivity. Upon the unions' filing of new general wage claims in March 1967, the Railways board seized the opportunity to insist upon concessions to effectuate the required new link to higher productivity. Its first step was to undertake a pay-and-efficiency review for the entire system.

By February 1966, the board was ready with an offer. Three basic elements were in its strategy: to merge job classifications and make them more flexible, by removing narrow work-separation definitions; to eliminate an obsolete and costly piece rate system in the workshops, replacing it with a work-study system of incentive pay; to revise upward the lower end of the pay scale, to bring these employees closer to the mean railway wage. Within

---

[30]   The guard is equivalent to a combined brakeman-trainman-conductor in American practice.

[31]   This was a Court of Inquiry, not a binding arbitration. The court functions as a factfinding body with the power to make recommendations.

[32]   McLeod, *All Change*, pp. 84-85.

[33]   The normal top body for negotiable issues is the Railway Staff National Tribunal. However, during the sixties the *ad hoc* Court of Inquiry procedure was used on occasion instead.

[34]   McLeod, *All Change*, pp. 86-90. Elimination of these vans in freight service put the guard up front, in the back of the locomotive. ASLEF immediately declared that this constituted "manning" not "riding" and claimed that it violated the 1965 Manning Agreement. ASLEF then ordered its drivers to "work to rule," which quickly led to a breakdown of service. Sir Jack Scamp was again called in and ruled against the union. To get this trivial issue settled and the trains moving again required the intervention of the minister of labour and then the prime minister, plus a promise of a manning and recruitment study. McLeod, *All Change*, pp. 90-91.

the "conciliation staff,"[35] the board proposed rationalization of the job structure for the traffic and supporting grades other than trainmen; the existing fifty job classifications in the lowest six grades were to be merged into two "versatility" classifications, Railman and Leading Railman, with Senior Railman and Chargeman (leadman or foreman) above these. Significantly, the railman was to get a 10.6 percent increase, to £ 12.50 per week. This proposal had a companion for the supervisorial grades and still another for the clerical side. Moreover, the board proposed to carry over the same approach to a merger and redesign of shop craft classifications, again to reduce narrow partitioning, which leads to idle time.[36]

Although agreement was reached for the clerical groups, negotiations became complicated in early 1968 by lodgment of renewed 1967 general wage claims by ASLEF and NUR, who asked that they be laid before the Railway Staff National Tribunal. At this level, the board urged the sterility of further general increases unaccompanied by specific measures, as in its pending pay-and-efficiency proposals, to raise productivity. In the upshot, the tribunal's recommendations leaned heavily in the board's direction, urging further specific productivity negotiations and special temporary increases to the lowest-paid groups. Both ASLEF and NUR rejected these unanimous recommendations. NUR then announced its intention to ban overtime working and to work to rule starting June 24. ASLEF followed, even subsequently moving up its date from July 1 to June 25.[37] Transportation chaos followed.[38]

Board Member Neal then took the drastic step of flying his team to the NUR annual general meeting at Penzance to get negotiations moving again. By hard informal bargaining, parallel deals were made with both unions providing tapered general increases (proportionately larger at the low end), in exchange for a promise to complete a pay-and-efficiency deal by September 2, 1968.

The parties then moved to informal continuous talks at BR's Windsor Staff Training College where, in an unprecedentedly relaxed and unstructured atmosphere, productivity settlements were reached basically along the lines of the board's February proposals. Even more, a number of older outstanding issues were dusted off and settled, such as single manning of runs during the deep-night hours and more flexible rostering (scheduling) for conciliation staff other than trainmen. Thus a productivity-pay link was finally forged, the wage structure was largely rationalized, the lowest paid were brought closer to the mean, and the concept of interindustry "wage-wage" comparisons, introduced by Professor C. W. Guillebaud in 1960, was finally put to rest.[39] By April 1969, the board had achieved most of its similar objectives for the shop groups, who are represented by NUR and CSEU. Indeed, 1969 proved to be a quiet year on BR, although tumultous for the rest of British industry.

To explain the 180-degree turn that negotiations took at Penzance, the following factors are relevant. Through its Prices and Incomes Board, the government had begun to convey its message that pay increases had to be linked to solid improvements in productivity. This provided a framework for bargaining, giving the board the initiative. Next, the chaos and hardship imposed by NUR's and ASLEF's resort to industrial action set the stage for drastic and dramatic leadership. British Railways Board proved equal to the challenge. For once negotiations were not conducted with the solemnity, rote, and rigor of what has been called in the United States — felicitously — a Kabuki play. Rather, they were opened up, made informal, and conducted with new-found regard for each side's needs. It remains to be seen whether so sharp a departure can become permanent. More recent experience would suggest the negative.[40]

STILL ANOTHER POINT OF STRAIN: NEGOTIATIONS OVER GENERAL PAY INCREASES

In essence the foregoing section centers upon disputes over technical and other innovations (and their effects) over the redesign of job and pay structures, and over the

---

[35] This term refers essentially to the blue-collar wage employees. It has its origin on the old North Eastern Railway during the period from 1899 to 1907, wherein a Conciliation Board was established on a bipartisan basis with the old Amalgamated Society of Railway Servants as an instrument for communication and for negotiations "as to conditions of service." Agreement between North Eastern Railway and Amalgamated Society of Railway Servants, dated November 6, 1908.

[36] McLeod, *All Change*, pp. 140-52. For the trainmen, the board proposed Conductor, to combine the duties of Guard and Ticket Collector.

[37] McLeod, *All Change*, pp. 152-55. Postwar, it has been standard for the railways to work overtime, both to overcome a chronic shortage of staff in an economy of inflationary boom and to hold down voluntary quits by means of the enlarged earnings.

[38] Each weekday a half million commuters pass through Victoria and Waterloo Stations in London alone, mostly travelling to and from Southern Region points.

[39] McLeod, *All Change*, pp. 158-62.

[40] The fact that a Labor government was in power also may have had some weight. As for the then pending Transport Act of 1968, which did not become law until October 25 and which was intended to make the railways self-sustaining, its influence is not clear. Sir Sidney Greene, general secretary of NUR, is reported never to have believed the system could be made self-supporting, while the typical union view was that the exchequer would always "fork over the lolly" anyway.

establishment of a real pay-productivity link. The remaining major point of friction concerns the postwar union practice of insisting upon annual general pay increases, throughout British industry, including the railways. For BR, of course, the consequences were particularly serious because the system has been chronically short of money.[41]

In truth, however, negotiations over general increases over the past fifteen years have not been confined to any such pure and simple topic. Always they have gotten interlocked with questions of wage structure, in good part because of ASLEF's habit of usually insisting upon something "on top" and NUR's quick response that, "Anything extra that ASLEF gets, we get too."

The pay system for ASLEF's footplate men goes back to 1919. It consists of a standard base rate plus a mileage supplement linked to distance. In its perception of wage matters, ASLEF stands for an equalized standard base rate for all of its drivers, with differentials in earnings to reflect varying distances run. ASLEF also thinks of itself as a craft union, with all members on the same plane. In consequence, it has developed the "link system" to provide for full rotation of runs and to equalize earnings within a given depot, an arrangement in which seniority does not count. A shunter in a marshalling yard and the driver on the Flying Scot both earn a base rate of £ 33 weekly. But the driver gets an additional £ 27 with his mileage supplement.[42]

One other aspect of ASLEF's wage policy is its firm belief that, although it is a craft and should be on top in pay, prestige, and power, its position has been eroding for years as regards relative pay. Partly its view reflects a two-thirds loss in membership since 1963. But it also derives from the pay-and-efficiency increases awarded to special groups usually at lower levels of pay. In the large, therefore, ASLEF consistently has asked for a differential over the going general increase. To get it the union has employed whatever lever might be at hand: increased single manning in 1957 and 1965, an overtime ban and work-to-rule in 1968, and one-day strikes and a "blacking" of the high-speed train trials in 1972-1973.

As noted earlier, NUR is a very different kind of union. Its structure is industrial rather than craft, although it includes craftsmen along with semiskilled and laborer grades. In consequence it is always concerned with job structure and relations among classification rates. For the same reason, it has been more friendly than ASLEF toward productivity bargaining. Perhaps because of the distribution of its membership, NUR tends to favor increases that are tipped in favor of the lower paid. Finally, because it is the largest organization on the railways, NUR regards itself as the wage leader. As such, it does not propose to allow ASLEF to extract any special advantages for itself.

As needs no elaboration, the going annual general wage increase is a phenomenon of postwar collective bargaining. Before the war, the only general link was between the wage and retail price levels, with each industry acting independently. With the Court of Inquiry headed by Lord Cameron in 1955, the railways were told that they had to pay "fair and adequate" wages, and this standard was linked to comparibility with other industries.[43]

By 1958 it was clear that railway wages were falling behind. The unions had submitted their claims, BR was pleading poverty, and the tribunal saw no solution. Both sides then persuaded the prime minister to set up a special Committee of Inquiry, headed by Professor C. W. Guillebaud, to look into the matter. The committee then adopted an approach resting essentially upon interindustry comparisons: the railway medians for comparable key jobs were set against those in other industries, while the spreads to the bottom end of the scales were also compared externally, to obtain a standardized criterion of "fair deviations." This exercise appealed to the unions and was employed effectively by them until it was finally overthrown at Penzance and Windsor in 1968. Beyond this structural principle, the Guillebaud committee also recommended a 10 percent general increase, in its report in 1960.

During 1962-1963, a 6 percent general increase was negotiated, after a complex period that included intervention by the prime minister. Then, in 1963-1964 negotiations over new claims occurred, with BR urging percentage increases tapered upward for the lower grades of pay, pleading financial stringency and the need to tie any increases directly to savings from increased productivity. Ultimately, the national tribunal recommended 9 percent for the Conciliation Grades, 5 percent for the supervisorial, and 4 percent for the clerical. This recommendation was accepted.[44]

This brings us to the labyrinthine skein of events during 1965-1968, in which general increases, structural adjustments, and special supplements were all tied together and emerged as the joint products of the Scamp inquiry, the tribunal, the price-wage freeze, and the Penzance-Windsor negotiations.

---

[41] BR's problem has not been made any easier by its high visibility as a leading public enterprise, supposed to set a national example in its wage settlements. Whitehall consistently keeps an eye on BR's wage policy.

[42] There are other adjustments for night, Sunday, and overtime work.

[43] McLeod, *All Change*, pp. 103-4. It was in this case that Lord Cameron coined the expression, "Having willed the end, the nation must will the means" — in short, if BR could not pay the increase, the Treasury should bail the system out.

[44] McLeod, *All Change*, pp. 123-26.

Many of these developments have been considered already under other rubrics, but the running disputes over pay structure and pay consolidation are important enough to require separate treatment. Among the major forces at work were the concern of management for costs and its desire for a more efficient wage structure, the intense rivalry and divergent ambitions of ASLEF and NUR, and the increasingly obsolete character of the old mileage bonus system.

At the Scamp inquiry of 1965, ASLEF was seeking a special deal for base pay, on top of a general increase, in exchange for relaxation of single-manning restrictions. Scamp, however, actually awarded a minimum bonus of forty minutes' pay, tapered upward with distance travelled. By 1967, L. F. Neal (now Sir Leonard Neal), board member for industrial relations, had become convinced that the mileage bonus system was now obsolete and counterproductive. The basic problem was the steadily decreasing relative importance of the base rate in total earnings, because of the multiplicative effect of higher base rates for the mileage bonus, which is calculated by bonus base-rate hours added relative to distance travelled. With the relative decline of base pay in total earnings, both pensions and holiday and sick pay had fallen far below desired levels, because all were linked directly to basic hourly rates rather than to total earnings. Moreover, differences in relative total earnings of drivers, for example, had ceased long since to bear any direct relationship either to relative efforts on the job or to "results" produced: the longer the run, the bigger the earnings, although diesel and electric traction has greatly reduced both the effort and the skill required, compared with steam, while the output (for example, ton-miles or passenger-miles per driver-hour) now depends far more upon capital and management (motive power, track, signalling, and schedules) than upon employees. By contrast, lower earnings go to the drivers of "stopping" (commuter) trains in the Southern Region who run much shorter distances and in the nature of the case do much more "work per mile." Finally, the footplate pay system, by yielding much lower earnings on the southern commuter network, has contributed to the growing shortage of staff in that region, where general wages are much higher.

Management, of course, had been aware for some time of these anomalies and encumbrances in the pay system for over-the-road personnel. Without a frontal attack on the time-honored mileage bonus system, however, it had to accept the system's growing disabilities, because it was compelled by economic weakness to restrain the rise of base rates. Otherwise, their rise would have enlarged the scale of total earnings, in this respect, costs.

During the Penzance-Windsor exercise in 1968, Neal developed a strategy for achieving pay consolidation (incorporation of earnings in base rates) that was economically bearable and that offered other benefits as well. His strategy was simply to insist that the issues of low pensions, holidays, and sick pay could not be addressed successfully so long as the parties were hobbled by an outmoded incentive system. Using this concept as a wedge, Neal was able to pry open the issue of mileage bonuses, convincing the NUR and ASLEF in turn that a freeze on these payments was essential if base rates were to be raised, and, through this, pension and other benefits increased.[45] In the outcome, a gradual transition to full pay consolidation became possible, to yield more realistic base rates and fringe benefits dependent upon them.

Under the rigorous incomes policy of 1969, further reconstruction of the pay system for train personnel was precluded, but by early 1970 the Wilson government dropped pay control. The rail unions then began pressing for both pay "restructuring" and general increases. Restructuring, however, got caught in the running rivalry between ASLEF and NUR, with ASLEF claiming entitlement to "something extra" for its purportedly "harsh" treatment at Penzance. The goal seems to have been a special addition to base rates above what NUR would get, in exchange for increasing the mileage minimum at which bonus would begin to some figure above the existing 124 miles. To this BR was sympathetic, but NUR was not.

The board then offered a study for drivers and secondmen only, which would mainly benefit ASLEF.[46] NUR then insisted that the traffic grades could not be ignored; impasse followed, and restructuring lapsed as a negotiating issue over the next two years.

BR, however, continued to study the problem, in an effort to find an economically supportable way to raise basic weekly pay to levels adequate to permit it to fill vacancies that began exceeding 5,000 over the system. In the Southern Region, with its dense commuter services, the problem had become particularly acute because industrial wages were much higher than BR's national scale, while its drivers could make little or no mileage bonus because of the preponderance of short runs. On this point, ASLEF and BR had parallel interests: a higher basic weekly rate for drivers. ASLEF, however, had no wish to abandon mileage bonuses for its long-distance drivers holding "star turns." Also, ASLEF was conducting a

---

[45] Under the system, there is a "pass-through" from each increase in the base hourly rate to fringe benefits (pensions, holidays, and sick pay), and to mileage bonus earnings. The freeze simply kept the basic rate for bonus calculation at its 1968 level. This permitted an increase in the basic rate for all other purposes, at a lesser increase in total labor costs than if mileage payments also were included.

[46] ASLEF represents about 29,000 footplate men and NUR 5,000, and there are some double registrations. NUR has the guards and railmen.

classic craft-union fight against an industrial union, NUR. For this, it continued to insist upon a special deal, and for the same reason NUR wanted an across-the-board package.

During August 1973, BR made its offer of a restructuring deal: bonus and mileage payments would be phased out by January 1976, with compensating increases in the weekly base ranging from £1.55 to £2.65; drivers would get a special increase of £1.50, and other grades would increase similarly; shift allowances of 4 to 6 percent would be added; and white-collar status would be awarded those with fifteen or more years' service, yielding improved pensions and sick pay, and a London allowance. ASLEF rejected the proposal, while unofficial action by local drivers banned the high-speed train trials.[47] Thus the gap between ASLEF and the other two bodies began to widen, as the drivers once more resorted to go-it-alone tactics.

While the restructuring deal was being discussed, all three unions lodged a substantial claim for a general pay increase as well, to take effect on April 29, 1974, when existing agreements would expire. By early December, restructuring was at impasse owing to ASLEF's intransigeancy. Late December 3, its Executive voted on official "industrial action" (a sanctioned strike) to start December 12 and to include bans on drivers working overtime, on Sundays, and on days of rest; and "total noncooperation" with management, meaning a go-slow strike achieved by working strictly to rule (for example, not taking out a train if the locomotive had no speedometer).[48] There followed some nine ghastly weeks of disrupted or suspended train services, involving a one-day official systemwide strike, two separate regionwide strikes with interregional repercussions; suspension of all services on nine successive Sundays; and enforced reductions at all times because of staff shortages owing to the ban on overtime working. Throughout the whole period, ASLEF never publicly disclosed its own demands. By contrast, NUR and TSSA were ready to settle in December. By February, Sidney Weighell, NUR's senior assistant general secretary, was denouncing ASLEF for "failing to come to grips with the twentieth century" by rejecting "a glorious opportunity to make our members among the highest paid workers in the country."[49] It was to no avail: ASLEF held out; in April BR finally took the issue to arbitration before the Railway Staff National Tribunal. Nor was this all, for late in March ASLEF also rejected an offer of a 7.5 percent general increase, which was entirely separate from the £52 million restructuring deal and worth another £33 million. Again ASLEF was

isolating itself from its two sister unions, both of whom were ready to settle. In this instance, probably in deference to the advent of a new Labor government, ASLEF itself took its claim for a 12 percent general increase to the national tribunal, where at this writing (June 1974) both issues are now being heard.

SOME CONCLUDING OBSERVATIONS

Over the past quarter century, BR has been transformed from a badly run-down, traditionally oriented network to a very modern railway, far better adapted to modern market opportunities. In quality and frequency, its long-distance passenger services are much superior to those offered by AMTRAK in the United States, and comparable to the best on the Continent. Its commuter operations are characterized by intricacy and reliability: they keep a huge volume of traffic off the road and put to shame the American East Coast services. On the freight side, perhaps retrenchment of small shipments has gone too far in view of newly recognized environmental considerations. As a strictly commercial undertaking, however, railways perform at their best with long hauls, block tonnage movements, and a minimum of terminal and reclassification operations.[50] Clearly, this has been the direction that BR has been taking from the start of the Beeching period.

British markets and distances of course are much more restricted than American, a fact that denies the railway the full potential of economies of scale, granting that much progress has been made. Historically, the rail freight business in Britain has involved a preponderance of short-haul traffic. Even today the average wagon moves only eighty-five miles for a given shipment, despite a

---

[47] *The Times* (London), September 10, 1973.

[48] The official BR rulebook for October 1972 requires "observance of standard operating procedures" for the safe and efficient operation of trains.

[49] *Daily Telegraph,* February 1, 1974.

[50] Block (or unit) trains eliminate the costs of breaking up and reassembling trains en route. In addition, the longer the haul, the more terminal costs can be spread with the increase in ton-miles produced, which lowers average cost per ton-mile. Haulage costs (mainly fuel and wages) increase with distance at an approximately constant marginal rate. Hence the direct relation between length of haul and size of profit margin relative to rates.

In long-haul economics, there is a degree of conflict between speed and volume of tonnage. Increased tonnage per train movement spreads haulage cost over more units, but also lowers speed, *ceteris paribus;* the result is fewer ton-miles produced per train-hour, hence higher unit haulage costs from this factor. Maintenance of the same speed with heavier trains can offset this influence, but raises haulage costs on its own: more motive power per train, more fuel, and more crew costs.

In the choice between speed and tonnage volume, some roads prefer a large number of relatively light trains, in part because this affords shippers greater promptness and flexibility. American practice, however, tends to favor the long "freight drag."

ten-year emphasis upon preblocked long-hauls.[51] Before the Second World War, this was even more strongly the case. Consequently, one wonders how the formerly private companies were able to cover their costs, as for the most part they did, whereas BR cannot, even after billions of pounds of new investment.

The solution to this intriguing puzzle is so complex as to require a monograph in itself. Here we can only cite the main reasons why BR continues to be a deficit operation. First, there is the problem of excess capacity, especially under the disastrous influence of highway transport economics. Before the advent of widespread motorization, even much of the railways' short-haul business was marginally profitable. Then as tax money began to pour into road building (with no charges for interest, depreciation, maintenance, or taxable value of the investment; with road access usually toll free; and, consequently, with no attempt to relate costs and returns) the railways' former rents of location and advantage began to be lost, first on the short-haul business, and later on most of the long-haul traffic as well. Indeed, this is the persistent dilemma of all railroads everywhere, how to make them commercially profitable undertakings when their principal competition involves services that are typically provided free of price entirely, and that do not bear a full share of long-run fixed costs. So far as BR is concerned, the result has been the emergence of a large amount of idle capital in terminal and line facilities. In the main, the shift to long-distance freight and passenger services has helped to cover variable costs. Investment capital, however, has never been adequately or consistently available since nationalization. This lack has hampered transformation of the system so that it cannot undertake new tasks.

Second, the emergence of excess capacity gave rise to the notion that "slimming down" or rationalization of the system would somehow take it into the Promised Land of profitability. In fact, this was the dominant theme of the Beeching Reshaping Plan. It is also the United States Department of Transportation's current proposed solution to the "Northeastern" problem. Yet this is not the way matters worked out on BR. True, there were cash savings on maintenance of way costs, salvage from scrap, gains from sale of real estate, savings on lineside personnel, and avoidance of capital replacements. But there were also strongly negative factors: some traffic revenues were lost, crew costs increased with use of more indirect routes, and

special capital expenditures for yards and passing tracks had to be made to handle surviving traffic on these other routes.[52] In a nutshell, the avoidable costs from line abandonments fell well short of revenue losses: accordingly, the system's cash-flow position emerged worse than ever.

Finally, the stop-go affliction of the British economy since the end of the war largely denied to the railways the opportunity to use their new managerial freedoms to produce a profit. Recurring price freezes and controls prevented increases in rates, while inflation was steadily and insistently raising costs. Rates could be lowered to attract new business, but they could not be raised quickly and fully as costs rose. In addition, stop-go economics were an important factor in denying BR a chance to formulate and execute a long-term investment plan.

Excepting 1971 and 1972, the deficits have continued and have resulted in a consistent handicapping of the ability of the system to negotiate with its unions. Whether the problem was investment funds for modernization or money to raise wages to competitive levels, BR has continued to depend upon the Treasury and, ultimately, the taxpayers.

Let us return now to our main concern, BR's industrial relations in this period. Given this very modern railway that has emerged in barely twenty years, the quality of its labor relations seems certain to be influenced favorably over the longer run if the government takes a firm decision to provide the capital needed to put BR's nine-year, $4 billion "interim strategy" in motion.[53] For, joined to the Tunnel undertaking, BR could exploit commercially its technical advantages in freight and passenger movements in the 300 to 500 mile range, and perhaps even for longer distances. Morale would be likely to improve on a property

[51] When British environmentalists talk about getting freight off the roads and back on the rails, their estimates tend to be grossly inflated by including in "freight" local cartage movements, bakers' vans, and similar items for which road is far better suited. The real place for road-to-rail transfer is the heavy long-distance lorry, which is heavily subsidized indirectly by current methods of financing road construction and maintenance costs.

[52] For analysis of the problem see Harry S. Meislahn, "But It'll Save $30 Million," *Modern Railroads*, June 1974, pp. 56-59. For dense networks in small countries or regions, the search for a "viable core" is probably a vain one.

[53] BR proposed an investment program of £1,787 million for the nine-year period beginning with fiscal year 1973-1974, for a yearly average of £198.5 million. These funds are separate from grant-aid payments and Treasury cover for operating losses. Late in 1973, the Heath government accepted BR's investment plan in principle, while shortening the period to five years. It pledged £891 million, starting with £140 million in 1973-1974, and rising to £225 million in 1977-1978, for an annual average of £178 million. The total includes £41 million for the Channel Tunnel. In June 1974, the new Wilson government in effect endorsed this capital-spending plan, "subject to the general economic situation." It also cut BR's funded debt from £439 million to £250 million, increased the system's authorized borrowing power to £600 million, and substituted assured Treasury funding of operating losses in the amount of £900 million (plus £600 million more on cabinet approval) for the former grant-aid system. *The Daily Telegraph*, June 13 and 25, 1974.

whose future were no longer in question and in fact were visibly expanding. The same factors would strengthen BR's ability to pay better wages. This is not immediately a matter of achieving commercial profitability, although even this is at least an eventual possibility. Rather, a decision to keep BR intact and to invest the desired capital would involve a novel long-run government commitment, hitherto denied railroad operations while unstintingly accorded to roads and aviation.[54]

Here note must be taken in passing of the formation, for the first time, of an organization whose purpose is to "pursue the development and promotion of rail transport within an integrated transport system."[55] It is known as Transport 2000 and owes its origin and survival largely to the joint leadership and support of NUR, TSSA, and ASLEF. Transport 2000 has attracted much attention and has gained the adherence of a large number of environmental groups. It is by no means a railway antiquarian society. But it does indicate that BR's leading unions have decided upon a sophisticated course of political action to insure their own future and that of BR's employees.

Looking over the entire record of industrial relations on the railways since 1948, one could say with confidence that the two most notable achievements were the redundancy policy for cutting the work force by nearly two-thirds, and the imaginative redesign of job and wage structure initiated in 1968 and 1969. Redundancy policy allowed a little noticed selective retention of the more productive employees, along with a humane program for separation of the rest. It also was essential to gaining relaxation of restrictions on manning and on work assignments.

Apart from locomotive manning and an inheritance of narrow and obsolete job classifications that promoted idle time through work separation rules, BR never had a problem of trade union restrictions to compare with the United States systems. Even the fireman was eliminated within ten years. There never was a "crew consist" issue, or a "yard versus road work" problem, or a restrictive seniority district issue, or full-crew and train-limit legislation, as there was in the United States.[56] Partly the

explanation may be differences in size, but the main factor seems to be that the British rail unions never felt an earlier need to pursue job protection in this way. Then, when the great cutback came, the redundancy program proved adequate to absorb the shock, while the savings on staff largely could be made available to the surviving employees.

There is also reason to believe that the rail unions did not impose extraordinary wage pressure upon BR in these years. Before the sixties, real wages actually fell. Thereafter they have barely kept up. Today the railways are no longer a top-paying industry. It is also significant that overtime working (now at an average of forty-seven hours weekly) and a high voluntary quit rate have been continuous phenomena since the war. Without the overtime, both the quit and accessions rates would have been far worse. The meaning of all this is that the railways are an industry with a chronic problem of recruiting and retaining personnel. Accordingly, their wages cannot be out of line on the high side. Indeed, on average they are not enough to balance the system's requirements with the supply of manpower on the market.

Until the year from 1973 to 1974, the railways did not experience a chronic strike problem, despite the pessimism and demoralization that have come with years of contraction and declining status. For a quarter century, the system has escaped lengthy national strikes. Its troubles have been confined to a few one-day stoppages, temporary bans on overtime working, and brief recourse to slowdowns achieved by work-to-rule exercises. Within the past year, however, the strike problem worsened seriously as ASLEF resorted to an aggressive program of industrial action, conducted at both the official and unofficial levels. ASLEF's goal seems to be to get a substantial increase in the basic weekly minimum from £33 to £40 without significant concessions on the mileage bonus; and to obtain a special deal on top of any increase granted to NUR and TSSA.[57] In short, left-wing influences in ASLEF's executive, joined to heady visions of recapturing the footplate men's lost glory as the aristocrats of craft unionism, have propelled the organization into an extremist strategy, in place of a coalition with its sister unions.

Yet, viewed as a whole, the railways' strike record has been remarkably good, and even this recent outburst of

---

[54] Concorde alone has already cost over $2 billion, without carrying a single paying passenger. Highway outlays per annum have been running at over $1.5 billion, but no one insists that the roads be made to pay or even be made commercially accountable.

[55] Transport 2000, *Policy Statement* (London 1972).

[56] There are other differences, also adverse to the United States railroads relative to BR. Except for periods of direct price control, BR has been free to set its own rates and fares; the United States companies are not. BR has been relieved of the burden of common carrier status (the duty to accept any and all freight offered) since 1952; the United States companies are not. BR can close any line it wishes, unless it is unable to prove losses or government provides full grant-aid;

the United States companies must take years in these proceedings, often losing, but without grant-aid in the event. BR is free to adjust train frequencies and type of service; the United States companies are hemmed in by federal and state regulation and, typically, must continue service even at an operating loss.

[57] The mileage bonus starts after the 124th mile and is calculated in increments of fifteen miles ("bands"). For the first band, the bonus is two and one-third hours; for succeeding bands, the premium is one hour's pay for each. BR wants to raise the starting minimum to 200 miles. *The Daily Telegraph*, January 3, 1974.

irresponsibility may be more an aberration than the advent of a permanent condition.[58]

Superficially, the explanation is that all sides in the industry are well aware of the catastrophic impacts of a railway strike and of the risks of quick and drastic government intervention. In the background, we may conjecture, is the traditional character of railway organization, which is military in structure and in discipline. As a technical matter, more than for any other form of transportation the railroad requires precise and reliable central coordination — of access to the line and of movements on the line. This coordination is achieved by a traditional chain-of-

---

[58] By spring 1974, however, ASLEF was declaring that it was not bound by any social contract between the Labor government and the TUC and was threatening to resume industrial action if the tribunal awarded no more than BR's offer. *The Economist*, June 29, 1974.

command, visible authority backed up by the rulebook, in a small version of the former empire. The habit of accepting orders, of discipline enforced fully by sanctions, follows. In this closed system, a strike is a challenge to internal authority and, as such, a breach of duty.

Accordingly, we have what a BR official perceptively refers to as this "ingrown railway world," a world of "we and they," of a "socially separated" work force struggling to survive against the common enemy, government and society. Thus the tradition of one's duty to keep the system going. Another of its consequences has been a subtle unilateralism in labor relations, a type of bargaining in which management customarily assumed a posture of saying no, rather than one of openness, imaginativeness, and a willingness at least to listen. Penzance was a new beginning here. It could well go much further if the railways' future is finally decided in a constructive and socially desirable way.

CHAPTER V

The Authority of National Trade Union Confederations: A Comparative Analysis

by John P. Windmuller, *Associate Dean and Professor,* New York State School of Industrial and Labor Relations, Cornell University

The most comprehensive element in the trade union structure is the national center or confederation, also sometimes called the central body.[1] In most industrialized Western countries the national center is a federative organization constituted by individual national unions whose number may vary from sixteen in West Germany and Austria to ·well over one hundred in Britain and the United States.[2] In a few countries, however, the national unions must share their position with regional bodies, sometimes even to the extent of equal or more than equal participation in confederal decision making.[3] The consequences of such dualism are for the most part extraneous to the subject of this paper.[4]

National centers are not only the most comprehensive but formally also the highest bodies in trade unionism.[5] Yet their position at the apex of the union structure does not necessarily express with accuracy the relationship with their affiliates as one of dominance and subordination. There are said to be strong (or centralized) and weak (or decentralized) confederations, but as a rule such terms or their synonyms are used so loosely as to have little meaning.[6]

---

[1] The term *federation* would be more consonant with North American usage, but in Britain a federation is a bargaining coalition of individual unions and in Romance countries it is usually an individual national union.

[2] As a long-term trend the number of affiliated unions is almost everywhere declining and average membership increasing.

[3] In France, the constitutions of all four major confederations (CGT, CFDT, CGT-FO, and CFTC) recognize the regional *unions départementales* as equals of the national unions and accord to them precisely as many votes in conventions and confederal governing bodies as are allocated to the national unions. For the text of the constitutions see Jean Pélissier, ed., *Documents de droit du travail* (Paris: Editions Montchrestien, 1971), pp. 24-62. Compare Jean-Daniel Reynaud, *Les syndicats en France,* 2d ed. (Paris: Armand Colin, 1966), p. 120, and Guy Caire, *Les syndicats ouvriers* (Paris: Presses Universitaires, 1971), pp. 393-94 and 399. Belgium, Italy, and Australia have similar situations. On Australia see J. H. Portus, *Australian Compulsory Arbitration 1900-1970* (Sydney: Hicks Smith, 1971), p. 110. For Italy see Daniel Horowitz, *The Italian Labor Movement* (Cambridge: Harvard University Press, 1963), p. 333, and Maurice F. Neufeld, *Italy: School for Awakening Countries* (Ithaca, N.Y.: New York State School of Industrial and Labor Relations, 1961), pp. 508-9 and Chart 1 following p. 554.

[4] Another complication that will also be disregarded arises from the prevalence of trade union pluralism in several countries. The term *pluralism* refers to the existence of more than one national center. Most of the time, pluralism arises

from ideological, philosophical, and religious differences that then form the basis for the creation of two or more national centers, each one identified with a particular set of beliefs distinct from and competitive with the beliefs underlying other national centers. France, Italy, Belgium, the Netherlands, and the Canadian province of Quebec are representative of this form of pluralism. Another kind of pluralism arises from conflicting organizational principles, as exemplified in the United States and Canada by the predominant support for craft unionism in the AFL and for industrial unionism in the CIO before the merger in 1955. A modified third kind of pluralism is based on occupational and status distinctions. It accounts for the existence of independent confederations for white-collar, managerial, and government employees in Sweden, West Germany, France, and other countries.

[5] As a portent the Dutch NVV has inscribed a provision in its constitution whereby the decisions of an international confederation will take absolute precedence; see NVV *Constitution,* 1971, Article 26.

[6] To exemplify, Derek Bok has made the circular observation that by comparison with Sweden, Belgium, and the Netherlands "the labor movement in America has remained markedly decentralized in the sense that the central confederation has had relatively little power over its member unions." "Reflections on the Distinctive Character of American Labor Laws," *Harvard Law Review* 84, no. 6 (April 1971): 1407-8. Everett M. Kassalow, *Trade Unions and Industrial Relations: An International Comparison* (New York: Random House, 1969), p. 114, has suggested that the French trade union confederations enjoy "more power than most other Western movements," but has furnished no criteria to support the assessment. While it may be true that in Belgium "both the Socialist and — even more — the Catholic confederation offices are strong," the assertion must be taken

The first object of this paper is to point out the existence of salient characteristics by which the internal authority of a confederation over its affiliates may be assessed. The second and more difficult one is the search for causal links that may explain why some confederations have more internal authority than others.[7]

First, some preliminary observations:

1. This study is limited to those industrialized Western countries for which adequate information is available from primary or secondary sources. Despite obvious differences, the countries in this group and their trade union movements are sufficiently similar that comparative analysis is feasible. Inclusion of less-developed countries would not only be technically unmanageable, but would also introduce an excessive degree of heterogeneity.

2. Central to the investigation is the relationship between confederations and their constituent national unions. The position of other bodies (state federations, trade councils, and similar ones) will be disregarded both for the sake of simplification and because in practice they occupy almost everywhere a subordinate role regardless of their formal constitutional rights. The main contestants in the competition for hegemony or dominance are the leaders of national centers and national unions.

3. In all Western countries save Austria and Israel the national centers are federative rather than unitary organizations.[8] The federative institutional form

safeguards the autonomy of national unions, for in federative organizations the center can exercise only as much authority as the constituent parts are willing to relinquish. Any increase in central authority entails a corresponding diminution of autonomy, a fact well understood among trade unions.[9] When the largest confederation in the Netherlands, the NVV, met in special convention in February 1973 to resolve a constitutional crisis over the proper balance of authority and autonomy, the preamble to the key resolution succinctly expressed the equation:

> The NVV is a federation of autonomous organizations, it being understood that their autonomy is limited precisely by the fact of federative cooperation. The individual unions delegate to the NVV a portion of their independent authority to make decisions. The extent of this delegation is determined by the NVV constitution.[10]

on faith, as it were. Val R. Lorwin, "Labor Organizations and Politics in Belgium and France," in *National Labor Movements in the Postwar World*, Everett Kassalow, ed. (Evanston, Ill.: Northwestern University Press, 1963), p. 145.

[7] Two recent studies addressed in part to the same questions have been prepared by R. M. Martin, "The Authority of Trade Union Centres: The Australian Council of Trade Unions and the British Trades Union Congress," *Journal of Industrial Relations* 4, no. 1 (April 1962):1-19, and Bruce W. Headey, "Trade Unions and National Wage Policies," *Journal of Politics* 32, no. 2 (May 1970):407-30. For an earlier comparison of the Scandinavian central bodies see Walter Galenson, "Scandinavia," in *Comparative Labor Movements* (New York: Prentice-Hall, 1952), pp. 128-52. On Germany there is a recent unpublished study by Gerhard Leminsky, "The Central Trade Union Organisation and the Individual Union in Federal Germany," prepared for the 3rd World Congress of the International Industrial Relations Association, London, September 1973 (original text in German).

[8] The ÖGB's sixteen individual unions are branches or subdivisions of the national center "having no legal personality of their own," as stated in the official commentary accompanying the constitution of the national center. Their jurisdictions are centrally determined, their individual constitutions require the approval of the center, and their employees and officers are legally deemed to be in the service of the national center. Moreover, an Austrian trade union member is first and foremost a member of the national center and only in a secondary sense a member of the particular

industrial union to which he has been assigned by virtue of his employment. See *Statuten und Geschaeftsordnung des Oesterreichischen Gewerkschaftsbundes*, 5th ed. (Vienna, 1961), p. 21. Compare Fritz Klenner, "Der Oesterreichische Gewerkschaftsbund," in *Verbaende und Wirtschaftspolitik in Oesterreich*, Theodor Pütz, ed. (Berlin: Duncker and Humblot, 1966), p. 444, and Ernst Lakenbacher, "White-Collar Unions in Austria," in *White Collar Trade Unions*, Adolf Sturmthal, ed. (Urbana, Ill.: University of Illinois Press, 1966), pp. 47-48. The other unitary national center is the Histadrut in Israel. A particularly good account of its internal government will be found in Ferdynand Zweig, "The Jewish Trade Union Movement in Israel," in *Integration and Development in Israel*, S. N. Eisenstadt *et al.*, eds. (New York: Praeger, 1970), pp. 162-84.

Transformation from a federative to a unitary structure has been a matter of active concern in the Netherlands for some time. The NVV came close to adopting such a scheme a few years ago. Currently the Protestant confederation (CNV) has it under consideration. It has commissioned a firm of management consultants to investigate the most desirable and most efficient organizational structure. According to its president, "if that investigation leads to a complete integration of all affiliated unions, the CNV will no longer be a confederation in the real meaning of that term but one big union inside of which the representation of interests will be divided according to groups and sectors." *S. E. R. Bulletin*, no. 48 (December 20, 1972), p. 40.

[9] Flanders seemed to see it differently: "In the eyes of the general public, the TUC has come to be regarded as so representative a body that the limits of its powers are frequently forgotten. Those limits are easily defined by the fact that a trade union in affiliating to the TUC does not yield up any part of its autonomy." Flanders, *Trade Unions*, 7th ed. (London: Hutchinson, 1968), p. 61. That does not seem to be a tenable position. In fact, in another place Flanders listed the various rules that confer explicit powers on the TUC over its affiliated organizations, *ibid.*, pp. 58-60.

[10] *Kort verslag van de 5de zitting van de NVV-Verbondsvergadering*, February 12, 1973, p.6.

4. Any assessment of internal authority must be an abstraction, for it can only express the composite of a series of individual relationships between the center and its parts. Any center is stronger when dealing with a small and weak affiliate, or even several of them together, than when facing its most important constituent organization.[11] Also, dependence on central services and on confederal support differs widely because each national union operates within a different market context and with different resources.

ATTRIBUTES OF AUTHORITY

In order to compare the extent of confederal authority this study relies on three attributes that appear most germane to the question. One is the share of total dues income collected by the national unions that the confederation receives for its own purposes; second is the control the confederation exercises over the internal affairs of its affiliates; third is the confederal role in industrial rule making, especially in collective bargaining.[12]

Admittedly the information for each category is sketchy, imprecise, and, at least for the second and third, subjective. The second category particularly lacks data. Nevertheless, it has seemed worthwhile to make this initial effort even if subsequent investigations should reveal errors of fact or inference.

Division of Resources

To meet their expenses, confederations depend on contributions from their constituent organizations.[13] They may have some independent sources of revenue, perhaps from sales of publications or interest payments from invested funds; but these are not likely to be significant. In any event, direct taxation of individual members by the center is not the practice, with the exception of unitary organizations. Obviously, direct taxation would diminish the financial dependence of the center on its affiliates.[14] The amount of the obligatory contribution may be expressed either as a percentage of the dues income received by affiliated organizations themselves, as for example in West Germany, or as a fixed sum for each reported individual member, as in the United States. We shall refer to the confederation's portion as its income share.

As a general proposition, the larger the confederation's share of the total income received by the movement, the stronger and more centralized it is likely to be in relation to its affiliated unions. After all, income received by the confederation is converted into central services, staff, benefits, and reserves. Their expansion tends to enhance the position of the center. Central strike funds have long been considered a key instrument of confederal control over the bargaining activities of affiliated unions. While only the stronger centers have usually managed to build up central strike funds, other central services, such as organizing, research, lobbying, and publicity, serve the same purpose. Their scope is limited only by the resources which the national center administers. As resources increase, so does authority.

The point, of course, is not a new one. Observers of British trade unions have frequently equated the low income of the Trades Union Congress, both in absolute terms and as a percentage of total trade union revenues, with its low level of authority, compared with confederations in other countries.[15] In his history of the American Federation of Labor Philip Taft regarded changes in its income "as some measure of the support the organization was able to gain."[16] William Leiserson took the financial arrangements when the Federation merged with the Congress of Industrial Organizations as evidence that the national unions had intended to retain most powers of union government firmly in their own hands.[17]

---

[11] See, for example, Michael Rogin, "Voluntarism: The Political Functions of an Antipolitical Doctrine," *Industrial and Labor Relations Review* 15, no. 4 (July 1962): esp. 529.

[12] The importance of the locus of control over internal union affairs and collective bargaining is underscored by Arthur Goldberg's observation on the division of authority in the AFL-CIO. In his commentary on the unification of AFL and CIO, to which he himself made an important contribution as negotiator and draftsman, he wrote: "The key conception underlying the AFL-CIO's structure is autonomy, which means the right of the constituent international [i.e., national] unions . . . to manage their collective bargaining and internal administrative affairs as they see fit." *AFL-CIO: Labor United* (New York: McGraw-Hill, 1956), p. 142.

[13] Only in exceptional cases do funds flow in the other direction. For many years, the central bodies in Italy subsidized their affiliated unions instead of being subsidized by them. As in France, some of the funds involved very probably came from outside the movement. Recently, however, the introduction of checkoff systems has reduced the authority of the central bodies, so that errant affiliates can no longer be disciplined by threats to cut off financial support.

[14] In 1913 the AFL polled its affiliates for their views on a proposal to levy a tax directly upon each member for support of a joint defense fund. The proposal failed. A number of opposing unions feared that it "would lead to too much concentration of power in the hands of the Federation." Philip Taft, *The A.F. of L. in the Time of Gompers* (New York: Harper, 1957), p. 118.

[15] See, for example, H. A. Clegg, *The System of Industrial Relations in Great Britain* (Oxford: Basil Blackwell, 1970), pp. 401-2, and Flanders, *Trade Unions*, p. 65.

[16] Taft, *The A.F. of L. in the Time of Gompers*, p. 52.

[17] William M. Leiserson, *American Trade Union Democracy* (New York: Columbia University Press, 1961), p. 345. Bok and Dunlop came to a rather different conclusion. To them the size of the staff at AFL-CIO headquarters,

Support for the usefulness of income share as a measure of confederal authority and particularly of changes in that authority appears in Table 1. It shows the percentage of total dues receipts the member unions of the Swedish central body LO have been remitting for the last forty years. The table indicates that with the passage of time the percentage has almost doubled. The absolute figures are even more impressive. In 1930, LO unions contributed about 2 million kronor to the national center; by 1971 the amount had risen to about 60 million. There seems to be a direct relationship between the timing of the relative increases and specific changes in authority relations. The disproportionately large percentage jump in the early 1940s coincided with the adoption of the constitutional reforms of 1941 that completed the concentration-of-authority movement of the second half of the 1930s. The second large percentage increase in the early 1960s probably reflected the institutionalization of centralized wage bargaining which had begun in 1956 and which, one may safely assume, imposed sizable costs on the national center.

Table 1: Percentage of Total Dues Receipts of National Unions Paid to the Swedish National Center LO, 1930-1971

Year	Percent	Year	Percent
1930	10.5	1951	14.3
1931	11.0	1952	15.7
1932	12.0	1953	14.6
1933	11.7	1954	12.2
1934	10.6	1955	12.9
1935	10.6	1956	13.4
1936	10.5	1957	16.7
1937	10.5	1958	16.0
1938	10.9	1959	15.6
1939	10.7	1960	15.7
1940	11.2	1961	15.1
1941	11.0	1962	19.7
1942	14.0	1963	20.1
1943	15.6	1964	21.0
1944	15.9	1965	20.3
1945	11.7	1966	17.9
1946	10.9	1967	21.8
1947	15.2	1968	21.0
1948	16.2	1969	19.9
1949	15.5	1970	19.1
1950	15.0	1971	18.4

SOURCE: Landsorganisationen i Sverige.

While the absolute level of financial support can be a useful measure of the scope of central body activities, intercountry comparisons based on relative income shares yield more insight into comparative balance of power relationships. Per capita taxes are transfer payments that diminish the amount of income controlled by the national unions themselves. The revenues are used for activities that may overlap or compete with the activities of individual unions.[18] Thus, it would seem plausible that relative income shares can serve as an approximate measure of confederal authority, however imperfect the measure may be.

Table 2 provides comparative data on income shares of national centers. No refined accuracy should be read into the figures. Trade unions of different countries do not use uniform accounting and reporting procedures, nor is there any coincidence of practice regarding the components of membership dues. There is not even any uniformity among unions within a particular country. Still, as far as it is available a single base of computation has been used in this study: the total dues receipts of national unions. Dues retained by local unions for local purposes have been excluded wherever possible.

Allowing a generous margin for probable error, the range of differences between national centers is striking. The central bodies in Australia, Great Britain, and the United States receive between 2 and 3 percent of total annual dues collected by their affiliates, as contrasted with much higher percentages in Austria, Belgium, Denmark, France, West Germany, the Netherlands, Norway, and Sweden. Without contrary evidence, one should conclude that confederal authority in the second group is greater, and perhaps substantially greater, than in the first.

An exception to this proposition is the West German central body, the DGB. Its 12 percent income share is constitutionally mandated and unquestionably permits a wide range of central services.[19] The percentage, however, is lower than that agreed to at the founding congress in 1949 when 15 percent became the compromise between advocates of national union autonomy and proponents of a highly centralized organization. Three years later the autonomists won out, and the contribution was reduced to

---

financed of course by the per capita payments of affiliated unions, indicated that the merged organization was "a much more significant body than the AFL of several years ago." Derek C. Bok and John T. Dunlop, *Labor and the American Community* (New York: Simon and Schuster, 1970), p. 192.

[18] The author of a recent study of the Canadian Labor Congress points out that "almost every function now performed by the Congress could be performed by the affiliates themselves. Many of the larger affiliates do in fact provide for themselves the services which the Congress performs for the smaller unions. Even in those areas in which the Congress can most plausibly claim to act on behalf of its affiliates and stake out a field for itself, it nevertheless finds itself in competition with them." David Kwavnick, *Organized Labour and Pressure Politics: The Canadian Labour Congress 1956-1968* (Montreal: McGill-Queen's University Press, 1972), p. 38.

[19] DBG, *Constitution*, 1972, Par. 4.

Table 2: Annual Contributions Paid to National
Centers as a Percentage of Total Dues Income
Collected by Affiliated Unions   (Various years)

National Center	Year	Percent
Australia (ACTU)[a]	(1966-1967)	2
Austria (ÖGB)[b]	(1972)	80
Belgium (CSC)[c]	(1972)	40
Denmark (LO)[d]	(1972)	9
France (CFDT)[e]	(1970)	21
(FO)[f]	(c. 1969)	13
West Germany (DGB)[g]	(1972)	12
Great Britain (TUC)[h]	(1964)	2
Netherlands (NVV)[i]	(1972)	15
(CNV)[j]	(1972)	18.1
(NKV)[k]	(1972)	18.5
Norway (LO)[l]	(1973)	18
Sweden (LO)[m]	(1971)	18.4
United States (AFL-CIO)[n]	(1966)	3

[a] Calculated from data in P. W. D. Matthews and G. W. Ford, eds., *Australian Trade Unions* (Melbourne: Sun Books, 1968), esp. pp. 93 and 139-40.

[b] Calculated from ÖGB financial report for 1972.

[c] Letter to the author from U.S. labor attaché, Brussels, September 20, 1973.

[d] Letter to the author from the treasurer of the Danish LO, June 1, 1973.

[e] Calculated from data in Guy Caire, *Les syndicats ouvriers* (Paris: Presses Universitaires, 1971), p. 412.

[f] B.W. Headey, "Trade Unions and National Wage Policy," *Journal of Politics* 32, no.2 (May 1970):428-29.

[g] DGB *Constitution*, 1972, Par. 4. See also Kurt Hirche, *Die Finanzen der Gewerkschaften* (Düsseldorf: Econ, 1972).

[h] Calculated from data in *Trade Unionism* (London: TUC, 1967), p.137, and *TUC Proceedings 1965*, p. 62.

[i] Letter to the author from the NVV chief fiscal officer, May 8, 1973.

[j] Letter to the author from the acting treasurer of the CNV, June 25, 1973.

[k] Letter to the author from the treasurer of the NKV, May 3, 1973.

[l] Estimate furnished by the treasurer of LO by letter to the author, November 23, 1973.

[m] From information supplied by Landsorganisationen i Sverige by letter dated May 17, 1973.

[n] Calculated from data in AFL-CIO, *Report of the Executive Council*, December 1967, p. 15; Edward P. Curtin, *Union Initiation Fees, Dues, and Per Capita Tax* (New York: Conference Board, July 1968); and *A Financial Survey of the Major National and International Unions of the United States* (Washington, D.C.: Chamber of Commerce of the U.S., 1966). There may have been a slight increase in the percentage in very recent years because of an increase in the per capita tax from 7¢ to 10¢ in 1971, but this depends on the extent to which the dues income of national unions may itself have increased.

12 percent. The ostensible reason was that increased wages and rising union membership figures still left the central body with an adequate income in absolute terms, which was true. In reality the cut was insisted upon by a few large national unions after the death of the DGB's first postwar president, a very strong personality.[20] Since 1952, all attempts by proponents of a strong center to restore at least a portion of the cut have failed, including a purely symbolic effort in 1971 to raise the percentage from 12 to 12.5.[21]

Austria also requires special comment. As a unitary body the national center, the ÖGB, receives 100 percent of dues income, for constitutionally it alone exercises fiscal authority *(Finanzhoheit)*. It is also responsible for paying all expenses of individual unions, including the salaries of their officers and staffs, their administrative costs, and the benefits paid to their members. In practice, however, the dues collected from individual members pass through the national unions which are permitted to deduct their approved expenses before transferring the balance. As an incentive to a high rate of dues collection and to economy of administration the national center allows its unions to retain for their own use an additional proportion of dues ranging from 5 to 22 percent (and averaging about 20 percent) for special programs under individual union auspices, such as the upkeep of vacation homes and various social programs.[22] Under these circumstances it may seem somewhat arbitrary to list the ÖGB's income share as 80 percent.

Intervention in Internal Union Affairs

Differences in income shares often parallel the distribution of power over internal union government. Unions prefer to view their central body not as a superior level of government, empowered to overrule their decisions, but as a useful instrument for common external action. One would, therefore, expect them to resist attempts by national centers to encroach on their internal rule making. Successful resistance preserves autonomy. Failure leads to increased confederal scrutiny and controls.[23]

Unfortunately, available information in this area is severely limited, but the record of four national centers (the Austrian ÖGB, the Swedish LO, the British TUC, and the AFL-CIO) indicates substantial differences in the

[20] Guenter Triesch, *Die Macht der Funktionaere* (Düsseldorf: Karl Rauch, 1956), pp. 21-22.

[21] Kurt Hirche, *Die Finanzen der Gewerkschaften* (Düsseldorf: Econ, 1972), pp. 302-4.

[22] Klenner, "Der Oesterreichische Gewerkschaftsbund," pp. 444-45.

[23] Although outdated, the following observations on Finland by Carl Erik Knoellinger, *Labor in Finland*

degree of confederal control over internal union affairs. Compulsory guidelines prevail in Austria and Sweden where the national centers collect high income shares. Their American and British counterparts, with proportionally much lower incomes, have far less control over the government of their affiliates.

The AFL-CIO constitution empowers the executive council to give directions to, and if necessary to suspend, an affiliated union that after investigation has been found to be "dominated, controlled, or substantially influenced in the conduct of its affairs" by corrupt or totalitarian (especially communist or fascist) elements.[24] The general council of the TUC holds similar authority to intervene when it has grounds to assume that the activities of an affiliated union "are detrimental to the interests of the Trade Union Movement or contrary to the declared principles and policy" of the TUC.[25] In both cases the grant of such authority is of fairly recent origin. It resulted mainly from events that had brought serious discredit on the unions: corruption in certain AFL unions, communist control in a number of CIO unions, and illegal tampering with election rules in the Electrical Trades Union of the TUC when that union was under communist control. Neither central body has yet sought to interpret its authority in a sweeping manner. What has been said about the TUC — "under this rule the General Council has a wide latitude, but it has exercised its discretion in an ultra-cautious manner"[26] — applies almost equally to the AFL-CIO, though the latter has invoked its power in four cases to discipline unions charged with corrupt practices,

including expulsion of the Teamsters Union, and once to expel a union for dual unionism.[27]

Rules governing membership admission are of central importance to unions seeking control over the labor market. Closed unions and unions with discriminatory membership policies have often embarrassed the labor movement in the United States, but proposals to adopt stringent central guidelines on admission standards have invariably been rejected as inconsistent with the autonomy of affiliates.[28] As a compromise, the constitution of the merged AFL-CIO declares that "all workers whatever their race, color, creed, or national origins are entitled to share in the full benefits of trade union organization."[29] Similarly, the TUC *Rules* hold it to be an aim of the congress "to assist in the complete organisation of all workers eligible for membership of its affiliated organisations."[30] Both instances should be regarded, however, as statements of principle or of intent rather than as enforceable policy. No explicit sanctions are tied to violations, though pressures to comply have sometimes been successful.

Austria and Sweden exemplify an entirely different approach. As a unitary organization, the Austrian confederation holds sweeping powers of supervision over its unions.[31] Its constitutional authority includes an obligation to control "the internal structure and activities

---

(Cambridge: Harvard University Press, 1960), p. 133, illustrate the point:

> That the SAK had secured an explicit right to control the constitutions of its member unions is indicative of the centralist tendencies of the Finnish trade union movement at the present time. Several other examples of this tendency can be found in the constitution of the SAK and even in the statutes of its member unions. Drafts of new collective agreements and other matters affecting the course of collective bargaining must be submitted in advance by the national unions to the executive committee of the SAK. Theoretically, this gives the executive committee unlimited possibilities of unifying the claims brought forward by different unions. But, what has happened in practice after the removal of wage restrictions (although experience has been limited) seems to indicate that efforts to coordinate the bargaining policies of different unions may cause serious discords between the SAK and the unions.

[24] AFL-CIO, *Constitution,* 1969, Article VII, Sec. 7.

[25] TUC, *Rules and Standing Orders,* 1971, Rule 13.

[26] John Lovell and B. C. Roberts, *A Short History of the T.U.C.* (London: Macmillan, 1968), p. 183. In September 1973 the TUC expelled twenty relatively small unions for refusing to adhere to a resolution under which TUC affiliates were not permitted to become or remain registered

organizations under the Industrial Relations Act of 1971. Although the drastic action would appear to indicate an assertion of substantial confederal authority, it seems more correct to regard it as the consequence of a policy of defiant noncompliance with the act adopted by a majority of TUC unions, especially some of the very largest affiliates.

[27] Gary N. Chaison, "Federation Expulsions and Union Mergers in the United States," *Relations Industrielles* 28, no. 2, (1973):343-60.

[28] Leiserson, *American Trade Union Democracy,* p. 344. Lloyd Ulman recalls that, while the Knights of Labor opened their membership to almost anyone who had ever worked for a wage, the national unions in the AFL defeated all "attempts to induce the AF of L to compel its affiliated unions to admit negroes to membership on equal terms with white workers.... The successful opposition invariably rested its case upon the inability of the Federation to meddle in the internal affairs of its autonomous affiliates." *The Rise of the National Trade Union* (Cambridge: Harvard University Press, 1955), p. 389.

[29] AFL-CIO, *Constitution,* 1969, Article VIII, Sec. 9.

[30] TUC, *Rules and Standing Order,* 1971, Rule 2.

[31] The official commentary accompanying the ÖGB Constitution declares that "the sixteen individual unions are subdivisions of the national center having no legal personality of their own." *Statuten und Geschaeftsordnung des Oesterreichischen Gewerkschaftsbundes,* 5th ed. (Vienna: 1961), p. 21. Although this commentary applies to the 1961 constitution, applicable provisions have not changed since that time.

of the individual unions."[32] To this end, the center decides on the acceptability of the constitutions and bylaws of affiliated unions; determines the level of dues for all classes of members; prescribes the conditions for admission, denial, and transfer of union membership; and generally acts as the guiding force of the movement.

To justify such far-reaching intervention, Austrian trade union leaders cite the importance of preventing a splintering of trade union strength and the shared gains of improved efficiency. A centralized treasury means that there are no affluent and impoverished unions, but that all are on an equal footing. They concede that a highly centralized administration may have some disadvantages, but insist that these are outweighed by the benefits.[33]

Structurally, the Swedish LO is a federative rather than a unitary body, but its powers of control are barely inferior to the Austrian center. The decisive change occurred in 1941 after sustained government pressure for greater centralization. That year's constitutional reform shifted the locus of power from the national unions to the LO.[34] Huntford overshoots the mark with his picturesque observation that "the LO commands obedience before the individual unions, as the bishop before the parish priest."[35] Elvander's more balanced assessment, however, registers essentially the same conclusion:

> A deeply rooted tendency exists among Swedish interest association, as in other spheres of society, toward the centralization of power and the development of larger structures. In recent years this tendency has become even more accentuated. Especially within organizations on the labor market decision-making power has shifted from the lower units — e.g., the individual unions and business firms — to the peak organizations. On the latter level the center of power has moved in turn from the representative organs to the various executive councils and leading officials.[36]

The LO imposes on its affiliated unions several specific obligations. In pursuit of structural reform it insists that unions must be open to all applicants, that they must accept all transfers from other unions, and that members whose change of employment involves a change of industry must change to the corresponding union.[37]

The most striking requirement, however, circumscribes the participation of individual members in ratifying the terms of collective agreements. LO requires the executive board of each national union to retain the power of "final decision in questions concerning the termination of collective contracts, the acceptance or rejection of proposals for agreement, or for resorting to direct action."[38] This rule eliminates binding contract ratification votes and enhances the authority of union officers.[39] The intent of the rule is neither arbitrary nor obscure. LO negotiates nationwide basic wage agreements with its counterpart on the employer side, the SAF, and these agreements establish the framework for subsidiary negotiations at the industry and the enterprise level. If a ratification vote could nullify a contract between an individual union and an employers' association, the basic wage agreement would be undermined and so would LO's long-term policy of wage solidarity that aims at a narrowing of wage differentials. It is far easier to obtain compliance with this policy from union officers than from individual members. The mandatory rule against binding ratification votes has frequently provoked controversy at LO congresses; nevertheless, it continues in effect as singular evidence of the concentration of authority in the Swedish national center.

Setting the Terms of Employment

Confederations exist ultimately because they perform functions useful to their constituents. Most functions fit one of four categories:[40] (1) representing trade union interests before government bodies, cultivating ties with political parties, maintaining links with foreign and international trade union movements, and, under plural unionism, safeguarding the special interests of one confederal group against the others; (2) providing services to the movement as a whole, or to those parts of it that cannot afford to provide their own, such as education and

[32] ÖGB, *Constitution*, 1971, Par. 4, Sec. 5.

[33] Fritz Klenner, *Die Oesterreichischen Gewerkschaften* (Vienna: Verlag des ÖGB, 1953), p. 1607.

[34] T. L. Johnston, *Collective Bargaining in Sweden* (London: Allen and Unwin, 1962), p. 44.

[35] Roland Huntford, *The New Totalitarians* (New York: Stein and Day, 1972), p. 58.

[36] Nils Elvander, "Democracy and Large Organizations," in *Politics in the Welfare State*, M. Donald Hancock and Gideon Sjoberg, eds. (New York: Columbia University Press, 1972), p. 303.

[37] Johnston, *Collective Bargaining in Sweden*, pp. 47-49. Similar rules are in effect in the Dutch NVV.

[38] *Ibid.*, p. 50.

[39] Actually, this rule is not entirely the outcome of developments in the second half of the 1930s. Elvander, "Democracy and Large Organizations," p. 305, has pointed out that already at the beginning of the century, Swedish "union leaders had begun to reserve the right of decisions for themselves, and the vote of members became only advisory."

[40] Concentrating on the AFL-CIO, Bok and Dunlop, *Labor and the American Community*, pp. 189-90, have identified five areas: the resolution of disputes between two or more member unions; the representation of the labor movement on matters of common concern; improvements in the image of the labor movement; the restraint of unions jeopardizing the interests of other elements in the labor movement; and the strengthening of weak links within the labor movement. That this is very much an American listing is indicated by the absence of any reference to collective bargaining.

leadership training, economic and social research, organizing backward sectors, and protecting the weakest segments of the labor force; (3) adjudicating interunion relations, including the settlement of disputes over members and work allocation and the legitimation of established territorial rights; (4) setting basic terms of employment through direct negotiations with employers and governments, coordinating the bargaining activities of individual unions, and intervening in industrial disputes to mediate or rally support.

The first three categories are virtually universal. Some involve only routine functions, and their centralization encounters little resistance from affiliates. Others are of some importance to constituent unions, but require centralized handling for efficiency, economy, or internal harmony.[41]

The fourth area is different. Setting wages and other terms of employment involves functions that, as Martin has noted, "affect the vital interest of unions and . . . to the extent that they are discharged by a central body, inevitably involve limiting the affiliated unions' independence of action."[42] Unions constrained by the terms of a central bargain have surrendered a significant degree of their autonomy. Strong unions give up even more than weak ones because central bargains tend to favor the lower-paid groups.[43]

The issue rests on the unions' own choice of priorities. In Western industrialized countries the principal function of trade unions is the representation of the interests of their members in all forums where the terms of employment are decided; all else is either subordinate or supplemental. It would, therefore, seem highly probable that the distribution of internal authority is closely related to participation in industrial rule making. Hence, a major change in the locus of industrial rule making toward the center should lead to a corresponding change in confederal authority. When centralized bargaining between a trade union confederation and a peak employer organization sets the ground rules for bargaining at lower levels, authority gravitates from national unions to national centers. The converse follows from movement in the opposite direction.

Confederal participation in bargaining can take various forms; not all of them confer an equal measure of authority.[44] Institutionalized top-level negotiations are more important than ad hoc interventions in crises. A central agreement contributes more to confederal authority than participation in developing wage guidelines. Control over strike calls and a central strike fund may be especially effective.

The Austrian ÖGB exemplifies central control at one extreme of the range. The central body has the exclusive right to conclude collective agreements, a right upheld by the Austrian Supreme Court.[45] In practice, the ÖGB only negotiates agreements on issues of economywide import, such as reductions in standard working hours, and allows individual unions to negotiate their own agreements. These agreements, however, are always concluded on behalf of the national center and are not valid without its approval.[46] Through membership in the tripartite Joint Commission on Wages and Prices, the ÖGB also participates in periodic reviews of the economy.[47] Recommendations of the commission serve as guidelines that union negotiators at industry and company level are expected to take into account. Impending strikes or lockouts must be brought to the attention of the central body in time for top officers to take appropriate measures that may include restraints on their constituent unions or permission to draw on the central strike fund.[48]

It would be difficult to carry central authority over collective bargaining much further without transgressing the limits acceptable in a democratic society. Yet, the national centers in the Scandinavian countries, especially Sweden and Norway, are almost equally powerful. There is, however, an interesting difference in origin. In Austria union authority became centralized during the reconstruction of the late 1940s. It did not stem from centralized control over collective bargaining because there was no bargaining then; and, by the time negotiations were resumed, the unions were already thoroughly centralized. In the Scandinavian countries, by contrast, the authority

---

[41] The settlement of jurisdictional disputes probably belongs in this category. It should be kept in mind, however, that in most Western industrialized countries disputes occur infrequently, are of relatively little consequence in industrial relations, and in any event are often resolved by amicable compromise. A major reason is the prevalence of industrial unionism which, though it cannot entirely avoid jurisdictional problems, tends to minimize them.

[42] Martin, "The Authority of Trade Union Centres," p.6.

[43] Unions without an effective presence at the workplace, a common problem in European countries, will be doubly squeezed because works councils and shop stewards will block their quest for compensatory functions in the plant if the level of bargaining moves upward to the central body.

[44] For a discussion of various forms of centralized wage negotiations see C. T. Saunders, "Lessons for Britain from European Experience," in *An Incomes Policy for Britain: Policy Proposals and Research Needs*, Frank Blackaby, ed. (London: Heinemann, 1972), pp. 89-98.

[45] Klenner, *Die Oesterreichischen Gewerkschaften*, p. 1622.

[46] Kurt Steiner, *Politics in Austria* (Boston: Little, Brown, 1972), p. 298.

[47] See James A. Ramsey, "Labor Management Confrontation: The Austrian Answer," *Columbia Journal of World Business* 7, no. 4 (July-August 1972):24-32. Compare Jack Barbash, *Trade Unions and National Economic Policy* (Baltimore: Johns Hopkins Press, 1972), pp. 49-52.

[48] ÖGB, *Constitution*, 1971, Par. 12, Sec. 3(e) and (f).

of the central bodies grew out of the transition to centralized bargaining. In Norway a milestone in this process was the negotiation, in 1935, of a master agreement between the central organizations of trade unions and employers; in revised form it is still in effect.[49] In Sweden the Basic Agreement of 1938, the well-known Saltsjöbaden Agreement, played the same role.

These central agreements are binding on affiliated organizations on both sides. They cover basic procedural matters and some substantive issues besides wages.[50] Distinct from them are the perennial centralized wage negotiations that, at least in Sweden and Norway, establish guidelines for subsidiary bargaining at the industry and the enterprise levels.[51]

In Norway the confederal constitution requires affiliated unions to adhere to a centrally determined wage policy.[52] Unions cannot give notice of termination of collective agreements, present new demands, or call a strike without approval of the central body.[53]

The Swedish confederation has its own observer at industry-level negotiations. In the event of an impasse he has the right to propose a settlement which the affiliated union must consider.[54] The confederation controls a central strike fund, and any national union wishing to draw on it must obtain advance approval for a strike if more than 3 percent of the union's members are likely to be involved.

In Denmark, where the formal authority of the central body is somewhat weaker than in the other Nordic countries, the central Rules for Negotiation stipulate that all agreements shall expire on the same date, a provision that enables the central body to coordinate the negotiations, even if it cannot control the terms of settlement.[55]

Although Austria and the Scandinavian countries are in the lead, confederations in several other Western countries are active participants in bargaining. In Belgium and France the national centers settle important issues of social policy (employment security, training and retraining, supplemental pensions, paid vacations, hours of work, and so forth) through top-level negotiations with employers, but questions of remuneration and specific working conditions still remain under the control of individual unions.[56]

In Australia, the low income share of the central body understates its participation in the determination of the basic terms of employment. The Australian Council of Trade Unions takes the lead in presenting national wage claims and "test cases" to the Commonwealth Arbitration Commission, coordinates collective bargaining in certain industries, and has some say over interstate industrial disputes. Martin, who carefully compared the Australian and British national centers, thought that the substantially greater industrial role of the ACTU enhanced its authority well above that of the TUC in spite of constitutional similarities.[57]

If participation in setting the terms of employment increases the authority of a national center, exclusion or circumscription must diminish it. Recent developments in the Netherlands show that centralization of authority is a reversible process.

For almost two decades after World War II the Netherlands operated a complex system of centralized

[49] Mark Leiserson, *Wages and Economic Control in Norway* (Cambridge: Harvard University Press, 1959), p. 13.

[50] Further "basic agreements" have been negotiated in Sweden and Denmark to cover special subjects, such as works councils, joint consultation, and the rights of shop stewards. For the current texts of the various documents see ILO, *Basic Agreements and Joint Statements on Labour-Management Relations,* Labour-Management Relations Series no. 38 (Geneva: ILO, 1971).

[51] In a Swedish study that has only recently become available in English the authors point out that, though centralized wage negotiations are an established feature of Swedish industrial relations, each round of central wage bargaining rests formally on an *ad hoc* arrangement, for "LO must on each separate occasion obtain the approval of the national unions before central negotiations can begin." The Swedish Employers Confederation (SAF) has proposed a formal agreement to institutionalize central negotiations, but for tactical reasons LO at this time does not wish to assume a permanent commitment. See Gösta Edgren *et al., Wage Formation in the Economy* (London: Allen and Unwin, 1973), p. 53.

[52] Mark Leiserson, *Wages and Economic Control in Norway,* p.13.

[53] Herbert Dorfman, *Labor Relations in Norway* (Oslo: Norwegian Joint Committee on International Social Policy, 1966), p. 57.

[54] Bo Carlson, *Trade Unions in Sweden* (Stockholm: Tiden, 1969), p. 69.

[55] It has been pointed out that the Danish LO "exercises much greater influence on wage questions than is theoretically provided for in the statutes. However, the question of the balance of responsibility between the Federation and the affiliated unions is still a bone of contention and from time to time it is the subject of lively discussion in the trade union movement." Albert Kocik, *The Danish Trade Union Movement* (Brussels: ICFTU, 1961), p. 40. Compare William Fellner *et al., The Problem of Rising Prices* (Paris: OECD, 1961), p. 289.

[56] For Belgium see Roger Blanpain, "Recent Trends in Collective Bargaining," *International Labour Review* 104, nos. 1-2 (July-August 1971):111-30. For France see Yves Delamotte, "Recent Collective Bargaining Trends in France," *International Labour Review* 103, no. 4 (April 1971):esp. 361-66.

[57] Martin, "The Authority of Trade Union Centres," pp. 9-14. Compare W. P. Evans, "The Australian Council of Trade Unions," in *Australian Trade Unions,* P.W.D. Matthews and G. W. Ford, eds. (Melbourne: Sun Books, 1968), pp. 117-18.

wage determination that concentrated unprecedented authority in all three national centers: socialist, Catholic, and Protestant. In the early 1960s, national wage setting began to disintegrate, and from that time on proponents of centralization and decentralization engaged in constant struggle, each view having supporters among trade unions, employers, and government agencies.[58]

Gradually, the decentralizers gained the upper hand, but it was not until 1972 that the full extent of their ascendancy became clear. With the active participation of a government deeply concerned about one of the highest rates of inflation in western Europe, the central organizations of employers and trade unions had negotiated the draft of a "social contract." Its comprehensive terms imposed obligations on the private parties and on government, on the latter especially in social legislation and budgetary allocations. The proposed terms, however, encountered vigorous opposition from the largest affiliate of the socialist confederation (NVV), the Industrial Workers Union. Its aggressive and somewhat leftist leadership rejected the wage provisions as insufficient in relation to projected profits, declared itself dissatisfied with half-baked measures to reduce income differentials, and deplored the alleged failure to initiate far-reaching changes in the distribution of power in society.

Without the assent of this one union, whose strength is concentrated in the key metals sector, no social contract could be implemented. When it became clear that its leaders would not budge, the president of the NVV resigned even though he had the express support of the leaders of all other unions in his own confederation, as well as the tacit support of the heads of the other two confederations.[59]

The conflict led to a thorough reappraisal of relations between confederation and affiliates, including a review of internal structures and decision making. The process is still under way, and, in the spirit of unhurried deliberation characteristic of Dutch society, various study groups have been appointed with instructions to report in two to three years. One need not wait for the results to recognize that a significant downward shift in authority has occurred, thus reversing a pattern of concentration after at least two decades of centralized authority.[60]

While the bargaining role of the Dutch confederation has declined, it still remains more significant than the position of the West German, British, and North American central bodies. The German DGB has the constitutional right to develop basic bargaining principles and may also establish guidelines for the conduct and support of strikes.[61] In practice, however, the individual unions bargain on their own and tolerate no central intervention of any consequence except, at most, confederal intercession in a major dispute.[62] In the mid-1950s, a DGB attempt to negotiate a national agreement on working hours was torpedoed by the powerful Metalworkers Union on the grounds of alleged interference with its bargaining autonomy.[63] The government's economic policies have contributed very little to the DGB's internal authority since they do not postulate centralized bargaining.

The authority of the British TUC to intervene in collective bargaining is very modest during periods of relative economic stability, but tends to increase during a crisis. In the immediate postwar period (1945 to 1949) its contribution to the maintenance of wage restraint was exceedingly important, but would not have sufficed without the consent of the major unions.[64] During a fairly brief period in 1965, when a Labour government sought to pursue a restrictive prices and incomes policy, the TUC obtained reluctant approval from its affiliates to scrutinize their wage claims. This "vetting" procedure, which was in any event voluntary, was intended as an alternative to more incisive government wage controls, but proved to be as unsatisfactory to the government as it was distasteful to the unions.[65] In the industrial relations and energy crises

within the exclusive control of individual unions in place of the active monitoring by the national centers that was once the practice.

[61] DGB, *Constitution*, 1972, Par. 2, Sec. 4(f) and (g).

[62] Kurt Sontheimer, *The Government and Politics of West Germany* (London: Hutchinson, 1972), p. 102. Sontheimer writes that "the leaders of the various unions have until now kept a careful eye on the Central Office of the DGB not becoming too powerful."

[63] Triesch, *Die Macht der Funktionaere*, p.22. The existing national agreement on conciliation procedures has no binding force on constituent unions.

[64] For a general review see Gerald Dorfman, *Wage Politics in Britain, 1945-1967* (Ames: Iowa State University Press, 1973). Dorfman maintains that the authority of the TUC declined in the 1950s and especially in the 1960s, but as a description of the general trend this is probably not correct.

[65] Concern over the economic effects of mounting wildcat strikes and lagging trade union efforts to bring them under effective control led the British Labour government in 1969 to prepare an industrial relations bill which included financial penalties for strikers and their organizations. Trade union

[58] W. Albeda, "Recent Trends in Collective Bargaining in the Netherlands," *International Labour Review* 103, no. 3 (March 1971):247-68.

[59] It should be noted that a slightly altered agreement was subsequently negotiated under the title "central agreement" rather than "social contract."

[60] A similar development seems to be under way in Italy. Aside from the growth of checkoff agreements that are making individual unions financially more independent of central control, collective bargaining has become increasingly a matter

of 1973 to 1974, the TUC sought to overcome the impasse regarding above-ceiling pay increases for the coal miners by pledging on behalf of its affiliates not to use the settlement in mining as a basis for wage demands in other industries. The government, however, expressed understandable skepticism about the TUC's ability to guarantee observance of its pledge.

A moderate shift toward greater central authority has occurred in labor disputes. Since 1955 the TUC has been constitutionally empowered to be informed of an impending or actual conflict, "including unauthorized and unconstitutional stoppages of work," especially where large numbers of workers are involved. "To effect a just settlement of the dispute" the general council of the TUC "may tender their considered opinion and advice thereon to the organization concerned."[66] Refusal to heed the advice could entail sanctions, even to the point of expulsion; but these have never been applied and are not likely ever to be. The TUC has, however, on several occasions exercised its right to intervene, notably in the nationalized industries and in disputes potentially damaging to the public image of the union movement.

The authority of the AFL-CIO in matters of collective bargaining requires few comments. It has no formal powers to intervene in the negotiations of its affiliates, seeks none, and has little precedent even for informal intervention. The emergence of coordinated bargaining in several major corporations has made no difference except perhaps for enhancing the role of the Industrial Union Department.[67] As regards industrial conflicts the constitutional position of the AFL-CIO is even weaker than the TUC's, although it has sometimes unofficially intervened to moderate the bargaining posture of an affiliated union if the dispute created a public relations problem. By and large, the role of the AFL-CIO in industrial disputes has consisted of mustering support for its affiliates. The short-lived participation in Phase 2 of the Nixon administration's inflation control program contributed no lasting increment

to the authority of the central body, and bargaining autonomy remains a cardinal principle.

A COMPOSITE PICTURE

The preceding review of three key attributes of the authority of national centers has shown the existence of substantial intercountry differences. It has also revealed a relatively high degree of internal correspondence. Centers strong in one area are likely to be strong in the other two, and the opposite is also true. There are, however, some inconsistencies. The West German DGB draws a respectable income share, but does not rank high in other respects. The Australian Council of Trade Unions plays an important role in national arbitration, but financially is kept on a short string and has little say in internal union affairs.[68]

In order to diminish the distortions resulting from reliance on a single measure, a rather elementary attempt at combination has been made by assigning a value of one to three points to each national center for each attribute. Three points signify a high degree of centralized authority, such as collecting a large income share, while one point designates a low degree (see Table 3). Although different raters might not agree on the proper value in each case, it is not very likely that the relative standings would be much affected.[69]

For fourteen national centers sufficient composite information is available to divide them into three groups according to the degree of central authority. The most centralized group consists of the Austrian, Norwegian, and Swedish central bodies. The least centralized organizations operate in Australia, West Germany, Britain, and the United States. Somewhere in the middle are the Belgian, Danish, French, and Dutch national centers.

Fragmentary information on fourteen other confederations in industrialized countries indicates that they would probably distribute themselves as follows: (1) highly centralized, the Israeli Histadrut; (2) moderately centralized, the Belgian FGTB, the Finnish SAK, the French CGT, the New Zealand Federation of Labor, and the three Italian confederations (CGIL, CISL, and UIL);

---

opposition to the bill was so adamant that it threatened the survival of Prime Minister Harold Wilson's government and forced it to negotiate a compromise. Under its terms the government dropped the bill in exchange for greater TUC authority to intervene in unauthorized disputes on the same basis as it was already able to do in union-approved disputes. The end result, however, fell short of the government's aims, for the relationship between the TUC and its affiliated unions was not materially altered. The story of the negotiations has been related in some detail by Peter Jenkins in *The Battle of Downing Street* (London: Charles Knight, 1970).

[66] TUC, *Rules and Standing Order*, 1971, Rule 11.

[67] Bok and Dunlop, *Labor and the American Community*, pp. 197-98, hazarded the guess that the AFL-CIO's authority could grow in the future through the use of coordinated bargaining and an increasing amount of government intervention in disputes settlement.

[68] It should be noted that under Australian law the registration requirements impose rules on individual unions that preempt rules that might otherwise have been devised by the central body. Furthermore, legal regulation of internal union affairs predates by many years the formation of the ACTU.

[69] It may also be argued that the rating device is too crude, first because it does not allow for a sufficiently wide range of distinctions and second because it assigns equal values to factors that should be given different weights on grounds of unequal significance. Even if these criticisms were valid and refinements were introduced, it is doubtful that the relative rankings would be substantially different.

Table 3: Composite Estimate of
Confederal Authority

	Income share[a]	Intervention in internal union affairs	Involvement in collective bargaining	Total
Highly centralized				
Austria (ÖGB)	3	3	3	9
Norway (LO)	3 (est.)	2	3	8
Sweden (LO)	3	2	3	8
Moderately centralized				
Belgium (CSC)	3	2	2	7
Denmark (LO)	2	2	2	6
France (CFDT)	3	2	2	7
(FO)	2 (est.)	1	2	5
Netherlands (NVV)	3	2	2	7
(CNV)	3	2	2	7
(NKV)	3	2	2	7
Decentralized				
Australia (ACTU)	1	1	2	4
West Germany (DGB)	2	1	1	4
Great Britain (TUC)	1	1	2	4
United States (AFL-CIO)	1	2	1	4

NOTE: 3 equals the highest amount of confederal authority;
1 equals the lowest.

[a] For income shares the following values have been assigned:

2 to 5 percent: 1
6 to 12 percent: 2
over 12 percent: 3.

(3) decentralized, the two largest Japanese confederations (Sohyo and Domei), the Swiss SGB, the Irish Confederation of Trade Unions, and the Canadian Labor Congress.[70]

Obviously, this distribution is neither precise nor frozen. Shifts have occurred in recent years and more will come in the future. For example, the resurgence of collective bargaining at industry and enterprise levels in the Netherlands has moved the Dutch national centers from the highly centralized to the intermediate category. George Meany believes that the AFL-CIO has achieved much greater cohesion, and presumably the authority that goes with it, than its predecessors. In an interview during

summer 1974 he said: "Now we have much greater cohesion at the national level. We don't have any more direct control. The unions are still autonomous, but the idea of a union running off by itself and defying the Federation or taking a position contrary to the Federation, that just doesn't happen anymore. We get much better cooperation now."[71]

Certain kinds of administered wage controls tend to strengthen the authority of central bodies, because it is through the central body that governments generally seek to enlist trade union compliance. The reverse can also happen. Yet on the whole there is sufficient stability in the overall pattern to preclude a sudden jump from the most- to the least-centralized group or vice versa as long as the basic fabric of the society remains intact.

SOME EXPLANATORY FACTORS

If there were an adequate theory of trade union government and structure or if organization theory had better clarified the concept of authority, it should now be possible to link the explanation of interconfederal differences to a coherent set of independent variables.[72] Unfortunately, that is not the case. The following discussion is, therefore, more ad hoc and impressionistic than a rigorous analysis ought to be, but at least it is a beginning in a relatively unexplored area of investigation. The focus is on six variables suggested by a review of the literature. Some of them appear to offer more useful insights than others, but there is hardly one in the group that could alone support a tenable explanation. That should not be surprising. Considering the diverse array of forces shaping the structure and government of trade unions in each country, singular causality is improbable and a combination of determinants seems more likely.

1. Antecedence has often been cited as an important clue. H. A. Clegg, for one, has sought to explain the limited powers of the British TUC in terms of its establishment "at a time when many of its constituents were already developed and mature. They wished to guard against any encroachment on their own autonomy and they had the strength to do so."[73] Neufeld has called attention to the same factor to explain why the CIO had

---

[70] The weakness of the Canadian central body is aggravated by the fact that certain functions normally performed by a confederation are exercised not by the CLC, but by the AFL-CIO (for example, the settlement of certain jurisdictional disputes), and further because "most of the larger affiliates of the Canadian Labor Congress are international unions whose leaders look to the AFL-CIO as their trade union centre." Kwavnick, *Organized Labour and Pressure Politics*, p. 61.

[71] Transcript of interview with George Meany, August 29, 1974, Department of Public Relations (AFL-CIO), p. 3.

[72] A recent study of authority in organizations concedes that "the concept of authority is as open to conflicting interpretations as any in the literature on organizations...." Gene W. Danton and Louis R. Barnes, *The Distribution of Authority in Formal Organizations* (Cambridge: Harvard University Press, 1968), p. 199.

[73] Clegg, *The System of Industrial Relations in Great Britain*, p. 396.

more internal authority than the AFL.[74] When more widely examined, however, the explanation loses some of its initially high plausibility. To be sure, it suggests why most central bodies started out as weak organizations.[75] Nevertheless, some confederations eventually became highly centralized, while others did not. Surely antecedence alone cannot explain that. Nor can it account for the wide disparity of strength between the West German DGB and the Austrian ÖGB, though both were reconstituted after World War II under fairly similar circumstances: a shattered movement and a military occupation.

2. Size of country also seems to be important. The most decentralized organizations are found in countries that are large in space or population or both, Australia, Great Britain, West Germany, the United States, and Canada. Conversely, it is striking that apart from France and Italy all national centers in the most centralized and intermediate groups are from small countries.

Other things being equal, it is probably easier administratively to impose central controls on a labor movement in a small and relatively homogeneous country than in a large and complex one. Economic desiderata may weigh even more heavily. Efforts to achieve wage restraint through centralized trade union machinery are likely to be most successful in those countries that most depend on foreign trade. In general, that means the smaller countries.

The propinquity often associated with smallness also tends to aid centralization. In smaller countries confederal and national union headquarters are almost invariably located in the same city and often housed in the same building. Contacts between leaders are therefore frequent, and hierarchical relationships perhaps develop more readily. In larger countries these personal contacts are likely to be more intermittent, and there is probably more geographic dispersion.[76]

3. Membership concentration can be significant. Galenson was probably the first to suggest that a relatively even distribution of confederal membership among affiliated unions contributes to central authority.[77] He pointed out that a single large union or a few large ones could frustrate central policy by pursuing their own objectives if in conflict with centrally defined objectives. Comparing the three Scandinavian national centers in about 1950, Galenson concluded that membership concentration was inversely correlated with central authority and that, on this reckoning, the Danish LO with a single very large affiliate was the weakest and the Norwegian LO with a more evenly distributed membership was the strongest of the three national centers.[78]

More recently, Turner has attributed the weakness of the British TUC to the fact that its affiliates "include a number which are quite powerful enough to pursue a solitary policy against the general will."[79] Although the designer of a giant merger scheme to amalgamate three of the largest British unions into a superunion, Turner maintains that conventional amalgamations of the kind usually advocated by proponents of a more rational British trade union structure would only increase the number of affiliates with independent strength at the expense of the TUC's authority.

In the Netherlands, as already mentioned, the NVV's central authority has been successfully attacked by its largest affiliate. In Germany, the Metalworkers Union with almost one-third of confederal membership has frequently acted as a rival center of power to the DGB.[80]

Though evidently of considerable importance, the concentration factor is no more completely explanatory than antecedence or size. The well-known weaknesses of the Canadian Labor Congress or of the several Japanese national centers have little or nothing to do with the competitive power of a large affiliated union or even several unions. Conversely, the Austrian ÖGB has been able to attain an extremely high degree of centralization in

---

[74] In this connection see the apt comments by Maurice F. Neufeld in "Structure and Government of the AFL-CIO," *Industrial and Labor Relations Review* 9, no. 3 (April 1956), pp. 378-79. Neufeld points out that the CIO as a central body exercised more influence over its affiliates than the AFL because nearly half the CIO unions owed their existence to the parent body. Neufeld also cites as an important factor "the overwhelming personality, ruthlessness, and prestige of John L. Lewis."

[75] Not all of them did. The Israeli Histadrut began as a highly centralized organization and remains so today. Zweig, "The Jewish Trade Union Movement in Israel," has pointed out that the Histadrut contains some unions with more independence than most others, and he links the explanation to the antecedence argument. He writes, p. 174, "They are mostly those which joined the Histadrut after they were fully grown. This is essentially true of unions of professional workers (academic) which assume greater independence, often defying the authority and discipline of the general Histadrut institutions. . . ."

[76] German trade union headquarters are dispersed among many cities, as pointed out by Pierre Waline in *Cinquante ans de rapports entre patrons et ouvriers en Allemagne* (Paris: Colin, 1970), vol. 2, p. 141.

[77] Walter Galenson, *The Danish System of Labor Relations* (Cambridge: Harvard University Press, 1952), pp. 31-32.

[78] *Ibid.*, p. 32.

[79] H. A. Turner, "British Trade Union Structure: A New Approach?" *British Journal of Industrial Relations* 2, no. 2 (July 1964):170.

[80] Richard J. Willey, *Democracy in the West German Trade Unions: A Reappraisal of the Iron Law* (Beverly Hills, Calif.: Sage Publications, 1971), p. 26.

spite of the long-standing presence in its midst of a large and powerful union, the metalworkers, and more recently the emergence of a second large union organizing white-collar employees in private industry.

4. Force of personality at the top increases the authority of the central body, but if the organization is basically weak the effects of strong leadership will be temporary. During the initial months of the reorganized German DGB after World War II the commanding presence of Hans Böckler, its first president, made the DGB appear to be a stronger central body than it really was.[81] Under his successors, the balance of power shifted rapidly to the constituent unions where it has remained to the present day. In the United States the authority of the AFL, very modest in its formative years, probably declined even further when William Green succeeded Samuel Gompers. More recently, George Meany's forceful personality has made AFL-CIO headquarters a highly respected element in American labor, but it remains to be seen whether his successor will be able to consolidate the enhanced status of the central body. In Australia, Robert Hawke's emergence as the dominant figure in the labor movement, first as the leading union advocate in wage arbitration and then as president of the central body, has conferred on the ACTU greater authority in dealing with its affiliates than it held under his predecessors. In Sweden, Arne Geijer ruled the LO without serious challenge from the national unions for over fifteen years, but LO's centralism was already well established when he took office. His retirement early in 1973 should presumably make little difference.

Important as it may be in certain periods, force of personality is thus more likely to be a transient than a permanent factor. Its explanatory value is, therefore, of only limited usefulness.

5. The close relationship between government intervention in the economy and centralization of trade union authority has frequently been noted. Historically, reliance on what Sidney and Beatrice Webb called the "method of legal enactment" has tended to strengthen the central body because in most political systems the concentrated application of pressure is more effective than dispersed efforts. In the contemporary period, economic controls or other forms of government intervention (planning, manpower policies, and so forth) once again tend to encourage centralization of trade union authority for reasons of common advantage. In other words, trade unions can influence policy makers more effectively through a joint spokesman, while government needs a representative body to consult with when necessary and to

use as an intermediary in applying pressure on individual unions to comply with the rules.[82] These considerations become particularly acute when an incomes policy has been promulgated.[83]

The adoption of an incomes policy does not necessarily result in immediate centralization of internal authority, although it tends to operate in that direction. The AFL-CIO and the British TUC have gained ground as central bodies during periods of wage controls, but on balance they are still among the least centralized of all confederations. The spearheading role of the Australian Council of Trade Unions in defending basic wage claims before the Commonwealth Arbitration Commission from the late 1950s on has not yet transformed it into a strong center comparable, say, to its Swedish or Austrian counterparts, though it has clearly gained a greater measure of authority than it held previously. Conversely, the absence of an official incomes policy in Sweden has not weakened the national center there; on the contrary, centralized bargaining through the central organization has been generally regarded as an incomes policy substitute acceptable to government and the parties alike.

The economic role of government is likely to remain one of the more important determinants of a national center's authority. It should be noted, however, that to the extent that expanding government intervention is the consequence of wage-push or cost-push inflation, the centralizing tendencies that emanate from it are really the cumulative result of individual unions' efforts to raise wages faster than productivity. In that sense, paradoxically enough, the constituent unions of national centers are actually fashioning their own centrally controlled restraints.

6. Centralization at the confederal level depends for its effectiveness primarily on the ability and willingness of individual unions to comply with central policies and directives. Where local or district bodies or, as the case may be, shop stewards act with a high degree of autonomy, compliance will be correspondingly difficult to obtain. It may even be impossible. In countries with a strong craft union tradition, usually based on local

---

[81] "The German Trade Union Federation operated successfully as long as its direction remained in the hands of a president who enjoyed undisputed authority and prestige both within and outside the organization." Otto Kirchheimer, "West German Trade Unions," *World Politics* 8, no. 4 (July 1956):493.

[82] Useful as a single spokesman may be, Daniel Bell has probably exaggerated the ability of AFL-CIO leaders to express the views of their constituents on issues of concern to the movement as a whole. He writes: "It is true that few constituencies in the American polity are 'corporative' in that some single spokesman acts for the interest of the whole — with the possible exception of labor, where a single body, the executive council of the AFL-CIO, formulates over-all policy, and George Meany expresses its opinion," Daniel Bell, *The Coming of Post-Industrial Society* (New York: Basic Books, 1973), p. 390.

[83] In this connection see especially Derek Robinson, *Incomes Policy and Capital Sharing in Europe* (London: Croom Helm, 1973), pp. 45-51.

autonomy, centralizing forces often meet the most tenacious resistance. Thus, it is no coincidence that the most highly centralized confederations are without exception explicitly committed to industrial unionism and contain a relatively small number of constituent unions, while the ranks of the least-centralized confederations (Germany excepted) are composed of a large number of more diverse union types.

Does centralization make a difference? Is there, for instance, a relationship between the degree of centralization and the incidence and distribution of industrial conflict? Are distinctive patterns of wage structure identified with a given degree of confederal authority? Do highly centralized movements achieve substantially higher overall levels of unionization? Perhaps these are more important questions than the ones to which this preliminary effort has been addressed. They will have to be explored some other time. There is at least a fair chance that some interesting results might be obtained. In a preliminary way the data in Table 4 would seem to suggest that there probably is a close, even if not a perfect, relation between the degree of centralization and the extent of unionization. These areas of inquiry deserve

Table 4: Confederal Authority and Degree of Unionization

Highly centralized confederations	Highly unionized countries (60 to 100 percent)
Austria (ÖGB)	Austria (65)
Norway (LO)	Belgium (71)
Sweden (LO)	Norway (65)
	Sweden (80)
Moderately centralized confederations	*Moderately unionized countries (40 to 59 percent)*
Belgium (CSC)	Denmark (58)
Denmark (LO)	Great Britain (48)
France (CFDT, FO)	Netherlands (41)
Italy (CGIL, CISL, UIL)	
Netherlands (NVV, NKV, CNV)	
Decentralized confederations	*Least unionized countries (20 to 39 percent)*
Canada (CLC)	Canada (34)
West Germany (DGB)	France (22)
Great Britain (TUC)	West Germany (38)
Japan (Sohyo, Domei)	Italy (33)
United States (AFL-CIO)	Japan (35)
	United States (30)

NOTE: Data on percentages of unionization are generally for 1971. They are approximations compiled by Professor Everett Kassalow, partly on the basis of information contained in Ivor L. Roberts, "Trade Union Trends in Seven Western European Countries, 1950-1968," *Industrial Relations Journal* 4, no. 2 (Summer 1973):45-56.

further study, and comparative research might well yield useful insights into the causes and consequences of the distribution of confederal authority. Further research might even help to identify what is cause and what is consequence, and that would be quite an achievement.

APPENDIX: HISTORICAL SKETCH

Although this study is concerned with the present rather than the past, some perspective on contemporary authority relationships may be gained by recalling the tenuous position that the founding organizations at first assigned to their national centers. In Britain, the Trades Union Congress (1868) was intended only as an occasional platform for publicizing the views of trade unions on labor issues and other social and political questions of the day.[84] To be sure, the Parliamentary Committee of the TUC soon demonstrated its usefulness to the unions by its influence on the passage of decisive trade union legislation in the 1870s, but various unions attending the annual meeting of the TUC in 1876 were still quite prepared to disband the congress.[85]

The German *Generalkommission* (1890), direct precursor of the contemporary DGB, was widely regarded "at first as a purely symbolic peak organization lacking significant power."[86] At its second congress in 1896 some of the individual unions proposed its dissolution because they wanted to use their contributions to build up their own organizations.

In France, the CGT during its early years has been described as "weak and uncertain" and its structure as a "hodge-podge of directly affiliated locals, regional and national bodies."[87]

The Swedish LO (1898) was designed as a loose coordinating body for defensive purposes. It was set up "after very little deliberation, for the main problem for discussion and decision [at the founding congress] was not so much the trade union aspects of a central LO, but rather the great issue of affiliation to the social democratic party, which had nurtured the unions over the past decade."[88]

The convention that established the Danish confederation (LO) in 1898 rejected proposals to

[84] A. E. Musson, *British Trade Unions, 1800-1875* (London: Macmillan, 1972), p. 62.

[85] B. C. Roberts, *The Trades Union Congress: 1868-1929* (London: Allen and Unwin, 1958), p. 95.

[86] Gerhard A. Ritter, *Die Arbeiterbewegung im Wilhelminischen Reich* (Berlin-Dahlem: Colloquium Verlag, 1959), p. 107.

[87] Val R. Lorwin, *The French Labor Movement* (Cambridge: Harvard University Press, 1954), pp. 23-24.

[88] Johnston, *Collective Bargaining in Sweden*, p. 24.

centralize power in the hands of an executive committee and deliberately chose a weaker type of national center.[89]

In the Netherlands, the principal national center (NVV), launched in 1906, appeared strong only by comparison with its syndicalist-oriented predecessor. The national unions retained full control over their internal affairs and relations with employers.[90]

By insisting on their own autonomy as "the ruling principle" in the American Federation of Labor (1886), the founding national unions meant to affirm explicitly their dominance "over the local federation, on the one hand, and the national federation on the other."[91]

Norway is one of the few exceptions, perhaps the only one. Created at a time (1899) when most national unions in that country were themselves just emerging, and formed without the balancing participation of the more self-sufficient unions in the metals and printing industries, the national center assumed from the outset substantial authority over the conduct of strikes and collective bargaining. This arrangement "left a permanent mark upon the organization," although later the central body had to relinquish some of its powers to the affiliated unions.[92]

During the decades from about 1900 until World War II, the national centers in most Western countries acted more as agents or instruments than as masters of their constituent national unions. Collective bargaining became increasingly the dominant form of rule making in industry, and its exercise was almost universally regarded as the foremost responsibility of national unions. Carl Landauer once observed that a strike "affects primarily, although not exclusively, the conditions in the industry in which it breaks out, and the particular group of workers that has to make the sacrifice and will obtain the gain wants to have the primary right to decide on any course of action."[93]

Such emphasis on the promotion of sectional interests receded only in times of grave national crisis when unions, too, came under exceptional stress.

The two world wars and the depression of the 1930s stand out as periods of centralization of union power. Most of the time the impetus came from governments eager to deal with a single recognized union authority through which nationwide agreements on wages, manpower allocation, restrictive trade practices, and the peaceful settlement of industrial disputes could be concluded. Thus, World War I became "the most important stimulus for the development of the TUC into the center of British trade unionism," as one observer recently expressed it, but the effect was only temporary.[94] Elsewhere, the war exercised parallel and, on the whole, equally impermanent effects on the authority of national centers. The normalcy of the twenties brought a return to national union autonomy, exemplified by the refusal of British unions in 1921 to delegate to the newly created general council of the TUC any of their traditional prerogatives.

Government intervention in the economy during the depressed 1930s reversed the pattern and strengthened many national centers. The consolidation of central power in the Swedish LO occurred largely between 1935 and 1941. It is generally acknowledged to have been a defensive response to government threats to impose controls on collective bargaining and internal union affairs unless the unions imposed administrative restraints upon themselves and jointly with employers found ways of curbing industrial conflict. In Britain the TUC's standing as the central body increased not only because of the Conservative government's intervention in economic affairs, but also because of the decimation of the Labour party leadership after the fall of the second Labour government. The vacuum was filled mainly by TUC General Secretary Walter Citrine and the leader of the Transport and General Workers Union, Ernest Bevin.[95]

Wartime mobilization extended the centralizing trend of the thirties. The Dutch trade unions, facing a particularly agonizing choice, responded to the pressures of the German occupation authorities by concentrating all major decision making in the executive boards of the three national centers for as long as these were permitted to operate. Elsewhere, the imposition of wage controls and the creation of disputes settlement machinery diminished the scope for free collective bargaining and generally contributed to some shift in authority from the national unions to the confederations.

---

[89] Galenson, *The Danish System of Labor Relations*, pp. 25-26.

[90] John P. Windmuller, *Labor Relations in the Netherlands* (Ithaca, N.Y.: Cornell University Press, 1969), p. 31.

[91] Lloyd Ulman, *The Rise of the National Trade Union*, p. 379. Many years later, according to George Meany's biographer, Walter Reuther tried during the negotiations leading to the merger of AFL and CIO to reverse the decision of 1886 by creating "a structure where all power rested in the national center." As told by Meany, he was opposed not only by the AFL negotiators with their historically greater commitment to national union autonomy, but also by the CIO's own Steelworkers Union. See Joseph C. Goulden, *Meany* (New York: Atheneum, 1972), p. 203. It is likely that the account overstates Reuther's perference for centralization.

[92] Galenson, *The Danish System of Labor Relations*, p. 12.

[93] Carl Landauer, *History of European Socialism* (Berkeley: University of California Press, 1959), p. 259.

[94] Dorfman, *Wage Politics in Britain, 1945-1967*, p. 9.

[95] For the impact on trade unions of government intervention in the British economy in the 1930s see Clegg, *The System of Industrial Relations in Great Britain*, p. 399.

Postwar scarcities and the requirements of economic and political reconstruction sustained the maintenance of confederal authority in most European countries for several years after the war. In a few countries, restrictions on wage bargaining actually continued for a very long time, almost twenty years in the case of the Netherlands. Elsewhere, centralized negotiations between top-level employer and trade union bodies helped to perpetuate the concentration of authority in several national centers, for example in Norway and Sweden.

More recently, the pendulum in several countries has swung toward more decentralization. This movement sometimes extends throughout the entire trade union structure down to the local level and is, in part, a reaction against the excesses of centralization or perhaps an expression of discontent with the industrial way of life. Whatever the reason, it exemplifies the impermanence of any particular set of institutional arrangements.

CHAPTER VI

Work: Some Observations

by **Irving Bernstein,** *Professor of Political Science and Associate Director, Institute of Industrial Relations,* **University of California, Los Angeles**

To transform an old adage, ambivalence is the price of life. This is nowhere more evident than in man's attitude toward work. It is an intense love-hate relationship. Work may be the source of profound gratification; it may also be a prime cause of alienation. Ambivalence toward work is not new with modern industrial man.

In Genesis, we are told, the Lord commanded Adam and Eve not to eat of the fruit of the tree in the garden; but the serpent beguiled Eve and she and Adam ate of the forbidden fruit. When the Lord learned of this defiance, He punished all three. To Adam, He said:

> Because thou has hearkened unto the voice of thy wife, and hast eaten of the tree, of which I commanded thee, saying: Thou shalt not eat of it; cursed is the ground for thy sake; in toil shalt thou eat of it all the days of thy life. Thorns also and thistles shall it bring forth to thee; and thou shalt eat the herb of the field. In the sweat of thy face shalt thou eat bread, till thou return unto the ground; for out of it wast thou taken; for dust thou art, and unto dust shalt thou return.[1]

Thus, in the beginning, work was a curse that the Lord visited upon man because of Adam's fall.

The Psalms and the Proverbs speak otherwise. The psalmist tells us in the prayer of Moses, "And let the graciousness of the Lord our God be upon us; Establish Thou also upon us the work of our hands; Yea, the work of our hands establish Thou it."[2] In his proverbs Solomon, again and again, praises hard work and its rewards:

> The soul of the sluggard desireth, and hath nothing; But the soul of the diligent shall be abundantly gratified.

> He that tilleth his gound shall have plenty of bread; But he that followeth after vain things is void of understanding.

> In all labour there is profit; But the talk of the lips tendeth only to penury.

> Slothfulness casteth into a deep sleep; And the idle soul shall suffer hunger.

> Go to the ant, thou sluggard; Consider her ways and be wise.[3]

By his labor, therefore, man performed the Lord's work and rewarded himself.

Already, in the Old Testament, work was both a curse and a blessing. The ancient Greeks shared this ambivalence. In the Aristotelian theory of the state, work, while necessary for survival, was degrading. Aristotle wrote:

> Since we are now investigating about the ideally best form of constitution—and that is the one which will make the state most happy; and . . . happiness cannot be present without virtue, it is clear from these premises that in the state that possesses the best form of constitution. . . the citizens must not live the life of either artisans or men of the market-place; for a life of that sort is low and adverse to virtue. Nor must those who are to be citizens be agricultural labourers; for leisure is required both for the growth of virtue and for political action. . . . The artisan element has no real part in the state, nor has any other class which is not a producer of virture. . . .The tillers of the soil must be either slaves or foreigners or serfs.[4]

But Hesiod sang the virtues of toil in *The Works and Days:*

> Love every seemly toil, that so the store
> Of foodful seasons heap thy garner's floor.
> From labour men returns of wealth behold,
> Flocks in their fields, and in their coffers gold:
> From labour shalt thou with the love be blest
> Of men and gods; the slothful they detest.[5]

It was said of Freud that he could not count beyond the number two because his thought was dialectical; he was preoccupied with the interrelations between opposites.

The author had the help in the preparation of this paper of two very able research assistants, graduate students at UCLA — Carol Vleck in animal behavior and Marta Whitmer in human behavior.

[1] Gen. 3:17.

[2] Ps. 90:17.

---

[3] Prov. 6:6, 12:1, 13:4, 14:23, and 19:15.

[4] Aristotle, *Politics,* trans. by W. E. Bolland (London: Longman's, Green, 1877), pp. 262-64.

[5] Hesiod, *The Remains,* trans. by C. A. Elton (London: Lackington, Allen, 1812), p. 160.

Freud invented the word "ambivalence." He had an intellectual attraction to the tension between polar pairs: love-hate, life-death, and so on. This was evident in his observations on work. On the one hand, "No other technique for the conduct of life attaches the individual so firmly to reality as laying emphasis on work; for his work at least gives him a secure place in a portion of reality, in the human community." But, on the other hand, "As a path to happiness, work is not highly prized by men. They do not strive after it as they do after other possibilities of satisfaction. The great majority of people only work under the stress of necessity, and this natural human aversion to work raises most difficult social problems."[6]

Ambivalence evokes curiosity: "Why," one asks, "should I have such opposing feelings about the same condition?" This paper is a partial answer to that query. The word "partial" is stressed. One could hardly deal comprehensively with so large a topic in this space. Rather, certain aspects of the problem of work are examined because they are especially interesting and important.

WORK AS A NATURAL CONDITION

Possibly something, perhaps a good deal, can be learned about contemporary man in the work context by comparing him with other animals and with primitive man. With respect to the lower animals, such a comparison is the premise of ethology, the comparative study of animal behavior. For many people this is a surprising, indeed shocking, idea. Perhaps, therefore, it is worth establishing the validity of such a comparison by quoting from an authority, N. Tinbergen.

Man is an animal. He is a remarkable and in many respects unique species, but he is an animal nevertheless. In structure and functions, of the heart, blood, intestine, kidneys, and so on, man closely resembles other animals, especially other vertebrates. Palaeontology as well as comparative anatomy and embryology do not leave the least doubt that this resemblance is based on true evolutionary relationships. Man and the present-day primates have only recently diverged from a common primate stock. This is why comparative anatomy and comparative physiology have yielded such important results for human biology. It is only natural, therefore, that the zoologist should be inclined to extend his ethological studies beyond the animals to man himself. However, the ethological study of man has not yet advanced very far . . . .

One of the main reasons for this is the almost universal misconception that the causes of man's behaviour are qualitatively different from the causes of animal behaviour. Somehow it is assumed that only the lowest building-stones of behaviour, such as impulse flow in peripheral nerves, or simple reflexes, can be studied with neurophysiological or, in general, objective methods, while behaviour as an integrated expression of man as a whole is the subject-matter of psychology .... It is of fundamental importance to recognize the utter fallacy of such a conception. As long as neurophysiology focused its attention on lower levels, there was such a gap between the spheres of interest of physiology and of psychology that the existence of the barrier somewhere in no-man's-land could neither be proved nor disproved. But neurophysiology has been including higher and higher levels in its area of work, psychology is beginning to look to the lower, instinctive levels, and ethology has settled in between and so meets neurophysiologists at its lower levels and psychologists at its highest levels. And one of the first results of this expansion is that we now realize that a barrier of this kind does not exist.[7]

Students of animal behavior are cautious fellows. They are especially wary of being charged with anthropomorphism. Doubtless for this reason, and because they employ a language different from that of social scientists, most of them do not use the word "work." There are exceptions, notably Edward O. Wilson in his masterful volume *The Insect Societies*.[8] By a reasonable definition, furthermore, there is no doubt that animals work, some in quite remarkable ways. Perhaps it is best to provide such a definition of work here, one very close to that set forth in the dictionaries: exertion, physical or mental, for a gainful objective. The last phrase in the definition is intended to distinguish work from play, which animals, including man, engage in. Both entail exertion, but only work is gainful. Anthropologists, of course, take it for granted that man in primitive societies works and use the word as do other social scientists.

Konrad Lorenz, in analyzing animal behavior, has referred to "the great parliament of instincts." In this body the main seats are taken by the "great" drives: hunger, sex, fear, and aggression.[9] It seems evident that all

[6] Ernest Jones, *The Life and Work of Sigmund Freud*, vol. 2 (New York: Basic Books, 1955), p. 422; Sigmund Freud, *Civilization and Its Discontents* (New York: Norton, 1961), p. 27.

[7] N. Tinbergen, *The Study of Instinct* (Oxford: Clarendon Press, 1951), p. 205.

[8] Edward O. Wilson, *The Insect Societies* (Cambridge, Mass.: The Belknap Press, 1971).

[9] Konrad Lorenz, *On Aggression* (New York: Harcourt, Brace & World, 1966), p. 67. It is worth noting that two aspects of the Lorenz position are controversial. The first is semantic: objection to the word "instinct" to describe innate, as distinguished from learned, behavior. The leading objectors are the American behaviorists, influenced by J. B. Watson. The Europeans, as the title of Tinbergen's book, *The Study of Instinct*, suggests, do not have this concern. The second is more serious, namely, whether aggression is an instinct or is learned, at least for man. For discussions of the controversy, see N. Tinbergen, "On War and Peace in Animals and Man," *Science* 160 (June 28, 1968):1411-18; R. Suthers and R. A. Gallant, *Biology:The Behavioral View* (Lexington, Mass.:

animals, including man, expend energy in a gainful manner to satisfy these fundamental instincts. That is, by this definition, all animals work. Work, therefore, is a natural condition of every animal species, including man; but, when one compares species, this work is performed in very different ways.

The social insects, in contrast with the primates, are very old on the evolutionary scale, tracing their histories back between fifty and at least one hundred million years. They spread across virtually the whole land surface of the earth, they embrace an extraordinary number of species, and their combined population is phenomenally large. The societies of ants, bees, termites, and wasps, according to Wilson, "are among the great achievements of organic evolution." While their social organizations are much inferior to man's because of "feeble intellect and absence of culture," they exceed man's in "cohesion, caste specialization, and individual altruism."[10]

Work is absolutely essential to the functioning and survival of these societies and many of the more advanced among them exhibit a sharply defined division of labor based upon sex and caste and, in some cases, slavery or parasitism. They have intricate systems of communication for the purposes of alarm, assembly, recruitment for work, recognition (of nestmates, castes, and life stages, including the dead), food exchange, and grooming. Many social insects have developed the capacity to build large and complex structures to house their colonies in the forms of combed hives, mounds, tree nests, and subterranean chambers and tunnels. Particular social insect species exhibit unusual construction capacities. Army ants build bridges of their bodies. The African termite *Macrotermes natalensis* erects a complex chambered nest that is thirty meters in diameter and provides a home for two million individuals. Honeybees, among others, regulate the temperature within the hive. On one remarkable recorded occasion the spread was 59°C.—from 31° inside to -28°C. outside.

An illustration of the work patterns of one species of the social insects may be illuminating. The honeybee *Apis mellifera* is selected for this purpose because it is the most extensively studied of the social insects; in fact, it is cultivated by man for his own purposes and is on about the same level of organization as the other high social insects though, unlike many others, the caste system is weak and a soldier caste is absent. The origins of the species seem to go back about thirty million years to tropical Africa. The honeybee appears to have spread naturally to the rest of Africa, to Europe except the far

north, and to western Asia. In recent times the white man has carried this animal around the world.

There are three distinguishable groups of honeybees: queens, drones, and workers, the last having internal functional specializations. The workers, usually 20,000 to 80,000 in a colony, construct a nest of hexagonal waxen combs in a hidden retreat, such as a hollow tree. In the spring, the queen's production and delivery of "queen substance" to the workers falls off and they build royal cells, large ellipsoidal chambers, along the lower edges of the combs. The queen lays one egg in each royal cell and nurse workers feed the larvae special foods to insure their development into queens. The growth period from egg to adult queen takes only sixteen days. During this period, the mother queen loses size, becomes agitated, receives less food from the workers, and meets with their hostility. She then flies off in the prime swarm followed by a large group of workers. Afterswarms behave similarly as new queens develop and fly away surrounded by workers. The swarms travel only a short distance and settle on an aerial perch. Scout bees move out from these bivouacs in search of permanent nest sites. They return to the swarm and, by the waggle dance, signal the direction and distance of the new site and the swarm moves there to found a new colony.

Meantime, the parental nest is briefly queenless, but the workers have already built drone cells into which the mother queen has laid unfertilized eggs that become males. When the drones develop, they fly off to await the approach of a virgin queen. If several new queens emerge, they fight until only one survives. The workers push her out of the nest for her nuptial flight. She gives off a distinctive scent, which attracts the drones. Each male explodes his genitalia into the queen and dies. She mates with about twelve drones and obtains sufficient sperm for her lifetime. She then either becomes the queen of the old nest or flies off in a swarm to form a new nest.

The caste system among honeybees, as has been suggested, is not especially complicated. It determines the division of labor. There are two basic female castes, queens and workers. The queens are much larger than the others and differ morphologically in many ways. The queen does not participate in the ordinary activities of the hive. Her most complex behavior occurs early in life when she challenges her sisters and makes her nuptial flight; for the rest, she is an egg-laying machine. The drones appear only to have a reproductive function. Among workers, the larger tend to become foragers and the smaller nest tenders and nurses. The latter construct the royal cells and in the spring rear the new queens by supplying the larvae with the royal jelly. Another jelly is provided that leads to the development of workers. Nurses spend a large amount of time in observing these development processes and in feeding. A breakdown of the labor of workers shows that they perform twenty-two separate functions related to

Xerox, 1973), pp. 540-43; P. Mussen and M. Rosensweig, eds., *Psychology: An Introduction* (Lexington, Mass.: Heath, 1973), pp. 842-44.

10 Wilson, *The Insect Societies*, p. 1.

construction, feeding, ventilation, and temperature control. This work is not constant; about two-thirds of the time is spent resting or wandering through the nest, the latter sometimes called patrolling. The idle and the patrollers provide a reserve labor force available for emergencies, such as defense against predators.

The waggle dance of the honeybee is remarkable, unique, and perhaps the most exhaustively studied form of animal behavior. It is the communications system by which a scout, having found a source of nectar and pollen, returns to the hive and informs the other workers of its location, with reference both to its angle to the sun and its distance from the hive, by the performance of a patterned dance, by rapid lateral vibrations (the "waggle"), and by emission of a distinctive buzzing sound. Those so informed then proceed to the site of the food. Honeybees also use the waggle dance to lead a swarm to a new nesting site, to gather resin for hive cement, and to obtain water for thermoregulation.

This last activity is not uncommon among social insects. Many species control temperature and humidity within the nest. Honeybees take account of thermoregulation in selecting a nest site, in sealing off all openings except the entrance hole with plant gums, in cooling the interior of the hive on hot days by wing-fanning and water evaporation, and in heating the nest on cold days by compact body clustering.[11]

Birds are prodigious workers and four of their activities are of interest in the present context: nest and bower construction, helping, tool using, and, in a different sense, parasitism or symbiosis. Birds build nests as an aspect of the mating process, as a repository for their eggs, and to protect themselves, their eggs, and their developing young against predators and the weather. Some nests are crude, holes scooped in the ground or piles of rocks; others are structures of delicate craftsmanship or, in the case of some colonial nesting, "apartment houses." Impressive commitments of time, energy, and ingenuity are needed for the latter types of building. Some indication of the work taken up in nest building is suggested by these observations: the ovenbird constructs a mud nest that is fifty times its own weight; the barn swallow makes 1,200 mud-carrying trips to gather material for a single nest; the nest of one long-tailed tit contained 2,457 feathers; the

nest hole for three broods of California, or acorn, woodpeckers required the continuous work of relays of from two to seven birds for three months. This great demand for work has led many species into systematic robbery of building materials from other birds.

A few illustrations of nest construction may be interesting. Hummingbirds, of course, expend enormous amounts of energy in relation to their weight. The females select sites for their inconspicuousness and build complex nests in the shapes of bowls, cups, or elongated pouches. They carefully choose the materials, usually spiders' webs, plant fibers, down, moss, or lichens and do not hesitate to steal them when they are in short supply. To maintain nest balance, the hummingbird sometimes weights one end with small stones or pieces of dirt. Some of the birds plait or glue materials as well. Hummingbirds sometimes use their bills like darning needles. A loose thread is drawn through the nest material and stitched into place.

The sociable weaver of the African veldt is a colonial nester. A group of birds begins by erecting a large dome of grass in an isolated tree. Pairs then build their own nests beneath the dome with downward-directed entry holes. Such "apartment houses" reach a size of 10 feet by 16.5 feet and may contain 120 families. Sometimes they become so heavy that the tree cannot sustain the weight.

The West African male village weaverbird has a masterful ability to weave such materials as elephant grass or palm leaves at great speed. He starts by forming a single strip into a ring, which serves as his perch for the entire job. He then moves on to the construction of the roof, the egg chamber, the antechamber, and the downward-facing entrance. All this work is performed in one day. He then displays in front of his structure. If a female is attracted, she enters the nest for an inspection. If she accepts his work she then brings the lining material to complete the nest before she lays her eggs.

The mallee fowl, who inhabits the arid parts of inland Australia, works prodigiously on nesting, the male, in fact, for eleven months of the year. Between February and June, he digs a hole three feet deep, ten feet in diameter, with an eighteen-inch-high rim. In the next two months, he fills the hole with vegetation and digs the egg chamber. Then, until December, he adds a layer of soil over the composting vegetation. He is constantly engaged in thermoregulation. In the spring, when fermentation raises the temperature, he opens the mound on cool mornings. On hot summer days, he adds soil as insulation. He does the same on cold nights to retain the heat. On dry autumn days, when composting heat falls off, he uncovers the mound at noon to allow the passage of warm sunlight. He will not permit the female to enter the mound to lay an egg unless the temperature is right. An observer timed this busy male at the mound for seven hours a day in the spring, thirteen in the summer, and ten in the fall.

The bowerbirds of Australia, New Guinea, and the

[11] The general observations on work among social insects are derived from Wilson. His specific references to honeybees are in *The Insect Societies*, pp. 94-102, 171-77, 262-71, 306-9. Karl von Frisch has made the basic studies of communication among honeybees, particularly the waggle dance. See his *The Dance Language and Orientation of Bees* (Cambridge, Mass.: Belknap Press, 1967), *Dancing Bees* (New York: Harcourt, Brace, 1954), and "Dialects in the Language of Bees," *Scientific American*, August 1962, pp. 2-7. See also Adrian M. Wenner, "Sound Communication in Honeybees," *Scientific American*, April 1964, pp. 2-9.

nearby islands are unusual in engaging in construction unrelated to nesting. The males build gardens, bowers, and ornamental turrets for display to court females. Their structures are quite varied and the following are observed examples: a cleared dance floor up to five feet in diameter covered with lichens and decorated with colored berries, snail shells, irridescent beetle wing cases, and flowers; a "maypole" of interlaced branches around a young tree to form a tower decorated with colored objects; an "avenue" of intertwined branches as walls connected at the top and decorated; a nine-foot-high bower decorated with living orchids; a hut fronted by a moss meadow and decorated with artfully arranged colored fruit and fungi. Perhaps most interesting, some bowerbirds "paint" their buildings. They mix berry juices with charcoal and saliva to form a liquid coloring material. With a fragment of fibrous bark held in the beak as a sponge, they then daub the "paint" on the bower.[12]

Many bird species have a division of labor which ornithologists call "helping." This activity goes beyond the frequent cooperation of the male and female in nest building, incubation, and feeding the young as well as the colonial nesting already noted for the sociable weaverbird and the woodpecker. "Helping" is defined as the work of a bird that assists in nesting another bird that is not its mate or feeds and attends a bird that is not its offspring. Helpers engage in such activities as feeding, nest building, incubation, brooding, and calling alarms. More frequently, helpers are intraspecific; occasionally they are inter-specific. A. F. Skutch has compiled a list of more than 130 species that have helpers. Among the examples he gives are: a wingless frigate bird fed by its neighbors; a wild goose guarding a duck's brood; a fledgling rock dove feeding a younger sibling; a cuckoo and a mourning dove laying their eggs and jointly incubating them in a robin's nest. Bluejays are said to care for the aged and infirm. The young of the Australian blue wren remain with their parents for up to three years to help raise their younger siblings. Emperor penguins keep the young warm in common and even fight for possession of the little birds. Adélie penguins, which live inland and must travel long distances to the sea for food, leave their young in nurseries where a few parents stand guard. The fruit crows of

Guyana form integrated social groupings for feeding, resting, preening, and, almost certainly, roosting jointly.[13]

A number of birds are tool users, though on a relatively primitive level. The employment of stones is quite common. The black-breasted buzzard of inland Australia drives the emu from her nest and then drops stones on the eggs to crack them open. The Egyptian vulture breaks open an ostrich egg by striking it with a stone held in the bill. Pacific gulls drop shells on rocky shelves to get at the animals inside. Australian bee eaters, which live in tunnels, may place bright objects (bones, mussels, shells) in their nests to increase illumination by reflection. Brown-headed nuthatches use bark scale as a wedge or lever to forage for insects under tree bark. Galapagos finches employ cactus spines or twigs for the same purposes. Northern shrikes impale insects, small rodents, and birds on fixed spines or forked sticks for food storage.[14] The "painting" of bowerbirds of Australia has already been noted.

There are several birds that avoid work by establishing symbiotic, especially parasitic, relationships with other animals, frequently of a different species. A number use the old or abandoned nests of other birds instead of building their own, for example, some owls, sparrows, starlings, and flycatchers. Ducks and the yellow-billed cuckoo occasionally lay eggs in other birds' nests. The most notorious parasite is the European cuckoo, which palms off its eggs on 125 other bird species. The female cuckoo observes the other birds building their nests and laying their eggs, selecting species with the same size eggs as its own. When the host bird is away, usually in the afternoon, the cuckoo removes one egg from the nest and then quickly lays one of its own in each of the host nests. Cuckoo eggs hatch more quickly than those of most birds and cuckoo chicks instinctively push solid objects out of a nest when they are ten hours old. The host mother will normally feed the surviving cuckoo.

Another form of symbiosis is related to feeding. A number of birds rely upon other species to provide them with food. For example, brown-headed cowbirds eat insects flushed out by bison or cattle; cattle egrets feed on

[12] J. C. Welty, *The Life of Birds* (New York: Knopf, 1972), pp. 261, 277, 279; W. E. Ritter, *The California Woodpecker and I* (Berkeley: University of California Press, 1938), p. 48; Gwynne Vevers, *Hummingbirds* (New York: Crowell, 1966), pp. 72-79; H. D. Dossenbach, *The Family Life of Birds* (New York: McGraw-Hill, 1971), pp. 42, 61; N. E. and E. C. Collias, "The Behavior of the West African Village Weaverbird," *Ibis* 112 (1970):457-80; H. J. Frith, "Temperature Regulation in the Nesting Mounds of the Mallee Fowl," *C.S.I.R.O. Wildlife Research* 1 (1956):79-95; A. J. Marshall, *Bower-Birds* (Oxford: Clarendon Press, 1954).

[13] A. F. Skutch, "Helpers Among Birds," *Condor* 63 (1961):198-226; A. F. Skutch, "Helpers at the Nest," *Auk* 52 (1935):257-73; David Lack, *Ecological Adaptations for Breeding in Birds* (London: Methuen, 1968), chap. 7; D. W. Snow, "Observations on the Purple-throated Fruit-Crow in Guyana," *The Living Bird* 10 (1971):5-17.

[14] A. H. Chisholm, "The Use by Birds of 'Tools' or 'Instruments'," *Ibis* 96 (1953):380-83; Jane and Hugo van Lawick-Goodall, "Use of Tools by the Egyptian Vulture," *Nature* 212 (1966):1468-69; D. H. Morse, "The Use of Tools by Brown-headed Nuthatches," *Wilson Bulletin* 80 (1968):220-24; David Lack, *Darwin's Finches* (Cambridge: Cambridge University Press, 1947), pp. 58-59; G. C. Millikan and R. I. Bowman, "Observations on Galapagos Tool-using Finches in Captivity," *The Living Bird* 6 (1967):23-41.

grasshoppers brought out by cows; hawks follow trains and eat birds flushed out by locomotives. One of the most interesting cases of symbiosis is the African honeyguide, which feeds on beeswax but is unable itself to break open the hive. It locates the hive and then finds a human, a baboon, a monkey, or a mongoose and leads this animal to the hive, sometimes up to five miles. This creature proceeds to open the hive to take the honey and the honeyguide gets the wax.[15]

Beavers have the reputation for being "busy" and "eager," which is deserved. They are notable lumberjacks, carpenters, and hydraulic engineers and feed on fresh wood and use timber, sticks, and mud to construct dams, lodges, and winter food stores. They usually live in families with the young departing at the age of two, though they occasionally form larger social groupings; it is possible that the latter was more common before the fur trade decimated their numbers. One beaver will cut a tree by himself, rarely will two do so. A pair will work together to transport a heavy log. The family usually builds the dam. A dam has been observed that was 12 feet high and 4,000 feet long and backed up a lake containing forty beaver lodges. This, obviously, was the work of a whole community. Lodges are built of sticks and mud and contain a dry room lined with wood shavings. They vary in size. An eighteenth century observation noted a huge lodge that housed at least thirty-four beavers. Their engineering is sometimes faulty, particularly in picking dam sites; but beavers do not hesitate to do extra work, overcoming error with persistence. Observation of beavers in New York State indicated that they worked between dusk and dawn, rarely during the day.[16]

Wolves have one of the highest forms of social organization among subhuman species, based upon the pack, a dominance hierarchy, and a sharing of labor. There is a rigid social order within the pack, arising from competition between individuals, and, once rank is established, the members are highly social. The capstone of this society is the dominant (alpha) male to whose leadership all the others submit. He breaks up fights between other pack members, guards the territory against intruders, and leads the hunt. Perhaps because of these duties and the submissiveness of all the females to him, which may inhibit copulation, he does not breed. The usual breeding pair, sometimes the only one, is the beta

male and the alpha female. All work seems to be performed cooperatively. Dens are dug for a pregnant female by the pack. All adults bring food to the pups. Sometimes a female without pups will guard another's pups while the latter hunts. If a lone wolf makes a kill, it may call the others to share the food. Normally, wolves hunt in packs led by the dominant male. Thus, they are able to bring down game much bigger than themselves, such as moose and caribou. Hunting packs have been credited with remarkable teamwork and sophisticated strategies, though these are only partly documented. If a pack makes a kill of more than the members can eat, they return later to finish it off. All adults in a pack join in defending a den against bears. Howling, evidently, is the means of communication, identifying the species, conveying information about other animals and the environment, and coordinating the social activities of the pact.[17]

Monkeys have a high degree of social organization based upon the troop and a dominance hierarchy. Since they are primarily herbivorous and frugivorous and often inhabit tropical jungle regions where food is plentiful except in dry spells, many need not work hard at feeding. They sleep in trees and some species have evolved special sitting pads to facilitate this. Thus, they have no need to construct nests. As a result, many monkeys have a good deal of time for rest, their young engage in elaborate play, and much of their activity goes into grooming. Monkeys often take a "siesta" when the heat of the day is most intense. In general, the higher a species is placed on the phylogenetic scale, the more frequent and varied the play among its young. Play has the functions of providing an outlet for physical energy, of socializing the individual, of integrating him into the troop, and of placing him on the dominance scale. As the young monkey moves into adulthood, play develops into grooming and monkeys spend a great deal of time in this activity, that is, grooming others. It serves a variety of purposes: keeping the skin and the fur clean, healing wounds, providing social intercourse, causing sexual arousal, and reinforcing the dominance hierarchy.[18]

Baboons are among the most interesting monkeys and some thirty savannah baboon troops in East Africa ranging in size from forty to eighty individuals have been studied in the field by Washburn and DeVore. The troop is a very

[15] Welty, *Life of Birds*, pp. 309-12; J. Van Tyne and A. T. Berger, *Fundamentals of Ornithology* (New York: Wiley, 1959), p. 253; H. Friedmann, *The Honeyguides*, U. S. National Museum Bulletin 208 (Washington: GPO, 1955).

[16] L. Lee Rue, *The World of the Beaver* (New York: Lippincott, 1964); L. Wilsson, *My Beaver Colony* (Garden City: Doubleday, 1968); L. Tevis, "Summer Behavior of a Family of Beavers in New York State," *Journal of Mammalogy* 31 (1950):40-65.

[17] David L. Mech, *The Wolf: The Ecology and Behavior of an Endangered Species* (New York: Natural History Press, 1970); M. W. Fox, *Behavior of Wolves, Dogs and Related Canids* (London: Baylis, 1971); G. A. Rabb, J. H. Woolpy, and B. E. Ginsburg, "Social Relationships in a Group of Captive Wolves," *American Zoologist* 7 (1967):305-11; J. B. Theberge and J. B. Falls, "Howling as a Means of Communication in Timber Wolves," *American Zoologist* 7 (1967):331-38.

[18] Desmond Morris, ed., *Primate Ethology* (Chicago: Aldine, 1967), especially chap. 5, Caroline Loizos, "Play Behavior in Higher Primates, A Review," and chap. 4, John Sparks, "Allogrooming in Primates, A Review."

cohesive social unit and provides the only viable way of life for its members. Baboons are highly responsive to fear of the dark, of falling, of lions, and of snakes. While they range fairly widely in search of food and water, they remain near trees, to which they can retreat before nightfall for safe sleeping. When they move on the ground in open country, the troop arranges itself with the adult males on the periphery to defend against predators and with the females and the young at the center. While the troop does not move rapidly, it will not slow down for the sick or the injured, leaving them in isolation for almost certain death. Only lions put a baboon troop to flight, forcing the monkeys into the safety of trees. Baboons are mainly herbivorous, though they occasionally eat meat, eggs, and insects. Baboons, with their sharp eyes, and such ungulates as impalas and bushbucks, with their keen sense of smell, form symbiotic relationships against predators and become almost impossible to surprise. Baboons spend a good deal of their time feeding and grooming, the latter in accordance with social dominance. The young, of course, play.[19]

The great apes, who also inhabit tropical jungle areas where food is plentiful, have social organizations and work patterns that resemble those of monkeys, but they seem more relaxed and there are differences between species. The gibbons of Indonesia, Malaysia, Thailand, and Burma organize themselves around the family in groups of three to six animals. They sleep in trees. At dawn, they feed for about two hours on fruit, insects, eggs, and birds. They take a siesta at midday for about three hours and then resume feeding during the latter part of the afternoon and at sundown move to the trees for sleep. There is no dominance hierarchy and the social bond seems to depend largely on grooming. The young, again, spend much time in play. The least is known about the orangutans of Sumatra and Borneo. They too seem organized about the family, though fairly loosely and usually in groups of only two or three. They feed mainly on fruit and build sleeping nests in the form of platforms in the forks of trees.[20]

Chimpanzees, of course, have been extensively studied in the wild and in captivity and are employed as laboratory animals. Their groups are loosely organized; individuals move in and out with some frequency; single chimpanzees have to look after themselves to a considerable extent; any adult male may become the leader and he plays no role in regulating conduct between the members of the group.

The chimpanzees observed by Jane van Lawick-Goodall in the Gombe Stream Reserve in East Africa spent the daylight hours alternately feeding and resting over a one-to-ten-mile range, with about half the time devoted to foraging. They ate vegetation, insects, eggs, and meat, including live monkeys pulled from trees. They put away an especially heavy meal before making their nests in trees for the night. Some of the nests are fairly complex, consisting of interwoven branches. Chimpanzees are tool users. They poke sticks and leaves into ant and termite nests, as well as beehives, and lick off the insects. They throw objects at or club other animals, though their aim seems better in captivity than in the wild. They use twigs and grass to probe into holes in the search for grubs and wasps, using their sense of smell to detect the presence of the insects. Chimpanzees have pried open banana boxes with sticks. They make sponges of leaves, food wads, dead blossoms, and chewed grass to suck up water and to wipe their bodies. Chimpanzees have been seen cracking open palm nuts with a stone against a flat rock surface. These animals are notorious food-beggars, although they are not always successful and then resort to stealing. There is a good deal of mutual grooming. Young chimpanzees are extremely playful and are imaginative in their play, sometimes with sexual connotations. There is an observation of an aged female, around forty, bald, infirm, and showing signs of senility, who was groomed and watched over by a young female. Chimpanzees are very noisy and their hoots, screams, and drumbeats seem to be signals to call the group together.[21]

The mountain gorillas of Central Africa are perhaps the most relaxed of animals. Excepting man, they have no predators. The fact that a silverback adult male is very strong and reaches a weight of 450 pounds in the wild may account for this. Gorillas appear to feed only on vegetation. By temperament, they are placid, stoic, and aloof, not easily aroused to anger. The African jungle areas they inhabit, now shrinking as man advances into them, are rich in food supplies and nesting sites. They organize themselves in groups of from two to thirty under the

[19] S. L. Washburn and Irven De Vore, "The Social Life of Baboons," *Scientific American,* June 1961, pp. 2-11.

[20] M. Kawabe, "A Preliminary Study of the Wild Siamong Gibbon at Frasers' Hill, Malaysia," *Primates* 11 (1970):285-91; G. B. Schaller, "Behavioral Comparisons of the Apes," in *Primate Behavior,* I. De Vore, ed. (New York: Holt, Rinehart & Winston, 1965), pp. 474-85; G. B. Schaller, "The Orang-utan in Sarawak," *Zoologica* 46 (1961):73-82.

[21] Jane van Lawick-Goodall, *The Behavior of Free-Living Chimpanzees in the Gombe Stream Reserve,* Animal Behavior Monograph, vol. 1, pt. 3 (London: Bailière, Tindall and Cassell, 1968); Jane Goodall, "Chimpanzees of the Gombe Stream Reserve," and V. and F. Reynolds, "Chimpanzees of the Budongo Forest," in *Primate Behavior,* De Vore, ed.; Jane Goodall, "Nest-building Behavior in the Free-ranging Chimpanzee," *Annals of the New York Academy of Science* 102 (1967):455-67; H. Beatty, "A Note on the Behavior of the Chimpanzee," *Journal of Mammology* 32 (1951):118; Toshida Nishida, "Social Behavior and Relationship Among Wild Chimpanzees of the Mahali Mountains," *Primates* 11 (1970):47-87; A. Kortlandt and M. Kooij, "Protohominid Behavior in Primates," *Symposium of the Zoological Society of London* 10 (1963):61-88.

domination of an adult male, but the hierarchy is loose. Since food is plentiful, they do not travel far in foraging, sometimes less than 300 feet a day. They feed at a leisurely pace in the morning, though some like to sleep late; they take a long midday siesta; and they do their heavy feeding in late afternoon. They do not share food. Gorillas often take a break to sunbathe. Though there are some reports of tool using, these animals have little or no need for tools. Nests are crude platforms of vegetation piled on the ground or in trees. Mutual grooming does not seem to be a prominent activity. While the young play, they do not appear to be as imaginative as playful young chimpanzees.[22]

When one turns from the lower animals to primitive man, one finds a similar propensity to work. Early anthropologists who studied nonliterate societies were given to the "coconut tree" theory, namely, that the "savage" who inhabits a territory in which nature is bountiful will exert himself only to the minimum necessary to sustain life. This view is no longer accepted. Melville J. Herskovits collected a substantial number of studies of work patterns among primitive peoples, mainly contemporary, and reached this conclusion: "Nonliterate peoples, like ourselves, do as much work as they feel they must to meet the basic demands of getting a living, plus as much more as their desire to achieve any given end not encompassed by these basic demands calls for."[23] Stanley H. Udy, Jr., using the Yale Human Relations Area Files, made a cross-cultural analysis of work in 150 nonindustrial societies covering virtually the entire world. While a few, such as Imperial Rome, were literate and provided historical records, most were preliterate and the information about them was taken from a great number of obervations by anthropologists or other outsiders. Udy found that work was universal in these societies. He broke down this work into seven categories: tillage, hunting, fishing, collection, construction, animal husbandry, and manufacturing.[24]

The conclusion one must draw from this evidence is that all species are compelled to work by their primal drives. While there are marked differences in the intensity and variety of work among species, no animal can escape

this compulsion in some form. It is, thus, a natural condition. Man, as an animal, is subject to precisely the same drives. He must work, as the current phrase goes, for "bread." For him, also, this is a natural condition.

Man's need to work goes beyond that of the instinctual forces that drive other animals. Because of his more powerful brain and his development of culture, he has placed another layer of necessity upon himself. This subject, of course, is extremely complex, and it is not necessary to enter into it for the present purposes beyond making the general point which was easily made by Albert Camus who wrote, "Without work all life goes rotten."[25]

Erich Fromm has reached the identical conclusion more affirmatively, rather romantically, and without the same economy of language:

> Work is not only an inescapable necessity for man. Work is also his liberator from nature, his creator as a social and independent being. *In the process of work, that is, the molding and changing of nature outside himself, man molds and changes himself.* He emerges from nature by mastering her; he develops his powers of co-operation, of reason, his sense of beauty. He separates himself from nature, from the original unity with her, but at the same time unites himself with her again as her master and builder. The more his work develops, the more his individuality develops. In molding nature and re-creating her, he learns to make use of his powers, increasing his skill and creativeness.[26]

Freud came to the same conclusion, but in a more complex and sour fashion. His principal comments on work appear to have been made late in his life in his rambling and prolix essay, *Civilization and Its Discontents,* originally published in 1930. His argument is hard to summarize, but summarization is worth the effort.

Freud defines "civilization" as the sum of man's achievements and regulations that distinguish his contemporary life from that of his animal ancestors. Civilization has two purposes, to protect man from nature and to adjust the relations between people. Civilization depends upon order, which allows man to use space and time efficiently and to conserve his psychical forces. Man first learned order from astronomical observation and its value became self-evident early on. Order, however, has not been achieved because "human beings exhibit an inborn tendency to carelessness, irregularity, and unreliability in their work." They do not follow "their celestial models."

Civilization, Freud continues, depends upon human community and community, in turn, is based upon two

[22] G. B. Schaller, *The Mountain Gorilla, Ecology and Behavior* (Chicago: University of Chicago Press, 1963); G. B. Schaller, "The Behavior of the Mountain Gorilla," in *Primate Behavior,* De Vore, ed.; Capt. C. R. S. Pitman, "The Gorillas of the Kayonsa Region, Western Kigezi, S. W. Uganda," *Zoological Society of London Proceedings* 105 (1935):477-94.

[23] Melville J. Herskovits, *Economic Anthropology, The Economic Life of Primitive Peoples* (New York: Norton, 1952), p. 90.

[24] Stanley H. Udy, Jr., *Organization of Work, A Comparative Analysis of Production among Nonindustrial Peoples* (New Haven: HRAF Press, 1959).

[25] Cited in *Work in America, Report of a Special Task Force to the Secretary of Health, Education and Welfare* (Cambridge: MIT Press, 1972), p. xx.

[26] Erich Fromm, *The Sane Society* (New York: Rinehart, 1955), pp. 177-78.

foundations, "the compulsion to work" (Ananke-necessity) and "the power of love" (Eros). Work, therefore, is indispensable to civilization, but it is also necessary for the individual. More than any other part of living, Freud observes, work links man to reality within a human community, and, thereby, it affords the individual the opportunity to displace "libidinal components, whether narcissistic, aggressive or even erotic."[27]

Freud, Fromm, and Camus are all saying that for the individual work performs functions that transcend "bread." There have been many efforts to systematize this point and that of the Department of Health, Education and Welfare Task Force in *Work in America* is about as good as any. This group says that work performs a number of functions beyond the economic: providing a place to meet people and form friendships; in traditional societies providing an apprenticeship for the child in preparing him for the economic and social role of the adult; determining the status of the worker and his family; conferring self-esteem upon the worker; establishing a sense of identity; and imposing order on the world in which the worker finds himself.[28] Thus, work potentially has a dual meaning for man: to satisfy his primal needs and to gratify his psychic needs. The first he shares with all animals; the second is unique to *Homo sapiens*.

TIME AND THE WORK RHYTHM

Modern industrialism is locked into the calendar and the clock. Economic operations, whether in mining, in manufacturing, in transportation, in distribution, or in the office, must be fitted into a schedule. Many of the more complex functions demand sequential synchronization; parts must meet at a particular moment so that they may be assembled into a larger unit, or function number one must be completed at a specific time or work may not go forward on function number two. The symbol of this link of time to output is Frederick W. Taylor and his followers in the scientific management movement holding stopwatches in their hands. For the Taylorites the second was too long a unit of time measurement for industrial processes; it had to be broken down into shorter segments.

In the scientific management system the worker becomes a function of the work rhythm. When he arrives for work, he punches the clock. He must be at his work station when the flow of work reaches him and he may not leave until it ceases. He is paid for the time he works, as the phrase goes, when he is "on the clock." The arrangement of his work in relation to time is a major function of management and of collective bargaining.

Examples from collective bargaining agreements will illustrate this function, but a few preliminary comments

are needed. The first is that time rules in industry have two basic functions: to systemize time itself and to employ this systematized time as a basis for compensation, that is, to trade off the hours the worker gives to the employer for the money the employer pays to the worker. In a piecework system of payment wages are exchanged for a combination of output and time worked. The second comment is that time is an essential function of a great range of factors in the employment relationship. In the typical collective bargaining agreement time appears most obviously in the provision, usually complex, that defines hours of work and overtime; but time measurement is also central to many other matters: the grievance procedure; seniority; promotions, transfers, layoffs, and recalls; leaves of absence; sick leave; pregnancy leave; hourly wage rates; shift premiums; cost-of-living escalators; progressions upward in job families; health and welfare benefits; old-age pensions; serverance pay; holidays; vacations; the duration of the agreement; and others. Finally, and this is related to the second observation, it would be cruel and unusual punishment to lay on the reader even a substantial summary, to say nothing of the full detail, of these time-related provisions, but a few highlights are needed to establish the point.

The first agreement I want to note is in the mining industry and is between United States Borax and Chemical Corporation and the International Longshoremen's and Warehousemen's Union (1972-1974); it covers the open-pit borax mine at Boron, California. Only a few of the working hours and overtime pay provisions and a clause called "benefit year" are of interest here. Employees must be at their work sites "at the start of their shift as signaled by the whistle." Employee schedules are of two sorts: those for "shift workers" and for "straight-shift workers." Those who work "around the clock" are called "shift workers" and must remain at their stations until relieved. Their shifts begin at 7:00 A.M., 3:00 P.M., and 11:00 P.M. They ordinarily rotate shifts; are entitled to a "reasonable period of time" for lunch, but at no set hour; and, in case of emergency, must "forego eating" until the emergency ends. Employees on straight shifts may work at variable times. The day shift, which is eight and one-half hours long, may start between 6:30 and 8:30 A.M. and there is half an hour for lunch, ordinarily at 11:30 A.M. The swing shift starts between 3:00 and 5:00 P.M. and the graveyard between 11:00 P.M. and 1:00 A.M.; the lunch periods occur approximately at midshift.

The benefit year under the U. S. Borax agreement is defined as the twelve-month period beginning February 1 and is used to compute sick leave, overtime equalization, and other benefits, except vacations. For vacation accrual, the benefit year begins on March 15.

A typical, though detailed, manufacturing agreement is that between Douglas Aircraft Company and the United Automobile Workers covering the facilities at Long Beach,

[27] Sigmund Freud, *Civilization and Its Discontents* (New York: Norton, 1961), pp. 27, 36, 40, 48.

[28] *Work in America*, pp. 3-10.

California, and Tulsa, Oklahoma (1968-1971). The workweek begins at the regular starting time of the employee's shift on Monday and ends "seven consecutive twenty-four hour days" later; the workday starts at the opening of the regular shift and terminates twenty-four hours afterwards; the standard workweek is "five consecutive workdays beginning on Monday"; the nonstandard workweek is five consecutive workdays beginning on a day other than Monday.

Shift schedules for most groups of employees are not in the agreement. An appendix to that document sets forth the schedules for Long Beach cafeteria employees. With some exceptions, the day shift is either 5:30 A.M. to 2:12 P.M. or 6:00 A.M. to 2:42 P.M.; swing is 1:48 P.M. to 10:30 P.M.; and graveyard is 11:00 P.M. to 6:00 A.M. The split shifts are 9:30 A.M. to 1:30 P.M. and 6:30 P.M. to 10:30 P.M. Bakers work days from 4:00 A.M. to 12:42 P.M. and swing from 11:30 A.M. to 8:12 P.M. The doughnut maker is on graveyard from 2:00 A.M. to 9:00 A.M.

The lunch period may be neither fewer than thirty nor more than forty-two minutes. The company retains the unilateral right to change the starting and stopping times of shifts provided the change in either direction does not exceed thirty minutes; if the change is more than half an hour, the union's agreement must be obtained. The company must give employees at least one week's notice of a shift change.

In the present context, it is worth quoting the daily overtime paragraph:

> Employees working on first and second shifts shall be paid time and one-half for all hours worked in excess of eight in any one workday or forty hours in any one workweek, whichever is greater. Employees working on third shifts of six and one-half hours shall be paid time and one-half for all hours worked in excess of six and one-half hours in any one workday or thirty-two and one-half hours in any one workweek, whichever is greater. The overtime compensation of third shift employees, regularly assigned to six and one-half hour shifts, shall be computed in accordance with the following formula: ($1\frac{1}{2}$ × working rate, which is 8 × (adjusted base rate plus 14¢)).

Payday is defined by shift. First- and third-shift employees are paid on the last regular working day of the calendar week for the preceding payroll week. Second-shift employees receive their wages on the next-to-last regular working day of the calendar week for the preceding payroll week, except when a recognized holiday falls on Thursday or Friday in which case they are paid on the last regularly scheduled workday in the week.

The Douglas agreement, which has 150 closely packed pages, contains, of course, a great many other time-related features. One of them deals with, in fact resolves, a problem to be covered later in this article. This short provision, entitled "Computation of Time," reads, "All time worked shall be calculated and paid for in units of six minutes' duration, that is, tenths of hours, beginning on the hour. Fractions of such units shall not be counted." The problem is that we measure time by a system based on the number sixty and we measure money by the decimal system. To accomplish the trade-off of time for money, it is necessary to have an arithmetic translation.

The time factor becomes even more important when one moves from mining and manufacturing industries to transportation. In part, this is because trucks, buses, trains, ships, and airplanes run on schedules. In addition, operating crews work not on fixed shifts of, say, eight hours, but for the duration of the trip. Also, they often move through more than one time zone, in the case of jet aircraft routes near the earth's poles through a substantial number; and in trans-Pacific voyages they cross the International Date Line. Thus, two kinds of time become significant: ground time, the hour at a specific point on the earth's surface, and elapsed time, the duration of the trip from the point of departure to the point of arrival. Finally, crews, particularly on ships, may be employed in two different conditions: while the vessel is in motion or while it is at rest.

The agreement between Hendy International Company and several other shipping firms with the Masters, Mates and Pilots (1969-1972) illustrates this last point. It establishes two basic types of time: sea watches and port time. At sea, of course, a ship must be manned around the clock. Deck officers stand the historic "sea watches of four (4) hours on and eight (8) hours off at any time except emergencies." Two watches constitute a day's work. On ships carrying three deck officers, the third officer stands the 8:00-12:00 watch, the second officer stands 12:00-4:00, and the chief officer, 4:00-8:00. When there are four officers, a third officer stands 8:00-12:00, another third officer stands 12:00-4:00, and a second officer stands 4:00-8:00. For such officers other hours worked are compensated at premium rates as are watch hours worked on Saturdays, Sundays, and holidays. Officers not required to stand watches at sea work eight hours between 0800 and 1700 with one hour off for meals. For other hours, with some exceptions, and for Saturdays, Sundays, and holidays they receive the overtime rate.

Sea time ends and port time begins thirty minutes after the vessel has anchored or moored in the vicinity of a port for certain designated purposes. Port time terminates thirty minutes before the time mooring lines are cast off or the anchor is aweigh for the purpose of putting to sea. Under port time, officers who are off watch are entitled to shore leave. Officers employed in port work an eight-hour shift between 0800 and 1700, Monday through Friday. They receive overtime for other hours, for weekends, and for holidays. A rotation schedule is set up to determine which officers will work under port time in which port. In United States ports, port-relief officers stand the watches between 1630 and 0800 on weekdays and on Saturdays, Sundays, and holidays.

This explanation sounds clear enough, but there are many complications, for example, emergencies, putting to sea before completion of the port-time shift, and shifting ship, which involves moving the vessel "in inland waters, bays, rivers and sounds." A ship that loads or discharges cargo at both ends of the Panama or Suez Canals is considered in shift; movements from Liverpool to Manchester, Montreal to Quebec, Philadelphia to Baltimore, among others, are not considered in shift. The condition of shifting ship has special systems of scheduling and compensation.

The ultimate in the management of time, of course, is the airline. The agreement between Pan American World Airways and the Air Line Pilots (1972) is literally a book. Section 14, Hours of Service, takes up thirty-five pages and an appendix; the Pilot's System Scheduling Manual consumes twenty-two pages. These are only two of many provisions that relate to time. It would be ridiculous to try to summarize these time-related rules, but a few highlights may be noted. A pilot may be scheduled for no more than eighty credited hours a month (reduced to seventy-five on July 1, 1973). If he surpasses this limit, the excess becomes "banked hours" upon which he may draw for specified purposes. February creates a complication in defining the "month." Under the agreement, nine months are calendar months, but January is January 1-30, February is January 31-March 1, and March is March 2-31. Flight time starts when the aircraft first moves for the purpose of flight and ends when it is secured at a ramp or unloading point.

Pilots perform ground duties before and after the flight and flight deck duties. Thus, the limitations on daily hours are expressed both in duty hours and in block-to-block hours and vary according to the type of aircraft, the size of the crew, and the type of flight, nonstop or scheduled for intermediate stops. Here is an example: when the flight is nonstop and the crew consists of two pilots and an additional member and the scheduled time of departure is between 0600 and 1359, the duty limit is thirteen hours and the block-to-block limit is nine hours. If departure is between 1400 and 2159, duty is twelve hours and block-to-block is nine hours. If the flight leaves between 2200 and 0559, duty is eleven and block-to-block is nine hours. There are two exceptions. On nonstop flights between Japan and San Francisco or Los Angeles, there must be three pilots and an added crew member in the cabin. On nonstop flights from Rome to New York, the usual crew size is allowed "notwithstanding the scheduled block-to-block time" on condition that the time of departure is between 0600 and 1359.

Most of the things that an airline pilot values, which all the rest of us would also value, depend upon his seniority. Unlike the other aspects of airline time management, this one is simple. "Seniority as a pilot with the Company shall begin with the pilot's date of employment as a pilot, and shall continue to accrue during such period of service and furlough." A pilot who is furloughed because of a reduction in force both retains his original seniority date for ten years of furlough and continues to acquire seniority during that period.

These agreements manage time effectively. In order that they do so, it is necessary to measure time precisely. A work-related society, therefore, is absolutely dependent upon the calendar and the clock. The calendar is quite old; the clock as a device for measuring accurately is a fairly recent invention.

Relatively ancient peoples were able to devise calendars because they are based upon simple astronomical observations that may be made with the naked eye. The cycles of the sun allow for two basic determinations, the day (actually the rotation of the earth on its axis) and the year (the orbit of the earth around the sun in 365 days, 5 hours, 48 minutes, and 46 seconds). The cycle of the moon's phases, which takes about 29.5 days, forms the basis for the month. A fundamental and unresolved difficulty, demonstrated by the Pan Am agreement's bout with February, is that the solar and lunar cycles cannot be fitted together with arithmetic precision. Thus, many early peoples, either by independent invention or by adjusting calendars derived from others, worked out varying systems of fitting days to months and months to years. The Moslems and Hindus did not even try. The Moslem calendar is purely lunar and the Hindu entirely solar.

The Chaldeans, evidently, invented the first calendar about three millenia before Christ. The number sixty had a special significance for the Chaldeans; they derived it by multiplying the then known five planets and twelve constellations. They used this number as the basis for dividing space, time, and quantity (including money). A sixty-based system was devised in antiquity for laying out the circle, 360 degrees, 60 minutes, and 60 seconds. It was then applied to the surface of the earth. The same sixty-based arrangement was extended to clocks when they were developed.

Astronomically derived calendars, while useful, are, of course, grossly inadequate for an industrial society. There are two critical deficiencies: the unit that falls between the day and the month (the week) and time segments smaller than the day. (The ancient Hebrews devised the week: in the Creation the Lord worked for six days and rested on the seventh.) Short time intervals are much more important in the present context and required the invention of the clock.

The need for an instrument to measure fractions of the day was recognized by the peoples of antiquity and a variety were devised, all with serious shortcomings. The sundial, which casts a shadow on a marked scale, is only moderately precise and is useless at night. The clepsydra was based on the principle of allowing water to drip at a predetermined rate, but was only roughly accurate. The hourglass was similar, using sand, and suffered the same deficiency. Candles and knotted ropes were burned as timing devices, again inaccurately. The first clocks, invented in the Middle Ages, were crude devices that announced the time by the ringing of bells.

The most sophisticated of these early devices was the astrolabe, which was invented in antiquity and gained widest use in the Middle Ages from India to Spain. It consisted of an axis with a series of rings, each containing astronomical information, which, when rotated, produced useful results. The astrolabe was used for astronomical observations, for surveying, for determining latitude and true north, for computation, for casting horoscopes, and, most important, for telling local time. For this last purpose it was effective both during the day and at night so long as the sun or a star marked on the instrument was visible. The defect of this remarkable device was that it was imprecise.

While inventors designed mechanical clocks as early as the thirteenth century, modern clockmaking begins with Christiaan Huygens, the Dutch mathematician and physicist. He invented the first effective pendulum clock about 1657 and the coiled hairspring in 1675; the latter was necessary for the watch. Others made improvements upon Huygens' work, and by the end of the seventeenth century the mechanics of clockmaking and watchmaking were perfected. Thus, only shortly before the Industrial Revolution did it become possible to measure intervals of the day accurately.[29]

These clocks and watches, of course, employed the Chaldean system of measurement based on sixty; but most of the nations of the world have opted for the decimal system for counting money. As has already been noted, it is necessary to translate time into money in order to pay accurately for work. This translation has been accomplished with the time clock that measures in both the Chaldean system as well as in intervals of tenths of an hour, that is, six minutes. It is a stroke of luck that sixty is divisible by ten.

While animals, including preindustrial man, work in relation to time, the rhythms are imprecise. Work locked into the clock and the calendar, such as that noted in the collective bargaining agreements cited above, is limited to modern industrial human societies.

Virtually all living creatures, unicellular as well as multicellular, plants like animals, have biological "clocks," with the possible exception of those that dwell in permanent darkness. These little understood mechanisms respond most dramatically to the twenty-four-hour alternation between day and night. They also react significantly to the annual cycle of the seasons, of course, more sharply nearer the earth's poles than at the equator. Some marine species are affected by the lunar month, by the moonlight and the height of the tides in the sea.

A few examples will illustrate these biological clocks in subhuman species. Bees time their visits to flowers as they start daily nectar secretion. This timing allows the bee to maximize the amount of food gathered and to assure flower pollination. Many species of birds accurately reckon complex problems of celestial navigation, taking account of the position of the sun in its daily cycle. Diurnal animals are active in daylight, nocturnal animals at night. The 8,000-mile annual roundtrip migration of the California gray whale follows the seasons, summer feeding in the food-rich Bering Sea and winter reproduction in the warm lagoons of Baja California. The flowering of plants is photoperiodic; the plant measures the hours of sunlight, a function of the season. The reproductive process of the grunion depends upon the tides. At the highest tide the female of this fish lays its eggs at the edge of the dry sand on a Southern California beach and the male deposits its sperm. Both return to the sea with the next long wave. The fertilized eggs then have a dry fortnight in which to develop. Two weeks later, at the next high tide, the larvae wash out to sea.

These and countless other time measurements of the day, the month, and the year by plants and lower animals are approximations. Thus, biologists who study these phenomena do not use the day defined as twenty-four hours; they refer to the circadian period (about a day), which may vary between twenty-two and twenty-six hours. For example, a flying squirrel in the wild had a customary daily period of high activity; when placed in constant darkness, he would engage in wheel-running in response to his internal clock in circadian periods of twenty-three hours and thirty-six minutes. Over time, of course, such a circadian period would become significantly desynchronized from the twenty-four-hour day. While circadian rhythms satisfy the functions animals need them for, including work, these periods hardly provide a foundation for human industrial processes. Biological clocks lack the accuracy of mechanical clocks.[30]

A number of studies of work patterns of primitive man demonstrate their irregular rhythm. Herskovits wrote, "Unlike workers in a machine economy, . . . they take their ease at their own pleasure."[31] Marshall Sahlins, who

[29] J. R. McCarthy, *A Matter of Time* (New York: Harper, 1947); American Council on Education, *Telling Time through the Centuries* (Washington: ACE, 1933); Eric Burton, *Clocks and Watches, 1400-1900* (London: Barker, 1967); J. D. North, "The Astrolabe," *Scientific American*, January 1974, pp. 96-106; H. Alan Lloyd, "Mechanical Timekeepers," *A History of Technology*, vol. 3 (New York: Oxford University Press, 1957), pp. 648-75.

[30] Michael Menaker, "Biological Clocks," *BioScience* 19 (August 1969):681-89; Suthers and Gallant, *Biology: The Behavioral View*, pp. 265-67.

[31] Herskovits, *Economic Anthropology*, p. 90.

collected work data on a substantial number of Stone Age peoples, who depend upon hunting and gathering, concluded that they work with great irregularity, that several put in only three to five hours a day on those days when they do work, and that they eat everything they gather right away and do not store a surplus for future consumption. "A good case can be made," Sahlins wrote, "that hunters and gatherers work less than we do; and, rather than a continuous travail, the food quest is intermittent, leisure abundant, and there is a greater amount of sleep in the day time per capita per year than in any other condition of society."[32] Paul Bohannan, who studied the Tiv of Nigeria, wrote as follows:

> I did not collect any precise data on the amount of time which Tiv spend in agricultural work. Though I made several attempts to do so, I found that collecting such data was disproportionately time-consuming. Tiv have no unit for measuring labor. Because they do not make any important connection between time, work and wealth, application of our quantitative notion of "man-hours" is in large part impracticable—if for no other reason than that it is impossible to collect accurate data by any means other than direct observation. The amount of time actually spent working in the fields is in many cases irrelevant, because different men work at vastly different rates of speed, and the same man works at different rates of speed in different circumstances. In addition, the amount of time spent in agricultural labour varies widely for both men and women at different times of the year. . . .
>
> Tiv are concerned with the results of labour, not with the amount of labour.[33]

The Alaskan natives fit this pattern. The Athabascan chairman of the 1972 state Democratic convention ran it on "Indian time," which he defined as "when everybody just feels like getting to it." A meeting of Kuskokwim Eskimos was closed with the motion, "Everybody in favor of adjournment, get up and go home."[34]

The same irregularity in relation to time is evident in man's satisfaction of his primal functions. In the absence of the industrial discipline, he eats when he is hungry, he sleeps when he is tired, he eliminates his wastes when he feels the need to do so, and he makes love when he and his partner feel like doing so.

Looking back to the Olduvai Gorge, it is evident that a regular work rhythm is very new indeed in human evolution. It has arrived with a jolt, as the process of industrialization demonstrates. When the Industrial Revolution came to England in the late eighteenth century, older workers in traditional jobs, mainly agriculture, refused employment in the factories because they would not subject themselves to industrial discipline. Instead they sent their children. In India currently, according to Gunnar Myrdal, the basic reason for low labor efficiency is that "the bulk of the labor force is unaccustomed to a rhythm of sustained and diligent work."[35]

There is no doubt that the regular work rhythm demanded by industrial discipline is a basic, if not the prime, souce of alienation from work. Although work is a natural condition for man, work locked into the clock and the calendar is unnatural. The taming of man to the time demands of a modern society requires powerful incentives and punishments. The propensity to work must be acquired. Some peoples develop it quite rapidly, others slowly, and still others not at all.

THE COMPARATIVE PROPENSITY TO WORK

Ethnic groups, national and religious, have differential propensities for work; this proposition and particularly its causation is not entirely popular in academic circles. It is extremely unpopular among some ethnic groups that are rated low. Nevertheless, I think it to be both correct and significant and so deserving of analysis.

Perhaps it is best to make clear at the outset that the subject under discussion is the propensity of an ethnic group *as a whole* to work, to accept what Max Weber called "the work ethic." Thus, differences between individuals within such a group (which, of course, are universal, are wide and have very complex explanations) are excluded from consideration. So too is that very small group of people who occur in all societies who are so gifted in intellect, in the arts, or in the complex crafts that they work hard out of a creative impulse.

Those ethnic groups with a high historic propensity to work include the northern and western Europeans, particularly those of the Protestant religions, the North Americans of the United States and Canada, the Jews, the Japanese, and the Chinese. The peoples with a moderate propensity to work include the Russians, the Italians, the Spaniards, and many Latin Americans. The groups with a low propensity to work include the Arabs, the Indians, and the other peoples of South Asia.[36] There are a handful of ethnic groups who deliberately avoid work, notably the

---

[32] Marshall Sahlins, *Stone Age Economics* (Chicago: Aldine-Atherton, 1972), p. 14.

[33] Paul Bohannan, *Tiv Farm and Settlement*, Colonial Research Papers no. 15 (London: 1954), p. 26.

[34] "Keeping Cool in Alaska," *The New York Times*, December 28, 1973.

[35] Reinhard Bendix, *Work and Authority in Industry* (New York: Wiley, 1956), chap. 2; Gunnar Myrdal, *Asian Drama* (New York: Pantheon, 1971), p. 291. See also Charles A. Myers, *Labor Problems in the Industrialization of India* (Cambridge: Harvard University Press, 1958), chap. 3.

[36] Much of Africa south of the Sahara, evidently, would also fall within this category. See *African Labour Survey*, Studies and Reports, New Series, no. 48 (Geneva: International Labour Office, 1958), pp. 144-46.

Gypsies and the Bedouins. These rankings are categorical and while all could be supported by documentation, only those discussed below will be. This is because the central purpose is not to place particular ethnic groups within one or the other of the ranks, but, rather, to seek to explain the reasons for differential propensities to work.

While many factors have historically affected the work ethic, it seems that three are central: climate, religion, and family.

The effect of climate on man's capacity to work, which has been extensively studied, is complex, for several reasons. One is that climate is composed of several elements: air temperature, humidity, air movement, and solar radiation, at least. Second, human tolerances differ in relation to these variables in accordance with the kind of work being performed. The common distinction between mental and physical effort is, of course, crude, because there are varying intensities and durations of each. The third reason is that man is adaptable. A person who is suddenly transported from a temperate zone where the climatic factors make him comfortable to a tropical area where these elements cause him discomfort, if not illness, may find it impossible at the outset to work at all. After several weeks, however, he becomes acclimatized, his discomfort diminishes or vanishes, and he is able to work. Fourth, there are moderately significant differences in tolerances between individuals, between the sexes, and, over time, in the same person.

Despite these qualifications, it is clear that there is a "comfort zone" in which working performance is at its highest. In Britain this is defined within the following ranges: air temperature of 60-68° F., relative humidity of 50 to 70 percent, and air movement of 50 feet per minute. In the United States, partly because lighter clothes are worn, the temperature may be pushed up four or five degrees. Presumably, exposure to sunlight under such moderate conditions would further add to comfort. When any of these factors deviates from these norms in either direction, the physiological capacity to perform work diminishes and, at a certain point, ceases.[37]

The conclusions to be drawn seem clear. People who live in temperate zones in which the conditions approximate the norms most of the time should on climatic grounds alone be capable of working hard. Those who inhabit areas with high heat and humidity or with high heat, aridity, and solar radiation or with intense cold and long periods of darkness are not able to work as hard.

Most of the world's population inhabit either temperate or tropical zones; relatively few people live in either deserts or extremely cold areas. As a practical matter, therefore, the significant question is what happens to the capacity to work in places where air temperature and relative humidity significantly exceed the norms. The answer is evident: man works at a slow pace because he is physiologically incapable of doing more. If he does work hard under these conditions, his body temperature rises, his heartbeat quickens, and he sweats profusely. If he continues to work hard, he experiences increasing discomfort and at a certain point, usually when body temperature reaches about 103°, he collapses. In the tropics, therefore, man adjusts to the climate; he slows his rate of work and he breaks the workday in half with rest, the siesta. As pointed out above, this is exactly what many other animals do.

This climatic analysis fits the rankings quite well. Those ethnic groups with a high propensity to work — northern and western Europeans, North Americans, Jews, Japanese, and Chinese — live primarily in temperate zones. In several of the countries with a moderate propensity to work, significantly, there are marked differences between the north and the south. This, of course, is dramatically illustrated by Italy. According to Luigi Barzini, the Milanese work hard in order to get rich; the Neapolitans, who want to be obeyed and envied, are not interested in hard work. The same is said to be the case in Spain. The pace of Barcelona is "European," that of Seville and Granada "Moorish." Seville, further, is the center for the Andalusian Gypsies. Frances FitzGerald writes in a similar vein of Vietnam. The northerners are industrious, like the Chinese; the southerners move at the easier pace of the south Asians.[38] The low-propensity peoples live in hot climates, both dry and wet, the Arabs, the Indians, other peoples of southern Asia. The Gypsies defy analysis, climatic or otherwise. The Bedouins fit the desert zone. It is also worth noting that the distribution of the world's major religions conforms roughly to these climatic patterns. Those religions that reinforce the propensity to work, Protestantism, Judaism, Japanese beliefs, and Confucianism, find most of their adherents in temperate areas. Those religions that do not support the work ethic, notably Islam, Hinduism, Buddhism, and, to a lesser extent, Catholicism, have more followers in the hotter zones.

---

[37] O. G. Edholm, *The Biology of Work* (New York: McGraw-Hill, 1967), chap. 4. The early studies gathered by Ellsworth Huntington suggest that mental work is more taxing than physical and demands lower temperatures. See his *Civilization and Climate* (New Haven: Yale University Press, 1915), p. 105. Huntington, of course, was an extremist who attributed such matters as the rise and fall of civilizations, racial differences, and sexual degeneracy to climate, conclusions that no one would take seriously nowadays.

[38] Luigi Barzini, *The Italians* (New York: Bantam, 1965), chap. 13; Frances FitzGerald, *Fire in the Lake* (Boston: Atlantic-Little, Brown, 1972), pp. 47-50. Raphael Patai has referred to "the general Mediterranean inclination" to take it easy. The Spanish word is *mañana*, the Italian phrase is *dolce far niente*, the Arabic is *buqra* ("tomorrow"). Raphael Patai, *The Arab Mind* (New York: Scribner, 1973), p. 276.

When one discusses religion in this context, of course, one must immediately confront Max Weber. It seems superfluous to say that *The Protestant Ethic and the Spirit of Capitalism* is the decisive work; in the judgment of many it is one of the greatest works of social science of the past century. This study, first published in a German journal in 1904-1905, has had an enormous intellectual impact. Its insights have inspired further scholarship, some relied on below, and have evoked great controversy, as every decisive book must. It is, of course, much the best known of Weber's works. What is not so widely recognized is that the sociology of religion was a major theme, almost an obsession, of Weber's intellectual life. Several other works, none of which he considered ready for publication, were brought out and translated after his death, *The Religion of China: Confucianism and Taoism; The Religion of India: The Sociology of Hinduism and Buddhism;* and *Ancient Judaism.* He had also done work that has not been published on Islam, early Christianity, and Talmudic Judaism.[39] *The Protestant Ethic* is much the most significant of these works for the purposes of this paper, mainly because Protestantism fits his theory more snugly than the other religions. Further, Weber's interest was broader than that of this paper. He was concerned with the emergence of capitalism; the interest here is in the work ethic, to use his phrase.

Weber's basic concept was that "rational bourgeois capitalism" emerged for the first time in human history in Europe between the sixteenth and nineteenth centuries, in large part because of the Protestant Reformation and particularly the impact of Calvinism. Calvin stripped Christianity of Catholic "magic" as the means of salvation. Man must seek his way by himself in this world. He would rest in the next. Here on earth man must work hard, he must not waste time, he must not fall prey to sloth or indulgence. By his unremitting labor, man was performing God's work. If he got rich, he became the Lord's steward. Protestant religion, therefore, reinforced the propensity to work, in fact, condemned man to damnation if he failed to do so. Thus, the work ethic: work is a "calling."

Weber, like many others, was struck by the differential in the propensity to work between Protestant and Catholic Europe, and his book was an attempt to explain it. Those Protestant Europeans, mainly British, German, Dutch, and Scandinavian, who emigrated abroad carried their religion and their work ethic with them to what were to become the United States, Canada, Australia, New Zealand, and South Africa.

With reference to the propensity to work, the mainstream of Judaism is much like Protestantism. There is no magic intervention to achieve salvation. The stress is on this world and on ethical rules for man's conduct. A key difference with Protestantism is that Judaism teaches that its followers are God's "chosen" people. This belief has been reinforced by the fact that the Jews for most of their history have been exiles wandering over the face of the earth, a small and often persecuted minority wherever they found themselves. Thus, they have had to work hard to prove their worth to their God, to the Gentile majority, and to themselves.[40]

This propensity to work is illustrated in the way of life of the Shtetl, the uniquely Jewish small-town community of eastern Europe, whose culture has migrated with the descendents of its former inhabitants to the United States, Israel, and many other lands. The saying went, "If no bread, then no Torah." Mark Zborowski and Elizabeth Herzog have written:

> The Covenant promises not only happiness in the world after life, but also Olam Hazeh, this world. It grants to the Jews the right to ask God for gezunt un parnosseh [health and livelihood], and to expect these blessings, provided they do their part.
>
> Their part includes not only fulfillment of the mitsvos [divine commandments], but also a prodigious amount of effort. One does not expect the Almighty to snare his gezunt un parnosseh for him, but merely to aid by smiling on his efforts to help himself. "Work, and God will help." . . .
>
> There is no leisure class in the Shtetl, except for babies in arms.
>
> Idleness is a sin and the loafer is scornfully dubbed "one who goes empty." A child who is not busy about something will be told sharply, "don't sit with empty hands!" If he is allowed to loaf he will grow up into a ne'er do well, a batln, and such a one is a disgrace to himself and his family. . . . The Shulkhan Arukh itself warns against lying in bed after one wakens in the morning, for rest should come only after hard work. It is against the background of constant effort that the peace of Sabbath takes on full flavor. . . .
>
> Waking hours are working hours, except for Sabbath and holidays. There is no official work day. One toils

[39] Max Weber, *The Protestant Ethic and the Spirit of Capitalism* (New York: Scribner, 1958); *The Religion of China: Confucianism and Taoism* (Glencoe, Ill.: Free Press, 1951); *The Religion of India: The Sociology of Hinduism and Buddhism* (Glencoe, Ill.: Free Press, 1958); *Ancient Judaism* (Glencoe, Ill.: Free Press, 1952). Also see Reinhard Bendix, *Max Weber, An Intellectual Portrait* (Garden City, N.Y.: Doubleday, 1960), particularly the bibliographical note and part 2.

[40] Philip S. Bernstein, *What the Jews Believe* (New York: Farrar, Straus and Young, 1950), p. 4. There has been a mystical strain in Judaism, represented by the Kabala and the Hassidic movement that does not fit this pattern. The sociology of American Jewry is set forth in detail in Marshall Sklare, ed., *The Jews: Social Patterns of an American Group* (Glencoe, Ill.: Free Press, 1958) and Nathan Glazer and Daniel Patrick Moynihan, *Beyond the Melting Pot* (Cambridge: MIT Press, 1963), pp. 137-80.

early and late, squeezing in extra time whenever possible.[41]

Robert Bellah had sought to do for Japan, in his book *Tokugawa Religion*, what Weber did for Protestant Europe. In their turbulent Middle Ages, the Japanese evolved a warrior-class ethic that absorbed influences derived from Confucianism and Buddhism. In the period of the Tokugawa Shogunate, 1603-1867, this became "the ethic of an entire people." The continuity of the imperial dynasty and a national religion supported this outlook. Bellah writes:

> Religion reinforced commitment to the central value system by making that value system meaningful in an ultimate sense. The family and the nation were not merely secular collectivities but were also religious entities. Parents and political superiors had something of the sacred about them, were merely the lower echelons of the divine. Fulfillment of one's obligations to these superordinates had an ultimate meaning. It ensured the continuation of future blessings and of that ultimate protection which alone could save the individual from the hardships and dangers of this transitory world....
>
> Finally, we must consider the relation of religion to that ethic of inner-worldly asceticism which is so powerful in Japan. The obligation to hard, selfless labor and to the restraint of one's own desires for consumption is closely linked to the obligations to sacred and semi-sacred superiors which is so stressed in Japanese religion, as also to that state of selfless identification with ultimate nature.... Japanese religion never tires of stressing the importance of diligence and frugality and of attributing religious significance to them, both in terms of carrying out one's obligations to the sacred and in terms of purifying the self of evil impulses and desires. That such an ethic is profoundly favorable to economic rationalization was the major point of Weber's study of Protestantism and we must say that it seems favorable in Japan.[42]

If Bellah's analysis is correct, the Japanese should have the highest propensity to work of any ethnic group in the world. This may well be the case.[43]

In the present context the Chinese, as in so much else, are a special case. My assault, and I use the word advisedly, upon Weber's *The Religion of China* was a total failure. This may be my fault or even Weber's, but I suspect it is China's. Other readings in Chinese religion tend to confirm

this suspicion. Aside from the obvious facts that China occupies an enormous land mass, has by far the largest population in the world, has the longest continuous history of any surviving nation, and has received many external influences, religious and otherwise, the Chinese are extremely complicated about religion. Many Chinese do not even regard their most important "religion," Confucianism, as a religion. It is a this-worldy code of political and personal conduct. The two other significant Chinese religions, Taoism and Buddhism, have value systems that one would expect to undermine the propensity to work. Thus, they could hardly explain one of the world's most industrious peoples. The key to the Chinese work ethic, obviously, lies elsewhere: in the family system. It has often been said that the real religion of China is "the cult of ancestors." The function of formal religion, particularly Confucianism, in the context of the propensity to work has been to reinforce the family. Mencius, the greatest of the Confucian philosophers, wrote, "The root of the State is in the family." For Confucius and his followers the family was the building block of society.[44]

Islam has undermined the propensity to work. "The traditional components of the Arab personality... fall into two main categories: a pre-Islamic Bedouin substratum, which continues to live on in the folk culture of the traditional majority; and the Islamic component, superimposed on the first one and often merging with it imperceptibly."[45] A central feature of the Bedouin outlook was aversion to manual work, the belief that dirtying one's hands was dishonorable, that work was a curse. This found reinforcement in Genesis in the fall of Adam. Mohammed and his followers incorporated this view into Islam. Allah both guides the world and predestines the fate of every man. The duty of man is to obey God. The root from which the word "Islam" is derived means total submission. Predestination is a basic doctrine of the Koran. It relieves the believer of both the obligation and the incentive to better himself. Predestination was carried to the extreme in that Mohammedan sect known as Sufism. Its followers surrendered themselves completely to fate, so that "they refuse every activity and effort to procure a regular livelihood."[46]

Another Bedouin concept that the Prophet absorbed was the distinction between "good" and "evil." It was not based on conduct. Rather, what was "good" was known,

[41] Mark Zborowski and Elizabeth Herzog, *Life Is with People, The Culture of the Shtetl* (New York: Schocken, 1952), pp. 239-41.

[42] Robert Bellah, *Tokugawa Religion* (Glencoe, Ill.: Free Press, 1957), pp. 183, 194-96.

[43] A Jew who was born and raised in Japan has written, "Of course, other peoples use plans and schedules in large-scale programs, but none carries them out with the split-second accuracy of the Japanese." Isaiah Ben-Dasan, *The Japanese and the Jews* (Tokyo: Westerhill, 1970), p. 48.

[44] Reginald Johnston, *Confucianism in Modern China* (New York: Appleton, 1935), p. 55; Olga Lang, *Chinese Family and Society* (New Haven: Yale University Press, 1946), pp. 8-9.

[45] Patai, *Arab Mind*, p. 309.

[46] Alfred Bonne, *State and Economics in the Middle East* (London: Routledge & Kegan Paul, 1960), p. 359.

familiar; what was "evil" was unknown, foreign. "The trend of thought fostered by this tribal heritage is thus an ultraconservatism. . . .Progress is tabooed."[47] Man accepts his condition and the state of the world as given. He need do nothing to change either.

These doctrines have corollaries that constitute barriers to the work ethic. To escape the curse of labor, man acquires riches "through a stroke of luck, by finding a treasure, by finding favor in the eyes of a king, by buying something cheap and selling it at a high price, by being helped by a jinni."[48] *The Arabian Nights,* which reflect Arab folk values, are filled with such tales of magical good luck.

Further, the measurement of time becomes meaningless. Islam looks out upon a static world. When time does not pass, there is no change or innovation. "The absence of exact tempora in the Arabic language appears to be correlated with the disregard of the time element and with the lack of a time sense that is an oft-observed characteristic of the Arab personality."[49] As has been stressed above, a work-related society must be based upon the measurement of time.

Religion has probably had a greater impact upon the Indian subcontinent than upon any other part of the world, and one of its effects has been to prevent the emergence of the propensity to work. The religious history of India is extraordinarily rich and complex and this is hardly the place in which to unravel it. Speaking generally, for nearly three thousand years the dominant religion has been Hinduism or Brahminism. It prescribed and was, in turn, reinforced by the caste system in which the Brahmins occupied the highest status and imposed their will in both the religious and secular areas. Early on, Hinduism was challenged by two heterodox doctrines, Buddhism and Jainism, both of which were contained, though Buddhism eventually spread widely to other parts of Asia. The central ideas of Hinduism are the transmigration of the soul, reincarnation, and retribution, paying the price in this life for the sins of the previous life. These doctrines support the caste system and lead believers into a passive outlook upon life in this world, in some cases, like Yoga, by withdrawal. There is, as well, an extraordinary stress on magic. Early Buddhism denied the concept of "mine" or "my possession." Time in India has had little meaning. Indians have written myths, not history. In classical Sanskrit the tenses are not clearly demarcated. In Hindustani the same word means "yesterday" and "tomorrow." Myrdal has noted the impact of these concepts upon the work ethic:

Western industrial experience was never complicated by the special factors that inhibit efficient utilization of labor in South Asia. Caste, religious, and ethnic stratifications impose artificial rigidities on occupational mobility in urban areas as well as in tradition-bound villages. Employers have at times been obliged to forego rational organization of the work pattern in order to adapt to these prejudices. . . . Unless he wants to risk serious labor disturbances an employer cannot confer upon an employee a status that would elevate him beyond his position in traditional society.[50]

The relation of family structure to the propensity to work can be stated in two basic propositions. The first is that in a society in which the family as an institution is weak, it affords no reinforcement for the work ethic. Second, when the family as an institution is strong, it may or it may not buttress the propensity to work. That will depend upon the goals the society attaches to the family, which appear to be determined primarily by religion. If these goals include the economic, a strong family system gives powerful support to the work ethic. If the goals are not economic, a strong family has a neutral effect upon the propensity to work.

The work of the anthropologist Oscar Lewis is illuminating with respect to the weak family unit. He studied intensively the poor in Mexico and the Puerto Ricans in San Juan and New York City and constructed the concept of "the culture of poverty." While most of the world's poor people, concentrated in the underdeveloped countries, fall outside this system, there is "a subculture of Western society with its own structure and rationale, a way of life handed on from generation to generation along family lines." This subculture crosses regional and national boundaries, appears in both rural and urban settings, and is characteristic of capitalist and colonial societies. A central feature of the culture of poverty is its family system. Here it is best to quote Lewis.

There is awareness of middle-class values. People talk about them and even claim some of them as their own. On the whole, however, they do not live by them. They will declare that marriage by law, by the church or by both is the ideal form of marriage, but few will marry. For men who have no steady jobs, no property and no prospect of wealth to pass on to their children, who live in the present without expectations of the future, who want to avoid the expense and legal difficulties involved in marriage and divorce, a free union or consensual marriage makes good sense. The women, for their part, will turn down offers of marriage from men who are likely to be immature, punishing and generally unreliable. They feel that a consensual union gives them some of the freedom and flexibility men have. By not giving the fathers of their children legal status as husbands, the women have a stronger claim on the

[47] *Ibid.,* p. 357.

[48] Patai, *Arab Mind,* p. 114.

[49] *Ibid.,* p. 308.

[50] *Asian Drama,* pp. 292-93. See also Weber, *Religion of India;* Bendix, *Max Weber, An Intellectual Portrait,* chap. 6; Hajime Nakamura, *Ways of Thinking of Eastern People* (Honolulu: East-West Center Press, 1964).

children. They also maintain exclusive rights to their own property. . . .

The family in the culture of poverty does not cherish childhood as a specially prolonged and protected stage in the life cycle. Initiation into sex comes early. With the instability of consensual marriage the family tends to be mother-centered and tied more closely to the mother's extended family. The female head of the house is given to authoritarian rule. In spite of much verbal emphasis on family solidarity, sibling rivalry for the limited supply of goods and maternal affection is intense. There is little privacy.[51]

An individual whose childhood has been spent in such a family develops strong feelings of fatalism, helplessness, and inferiority. His physical world is bounded by the neighborhood he resides in; he knows next to nothing of what lies beyond it. His time orientation is the present moment; he knows no history of the past and makes no plans for the future. Though Lewis does not directly say so himself, it seems clear that such a person would have a low propensity to work, particularly in a time-related work setting.[52] The work of Nathan Glazer and Daniel Patrick Moynihan on the Negro family, while written from a different viewpoint, tends to confirm the conclusion that a weak family system inhibits the work ethic.[53]

There can be no doubt that the strong family in a society which attaches value to an economic goal reinforces the work ethic. This is characteristic of the peoples with a high propensity to work, the northern and western Europeans, the North Americans, the Jews, the Japanese, and the Chinese. The European and North American model of the family is so familiar as to need no elucidation beyond noting that it casts the husband-father in the role of "breadwinner." The cement that binds the Jewish family is equally well known, but the Japanese model is not so familiar. The studies of Ruth Benedict and others stressed that the social structure of the whole nation was based upon the concept of kinship in accordance with hierarchy. This kinship was extended far beyond blood relationships. As J. C. Abegglen has pointed out, the idea of the family provides the underpinning for the traditional Japanese factory. Both the employer and the employee have entered into a lifetime commitment. Wages are "patriarchally" determined, not so much in relation to the work performed, but, rather, on such factors as age, education, size of family, and fidelity to the enterprise. In the West the worker trades off his work for pay in an impersonal exchange; in Japan the employer becomes responsible for the worker's "total functioning." Among other things, the traditional Japanese employer is obliged to see to it that his female employees are married by age thirty, either by arranging a marriage or by putting pressure on them to quit or, at the least, by denying women advancement.[54]

It seems that the historic Chinese concept of family is the most powerful in the world and so deserves more extended discussion. As noted above, it finds primary reinforcement in China's dominant religion, Confucianism. Confucius (551-479 B.C.) lived in an age of chaos and his teachings, therefore, sought to unify and stabilize China with a code of political and personal conduct. Confucianism dominated Chinese thought and behavior for two thousand years, at least to the close of the nineteenth century, and continues to maintain a hold upon the Chinese people into the present century, particularly in rural areas.

The family is the heart of Confucianism, for its own sake and also as the way to strengthen the state. Of the Five Cardinal Relations of Humanity, three involve kinship, father-son (filial piety), husband-wife, and elder brother-younger brother. The student was to pay respect to his teacher as though he were his father. The old man, who represented the accumulation of wisdom, was revered. Dead ancestors were venerated, if not worshipped. There were, in addition, six formal kinship relations, the last of which extended to the great-grandchildren of brothers. The ritual for mourning embraced twenty-one categories of relatives. The concept of family was extended to the state. The emperor stood in the position of the father to his scholars and ministers, who were his sons and grandsons. The local civil servant was assigned a certain number of families to administer and tax. The main forms of corruption were nepotism and advancing the interest of the family against the state. Social and economic organizations patterned themselves after the family. Secret societies would initiate a new member by the drinking of a few drops of another's blood to establish a "blood tie."

The family provided the economic base for an overwhelmingly peasant society. A whole village was often linked by kinship. Within the family there was a sharp

---

[51] Oscar Lewis, "The Culture of Poverty," *Scientific American*, October 1966, p. 23.

[52] See in particular the harrowing story of Roberto in Lewis, *The Children of Sanchez* (New York: Vintage, 1961), pp. 60-87, 191-233, 371-402. When Roberto's father told him that he was now a man and should go to work, Roberto said, "Unfortunately, that's the way I have been. I worked at a job until I had some money in my pocket, and then I quit." (p. 383).

[53] Glazer and Moynihan, *Beyond the Melting Pot*, pp. 50-53, 122-29; *The Negro Family, The Case for National Action* (Washington: Department of Labor, 1965). The latter, the so-called "Moynihan Report," has been severely criticized. The classic and more favorable view of the black family is E. Franklin Frazier, *The Negro Family in the United States*, rev. ed. (New York: Holt, Rinehart & Winston, 1948). See also Jessie Bernard, *Marriage and Family among Negroes* (Englewood Cliffs, N.J.: Prentice-Hall, 1966).

[54] James C. Abegglen, *The Japanese Factory* (Glencoe, Ill.: Free Press, 1958).

division of labor between the sexes. The males worked the fields under the leadership of the father with occasional help from the women at the harvest. The females ran the household. The mother was responsible for young children of both sexes and the instruction of the girls in housekeeping duties, while the father took the responsibility for training the boys. In agriculture the family sought to be as self-sufficient as possible in both production and consumption as an economic unit. In the towns the stores and handicraft enterprises were overwhelmingly run by families.[55]

The traditional Chinese family in a very poor peasant society demanded unremitting labor from its members. The pressures bore in upon them from all sides, from the kinship collectivity, from the dominant father, from the dead ancestors, from the obligations to the young and still unborn, from the state, from Confucianism. There was almost no escape.

The strong family does not *necessarily* produce a high propensity to work, as the Italian family, particularly in the south, illustrates. According to Barzini, the Italian family is "a stronghold in a hostile land." The world outside this institution is "unruly and unpredictable," a sea of "anarchy." For the Italian the family is the real Italy; the laws and institutions are make-believe. Within the family Italians are truthful, reliable, and generous; outside it they deceive, procrastinate, and grab what they can. A man will die to protect the honor of his family; he is rarely willing to do so for the nation. Nepotism is one of the greatest of Italian arts, practiced by dukes, kings, and popes as well as by shopkeepers and peasants. In Sicily, the Mafia is run by an intricate network of families which extends to the United States. While the man appears to be the proud head of the family, "Mamma" runs it. Despite its strength and warmth, perhaps because of them, the Italian family is an institution designed primarily to protect its members, not to push them outward and upward. A south Italian proverb says, "Do not make your child better than you are." Among Italian-Americans, the youngster who wanted to go to school to better himself was considered to have deserted his family.[56]

One could hardly conclude this discussion of ethnicity in relation to the work ethic without a few words about the Gypsies, of whom there are said to be between six and ten million around the world. Their history is shrouded in mystery, in part because they have been mainly illiterate,

in part because they have made up fairy tales about their past (for example, that they came from Egypt, hence their names Gypsies) and in part because most Westerners who have written of them have been romantics enchanted by the free nomadic life of this wandering people. There seems no doubt that they originated in India and that their spoken language, Romany, is an Indian tongue. They appear first to have migrated to Persia, where they became known as Luri, or minstrels, because of their music. In the fifteenth century, they probably entered Greece and thereafter spread over much of Europe. It is possible that another stream crossed North Africa and settled in southern Spain. The Gypsies later migrated to North and South America, as well as to Asia, Australia, and New Zealand.

Aside from Romany, several Gypsy characteristics suggest their Indian origin: an indifference to time, a strong emphasis upon magic, and an extremely low propensity to work. As to the last, Walter Starkie wrote of the Andalusian Gypsies: "The humblest Gypsy picaroon in Seville and the most blue-blooded noble still have this in common: both firmly believe that to work for the sake of work is to be unworthy of the dignity of man."[57] What little work is performed, evidently, is mainly the burden of women. The Gypsy fortune-teller is the classic female figure. Insofar as men are concerned, there seems to have been one notable exception, a tradition of handicraft metalwork. They have been coppersmiths and tinsmiths and have produced pots and pans and big buttons to adorn their coats.

The consequences upon the Gypsies of both the nomadic life and the aversion to work have been poverty and reliance on their wits to survive. In Spain they became sharp "horse-traders" with the peasants in the south, particularly of asses and mules. They were skilled thieves and con artists. There was a school in Seville, known as the Rogue's Academy, where the young were instructed in these arts. Because of such characteristics and their life style, Gypsies have usually been regarded with fear, suspicion, and loathing in the settled communities into which they have wandered. Many nations passed laws to keep them out or to contain them, and they became objects of persecution, most notably by Hitler who sent them to the gas chambers, along with the Jews, for extermination. At the same time, they have had a romantic appeal to the free spirit. "The Gypsy is a natural man," Starkie wrote, "unspoilt by civilization, and his character, like that of Shakespeare's Caliban, springs from the soil where it is rooted, uncontrolled, uncouth and wild, uncramped by any of the meannesses of custom."[58]

[55] Johnston, *Confucianism in Modern China*, pp. 43, 55; Lang, *Chinese Family*, pp. 8-11, 18-21; C. K. Yang, *The Chinese Family in the Communist Revolution* (Cambridge: MIT Press, 1959), pp. 6-10, 138; Marion J. Levy, Jr., *The Family Revolution in Modern China* (Cambridge: Harvard University Press, 1949), pp. 210, 214, 223-24.

[56] Barzini, *The Italians*, chap. 11; Glazer and Moynihan, *Beyond the Melting Pot*, pp. 194-202.

[57] Walter Starkie, *In Sara's Tents* (London: Murray, 1953), p. 65.

[58] *Ibid.*, p. 285. See also Walter Starkie, *Raggle-Taggle* (London: Murray, 1933); Brian Vesay-Fitzgerald, *Gypsies of*

In conclusion, this comparative analysis of the propensity to work has been essentially historical. If it had been written when Weber wrote, at the turn of the century, it would have had a contemporary significance. But the twentieth century has wrought great changes, particularly in the period since the end of World War II, which have eroded the three factors stressed.

While climate itself has not changed in any important way, man has altered the conditions under which climate affects work. For one thing, it is now possible to create artifically temperate enclosed spaces, both above ground and in underground mining, in the tropics with air conditioning. In these work places air temperature, relative humidity, and air movement, though not sunlight, can be regulated to fit into the "comfort zone." In addition, peoples from temperate areas with high work propensities have migrated into hotter climates. Large numbers of European Jews have settled in Israel and many Chinese have migrated to Southeast Asia. The result has been a marked increase in the pace of work. Reverse migrations have had the same effect. Many southern Europeans, North Africans, and Turks have moved to the colder countries of northern Europe and in the United States blacks have left the rural South for the urban North.

Religion appears to have lost ground all around the world in an increasingly secular period. Communist governments have attacked it directly. In the West, Catholic dogma has been diluted and the hold of Protestantism, Catholicism, and Judaism upon their adherents has loosened. In the Arab countries, the educated, westernized elite groups have moved away from orthodox Islam. Similar tendencies are underway in southern Asia and Japan.

The family as an institution is also eroding. Communism has sought to undermine the traditional Chinese family on the theory that its local autonomy is inconsistent with a centralized, industrialized, urbanized, and Communist system. Cracks are visible in the Japanese family and the traditional Japanese factory system is giving way to the impersonality of the Western model. In the United States and in Europe many think the historic family system is disintegrating. Even the Italian family has loosened its hold, particularly in the north and in the cities, as well as among Italian-Americans.

Insofar as the work ethic is concerned, we are in a period of tension between traditional institutions and the forces of change. Where the former retain their hold, they still exert the old influences. Even where they have relaxed, the momentum set up earlier continues, though at a slower pace. Where the forces of change have taken over decisively, where the backs of religion and family have been broken, one of the results has been alienation.

Britain (London: Chapman and Hall, 1946); Norman N. Dodds, *Gypsies, Didikois, and Other Travellers* (London: Johnson, 1966); Grattan Puxon, *On the Road* (London: National Council for Civil Liberties, 1968).

ALIENATION FROM WORK

Alienation from work is a central problem of our time in America and in other advanced industrial societies. It is a major preoccupation of management in maintaining the industrial discipline that is needed to produce an adequate quantity and quality of goods. A large proportion of the grievances unions process involves the discharge, suspension, or reprimand of workers who refuse to conform to that discipline. Arbitrators find that a growing share of their cases arise out of such disciplinary actions.

Criticism of the work ethic has been a basic theme of the New Left, the counterculture, call it what you will. In *The Greening of America,* for example, Charles A. Reich wrote:

> Work and living have become more and more pointless and empty. . . . Our working days are used up in work that lacks meaning; making useless or harmful products, or servicing the bureaucratic structures. For most Americans work is mindless, exhausting, boring, servile, and hateful, something to be endured while "life" is confined to "time off.". . .
>
> But the real tragedy of the lost self in America is . . . the tragedy of the white-collar and blue-collar worker, who never had any chance. . . . Imprisoned in masks, they endure an unutterable loneliness. Their lives are stories of disappointed hopes, hopes disintegrating into the bitterness and envy that is ever present in even the most casual conversation of the worker.[59]

These views are not unique to radical critics of the establishment. Those who cherish respectability will find them more acceptably expressed in the report of the Special Task Force of the Secretary of Health, Education and Welfare:

> Our Nation is being challenged by a set of new issues having to do, in one way or another, with the quality of life. This theme emerges from the alienation and disenchantment of blue-collar workers, from the demands of minorities, for equitable participation in the "system," from the search by women for a new identity and by the quest of the aged for a respected and useful social role, from the youth who seek a voice in their society, and from almost everyone who suffers from the frustrations of life in a mass society. . . .
>
> Significant numbers of American workers are dissatisfied with the quality of their working lives. Dull, repetitive, seemingly meaningless tasks, offering little challenge of autonomy, are causing discontent among workers at all occupational levels. This is not so much because work itself has greatly changed; indeed, one of the main problems is that work has not changed fast enough to keep up with the rapid and widescale changes in worker attitudes, aspirations, and values. . . .
>
> The productivity of the worker is low — as measured by absenteeism, turnover rates, wildcat strikes, sabotage,

[59] Charles A. Reich, *The Greening of America* (New York: Bantam, 1971), pp. 6-7, 164-65.

poor-quality products, and a reluctance by workers to commit themselves to their work tasks. Moreover, a growing body of research indicates that, as work problems increase, there may be a consequent decline in physical and mental health, family stability, community participation and cohesiveness, and "balanced" sociopolitical attitudes, while there is an increase in drug and alcohol addiction, aggression, and delinquency.[60]

These are but two of many expressions of work alienation which could be culled from the contemporary literature. One need not accept all the specific points that are made or the apocalyptic language in which the criticism is often couched to acknowledge its main tenor, that alienation from work is a fundamental problem. There are few, if any, serious students of American society, and particularly of its industrial relations, who would agree with the message President Richard M. Nixon delivered on Labor Day, 1971, when he said, "The work ethic of this people is alive and well. . . . The dignity of work, the value of achievement, the morality of self-reliance — none of these is going out of style."[61] While the work ethic is certainly alive, it is not well.

A basic problem is that "alienation" is an extremely slippery term. There are several reasons for this. One is that it involves *feelings,* how people feel about their experiences in relation to social situations or institutions. According to Melvin Seeman, who has proposed a definition of alienation in the sociological context, it consists of five states of mind: powerlessness, meaninglessness, normlessness, isolation, and self-estrangement.[62] Each is a feeling that the individual has about his condition. Feelings are not readily quantifiable. People change their feelings; they may dislike the boss on Monday and get along with him on Friday, both with good reason. Many people, unless goaded, are neutral in their feelings toward their work situation, neither contented nor alienated. A second difficulty is that those who write about alienation from work are usually literate intellectuals who have a different perspective from that of industrial workers. They tend to identify with Charlie Chaplin in *Modern Times* and would be miserable working in a factory. It is not clear that most industrial workers are alienated from factory work, assuming that the pay, the hours, and the working conditions are acceptable.[63] Third, alienation within the individual may

grow out of one, several, or all of his relationships with himself, with others, or with the social institutions of which he is a part. Similarly, he may aim his negative feeling diversely. For example, an employee may come to work drunk because his supervisor is a callous brute or because he is himself emotionally disturbed or because his marriage has broken up or because, having just read *The Greening of America,* he thinks the whole society is rotten. Sorting things out is difficult, if not impossible. Fourth, and perhaps most important, though the word "alienation" is now in common usage, it has no commonly accepted meaning. It is applied in different contexts — philosophical, psychological, sociological, political, economic, cultural, and historical — in different ways. Thus, it is easy to start an argument over alienation. All that one need do is to use a different definition or a different perspective.

It seems to me that much of the current controversy over alienation from work in the United States falls into this semantic trap. The HEW Task Force study made an essentially sociological study and concluded, as pointed out above, that "significant numbers of American workers are dissatisfied with the quality of their working lives." That is, they *feel* that in their work, in Seeman's definition, they are powerless, meaningless, normless, isolated, or self-estranged. Harold Wool, an economist, has written a closely reasoned attack upon this thesis that shows that the statistics on labor turnover, absenteeism, strikes, productivity, and labor-force participation do not support the alienation hypothesis.[64]

I think that both are right and that the major findings of this paper explain why they are. Assuming that jobs are available, most people are eager to get them and, to a lesser extent, to hold onto them in order to satisfy their primal animal drives and, it is to be hoped, to fulfill their psychic needs. At the very least, the latter include the feeling of being sufficiently needed that employers are willing to pay for their services. When workers are asked whether they are "satisfied" with their jobs, and 80 percent usually say they are, this, I think, is essentially what they are saying and nothing more. Many of them, perhaps most, expect from a job only a paycheck, a way to keep busy, and a chance to talk to other people. If they need greater fulfillment, they seek it away from the work place. Many others, including both some of the 80 percent and, presumably, the residual dissatisfied 20 percent, feel one or more of the states of alienation that Seeman has pointed out. Virtually everyone, I think, resents the time demands of work in a modern industrialized and urbanized society.

Thus, there is a tension between the need to work and the burden of work, and a very large part of the latter

[60] *Work in America,* pp. xv-xvi.

[61] The President's Address, September 6, 1971, *Weekly Compilation of Presidential Documents,* September 13, 1971.

[62] Melvin Seeman, "On the Meaning of Alienation," *American Sociological Review* 24 (1959):783-91.

[63] For a differentiated analysis of this problem, see Robert Blauner, *Alienation and Freedom, the Factory Worker and His Industry* (Chicago: University of Chicago Press, 1964). Several studies indicate that most industrial workers prefer repetitive tasks that demand little attention so that they can think of more pleasant things while they work; see Hannah Arendt, *The*

Human Condition (Chicago: University of Chicago Press, 1958), p. 146.

[64] Harold Wool, "What's Wrong with Work in America?" *Monthly Labor Review,* March 1973, pp. 38-44.

consists of endless wrestling with the clock and the calendar. It is a fundamental problem. The bureaucratic organizations for which most of us work are of necessity locked into time schedules. Evolution, however, has not prepared us to work under this condition. While most workers do not appear to be fundamentally alienated from work, the great majority is alienated from the way in which work is regulated in relation to time.

The existence of this resentment of the time requirements of work may be a helpful finding to those who are seeking remedies to the problem of alienation from work. Historically those seeking remedies have fallen into three categories: those who try to remold the worker, those who want to reshape the job, and those who want to improve the conditions of work.

"One of the first requirements for a man who is fit to handle pig iron as a regular occupation," Frederick W. Taylor wrote, "is that he shall be so stupid and so phlegmatic that he more nearly resembles an ox than any other type."[65] Taylor did not succeed in converting men into oxen, and the one thing that virtually everyone who has written about work in the past half century agrees about is that Taylorism is bankrupt insofar as the human factor in work is concerned. The movements for human relations, group dynamics, and sensitivity training have taken the opposite tack. They have sought to promote self-understanding and the understanding of others on the theory that these will make workers more contented and more productive. While there is nothing wrong with promoting understanding, it seems extremely difficult to accomplish and, even if it is successful, there is no necessary connection between its achievement on the one hand and contentment and output on the other. Further, those attempting to remold the worker must confront the fundamental fact that evolution moves with glacial speed. This does not seem to be a very hopeful remedy for work alienation.

Reshaping the job (programs for job enrichment, enlargement, and redesign) offers somewhat wider room for maneuver. There have been a number of interesting and, evidently, successful experiments of this sort.[66]

There must be many other work situations to which such remedies may be applied; but the number, clearly, is limited, perhaps severely so. Employers are willing to pay workers to perform an enormous amount of fundamentally uninteresting work, and, no matter how it is rearranged, it will continue to bore people who seek challenge in their work. Further, as Blauner has stressed, the critical determinant in building alienation is the technology of the industry in which the factory worker finds himself. If the job is shaped by the machine, there is little possibility for reshaping the job.[67]

The greatest possibilities, clearly, lie in improving the conditions of work. This is hardly a new discovery. Those who advocate collective bargaining and social legislation have been proceeding on this theory for a century and a half. In an advanced industrial nation such as the United States much remains to be done to overcome substandard conditions of pay, safety, sanitation, noise, and arbitrary and discriminatory employment policies. Even in those situations in which these elements are standard, workers are overwhelmingly locked into the clock and the calendar. As pointed out above, time is measured in numbers. Arithmetic offers almost endless opportunities for manipulation. The greatest potentiality for diminishing alienation lies in this area, in reducing working hours and working years and in rearranging work schedules. This can often be done while still assuring the employer that a work force will be available at the times he needs labor.

A quotation from the concluding paragraph of Udy's comparative study of work in primitive, traditional, and contemporary societies might be appropriate for this conclusion:

> Perhaps the most striking feature of organized work is that it occurs at all. Organized work is everywhere a major ongoing activity. Nevertheless it is always unstable and borders on the impossible.[68]

This instability arises from the ambivalent feelings man's involvement with work evokes in him.

---

[65] Cited by Daniel Bell, *The End of Ideology* (New York: Collier, 1961), pp. 232-33.

[66] *Work in America*, pp. 188-201. For a collection of readings on this topic, see Louis E. Davis and James C. Taylor, eds., *Design of Jobs* (Baltimore: Penguin, 1972).

[67] Blauner, *Alienation and Freedom*, p. 6. See also Sar A. Levitan and William B. Johnston, "Job Redesign, Reform, Enrichment — Exploring the Limitations," *Monthly Labor Review*, July 1973, pp. 35-41.

[68] Stanley H. Udy, Jr., *Work in Traditional and Modern Society* (Englewood Cliffs, N.J.: Prentice-Hall, 1970), p. 129.

Contributors

IRVING BERNSTEIN, professor of political science and associate director of the Institute of Industrial Relations at UCLA, joined the UCLA faculty in 1948 after service with the Bureau of Labor Statistics, the War Labor Board, and the U.S. Conciliation Service. Among his publications are *The New Deal Collective Bargaining Policy* (1950), *The Arbitration of Wages* (1954), *Emergency Disputes and National Policy* (coeditor; 1955), *The Lean Years* (1960), and *Turbulent Years* (1969).

HARRY T. EDWARDS, professor of law at the University of Michigan, joined the Michigan law faculty in 1970. In 1974 he was a visiting professor at the Free University of Brussels. A 1962 graduate of the ILR School at Cornell University, Professor Edwards was a student in courses taught by several of the retirees honored in this volume. He has published numerous articles on labor law and collective bargaining and is coauthor of *Labor Relations Law in the Public Sector: Cases and Material* (1974).

SIDNEY FINE, Andrew D. White Professor of History at the University of Michigan, joined the Michigan faculty in 1948 and received the university's "Distinguished Faculty Achievement Award" in 1969. He is past president of Labor Historians and a member of the board of editors of *Labor History*. Among his publications are *Laissez Faire and the General-Welfare State* (1956), *The American Past* (2 volumes; 1961), *The Automobile under the Blue Eagle* (1963), and *Sit-Down: The General Motors Strike of 1936-1937* (1969).

GEORGE H. HILDEBRAND, Maxwell M. Upson Professor of Economics and Industrial Relations at Cornell University, previously taught at the University of Texas at Austin, the University of California at Berkeley, and UCLA. He joined the Cornell faculty in 1960. In 1969-1970 he was deputy undersecretary of labor for international affairs and chief of the American delegation at the International Labor Organization. He is past president of the Industrial Relations Research Association. Among his publications are *The Idea of Progress* (editor; 1949), *The Pacific Coast Maritime Shipping Industry, 1930-1948* (2 volumes; 1952-1954), *Manufacturing Production Functions in the United States: 1957* (with T. C. Liu; 1965), and *Growth and Structure in the Economy of Modern Italy* (1965).

HARRY H. WELLINGTON, Edward J. Phelps Professor of Law at Yale University, previously taught at Stanford University. He joined the Yale law faculty in 1956 after serving as a law clerk to Supreme Court Justice Felix Frankfurter. Among his publications are *Contracts and Contract Remedies* (with Harold Shepard; 1957), *Cases and Materials on Labor Law* (with Clyde Summers; 1968), *Labor and the Legal Process* (1968), and *The Unions and the Cities* (with Ralph Winter; 1971).

JOHN P. WINDMULLER is associate dean and professor in the School of Industrial and Labor Relations at Cornell. Dean Windmuller received his graduate training from several of the retirees honored in this volume. He joined the ILR faculty after receiving his Ph.D. from the school in 1951. He is a past Fulbright scholar and visiting professor at the Free University of Amsterdam. Among his publications are *American Labor and the International Labor Movement, 1940 to 1953* (1954), *Labor, Management, and Economic Growth* (coeditor; 1954), *Labor Internationals: A Survey of Contemporary International Union Organizations* (1969), and *Labor Relations in the Netherlands* (1969).